The
New Music Theater

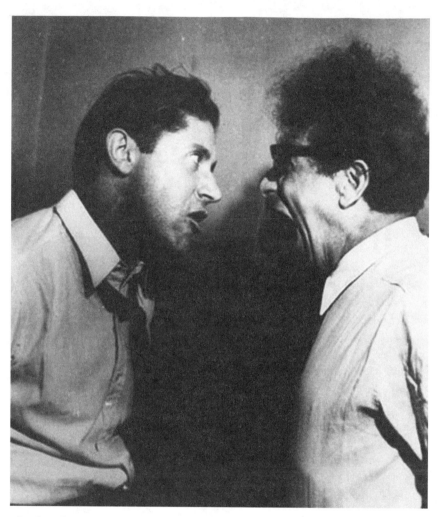

The founders of extended vocal technique (see Chapter 17): Roy Hart (l.) and Alfred Wolfsohn (r.); London, 1954. Photo: Reg Coote.

The
New Music Theater
Seeing the Voice, Hearing the Body

Eric Salzman and Thomas Desi

OXFORD
UNIVERSITY PRESS

2008

OXFORD
UNIVERSITY PRESS

Oxford University Press, Inc., publishes works that further
Oxford University's objective of excellence
in research, scholarship, and education.

Oxford   New York
Auckland Cape Town Dar es Salaam Hong Kong Karachi
Kuala Lumpur Madrid Melbourne Mexico City Nairobi
New Delhi Shanghai Taipei Toronto

With offices in
Argentina Austria Brazil Chile Czech Republic France Greece
Guatemala Hungary Italy Japan Poland Portugal Singapore
South Korea Switzerland Thailand Turkey Ukraine Vietnam

Published by Oxford University Press, Inc.
198 Madison Avenue, New York, NY 10016

www.oup.com

Oxford is a registered trademark of Oxford University Press

Library of Congress Cataloging-in-Publication Data
Salzman, Eric.
The new music theater : seeing the voice, hearing the body /
Eric Salzman and Thomas Desi.
p.   cm.
Includes bibliographical references (p.   ) and index.
ISBN 978-0-19-509936-2
1. Music theater—20th century—History and criticism.
I. Desi, Thomas, 1967–.   II. Title.
ML1706.S26 2008
792.6—dc22
2007042353

9 8 7 6 5 4 3 2 1

Printed in the United States of America
on acid-free paper

contents

part iii: Putting It All Together: *La Mise en Scène*

part iv: After the Show: Taking It Apart

preface

THE EMERGENCE OF A NEW MUSIC THEATER in the past half century in both Europe and North America is a tale that has not been well told. Few conservatories, arts organizations, funders, universities, publishers, publications, or media organizations have music-theater departments or music-theater specialists, although there are active music-theater creators and music-theater works being created every day and in many parts of the world. The lack of categorization and lack of definition is at once the glory of music theater and its problem. It is not easy to put in a labeled box, but then again the opportunities are limitless. Innovation and individuality are major characteristics of an art form that eludes institutionalization and sometimes seems to be perpetually coming into being.

Our job as we see it is to try to connect the dots, draw lines, follow ideas, interweave details, pick up the bits and pieces, and set them into a large picture. We are not musicologists, nor music historians in the philological sense, but practitioners, hands-on composers, sometime writers and directors, defenders of "the art form that never happened." For us, this is an opportunity to tell a story that has needed and still needs telling.

We have a lot of people to thank but only a few of them can be mentioned here: Giorgio Battistelli, Cristina Berio, Victoria Bond, Sylvano Bussotti, Guy Coolen (Muziektheater Transparant), Michael Dellaira, Paul Dresher, Mark Feldman, Heiner Goebbels, Mark Grant, Martin Hennessy, Mimi Johnson (Artservices), Dragon Klaic, Laura Kuhn (John Cage Trust), Antoine Laprise, Jason Loeffler (Byrd/Hoffman Foundation), Richard Marshall (Center for Contemporary Opera), Isabelle McEwen, Zaidee Parkinson, David Pountney, Ozzie Rodriguez (La

Mama), Michel Rostain, Michael Sahl, Kenny Savelson (Bang on a Can), Dave Stein and the Kurt Weill Foundation, Jon Szanto, Pauline Vaillancourt (Chants Libres), Valeria Vasilevski, as well as Norman Hirschy at Oxford and, back home, Lorna Salzman and Sophie Cwikła. We couldn't have done it without you.

Eric Salzman and Thomas Desi

The
New Music Theater

Introduction: What Is Music Theater?

WHAT IS MUSIC THEATER? Since this usage, although known in various European languages, is relatively new in English, the question has been posed in various ways.

Opera is an abbreviated form of a still-current Italian expression, *opera lirica*, which can be translated as "lyric work" or "works that are sung" (*opera* itself being the plural of *opus*, the Latin word for "work"). The term has been used to represent many "classical" forms of sung theater, even when the connections to European opera are slight (hence "Chinese opera" or "Peking opera"). By extension, popular theatrical forms containing music (some of them older than opera itself) have come to be designated as operetta (or "little opera"), light opera, comic opera, *opéra comique*, or *opéra bouffe*, all variable and somewhat awkward expressions that try to marry terms for relatively small-scale popular or comic (i.e., nontragic) art with a word whose historically developed character is closely connected with notions of "big" and "grand."

In fact, the term *opera* itself has sometimes inspired doubts among composers and librettists. Reformers and innovators of serious opera as well as the creators of popular forms have often preferred to use other terms such as *musical comedy*, *the musical*, *Singspiel*, *dramma per musica*, *favola in musica*, *dramma giocosa*, *pastorale* and lyric drama, all terms from which the word *opera* is missing. Wagner, who associated "opera" with Meyerbeer and the Italians, referred to his work as "music drama." Bertolt Brecht, who disliked opera and wanted to draw on the popularity of musical theater, invented new terms for his works and essentially broke with Kurt Weill over the operatic dimensions of *Mahagonny*.[1]

New music theater was created outside these categories. It absorbed the musical and artistic revolutions of the early twentieth century as well as the technological innovations of stagecraft and stage design, machinery and light, audio and video. When we say that the new music theater is distinguished by innovation and revolution, we do not mean to imply that everything was reinvented simultaneously. Some aspects (say, the standard pit orchestra) might be retained but others (for example, singing style, subject matter, or text) might be quite new. Some works might still fit the operatic model because they use operatic voices or because they integrate well into the standardized process of operatic production. But a good deal of music theater (or even small-scale opera) rejects the grandeur of grand opera for many reasons including economics, the preference for nonpro-jected voices (extended voice, pop, non-European styles or other kinds of singing that need to be amplified), a desire for audience immediacy, or a general esthetic or philosophical preference for small-scale, unpreten-tious, small-theater work—closer in many ways to contemporary dance, dance theater, new theater and new performance art than to traditional opera. Small voices and small budgets require a small theater concept, a small theater, a small ensemble, and, probably, amplification. These needs combine with esthetic preferences to produce the kind of piece that works well in a small theater but which is difficult, if not impossible, for a large opera house or company to swallow.

Nevertheless, some terminological problems seem unavoidable. In English, "music theater" is essentially a coinage taken from the Germanic form *Musiktheater*, which can refer to a building but which also came to desig-nate a kind of instrumental or instrumental/vocal avant-garde performance associated with composers like Karlheinz Stockhausen and Mauricio Kagel. In the English-speaking world, it was first applied to small-scale sung theater in the Brecht or Brecht/Weill tradition but it has been widely appropriated

---

1. On the other hand, the word *opera* has sometimes been used to designate forms of theater that are remote from the traditional meaning. Perhaps the most extreme examples of this are the early Robert Wilson works, which were called operas even though they contained no music at all; they were "operatic" only in their scope and extreme length.

for almost any kind of serious musical theater. Hardly anyone on Broadway or in London's West End uses the term *musical comedy* anymore, and ambitious modern musicals with a pretense to do more than merely entertain are as likely to be designated "music theater" as anything else.

Music theater or opera? Exclusive or inclusive?

In short, "music theater" has come to have two opposing uses: one inclusive, the other particular and exclusive. The inclusive meaning of the term can encompass the entire universe of performance in which music and theater play complementary and potentially equal roles. In this sense, *opera* can be viewed as a particular and historical form of music theater. Music videos, to choose a radically different example, might be another.

However, when we say *new music theater* in this book, we use the term in a way that is almost always meant to exclude traditional opera, operetta, and musicals. This meaning is partly historical but mostly categorical. New music theater can be compared to modern dance and it is in an evolutionary place that is close to where modern dance was in the mid-twentieth century. In other contexts, it has sometimes been designated as fringe or experimental opera or even as the off-Broadway of opera. Since it is in mid-evolution and comprises different streams and styles, it is most easily defined by what it is not: not-opera and not-musical. A slightly less negative definition would describe it as the wide and evolving territory that lies between opera and the musical. Music theater is theater that is music driven (i.e., decisively linked to musical timing and organization) where, at the very least, music, language, vocalization, and physical movement exist, interact, or stand side by side in some kind of equality but performed by different performers and in a different social ambiance than works normally categorized as operas (performed by opera singers in opera houses) or musicals (performed by theater singers in "legitimate" theaters).

Does the archetype hold in all forms from the most traditional to the most contemporary?

What if a work or a performance requires a mixed cast of singers? What happens when a musical is performed in an opera house or an opera appears on Broadway? The movement from theater to opera house is a kind of appropriation and institutionalization of works that might have had quite different origins and even different meanings at an earlier stage of their existence. Without any viable in-between, a work that began as a literary or theatrical protest may be appropriated to represent something very different in the opera house. Mozart's *Die Zauberflöte* started life as a *Singspiel* or musical comedy—a mixture of slapstick and occult symbolism—and retains its original number form with spoken dialogue even in the opera house. Bizet's *Carmen* was originally a serious *opéra comique* with spoken dialogue, but after the composer's death recitatives were added to obtain its acceptance in the opera house; although various attempts have been made to recapture the work as music theater, the operatic version with recitatives is almost universally performed. *Parsifal* was written as a festival music drama and was not supposed to be performed anywhere except in the Bayreuth *Festspielhaus*; today, like all the Wagnerian music dramas, it is "just" opera (its origins are revealed only by the tradition that—in certain houses at least—applause and curtain calls take place only after the secular second act). Stephen Sondheim's *Sweeney Todd* started life as serious musical theater but has turned into an opera and had to be recaptured for the theater in the form of a post-Brechtian music-theater style production in which the actors play musical instruments (and, with revisions, has now turned into a decidedly nonoperatic musical film). As already mentioned, the argument over whether *Mahagonny* was to be an opera or not was a major cause of the breakup of the Weill/Brecht collaboration (they collaborated only once more afterward); history seems to have decided definitively that it is indeed an opera.

Are we just arguing semantics here? Evidently, contemporary opera, music theater in its various forms, and the modern musical coexist on a continuum and the lines between them are often blurred. But even though the boundaries between species are often fuzzy (an inevitable result of any evolutionary process), this does not mean that valid species do not exist (they clearly do) and should not lead us to deny that differences exist—differences of purpose, of category, of social setting, of casting, and of vocal type.

A recurrent theme throughout this book is the question of what music theater has been, is or might be. We often return to early or non-Western forms of music theater and performance art, not in an attempt to prove that new music theater is merely a return to origins but rather to find universals, untainted perhaps by the recent domination of traditional Western forms. We also sketch the largely unwritten and shadowy history of "alternate opera" going at least as far back as the period between the two world wars as well as the second and third waves of the 1960s and the 1980s to the present. In all these periods, new forms of music theater were proposed—initially at least—as a protest against opera or a conscious attempt to create new musico-theatrical forms outside the physical and esthetic precincts of opera.[2]

2. But in spite of occasional proletarian pretensions, generally revealing itself as an art form for the upper levels of society.

Music theater has a difficult but inspiring past whose story is still being written; it is also still evolving, not to say constantly redefining itself.

Music theater is the oldest and newest of theater forms

If you go far enough in any direction, historically or culturally, you eventually arrive at some form of theater based in music and dance. The origins of theater in ritual, religion, and myth have been extensively explored and surviving examples can be cited from many cultures.[3] Given the antiquity and ubiquity of these forms, it can be said that singing accompanied by physical movement is at the base of the performing arts family tree. At some unknown point, language—ritualistic or storytelling—is added to the mix. As music-plus-text seems to be stored in a different area of the brain than words alone, the combination of the two facilitates the memorization of extended passages of text. Thus, religious texts are chanted in virtually all cultures and extended poetic and dramatic texts almost as universally. The separation of spoken and sung theater (and of dance) was an achievement of Renaissance Europe and is recent in other cultures as well.

Opera (the classical European form of nonreligious sung theater) was invented only in the seventeenth century[4] and ballet, in its modern form as a truly separate art form, only in the nineteenth. Modern spoken theater has its roots in the sixteenth century and came to dominate all but the most popular forms of theater only in relatively recent times.

As opera established its independence from religious ritual, from spoken theater, and from other presentational forms using accompanied song, it began to spread outside of Italy and take on a special role—that of representing the wealth and the accomplishments of the sponsoring court, town, or society. As a form of "conspicuous consumption," it tended to grow to maximum dimensions in length, scope, size of performing forces, and, of course, cost. The use of a wide and deep frontal stage with a large orchestra pit beneath and the development of certain types of dramaturgy and subject matter all contributed to its growth as a large form. Serious opera also deals with large-scale subjects and emotions. It is often "over the top" musically and vocally, and it typically deals with violence and violent emotions stylized

3. The still-visible theater of Priene in the Gulf of Milet in Greece dates from 400 B.C. Greek theater evolved from choral dancing as part of religious rites for the God Dionysius.

4. The first recitative operas were privately performed in Florence in 1598, 1600, and 1602. Monteverdi's *Orfeo*, the earliest opera still regularly performed, appeared in Mantua in 1607. The first major public theaters built to accommodate opera were opened in Rome and Venice in the 1630s.

in musical form. As was the case with Greek tragedy, opera is allowed to show antisocial behavior, taboos, and bloodshed as well as the extreme emotions that accompany them. Thus it has a cathartic function in which the omnipresence of music becomes an essential feature.

In spite of the fact that opera trades in extremes, it deals with them in a highly controlled manner. Serious opera—expensive, elaborate, traditionally dealing with larger than life characters—has always been a highly subsidized, aristocratic art form, closely associated with the status quo of society. Its protagonists are rulers and heroes in a society in which rule and order are threatened by extraordinary events and out-of-control passions.[5] These cautionary tales, the expensive form of their presentation as well as the social institution itself, all reflect conservative tendencies, which from time to time have provoked periodic renovations and reforms. These have had the aim of keeping opera from losing its central place in artistic life, allowing it to hold on to (or helping it restore) its ability to function dramatically and speak a more contemporary language to the society in which it must function. These changes have come about through aggressive programs of reform (Gluck, Wagner) or through the infusion of popular forms into the serious opera house (the various manifestations of comic opera or *opera buffa* which have popular origins and are generally concerned with issues of class, gender, and social structure).

By the mid-twentieth century, however, due perhaps to the impact of mass media (notably film),[6] opera seems to have lost its keystone position at the apex of the arts. The much-discussed "crisis of opera" is sometimes dated to the period just after World War I and the political and economic upheavals that followed: 1924 is the year of Puccini's and Lenin's death and the year that Berg's *Wozzeck* appeared; it is also only a few years before the economic crash of 1929 and the appearance of sound film. Others put the crisis point a quarter of a century later, just after World War II.

The twentieth century developed into an age of specialization. The *Gesamtkunstwerk* of late romanticism was once more teased apart. In classical Aristotelian theory, art was believed to derive from the imitation of the real world. Music, notably instrumental music, challenges that view. Under the influence of German idealistic philosophy, music came to be viewed as the purest of the arts and a model for all the arts precisely because it is presumably the most abstract and the least contaminated by the "real

5. Unlike the original Greek tragedy, the status quo is usually preserved in opera through the intervention of a kindly monarch or a benevolent god— the deus ex machina leading to the happy end.
6. The notion that cinema came to fill the place in the twentieth century that opera occupied in the nineteenth has been proposed by a number of critics since the advent of the sound film at the end of the 1920s.

world" or by everyday life. This idea comes to the fore once music's ancient connections with language and storytelling have been severed. The classical tradition, with its fugues and sonata forms, appears as a veritable fairyland of Platonic ideals. In this universe, now dominated by atonal and nonfigurative art, instrumental music seems more important than vocal music and concert performance is accorded a much higher status than the theater. Wagner once remarked that having created the invisible orchestra, he now had to invent the invisible theater. The rift between new music and the old operatic theater—culminating in Boulez's 1963 interview in *Der Spiegel* in which he suggested that "the most elegant solution would be to explode the opera houses"—appeared to be unbridgeable. The utopian reinvention of postwar society seemed to be possible through an enlightened modernism within which opera was not seen to play a role.

The most significant challenge to this view—that the highest forms of art were the most abstract—came from artists involved with the political left; these included Stalinist and Maoist cultural commissars in the communist world but also Bertolt Brecht, his various collaborators, and a later generation of intellectual populists. Brecht, Kurt Weill, and their followers (Eisler and Dessau in Europe; Blitzstein, Bernstein, and Sondheim in America) went to the place where the music-theater ideal still remained strong: the popular theater of operettas, *operas bouffes*, musicals, vaudevilles, and music hall entertainments. The so-called *Zeitoper* and its theatrical counterparts (Brecht coined the terms *Songspiel* and *Lehrstück;* sometimes other terms such as *theater opera* or *opera for actors* are used) were "anti-opera" operas that traded on the political and social issues of the day.[7] These ideas returned after 1968 when political and artistic avant-gardism merged with a new and serious interest in popular forms and also in non-Western art. The appearance of performance and concept art, the new tonalities of the minimalists, and a broad expansion of the idea of vocalism all set the stage for the development of a new music theater in the final decades of the twentieth century.

The conflict between the Aristotelian notion of music as mimetic and the Platonic purity of music in idealized and nonrepresentational forms had to be abandoned (or reconciled) before the new music theater could develop. A more useful dialectic might be found in the contrast between the biological nature of music (primarily as sexual behavior) and its scientific or mathematical/Pythagorean character. Music theater cannot avoid these conflicts. It is obliged to combine the kind of mimesis routinely found in the visual

7. Roman Haubenstock-Ramati's *Comedy* is actually subtitled *"Anti-Opera."* Luciano Berio's *Opera* and the John Cage *Europeras* are in effect meta-operas, in effect a whole subgenre self-reflexive of contemporary opera.

and performing arts with the nonmimetic "science" of music just as it may also combine the notion of sexual behavior—as found in popular and world musics everywhere—with the old idea that music can tell its stories.

This last turn of the wheel brings us to the subject matter of this volume. Every revolution revolves through a 360° cycle and reaches its starting position but always further down the road. The revival of music theater was the return of something older than opera itself but also something quite new. It happened in many places, often at the same time, sometimes without conscious collusion, sometimes with an explicit exchange of ideas and influences.

Further Reading

Boulez, Pierre. Interview in *Der Spiegel* 40 (1967): 166–74. In this interview, Boulez also mentioned plans to write an opera himself—which he never did.
Wagner, Richard. *Oper und Drama*. 1852. Translated into English by William Ashton Ellis, London, 1893. It was called "the book of books about music" by the other operatic Richard—Richard Strauss—and it sums up musical romanticism and shows Wagner's own philosophical conceptions of a new music theater.

part i   Music in Music Theater

chapter 1

The Voice

The actors need to go back to that rare and inexhaustible school, the life of the people, to regenerate and purify themselves. Until a time when we have completely purified our language, an actor or an actress must not intrude with a distinctive, individual tone of his or her own, i.e. we must not be able to "recognize" the voice of Mr A or Miss B, whether he or she plays this or that part.

Leoš Janáček, *The Language of Our Actor and the Stage*, 1899

Language and music; song and speech

Music theater can be considered the confluence or adding up of language-like expressions: verbal or spoken language (the story; the libretto), physical movement or body language (gesture, dance), images or visual language (*décor* or design), and sound or musical language (pitch and rhythm; vocal and instrumental). The word "language" is used here in the general sense of an organized communications system. We will avoid the traditional arguments about what nonverbal language systems like music can express or signify and how they function. The classical idea of *mimesis*—the imitation of real life in art—has at best a minuscule role in music, which has usually been regarded as either a science of numbers and proportions, as a grammatical form (like spoken language but with sounds instead of words) or merely as a "from-the-belly" way to express feelings and emotions.

Yet another (and perhaps more useful) way to look at music is from an evolutionary point of view. If the evolutionary record offers us any clues, music is older than spoken or verbal language and has an independent history. The origins of music (including rhythmic signaling and dance movement) almost certainly derive from sexual display and communication; Darwin himself made this proposition.[1] These activities can be found in many species and have an evolutionary origin that predates the emergence of *homo sapiens*.[2] On the other hand, language, as currently understood, is a universal human acquisition and defines *homo sapiens* as a social animal; it is now widely accepted that all humans are born with or develop a template for the grammatical structures of language. In most societies, the stylized, intoned delivery of language accompanied by rhythmic display (often with some element of physical movement or dance) is the most basic and widespread musical form. It is associated with courtship but also with community rites and celebrations including religious practice. It is striking that the lines that separate the erotic, the tribal, and the sacred are not always very clear, and it is at the conjunction of the three that the first presentational theater forms develop. The shaping of vocal expression through language, addressed to a second or third party, is the origin of song but also of various forms of storytelling and, with the addition of physical movement, of theater.

All kinds of singing can take the form of public address, but in most times and places, public vocal projection can have only a relatively limited compass. The invention and elaboration of physical structures like the ancient great Greek theaters, designed to amplify projection and maximize the size of the audience that can gather within hearing distance, played an important role in the development of sacred and secular architecture. These buildings were meant to serve as gathering places with important community functions (religious ritual, rites of passage, dissemination of information, entertainment, etc.). Loud, public vocalizing, rooted in verbal communication, is very closely connected to singing as a way to amplify and project speech and it is used that way in public rituals and performances in almost all human societies. Part of this is simply a matter of projection, but there may be other factors involved. The continuous repetition of verbal phrases in a public setting almost invariably turns a speaker into a singer (examples would include auctioneers, street sellers, cheerleaders, organizers of political rallies, and so forth).

1. "The impassioned orator, bard, or musician, when with his varied tones and cadences he excites the strongest emotions in his hearers, little suspects that he uses the same means by which his half-human ancestors long ago aroused each other's ardent passions, during their courtship and rivalry." *The Descent of Man, and Selection in Relation to Sex* (London, 1871).
2. Although debates rage about the evolutionary origins of language and its antecedents in nonhuman communication, there is little doubt that musical communication exists in birds and some mammals other than *homo sapiens*.

Singing in the classical age of opera

Although we cannot be sure about singing styles before the invention of sound recording, it is possible to tell a great deal from written accounts, from the musical instruments and physical spaces that survive, and from musical notation. Early opera singing was a kind of chamber music designed to reimagine ancient Greek theater in relatively small indoor performance spaces. The vocal qualities that were most prized were focused tone, delivery of text, flexibility, expressivity, and the ability to ornament and improvise—all qualities that have more in common with latter-day jazz vocalization than with either Greek theater or what we traditionally think of as opera singing. Early opera was largely (but not entirely) based on high voice singing of great clarity and focus and with an exceptional degree of virtuosity that came out of the late Renaissance and evolved throughout the baroque and early classical period. For most of the seventeenth and eighteenth centuries, this style of singing was exemplified and dominated by the *castrati* who were often paired with outstanding female singers. The modern distinctions between sopranos and mezzo-sopranos and between baritones and basses did not exist. Basses and female altos generally appear in secondary roles.

Although opera seems to have relegated spoken drama to a minor role in Italy (until the end of the eighteenth century, it survived largely as popular, improvised theater), the two flourished side by side in France, Spain, England, and the emerging German-language theater. Until quite recently, the typical projection of an actor's voice in a public space would probably seem to us more like opera singing than our contemporary notions of acting, which are based on performing for the camera rather than the upper balconies of a large theater. The "realism" of amplification and cinematography (close-up acting for the camera and the microphone) has provoked the disappearance of the traditional actor's style of projected vocalization, leaving operatic projection and ballet dancing *en pointe* as the last remaining exemplars of romantic performing style.

The nature of the instrumentation and the performance spaces used in the early history of opera indirectly tell us a good deal about vocal practice. Orchestras in the seventeenth and eighteenth centuries were small and dominated by strings and continuo keyboard. Even the string instruments themselves were much softer than their modern counterparts because of the use of gut (not metal) strings, lower tension on the strings, and different forms of the bow, with the horsehair held at lower tension. Performance spaces were originally large palace rooms, but especially designed theaters for spoken drama and other entertainments appeared in the sixteenth century and houses expressly designed for operatic performance were in widespread use in the seventeenth. Eventually a standard design was developed and adopted almost everywhere. This consisted of a shallow horseshoe with several levels of boxes in concentric rings above a relatively small area of public seating on the ground floor or *parterre*. The proscenium arch was relatively high and the small orchestra was generally well in front of the stage and at the same level as the groundlings in the *parterre*, an area that, confusingly, is also known as the "orchestra."[3] This layout, which originated in early opera house architecture, is still known as *à l'italienne*. One important characteristic was the closeness of the public to the stage; another was that singers, orchestra, and public were all more or less in the same acoustic space. These theaters were not large. When *La Fenice* was built in Venice in 1800 it was considered to be, at about 1,000 seats, the largest in Europe; today it is one of the smallest of the major houses.

Although it is certain that singing styles evolved considerably over a period of more than two hundred years, some generalizations apply. The penchant of singers (with the encouragement of the public) to indulge in more and more highly elaborated ornamental displays is well known. If the composer did not supply sufficient quantities of ornamentation or *fioritura (canto fiorito)*, the performer was expected to add his or her own to the score through improvisation. The *da capo* aria, the dominant musical form of the period, was an open invitation to singers to practice the art of variation, generally in the form of highly elaborated melodic repetition but also including interpolated cadenzas at key points. Written-out examples of performer ornamentation survive and give us an idea of this common practice. One of the recurring features of various tries at operatic reform was the attempt by composers to control or even suppress these tendencies toward exaggerated embellishment and improvisation. The most famous example was the eighteenth-century opera reformer Christoph Willibald Gluck who, for esthetic and dramatic as well as musical reasons, was apparently successful in eliminating or greatly reducing gratuitous embellishment. Rossini, not usually thought of as a severe taskmaster in this regard, was known for his insistence on writing out his own *fioritura*. However, only a handful of composers were powerful enough to impose their point of view, especially in an age when singers were more famous and more in demand than composers or music directors. Nineteenth-century *bel canto* composers who followed Rossini tended more and more to write out their embellishments apparently because the ability of singers to provide appropriate embellishment and improvisation was on the wane.

3. The modern, looming figure of the stand-up conductor did not exist, as the musical director was either the concertmaster (first violin) or was seated at the keyboard.

The disappearance of the *castrati* or *evirati* was part of a major change in singing practices. Did the *voci bianchi* vanish because of a growing sentiment against the castration of young boys or was it that the taste in singing voices was changing as the super virtuosity of the white voice give way to a bigger and richer kind of singing? In any case, certain traditional elaborations and interpolations survived well into the twentieth century although, ironically, they now had to be taught by singing teachers as part of the score rather than actually improvised.

While we cannot know with any certainty what the operas of Monteverdi, Handel, Gluck, Mozart, or Rossini sounded like to their contemporaries, it is likely that the voices were relatively small by modern operatic standards, that tone production was simple and dominated by the so-called head voice, and that singers were expected to compete with instruments in matters of quickness and flexibility. Outside of Italy at least, the projection of both the speaking voice and the singing voice seem to have been based on similar techniques. The distinctions between operatic and theater singing were not always as clear as they later became and some performers moved easily from the theater to music theater and opera. Handel is known to have used well-known actors as singers in performances of his *Messiah*; Mozart wrote a high and florid part for the actress/singer who performed Blonde in *Entführung aus dem Serail*; the Irish tenor Michael Kelly was the first Basilio in *Le Nozze di Figaro;* and the *impresario* Emanuel Schikaneder, an actor, singer, director, and musical comedy star rather than an opera singer, performed Papageno in *Die Zauberflöte* in 1791.

Bourgeois opera singing in the nineteenth century

Opera began as aristocratic entertainment performed in court precincts, and opera houses long preserved the royal or aristocratic connection. Public opera houses appeared early in Italian operatic history, but the very structure of the opera theater *à l'italienne* provided for tiers of private boxes that were typically purchased for the season by well-to-do subscribers. Elsewhere, opera houses and companies were supported by court establishments of which they were often physically a part. After the French Revolution and the Napoleonic period, patronage passed out of the control of the aristocracy and into the hands of commercial impresarios and managers. Public theaters and opera houses were constructed all over Europe, most of them with government funding or with an aristocratic subscription base. Nevertheless, the commodification of opera and the rise of the bourgeois ticket-buying public in the nineteenth century brought many changes in the creation and production of opera. Above all, the need and desire for larger and larger houses was driven by the professionalization of opera as a business but also by population growth and new wealth flowing into Europe from industrialization and colonialism. Opera became the focus, the lynchpin, of cultural life. More clearly than any of the other performing arts, opera came to represent the expanding European economy; cultural and economic domination were, not for the first time nor last, inextricably intertwined. For composers, newly cast adrift in what we would call the entertainment marketplace, opera was a cash cow and also a field of seemingly unlimited expressive possibilities. But, as is often the case, there was a price to pay. The subject matter itself had to follow clear rules involving virtuosity, showmanship, and glorification of the *status quo*. Although most theaters and artists accepted these limitations, there were also controversies, breakaways, and reform movements.

The nineteenth-century transformation of baroque and classical opera into "grand opera" required bigger houses both for economic and esthetic reasons. The increase in the size of the audience and the growing taste for larger, more expressive, and more sonorous orchestras and for bigger stage spectacles required larger and more elaborate houses, and this in turn required the development of an appropriate singing style. The new vocalism of grand opera had to ride above the sizable romantic orchestra and fill cavernous houses up to the highest balcony. But this was not merely a practical necessity. The new operatic vocalism appealed to audiences who came to appreciate its power and, at its best, its transcendent qualities, eminently suitable for romantic opera. As always, major singing stars dominated, but the size and quality of their vocal endowments now replaced agility as the prime vocal requisite for stardom. The supported voice with a big throw became the dominant technique of opera singing.

Vibrato was originally an expressive device based on the idea of small and rapid changes of pitch (rather than dynamics) in vocal production; its ability to magnify and project sound came to be appreciated only later. It was also used in instrumental music, notably when string and wind players tried to imitate the expressive and singing qualities of the voice. Although it is rarely explicitly required in string music, it eventually became the normal method of tone production for violinists, violists, and cellists (and remains so to this day). It was a common technique in clavichord playing, and the *vox humana* is a well-known organ stop, which produces a "trembling" of sound. Indications requiring singers to use vibrato can be found in early nineteenth-century vocal scores such as the early works of Meyerbeer, which tells us that it was not automatically assumed to be a normal method of vocal production, even in the largest operas and theaters of the period. These techniques were associated with and popularized (if not actually introduced) by certain singers at the Paris Opera who developed a way of supporting and projecting the voice using the *voix de poitrine* (chest voice) or a chest/head mix. The resulting sound has been described as an elegant and controlled form of shouting. It thrilled audiences, carrying vocal sound at top volume, riding up and over the big romantic orchestras and traveling to the farthest reaches of larger and larger houses.[4]

This technique quickly came to be not just a special expressive device for selected musical passages and theatrical moments but the normal, ongoing foundation of operatic vocalism. Although originally French, it quickly spread to Italian opera. Rossini, who retired from opera at the height of his career, said that the new generation of opera singers could not sing his music, which required a clearer, cleaner method of tone production and a very different esthetic. On the other hand, late romantic opera, especially the music dramas of Wagner, would have been inconceivable without this kind of singing. The big, sometimes unwieldy voices that came to dominate opera (and which, in spite of some changes of taste, remain the paradigm of operatic singing) could not manage most baroque or classical opera and, with a few exceptions—an opera or two of Gluck, Mozart's *Don Giovanni* (works that were drastically reinterpreted in the period)—the entire first two centuries of operatic history disappeared.

The appearance and dominance of projected, vibrato-based singing can be compared to parallel developments in the dance (dancing *en pointe* or on toe) and theater (the heavy makeup, large gestures, and vocal throw of acting styles in the romantic theater). Relics of romantic acting style survive in early film, ironically a silent, close-up medium for which it was utterly inappropriate; they can also be seen in parody form in animated cartoons. Otherwise, these larger-than-life techniques have entirely vanished from the theater and survive only in traditional opera and ballet.

Changing vocal styles

The European-trained operatic voice—supported, vibrato-based vocalism—was the gold standard of singing. It dominated opera for over a century and

---

4. The use of vibrato as the structural basis for vocal tone production has its parallels in the choral voicing of romantic cathedral organs, in the use of multiple strings for each note in nineteenth-century pianos, and the chorus doubling of the violins in the symphony orchestra (up to sixteen players on a part). Vibrato, like chorus doubling, produces the broader but less focused tone that became the hallmark of romantic performance practice. The orchestra, which was becoming larger and larger, and the orchestral instruments, which were becoming louder and louder, were always threatening to overwhelm the singers and had to be moved farther and farther under the stage to the point where, as in the Bayreuth *Festspielhaus*, they had become invisible.

a half and suppressed other styles of singing or relegated them to second-class status. Its claims to preeminence were vast, and although other singing styles continued to exist in the popular theater, operetta, cabaret, and music hall, they lacked the prestige of opera singing. The widespread tradition of theater singing in the era before recordings is difficult to trace with any assurance, but we can be fairly certain that high voice singing dominated and that some influence from classical/operatic high-art vocalism filtered down to the theater. Other singing techniques existed at the not-quite domesticated fringes of European culture, notably Slavic/Gypsy/Spanish styles and the Anglo-Irish tradition, both of which had an influence on art music at the end of the eighteenth and early nineteenth centuries but then went underground to reappear only at the very end of the nineteenth century. The point can be illustrated by the Irish tenors Michael Kelly and John McCormack, who both sang Mozart—the former for the composer himself, the latter into the age of recording. Irish songs, arranged by late classical and early romantic figures like Beethoven and Thomas Moore[5], were popular throughout the period. Although Anglo-Irish (or, more accurately, Anglo-Celtic) music has had a major revival in recent times, one can only guess what ancestral Celtic singing was like. On the other hand, the Gypsy-derived and Islamic-influenced forms of Eastern European and Hispanic vocalism survived into contemporary musical life even after having to compete with classical singing from Central Europe and then being eclipsed by the emergence of Afro-American popular music.

It is worth noting that these "survivor" traditions have returned and influenced the Afro-American mainstream of popular music. Irish song, which was popular in America well into the twentieth century and came to influence popular and theater music, showed how pentatonic melodies could be tamed and controlled with chord structures and instruments derived from European practice. These same principles were then applied to African-American music as it gained steadily in popularity through the early years of the century. Because vaudeville and music-hall arrangements of Afro-American music were arranged with the same methods as had been used for Irish songs, they were once known by the jarring and seemingly inexplicable label of "Irish Coon Songs."

Parallel influences from Spain and Portugal can be found in Afro-Latin music. The history of how colonized cultures survive by assimilating elements from other cultures and taking what is needed from the colonizers

---

5. Moore wrote new lyrics for old melodies and accompanied himself on the piano on the parlor and salon circuit of the day. When *Moore's Irish Melodies* came to be published—for voice and piano in ten volumes starting in 1807—the arrangements were made by Sir John Stevenson.

has only begun to be written.[6] What we can say is that this process produced the elements of popular culture that were later liberated and diffused by the colonizer's own technology. From a purist's point of view, the original musical styles were corrupted, but it was almost certainly this history of acculturation that enabled them to gain such a wide audience and influence.

Most of these musical styles were based on so-called natural voice singing, that is, singing in chest registers and close to the speaking voice. These were musics created and evolved in the context of small social gatherings, sometimes with specific social functions. Church singing and religious camp meetings (where high voice singing was also employed in choirs) played an important role in the development of that primarily vocal style known as gospel. Early jazz and blues performances typically developed in honky-tonks, juke joints, and whorehouses but also appeared in public rituals such as funerals and political rallies. These musical and singing styles lent themselves to performances in clubs and other gathering places, originally in the American South but afterward in the large Midwestern and Eastern cities. The popularity of this music was evident from a very early period. Sheet music arrangements were published before the end of the nineteenth century, and recordings began to appear in the early years of the twentieth. The famous *Memphis Blues* was written by W. C. Handy in 1909 for a Memphis politician to attract attention to his political campaign. By the 1920s, American performers were appearing in Europe, and European jazz performers began to make a name for themselves shortly thereafter. Concert composers—Debussy, Ives, Stravinsky, Milhaud, Copland, and their successors—consciously used jazz and pop elements in their symphonic and chamber music. The Afro-American bandleader and composer James Reese Europe organized his Clef Club Orchestra to play symphonic jazz before World War I, and cross-over composers like Scott Joplin, James P. Johnson, and George Gershwin were major figures.

The cross-over phenomenon was mainly instrumental, however; the influence of jazz and pop vocal styles took longer to be felt. In addition to resistance from the worlds of "serious music," there was a more difficult problem: jazz and pop vocalism needed the development of appropriate technology to enter the marketplace. Recordings and radio brought these popular musical styles to a large public at a fairly early date, but for unsupported singing to be heard in large halls, some kind of amplification was needed. At one point, acoustic megaphones were actually employed. Eventually the development of public address microphone/amplifier/loudspeaker systems was essential.

6. See, for example, Christopher Small's *Music of the Common Tongue* (Hanover, NH, 1998); also see Further Reading at the end of the chapter.

Amplification was long a major problem in the theater. It was strictly disallowed in the opera house where it is still vigorously opposed and where, as a result, alternate and "natural voice" singing styles have been largely excluded. Non-vibrato singing styles (so-called white-voice styles) have only recently penetrated the opera world as a result of the new interest in seventeenth- and eighteenth-century repertoire. Whether this is truly a return to baroque and classical style (parallel to the so-called original instrument movement in early music performance) is a matter of debate but the advent of countertenors and Mozart sopranos on the opera stage certainly represents a change in taste. A cleaner, whiter sound can also be heard in many modern and contemporary works. These changes represent a small window through which various kinds of singing have become part of new music theater and may yet slip onto the operatic stage.

In the theater, as opposed to the classical opera, there has never been a big prejudice against technological innovation. Classical theater singing (i.e., before electronic amplification) is derived from the operetta; it is essentially a simplified version of operatic high voice singing, modified to permit clear articulation of the words, especially in the high registers. Theater sopranos and tenors dominated the casts of operettas and popular musicals for many years. High voices were popular, perhaps because they were youthful in character and simultaneously sexy and refined. But there was also a practical reason; they could soar more easily above the orchestra and be heard in the second balcony. Even theater baritones tended to sing mostly in the upper part of their range (there are even singers who define their voice types as "bari-tenor"). And some theater altos managed a loud, forced high extension of their chest register (or a chest/head mix), the so-called *belt* voice, which became a hallmark of musical comedy performance before the days of wireless microphones. Exponents of high *belt* like Ethel Merman could be heard nightly singing Gershwin's *Girl Crazy* without amplification over a twenty-four-piece pit orchestra playing with full force in a 2,000-seat theater.

Before wireless or radio microphones, the effectiveness of amplification in the theater was limited by the need to cover the stage with microphones or for singers to move into fixed positions. The introduction of wireless microphones in the latter part of the last century was a big technological advance as performers now had their own individual microphones (and transmitters) that could move with them. This allowed performers to move about the stage freely and led to major changes in musical staging. However the purely musical results were decidedly less than ideal for a long time. There were technical problems such as unwanted noise (microphones rubbing against fabric, police radio transmissions picked up in the theater) and strange acoustic effects (when lovers sing in close embrace, their voices are cross amplified by their partner's microphones). New specialists now became part of the production team: a sound designer and a sound engineer had to monitor and control the sound volume and mix on a continuous basis. The esthetic sound ideal of the commercial musical became that of the recording studio, and there are times in these over-amplified environments when it is difficult to figure out exactly who is singing what. In some particularly energetic musicals, prerecorded sound with lip synching has been used to a greater or lesser degree to avoid the huffing and puffing of out-of-breath voices and create the seamlessness of commercial recorded sound. Some American critics of the contemporary Broadway musical theater (Michael Feingold, Mark Grant) have taken the position that amplification and the influence of amplified pop music has been a major negative influence on the evolution of the popular musical.

The microphone and the singing voice

Whatever the problems, the domination of microphones and loudspeakers has had a very large effect on popular music and musical theater of all kinds. The full range of folk, pop, blues, gospel, and jazz voices is now regularly heard in the theater, and even actors or actor/singers with very small voices can be heard in the upper balconies. The "natural voice" sound of a lot of traditional jazz singing (closely bound to the speaking voice), the strength of African-derived New World styles, the growing influence of other kinds of non-Western music, and an interest in vocal improvisation has led to the development or incorporation of radically new techniques not previously considered to be a legitimate part of formal vocal performance.

Most of these developments are dependent on the artful use of the microphone and amplification. Not only does this permit nonprojected vocal sounds to be heard in large spaces but it also enables the artistic use of close-up sound and makes expressive intimacy (not to mention true *pianissimos*) part of the singer's repertoire. It also allows and encourages the differentiation of style to the point of individualized vocal sound and technique. Even in an age of sound synthesis and computerization, where instruments have been imitated with ever-increasing accuracy, the human voice has remained individualized. As is well known, we can recognize the sound of individuals talking and singing almost as easily as we recognize faces, a fact that creates the necessity to know the face that goes with the voice. Amplification and recording encourages the notion of individuality in vocalism so that identifiable (sometimes strange and unique) voices are often more appreciated than uniform or prototypical voices. The microphone, a kind of aural magnifying glass, brings individual vocal artifacts and artistic detail to our attention with great clarity.

Understanding the influence of microphones and loudspeakers on vocalism requires a more general consideration of the impact of sound transmission and reproduction on musical culture. The transmission and diffusion of sound through microphones went through several phases starting with telephone transmission, recording, and radio broadcasting. From the beginning, these transmissions provided an intimacy and close-up detail on a performer-to-listener basis that annihilated distance. The enlargement or amplification of the voice in large spaces and for large audiences was at first almost a side effect but it quickly became important for spoken voice and pop singing.

Operatic projection that is also miked produces a strange amalgam, a redundancy that actually strains the technology. In the end, the microphone in the theater does what nineteenth-century vibrato-based singing technique was designed to do: it throws the voice outward to places it could not previously reach. It is therefore somewhat logical that, except under special circumstances, any form of electronic enhancement is forbidden in the opera house. Amplification quickly came to dominate virtually most other forms of public vocal performance from a relatively early date. Audiences are, in fact, used to hearing speaking and singing voices through loudspeakers. When wireless microphone technology finally improved to the point that it could be used efficiently and with some degree of confidence, it was very widely adapted in the theater.

One immediate result was a major reaction against the high, trained singing voices that had dominated for so long. Low voices were suddenly everywhere. Nonprojected singing styles now commonly used in the theater include those associated with folk and non-Western music; the familiar throaty half-voices of pop, blues, and jazz styles; and various forms of the traditional mid-range theatrical belt. To this list, we can also add various forms of rhythmic speech ranging from Rex Harrison to rap. This is a huge range of possibilities, some quite traditional and some of recent vintage. Folk and popular styles that were originally meant to be used in close, intimate settings have been projected to larger and larger audiences.[7] Miking also offers the possibility for singers to move and play on stage without always observing the traditional operatic necessity of continuously facing the audience.

As both microphones and the required body transmitters have become smaller and smaller, it has become easier to hide them in the performer's

7. In fact, it is probable that the limits of the effective use of this amplification technology may have already been reached. It is obviously possible to see and hear a lot more with a DVD and 5.1 Dolby Surround Sound than can be experienced from the last row of a concert in a 50,000-seat arena that is heard through a blasting public address sound system.

costume or hairdo. But ironically, it has also become common practice to let them be seen, even in situations when their appearance might be thought inappropriate. The effect is to make all the characters in a musical play look and sound like rock performers or rappers.[8] This has made vivid the contrast between the operatic ideal of beautiful, high-level performance by unplugged singers and the seemingly endless possibilities of wide dynamics, interpretative subtleties, intimate close-ups, expressive detail, and sound manipulation—all qualities made possible in large spaces through the use of microphones.

The discrepancies and contradictions between singing styles that were developed in pretechnological and even preliterate societies and their extensive uses in contemporary society though larger-than-life technological amplification present a paradox that has many implications. Intimate performance styles and a huge dynamic range can be presented and understood by audiences of thousands, in part because the loudspeaker transmission of music has been accepted as normal, thanks to the already widespread use of recorded music. Amplified singing is the principal method of musical transmission and remains a natural mode for both performers and listeners. This has also promoted the appearance of singing stars with individually recognizable voices in the theater. The result is that some elements of the community bond—represented in its earlier pretechnological form by this kind of musical expression—have been preserved or at least alluded to.[9]

From this point, the use of amplified sound—amplified vocal sound in particular—has taken off in unexpected directions. The range of available singing styles is very great and in an almost continuous evolution. There are, for example, lines of connection between the vocal techniques of Louis Armstrong, Bobby McFerrin, and Tom Waits; experimenters like Roy Hart; and contemporary extended voice singers like Meredith Monk, Rinde Eckert, Diamanda Galás, and Theo Bleckmann. Although much of this kind of singing originally took place in clubs, performance spaces, recording studios, concert halls, and festivals, it has also become an important element in the evolution of alternative music-theater performance styles.

8. This fashion has now spread to the street where people talk on cell phones while walking or driving with seemingly permanently implanted headsets.
9. The new popularity of low voices overwhelmed the traditional theater soprano and tenor sound, which virtually disappeared for a few years and seemed to be on the verge of extinction. More recently, however, the return of romantic opera and operetta in the theater has created a new market for trained voices—that is, theater sopranos, tenors, and baritones, often with operatic backgrounds (see especially the Euromusicals of Andrew Lloyd Webber and Claude-Michel Schoenberg).

The esthetic of amplified sound has itself become part of the musical sound of certain composers and styles. Performers have learned to use the microphone as part of their performance technique, and a whole repertoire of electronic equipment has been developed to alter live sound in performance as part of the musical expression. Some of this was an outgrowth of electronic and electro-acoustic music that started after World War II in European public radio stations and American universities, and was picked up by the large record companies for multitrack pop recording, developed through electro-acoustic research centers (IRCAM and CEMAMu in Paris; STEIM in Amsterdam; ZKM in Karlsruhe; Stanford, MIT, and other universities in the United States) and carried into the (largely pop) marketplace by private corporations in the form of synthesizers, samplers, and other performance-adapted electronic gear. What began as an attempt to explore the artistic possibilities of sound processing and electronic/digital media was eventually sidetracked or rendered obsolete by commercialized hardware and software.

Microphone techniques, sound modification, and nonstandard vocal usages are widespread in the more experimental forms of jazz and pop as well as in more experimental forms of contemporary music. Formerly, sound modification and processing took place through the use of specially designed analog equipment but, as with other electro-acoustic musical developments, most of the technology associated with this kind of performance has now been digitalized. The processing and modification of vocal sounds in performance are accomplished with the use of computers and specially developed software programs. These actions can be preprogrammed but they can also be used live and even improvisationally as part of the action of performance. Using programs such as MAX/MSP (originally developed at IRCAM in Paris) to control the parameters of live sound in performance turns the computer into a musical instrument.

All methods of processing the voice through technology—from the most primitive microphones, recording equipment, and loudspeakers to the most sophisticated—transform the reality of what they propose to transmit. In spite of the claims of the inventors and manufacturers of these technologies (starting with Edison), the type of microphone employed, the recording technology itself, the loudspeaker system, and the storage devices used (LP, CD, audiocassette, DVD, flash memory) all have a major impact on the quality of sound that passes through them. Although the history of sound technology is sometimes described as an inexorable march toward greater and greater "realism" or higher and higher "fidelity," the case could also be made that much of the change is simply from one style to another. Indeed, low-fi (low fidelity) has even become a style on its own and is often preferred as more honest than the blandishments of sophisticated sound technology.

As the center of musical culture has moved away from live, acoustic sound toward loudspeaker sound, there has been an inevitable effect on the way music is written, performed, produced, and received. In a very general way, we can note the tendency for live music to sound like recorded music, an esthetic preference that can be found in concert performances of classical music and in the opera house just as much as in rock concerts or popular musicals. In new music and music theater—once the old prohibition against amplification has been superseded—all this offers a wide range of choices in the creation and performance of new work.

New vocal styles

The history of the development of new vocal techniques has yet to be written, but as suggested above, it has roots in the improvisatory nature of jazz (notably the technique of scat singing), in the growing influence of non-Western or world-music styles, and in the experimental work of modernists like John Cage, Harry Partch, Karlheinz Stockhausen, Mauricio Kagel, and György Ligeti who mixed abstract musical or philosophical concepts with an expanded view of voice. These extended vocal techniques include a substantially enlarged range with a variety of techniques of voice production; the use of verbal, subverbal, and emotive sounds; and the inclusion of unconventional sounds including, among others, throat singing, harmonics, multiphonics, and the so-called vocal fry (a generalized name for nonpitched, nonverbal, low-pitched, and throaty vocal sounds).

The most important early exponent of a vastly enlarged vocal technique was the English singer Roy Hart. Hart, in turn, was the major pupil and disciple of Alfred Wolfsohn, a singing teacher from Berlin who taught in London in the later part of his life and who was the first to study, organize, and teach the practice of what became known as extended range or extended voice. Peter Maxwell Davies' *Eight Songs for a Mad King* was written for Hart and is a compendium of his technique. Hans Werner Henze also wrote his *Versuch über Schweine* for Hart, and Karlheinz Stockhausen studied Hart's vocal methods and was influenced by his ideas and practices. In the latter part of his life, Hart formed a company that performed in England and France, eventually settling in the south of France. Since his death in 1975, Hart's disciples have continued to espouse his principles and techniques.

Another important early practitioner in this area was Cathy Berberian, who worked with Cage and, notably, Luciano Berio (to whom she was married for a time). She also produced work of her own (*Stripsody* is the best known), and her performances of the Cage *Aria with Fontana Mix* show the range as well as quality of her vocal performance. Starting around

1970, a number of experimental ensembles devoted themselves to this kind of work. Roy Hart's ensemble has already been mentioned. Others include Kirk Nurock's Natural Sound Workshop; Eric Salzman's Quog Music Theater; and Meredith Monk's The House and, later, her vocal ensemble (all in New York); Georges Aperghis's ATEM (in Paris); and Pauline Vaillancourt's Chants Libres (in Montréal). Many of these groups functioned or function in the manner of contemporary improvisational theater or dance ensembles, developing sounds and new vocal forms through a rehearsal process and often using ensemble improvisation.

A central figure in new performance art (known in Europe simply as "performance") was the monologist or storyteller who now reappeared as a solo vocal composer/performer/improviser. The background of much of this work is semi-improvisatory and built on storytelling (Laurie Anderson, Robert Ashley), improvisational theater performance (Lynn Book), physical movement and voice (Meredith Monk), jazz, electronic, and radio (Theo Bleckmann, Pamela Z, Joe Frank), the serious side of pop culture (Rinde Eckert, John Moran, Mikail Rouse, David Moss), and even classical music and opera (Diamanda Galás, Kristin Norderval). (See Chapter 17 for more details on extended-voice performance and its practitioners.)

The use of nontraditional vocal styles and techniques in new music performance and music theater has a number of meanings. Speech-derived sounds and rough singing challenge the tradition of *bel canto* or beautiful projected song. Soft, amplified sounds provide intimacy, and a wide range of emotionally expressive sounds can be used improvisationally or even organized into musical structures. Language can function as music and music as pseudo-language. The projection of rhythmic breathing and subarticulate sound with shades of directed or rhythmic speaking may serve the outward projection of inner states; nonverbal vocal sounds can be highly emotive. Microphones permit the use of a range of dynamics and the projection of nuances; even very small and inward elements of dialogue and expression can carry a lot of force. And the simultaneous use of different vocal styles may be used to characterize different performers as a kind of vocal costuming. Some of this music is composer driven and involves traditional or nontraditional notation but, as already suggested, much of it is improvisation based.

Microphones and loudspeakers allow not only projection but also processing. It is now possible, quickly and easily and with relatively simple means, to alter vocal sounds and manipulate fragments of vocal sound to create electronic or electro-acoustic extensions in performance and to use these to further enhance, distort, amplify, or accompany the live voice. The best known of these techniques is looping, originally performed with tape loops but now accomplished electronically with methods that permit changes of speed without affecting pitch. The use of digitalized sound and the development of computer programs suitable for sound manipulation, live and otherwise, have facilitated this process. A wide range of other alterations can be introduced in real time for many purposes, offering a dramatic series of amplifications of the notion of extended voice. Performers like Pamela Z, Theo Bleckmann, and Kristin Nordeval create improvisational works in live performance, using recorded elements taken from their own singing that are then processed in live performance, by their own activities and actions, to create real time accompaniments.

Further Reading

Feingold, Michael. *New American Theater*. New York, 1993.
Grant, Mark. *The Rise and Fall of the Broadway Musical*. Boston, 2004.
Small, Christopher. *Music of the Common Tongue: Survival and Celebration in African American Music*. Hanover, NH, 1998.

chapter 2

Where the Sound Comes From

The make-up of the average theater orchestra of some years ago... was neither arbitrary nor a matter of machinery. It depended somewhat on what players happened to be around. Its size would run from four or five to fifteen or twenty, and the four or five often had to do the job of twenty without getting put out.... Its scores were subject to make-shifts, and they were often written with that in mind. There were usually one or two treble Wood-Winds, a Trombone, a Cornet, sometimes a Saxophone, Strings, Piano and a Drum—often an octave of High Bells or a Xylophone.

Charles Ives, from his Introduction to his *Set of Pieces for Theatre or Chamber Orchestra* (1932)

Ensembles and instrumental groups; bands and orchestras

Archeological evidence tells us about the antiquity of musical instruments but not about their use. There is an assumption that instrumental music has been used, with or without voices, to accompany physical movement or dance, starting with rhythmic elements such as hand claps and drum beats. Instruments may also accompany performers singing or speaking, solo or in groups. If storytelling or ritual is the essential goal of the performance, then the voice dominates, although it may be accompanied by string or wind instruments with the minimum basic aim of giving the tonality and holding the voice to a steady level of pitch. The instrumental line can embellish the vocal delivery or, in more complex forms, underline it, comment on it, or even contradict it. Accompanied song and dance arise from the fusion of these elements.

The truly independent instrumental ensemble has developed only a few times in musical history and its evolution has many associations with storytelling dance and theater. The formation of large orchestral ensembles in

Europe was based on harmonic togetherness. The idea is that different pitches sound simultaneously to form complex vertical aggregations that not only color the music but also help drive it forward, pushing it away from and back to a basic tonality or tonal base. This is a principle of musical narrative that has strong connections to storytelling and it requires rhythmic simplicity and regularity. In its earlier forms, chordal and melodic instruments are used to accompany voices while instrumental ensembles alternate with the voice but accompany dance. Most of the "modern" notions of chords, chord progressions, and tonality grew out of the invention of the *stile rappresentativo* in the late sixteenth century and the early experiments in *opera lirica*. Opera came to be defined as dramatic action propelled by a form of chanted narrative recitation or recitative, accompanied by *basso continuo:* a bass instrument plus a keyboard or a plucked string instrument playing chords from a melodic chart (or lead sheet) with shorthand notations (melody + bass with chord symbols). This music, molded around the words, is almost always rhythmically flexible. The complex rhythms of spoken language, bearing both grammatical logic and meaning, create their own dramaturgical tempo while the chords underneath define an internal tempo under the verbal surface.

In the earliest opera, only some of the choral interpolations and dance music are likely to be rhythmically regular, and it is for these numbers that the larger instrumental ensemble joins in. These instrumental ensembles were used to provide mainly dance music but also to accompany scenic effects. Eventually the two elements, vocal recitative and the instrumental dance, coalesced into accompanied solo song—the "air" or aria—which quickly became the main focus of early operatic form. Accompanied solo ensemble singing has a sporadic history in the theater[1] where the music must be memorized; it is more common in concert performance where the performers can hold the music in their hands and therefore fewer rehearsals are necessary. Complex ensembles occur in religious music in the late Renaissance but they do not appear on the operatic stage until the late eighteenth century.

Early orchestras consist mainly of continuo (a keyboard instrument and a bass instrument or two that perform throughout) and a string ensemble that performs only sporadically. Larger orchestras with wind instruments turn up after the Renaissance, mostly in sacred works performed in large spaces. Many such works follow operatic form and occasionally were performed with simple staging. These cantatas and oratorios were popular during Lent when the theaters and opera houses were closed.

---

1. Even in the operas of Handel, at the end of the baroque era, there are few duets and almost no larger ensembles at all.

Houses built for opera first appeared in the mid-seventeenth century and tended to grow as audiences and patronage increased. The physical theater, the stage, cast size, the orchestra, and the works themselves grew larger and larger in parallel fashion. The evolution of musical style, of vocal technique, and of the orchestra is theater driven from 1600 until well into the twentieth century. The baroque, rococo, and classical styles were largely formed in the opera house, which remained important in the evolution of romanticism and post-romanticism, almost to the edge of modernism. Many orchestral innovations appear first in the opera house. By the early part of the eighteenth century, winds—woodwinds plus domesticated hunting horns—had become part of the opera orchestra in many places, and in subsidized opera houses at least (notably in French opera but also in some of the wealthier German courts), larger casts including choruses had become fairly standardized. Nevertheless, it is striking that the continuo orchestra, built around a central keyboard (and often conducted from the keyboard) and a string section with a few optional winds, dominated opera well into the nineteenth century. It had a long afterlife in the popular theater where it eventually incorporated or merged with another continuo ensemble, the rhythm section of the jazz or dance band (piano, bass, and drums).

Musical forms in the opera between 1600 and 1900

Although the history of musical theater since 1600 has been usually regarded as a history of opera, that is probably a distorted view due to the disappearance of the much less well-documented popular forms. Traditional opera or opera seria was conservative and not just politically. The same stories, even the same librettos, based on classical tragedy (but with happy endings often added on) and dominated by larger-than-life figures from mythology or history, were used for generations. These operas were about such subjects as fate and predestination, the conflict between desire and duty, unleashed passion versus controlled artifice, and, above all, the triumph of order and duty over emotion and desire. It was a highly sophisticated, *recherché* art form dominated by some of the most cultivated vocal artists who ever existed and by a highly developed art of décor and scenography. The musical form is based on the alternation of recitative (accompanied only by continuo most of the time but occasionally by the orchestra as well) and the *da capo* aria with its set structure: main section, contrasting middle, and embellished repeat.

As opera evolved and grew as a public art form, changes in taste and economics resulted in its taking on influences from the popular culture. Many of these changes came about through the increasing success of comic opera or *opera buffa* and its related vernacular forms: *Singspiel, opera bouffe,* and *opéra comique.* In contrast to *opera seria,* the various kinds of comic opera used contemporary subjects and realistic action, often based on contemporary stories and plays (the novels of Richardson, the plays of Goldoni). *Opera buffa* was about the interaction of social classes, the cleverness of individuals who learn how to manipulate the system, and even the possibility of change. Whereas *opera seria* tended to feature *castrati* and tenors, *opera buffa* preferred female sopranos and low male voices and was far more open to innovation on all levels. The ensemble number in which different characters express differing simultaneous points of view as well as the use of musical continuity to set the scene, help narrate the plot, underscore character, show conflict, or even contradict the vocalist are all contributions of *opera buffa* that eventually came to have a major influence on *opera seria*.[2]

The forms changed as well. By the eighteenth century, the circular *da capo* aria gave way to the more directional and less formulaic slow-fast format of *cavatina/cabaletta*: a reflective opening section, moderate in tempo and highly melodic, was followed by a fast and virtuosic second half. By the end of such a progression, we are, dramatically as well as musically, in a different place from the one where we started. Key contrasts began to be used to create a dialectic in the music that corresponds to conflicts or changes in the narrative. Larger scenes and in particular finales tend to be more through-composed, creating larger musico-dramatic units. The notion of linked dramatic musical forms was most notable in French opera, which descended directly from the Monteverdean model through Jean-Baptiste Lully—originally Giovanni Battista Lulli from Florence, the city that was the cradle of opera.[3] Through-composed opera with major dance elements throughout and elaborate orchestral scene music remained important in France during the seventeenth and eighteenth centuries and, through the wide diffusion of the operas of Gluck,[4] came to have a European-wide influence. Although the influence of *opera buffa* is not obvious to our ears in the high-minded works of Gluck, that grand simplification of style we

2. The most notable example of the mixture of *buffa* and *seria* is, of course, Mozart's (and Lorenzo da Ponte's) *Don Giovanni,* which the creators designated neither as an *opera seria* or *buffa* but as a *dramma giocoso.*
3. French opera, which was heavily subsidized by the royal court, also tended to include more ensembles, more dance numbers, and more pageantry than contemporary Italian opera.
4. Gluck was born in Bohemia and worked in Austria, Italy, England, and Germany, but it was in Paris that his reform opera was particularly well understood and supported. It should also be noted that he wrote both comic and serious operas in German, Italian, and French.

call classicism actually began with the bourgeois comedies of Pergolesi and Piccini (both popular in France) and was only later codified in the symphonies of Haydn and the serious operas of Gluck (who also wrote comic operas). The symphonic and sonata forms of classical instrumental music were born in the theater.

Other forms of comic opera flourished in the eighteenth and nineteenth centuries, notably the German *singspiele*, the French *operettes* and *operas bouffes,* and the English light or ballad opera. These works were theatrical entertainments with spoken scenes embellished with songs and dances. They were often influenced by opera, especially by *opera buffa*. Much of this literature is lost or forgotten except when high-art composers such as Purcell, Gluck, Mozart, Beethoven, von Weber, Offenbach, Johann Strauss, or Sir Arthur Sullivan took up the popular form. In a less musically sophisticated fashion, John Gay's *Beggar's Opera* put new words to dozens of popular melodies of the day. The ballad opera, operetta, and musical theater of earlier times pass imperceptibly into the modern musical.

Many "modern" (i.e., nineteenth-century) ideas about music come directly from the opera and the theater. The international terminology of music is due to the diffusion of Italian opera throughout Europe in the baroque and early classical periods. The notion of "the score" and the classical orchestra of the late eighteenth century have their origins in the operas of composers like Jomelli and Gluck, and the evolution of the classical and romantic orchestra continued to evolve in the operas of Mozart, Weber, Berlioz, and Rimsky-Korsakov and the music dramas of Wagner and Strauss.

Pit orchestra and stage musicians

As opera houses and opera orchestras both got larger, the orchestra was gradually moved out of the main space, down into a pit, and increasingly under the stage. This culminated in Wagner's construction of the *Festspielhaus* in Bayreuth where the huge orchestra is completely out of sight under the stage.

After Wagner and early Richard Strauss, the opera house lost its innovative status and instrumental music replaced vocal and theatrical music at the center of musical evolution. Nevertheless, new ideas continued to turn up in some radically rethought ideas about opera and music theater. After 1900, a reaction set in against the hugeness of late romantic opera and Wagnerian music drama. The small mixed ensemble used by Schoenberg in *Pierrot Lunaire* and by Stravinsky in *L'Histoire du Soldat*, the chamber orchestra scoring of the so-called *Zeitoper* of the 1920s, and the band that accompanies the Kurt Weill/Bert Brecht *Dreigroschenoper* are examples of adaptations and amalgamations of the chamber ensemble with the popular theater orchestra that came into vogue in the twentieth century and had a lengthy currency. Such works, connected with the theater and the cabaret rather than with the big opera, use contemporary subject matter, often with psychic or political significance.

After two centuries of straight line development, the opera house orchestra was now starting to deconstruct radically into the small mixed ensemble. As suggested above, the mixed ensemble had another ancestry and kept its close relationship with the popular, jazz, theater, and music-hall orchestras which, for historic or purely musical reasons, are themselves descendants of the baroque continuo-based ensemble. The classic mixed ensemble is usually centered on a keyboard with a bass instrument, drums, or percussion and a fluctuating number of melodic instruments representing the string and wind (woodwind and/or brass) sections. The mixed ensemble may also use nonstandard orchestral instruments including (but not restricted to) guitars, saxophones, and a wide range of percussion.

Since much of the history of popular musical theater is lost, it is difficult to connect past and present. The notion of continuo as the basis of the orchestra, operatic and otherwise, disappeared from classical and early romantic instrumental music but, as suggested earlier, remained current in the opera house well into the nineteenth century and never really disappeared from the popular theater. Operetta and musical comedy scores were generally published in and conducted from "piano-conductor" scores—essentially vocal scores with cueing indications. The pit orchestra, based on keyboard-and-drums, often of reduced size and mixed character, easily incorporated jazz instrumentation. The popular character of this instrumentation as well as its reduced size serves the needs of a popular and inexpensive musical theater that was and is a direct challenge both to the high status of opera house opera and to the pretensions of the big-scale bourgeois musical.

Onstage and offstage sound; projecting sound in the space

Like the Wagnerian orchestra, the small or mixed ensemble is not restricted to mere accompaniment. Although traditional theaters (such as opera houses) place the musicians in a more or less deep pit, many smaller theaters and performance spaces put their instrumentalists on the same level as the audience or even on the stage where they become participants in the theatrical action. As the pit orchestra grew larger and deeper and traveled farther and farther underneath the stage, part of it sometimes broke off to form a smaller stage ensemble. This idea, which had already been discovered by Mozart, Verdi, Alban Berg, and others, most often has a social context and meaning. The band or small orchestra becomes a featured part of the performance and is integrated on the stage with singers and dancers. Even in grand opera, the small or mixed ensemble may provide stage music that is expected to evoke the sound of "real" (the technical term is *diegetic*) music that is part of the scenic action; this music is either popular in nature or is meant to evoke popular forms such as military marches or social dances. In such cases, the pit orchestra provides a larger musical context and retains its high-art function. However, when the small stage ensemble becomes the orchestra itself in its entirety, its role becomes much more complex. It must, at the same time, provide the "real" or diegetic stage music (dance music, phone or door-bell ringing, sound of thunder, etc.) as well as give the context or commentary expected from an ongoing, through-composed score.

Set numbers versus through-composed

The classic formal issue in opera and music theater is the old contrast between a through-composed score and a score composed in set numbers separated by recitative, dialogue, or perhaps just silence. The traditional view is that the classical operatic form consists of set numbers separated by "dry" recitative whereas Wagnerian and post-Wagnerian music drama and most modern opera are through-composed; popular operettas and musicals are, like early opera, supposed to use set numbers separated, however, by dialogue, not recitative. This is vastly oversimplified, however, and has not corresponded to reality for a long time. The operas of Monteverdi, French baroque opera, and the reform operas of Gluck are essentially through-composed. Many music-theater works in the Stravinskyian or Kurt Weillian traditions use set numbers while many recent musicals, especially of the more serious or ambitious type, are more or less through-composed without dialogue scenes (although they may use dialogue over music and will often pause at crucial moments for a set number).

The number opera versus through-composed dialectic is also reflected in the dual role of the instrumental ensemble. In a work that is made up of set numbers, the orchestra's main tasks are accompaniment plus a simple, clear delineation of form through the use of introductions, interludes, and codas. In the traditional popular form, with its alternation of dialogue scenes and musical numbers, the orchestra's function is largely restricted to introductions, song-and-dance accompaniments, scene music, and some mood setting (and most of this music is provided by an arranger). This is in contrast to the development of through-composed forms in grand opera (or Wagnerian and post-Wagnerian music drama) in which the orchestra frames or even drives all the action as well as the thoughts, intentions, emotions, and interactions of the characters being portrayed. This complex assignment therefore includes a carrying forward of the narrative action as well as commentary on the action and the motives or mental states of the protagonists. The commentary itself works on many levels and can serve many purposes including a reinforcement or doubling of text and action (including character delineation) or, on the other hand, subverting the stage action by telling us (behind the performer's backs so to speak) what is really going on. It can also be used to color the scene, cue the audience as to how to react to the characters in the drama, simply direct the audience's emotions, or some mixture of the above. Sometimes characters are connected to specific instrumental sounds or combinations, which gives the composer the opportunity to remind us of a character without that character having to appear on the scene.

It is precisely because the orchestra plays a much more involved role in all these latter cases that the modern orchestra has grown in size and in color potential. Many of the great orchestrators of the nineteenth and early twentieth centuries were opera composers (Gluck, Mozart, Berlioz, Wagner, Richard Strauss, Rimsky-Korsakov) whose desire or experience in the opera theater led them to orchestral innovation and expansion. It should be noted that the large pit orchestra was developed to be used with big "modern" vibrato-supported operatic voices in large spaces and it has remained primarily an acoustic resource, relatively little changed since the beginning of the twentieth century. As discussed earlier, neither singers nor orchestra are amplified in traditional opera and the prejudice against it remains in force. Musical balances are therefore dependent on some combination of the sensitivity of the performers themselves, the musical direction, and the acoustics of the house.

Smaller ensembles performing in other kinds of spaces have been less inhibited in the use of microphones, loudspeakers, and other electronic gear. Pop and jazz ensembles began to amplify their sound relatively early in their history. Partly because of the varied acoustics of nonstandard performing spaces, partly because the strong presence of drums and percussion makes acoustic balances difficult, and partly because jazz clubs tend to be noisy places, instrumental soloists and band singers have used many different methods of amplifying themselves over the years. The introduction of instruments with built-in amplification—notably guitars of various sorts, strings, and winds with attached pickup microphones—eventually led to a situation where the entire band sound was miked and where the sound engineer rather than the composer, arranger, music director, architect, or acoustician controls the balances. The relationship of stage to pit began to change as the ratio of live (acoustic) sound versus loudspeaker sound shifted to the latter. Stage aprons were extended over the pit, reducing still further the acoustic element or even the awareness of the presence of live musicians. At a certain point, the need for the band to be even in the same space as the stage performers began to diminish. With the aid of TV monitors, the musicians (music director included) could be almost anywhere—and sometimes they were. Orchestral simulation via sampling and other digital techniques is of course the pit musician's nightmare. At this point, the need for live musicians in the popular theater has been called into question and their presence is sustained largely by union contracts.

Breaking the stage/audience barrier: Live electronics; synthesizers and samplers; tape and CDs

The electronization of ensemble sound took place almost everywhere outside of the classical music establishment—in popular music, rock, jazz, contemporary, and theater music of all kinds. This was, at first, simply a matter of the extension of live vocal and instrumental sound with stand microphones, pickups, and loudspeakers. Recorded sound, originally confined to special effects (sound effects, *bruitage*), became much more flexible as tape replaced vinyl discs and then as digital recording—on tape or disc—replaced analog tape. A third step was the introduction of sound generators, originally in the form of synthesizers, studio instruments meant to create (as opposed to copy or store) sound on tape but afterward adapted with keyboards or other devices in the form of musical instruments that could be used in live performance. Digital technology actually combines many of the elements of sound synthesis, alteration, and reproduction into a single technology and, as with other such technologies, there has been a consistent trend toward ease of use and lower cost.

A number of aspects of these new musical technologies are relevant to their use in music theater. The tremendous reduction in size and bulk that has accompanied the turn to digital is a major factor. Another is the narrowing of the distinction between musical sound, noise, and sound effects, already anticipated in the predigital age by composers like Edgard Varèse and John Cage. In fact, the ease with which it is now possible to endow any sound with desired musical characteristics (rhythm, timbre, even pitch) has put all sounds—voice included—on a continuum or series of continua. The control of such parameters as loudness or the projection of sound in space can be extremely precise, and even nonpitched sounds can be given musical characteristics. Also, the physical placement of performers and instruments is much less dependent on the acoustics of the performing space. This permits the use of nontraditional spaces that were previously considered ill-adapted to opera or music theater and it has facilitated a good deal of experimentation (singers mixed in with the audience; audience participation or interaction; physical movement from place to place, etc.). In a "difficult" space, it is possible to create an artificially optimized acoustic that can supplement (although not entirely defeat) the natural acoustic of the room. At this point, the use of these technologies in performance and in the theater becomes something more than a mere series of technical devices and begins to have major implications for theatrical possibilities as well as for the relationship between the performers and the public.

Further Reading

Biancolli, Lorenzo, and Giorgio Pestelli, eds. *Opera on Stage*. Translated by Kate Singleton. Chicago, 2002.

Biancolli, Lorenzo, and Giorgio Pestelli, eds. *The History of Italian Opera*. Chicago, 2003. A multi-volume documentary history.

Ives, Charles. *Set of Pieces for Theater or Chamber Orchestra*. New Music Quarterly. San Francisco, 1932.

Is there such a thing as progress in
opera or music theater?

In August 2006, the Berlin Opera cancelled performances of Hans Neuenfels's production of Mozart's *Idomeneo,* which featured the decapitated heads of religious leaders including the prophet Mohammed. The official reason was fear of a terrorist attack, but there was also more than a hint of "political correctness." An avalanche of protest followed from all sides—protests from the right and the left, from religious groups and free-speech advocates, opposing the production or opposing the cancellation of the production. This may well demonstrate the limits of relativism and the excesses of a director's theater. It should be pointed out that there is nothing in the Mozart work—an *opera seria* set in ancient Greece—to suggest an appearance by the prophet, with or without his head. Is this progress or a dead end?

Does "progress" or sequential artistic improvement actually take place in opera and music theater, and if so, why? It is easier to follow the way visual, textual, and musical elements are shaped and changed than it is to retrace the motivations of these changes. And it is certainly difficult to prove that these changes are necessarily for the better.

Music-theater forms, including opera, are large in scale; they are "consumptive" and also very social art forms. Not surprisingly, they both depend heavily on funding and funders, and those who give the money (or invest it) always want to have their say. The history of music theater is a balancing act between demands: circus-like virtuosity, entertainment, grand tragedy, moral lessons, and so forth. A huge social enterprise masquerading as an art form inevitably has a complicated history.

In comparison to spoken theater, where communication works through the mechanisms of decoding verbal language, music theater hits its audience largely through its emotional and visual impact. Music has little or no command over precise significations but it has the ability to reach the emotions very quickly. Music as a social act always has a more or less obvious theatricality. The more this theatricality is unleashed, the less the music seems to have to say on its own, independent of its social and theatrical context.

For a contemporary audience, it is difficult if not impossible to imagine a world without close-up recordings of nearly everything in sound and image; the need for any imagination on the part of the listener or viewer has become increasingly irrelevant. Before such recordings were possible, it was theater's job to double the real world through imitation—the *mimesis* of the Greeks. Using various theatrical means and tricks, theater tried to surprise its audience with reality effects calculated to move its spectators by frightening, surprising, amusing, or teaching. But this whole complex of theatrical *mimesis*, reality, and imagination tends to be dumped when reproductive technologies like film, television, and video arrive. But is this progress?

The striking artificiality of opera in comparison to film or television (especially such genres as reality TV, TV news, or even action movies) creates a contradiction to the *verismo* tendencies of operatic forms of music theater in the nineteenth and twentieth centuries. Theater—and therefore also music theater—still has to deal with the imagination of the spectator to break the limitations of theatrical space. This kind of theater is actually closer to the tradition of the ancient storyteller than it is to the motion picture. Storytelling uses the spectator's imagination to open up the magical, the impossible, the fantastic. It can access psychological depth through artificial image and through sound. And insofar as singing is still the main issue in music theater, the close correlation between emotion and voice remains intact.

The "search for reality" in opera and music theater (in contrast to traditional stage "realism") has to be understood in terms of historic development. Before the motion picture era, opera—as represented by the Wagnerian music drama and Italian *verismo*—was the most representative and complete of all the art forms but it has now lost its supremacy in these fields to mass media. In consequence, two things took place: there was a concentrated and artificial preservation of historic pieces (the creation of "the repertoire")—a conscious opposition to realism through theories like those of Meyerhold or Brecht/Eisler/Weill—and subsequently, a proliferation of abstract or fantastic styles in productions by great modern eccentrics like Robert Wilson, Peter Brook, or Jérôme Savary. Theater had to find its own generic possibilities in areas where film and television could not compete.

One result of this has been the creation of theater as an elite meeting spot for a marginal or niche public. Actually this has meant a variety of theaters, often seemingly opposed to each other politically, ideologically, and sociologically. But they all deal with the same problem: is theater good for anything except as a pretext for the coming together of people from similar social backgrounds and interests? Artistic history, like political history, is always an interaction of manifold activities and conditions. Although the omnipresence of mass media might seem to date only from the period after World War II, the technical and sociological predispositions have existed since the early years of the century and these issues were already being discussed by Walter Benjamin, Miguel de Unamuno, and others. But the terms of the discussion have changed. Leading tendencies and key positions, the notion of progress, the whole discourse about

"The New," "Avant-garde," even terms like *radical* and *conservative*, all these have become stale, inherited subjects.

The ancient idea that there is nothing new under the sun gets support from the question of whether the massive arrival of technology has contributed anything essentially new to theater and opera. Of course, electronic music did not exist before the twentieth century. But musical automata existed already in the eighteenth century. In fact, the first person to pick up a hollow bone and play it like a flute was a technological innovator. So were the Galli Bibbienas who invented, designed, and ran the machinery of opera scenography for more than a century. Does the use of electronic technologies—not just in music but overwhelmingly in stagecraft—really constitute progress? And has technology significantly conditioned the content of new work leading to the creation of significant new genres of, say, science fiction operas? Peter Sellars staged Handel's *Orlando* as an astronautical expedition from Cape Canaveral to the moon virtually without any modern technology in the production.

Does technological innovation (which runs throughout the history of music, opera, and music theater) create artistic innovation in any deeper, meaningful sense? Perhaps we can contrast the image of the turning wheel revolving steadily down the road with the chain of explosive revolutionary events intended to produce the illusion of change even as it must conceal its dependence on tradition. Both images interpret the same facts. The revolutionary bombs make a lot more noise than the squeaking wheel but don't necessarily take us anywhere!

Further Reading

Brecht, Bertolt. *Brecht on Theatre: The Development of an Aesthetic.*
   Translated by John Willett. London, 1964.
Brook, Peter. *The Empty Space, A Book about the Theatre: Deadly, Holy,*
   Rough, Immediate. New York, 1968.
Holmberg, Arthur. *The Theatre of Robert Wilson.* Cambridge, 1996.
Meyerhold, Vsevolod. *Meyerhold on Theatre.* Edited by Edward Braun.
   London, 1978.

chapter 3

The Music

*Changes in music precede equivalent ones in theater,
and changes in theater precede general changes in the
lives of people. Theater is obligatory eventually because
it resembles life more closely than the other arts do,
requiring for its appreciation the use of both eyes and
ears, space and time. "An ear alone is not a being."*
HAPPY NEW EARS!

John Cage: *A Year from Monday* (1967)

Verismo/realismo to expressionism

The notion of history as a progression (if not actually as "progress") has been somewhat awkwardly adapted from art history and applied to the sequence of styles that followed romanticism: post-Romanticism (Wagner, Strauss, and Mahler), *verismo* (post-Verdian Italian opera, Janáček), impressionism and expressionism (Debussy, the post-Mahler Second Viennese School). It is from the last-named that modernism, abstraction, and atonality are derived. The dialectic of modern opera after Wagner and Verdi hovers between slice-of-life stories from the outside world (*I Pagliacci* was based on a newspaper clipping) and dark internal dramas of dreams and nightmares (did that woman in *Erwartung* really find the body of her dead lover or did we just take a journey into the hidden regions of her subconscious?).

The style categories of art history—to which *verismo/realism* and *expressionism* really belong—must be understood above all as specific historic categories. The basic feelings are universal but they undergo a lot of filtering in the process of being created by artists from specific societies at specific times. Some stories evoke a certain style that belongs to a particular age but there are also universal stories that remain beyond any historical viewpoint. That is why tendencies and similarities in art are grouped together. Compare the explosive emotions generated by social or political pressure in a piece of *verismo* like *Pagliacci* or *Tosca* to the works of Zemlinsky, Janáček, or Korngold coming out of a different society in Austria at more or less the same period and also attempting a kind of heightened operatic realism. In an era before mass media, theater with the missing fourth wall served an important social function by bringing site-specific social problems to the stage. For a brief moment, it was possible to extend that reality (or the illusion of reality) with music and continuous singing.

Against these forms of realism, there is the tendency to go beyond reality in various directions: morally, historically, psychologically, or simply in size. Today we might say that the duty of art—the function of opera in particular—is to exaggerate, to go over the top and take us far beyond ordinary visions of real life. We are not just talking about dada here. Compare the larger-than-life narratives of Wagner and the exotic narration of Debussy/Maeterlinck with the retreat to inner space in the music of Berg or Schoenberg (or is it outer space, Stefan George's *Ich fühle luft von anderem planeten* as set to some of the first atonal music by Schoenberg in his second string quartet). These examples are very different from each other but they all show the same tendency to flee from the banality of daily life. The early years of the century generated many new movements in art, some of them certainly due to the explosive technical developments that put the whole world of the arts and artistic expression into question. What had been a relatively slow evolution quickly accelerated into a strategy of radical difference and revolution.

Most of the principal motifs of European modernism were introduced in a relatively few years[1] just before World War I: cubism, expressionism and abstract art, atonal music, the birth of cinema and its various genres, radical theater such as that of Meyerhold in Russia (and, a little later, Brecht in Germany), the first music-theater reforms (Stravinskian chamber opera and parallel works from the second Viennese school), and even the first glimmers of the modern musical. All of these were initiated before World War I and carried forward into the 1920s before they were rolled back in

---

1. Approximately 1907–1913. These are the years of the *Fledermaus Kabarett* in Vienna, which included major post-secessionist and pre-expressionist artists of the time as habitués and contributors. The *Fledermaus Kabarett* in turn was modeled on the famous *Chat Noir* in Montmartre, Paris, which, starting in the 1880s, was frequented by avant-garde writers, artists, and musicians. The avant-garde cabaret played an important role in establishing a "Gesamtkunstwerk" attitude that had an important influence on new forms of music theater that arose shortly thereafter.

that period of retrenchment represented by rampant neoclassicism, epic theater, the jazz musical, chamber opera, the *Lehrstück* (teaching piece) *Schuloper* (school opera), and that series of music-theater pieces classified as *Zeitoper*—opera updated or opera for our time. This pattern was then repeated after World War II and, even more strongly than before, the freedom of art became the possibility or even the necessity to create provocative events that would hardly be allowed anywhere outside the framework of a defined art event.

Musical modernism and its terminology

The practice of using extra-musical terminology to name musical styles and movements continues right up to the present with such designations as expressionism, futurism, neoclassicism, avant-gardism, minimalism, conceptual art, and others. Expressionism arrived as the result of a breakaway from academic representative art in turn-of-the-century Berlin where younger artists were looking for a greater reality and truth in their works than that afforded by academic realism. The emperor called their works "gutter-art," which prompted the group to describe themselves as "Secessionists." Something similar happened in Vienna with a group of artists around Gustav Klimt. These movements, associated with *Jugendstil* or *art nouveau*, led quickly to the idea of an art that used immediacy, simplification, abstraction, vivid colors, and even "posterization" to depict inner states of mind and feeling. Art makes visible what cannot be otherwise seen, said Paul Klee, who was in close contact with Arnold Schoenberg during those years. Schoenberg himself painted—mainly anguished self-portraits in an extreme expressionist style. A straight line can be drawn connecting the visual and musical compositional styles of those years through artistic sympathies, parallel theoretical ideas about abstraction (for example, the familiar analogy between the theories of painterly abstraction of Wassily Kandinsky and Schoenberg's twelve-tone method) and the construction of artworks according to abstract rules.

Something similar took place in Paris during those same years between the end of the nineteenth century and World War I. The term and concept of *avant-gardism* came to art history from Napoleonic military theory. The notion that artists and writers are ahead of the mainstream entered the standard critical vocabulary in late nineteenth-century Paris and was long an article of faith and even a rallying cry in both Europe and the Americas (and still retains much of its power in a good part of both the critical establishment and the popular mind). The first French composer to apply notions of originality and idiosyncrasy was probably the unclassifiable Erik Satie. The so-called musical impressionism of Debussy and Ravel—really more closely allied to *art nouveau* than to impressionism in painting—and the early ballets of Stravinsky, notably *Sacre du Printemps*, proposed a series of innovations in harmonic discourse and in rhythm that were as subversive of the old tonal system as Viennese atonal expressionism but without the psychological element. Note that many of the seminal works were created for theatrical performance—in a theater, on the dance stage, or in the opera house: Debussy's *Pelléas et Mélisande*, several works of Ravel, and the Stravinsky *Sacre du Printemps* are examples. Theatrical form can also be found in Schoenberg's *Pierrot Lunaire*, his monodrama *Erwartung*, and his unfinished oratorio *Jacob's Ladder*. *Wozzeck* of Alban Berg is a word-for-word setting of scenes by Georg Büchner that had long been considered a prototype of theatrical expressionism. All of these works (and others) continue the European tradition of associating new musical ideas with theatrical performance.

A word about the term and movement known as *futurism* is in order here. The Italian artists who, around 1910, called themselves futurists were visual artists with a passion for technology and mechanization and also a major interest in sound and music. This led them to organize some of the first concerts dedicated to noise and percussion. *Futurism* had an important influence in the Soviet Union (during a brief experimental period, later suppressed by Stalinism) and America (especially through the work of Edgard Varèse). It had a mystical association with speed and the machine, with the power of technology and human technical ingenuity, with Fascism, and with the early, idealistic period of communism in the Soviet Union. Given the connections of *futurism* to the destructive forces that swept Europe and the world only a few decades later, it is perhaps not surprising that the futurists were largely excised from the standard histories of the triumph of modernism. Nevertheless their importance in the evolution of modern art is undeniable and they are more than a footnote in musical history.[2]

Although atonal expressionism is usually (or used to be) considered the dialectical opposite of neoclassicism (see below), it had its own period of synthesis in the development of twelve-tone music, both as a technique and as a style. In many ways, the development of twelve-tone music represents a rapprochement of twentieth-century music with the historical past just as much as neoclassicism. However, in spite of a number of important twelve-tone operas (most notably, Schoenberg's *Moses und Aron* and Berg's *Lulu*), these developments ultimately had limited resonance in opera and still less

---

2. Futurism produced only a few works for the stage, mainly in the early years of Soviet Russia. Varèse's *Astronome*, on a text of Antonin Artaud, remains only as a fragment.

in theater and music theater (see, however, the discussion of the works of Luigi Nono in Chapter 10).

Neoclassicism, presentational theater, and chamber opera

Neoclassicism and the various forms of neo-tonality that appeared after World War I would seem to contradict widespread notions of linear historical progress (Schoenberg certainly thought so; see his Stravinskian parody of 1925 entitled *Der kleine Modernsky*). Neoclassicism, especially as represented by the works and influence of Stravinsky, was overtly opposed to the notion of musical innovation for expressive purposes. Stravinsky and Hindemith both thought of themselves as medieval craftsmen and consciously initiated a dialogue with the historical past. Both also helped create, well before Brecht and Weill, a small-scale presentational theater in music. In works like *L'Histoire du Soldat, Les Noces, Pulcinella, Renard,* and *Mavra,* Stravinsky proposed an original form of music theater or chamber opera combining elements of dance, voice, mime, and chamber music, based on traditional models and influences that ranged from Russian folk art to baroque music to Italian opera. Equally significant is what is not there; the psychological element and the notion of an intensely personal artistic expression are intentionally omitted. The presentational style of these works can be represented by *Renard* in which dancers mime the fable with a separate set of singers performing to one side. Another example is the "opera oratorio" *Oedipus Rex* (with Jean Cocteau) in which a narrator explains in the local vernacular what is about to happen in each scene *before* we see it represented while the text of the Greek tragedy is sung in Latin, a language familiar to singers but understood by almost no one.

Stravinsky's long neoclassical period culminated in a series of ballets on classical themes for George Balanchine and *The Rake's Progress*, a Mozartean opera with a libretto by W. H. Auden and Chester Kallman based on eighteenth-century engravings by William Hogarth. Although this work and a few others entered the repertoire of the larger opera houses, the chamber opera idea has flourished mostly as an alternative to grand opera. The notion of a small-scale music theater made economic sense in a period of financial crisis. The scale and cross-influences with jazz and pop made many of these pieces accessible to a popular theater audience. Among the results was the creation (or rebirth) of opera in the theater and the introduction of contemporary subjects to the opera house, often in a satirical style that suggested social or political commentary. In German-speaking Europe, such works were known as *Zeitopern;* among the composers who wrote them were Hindemith, Ernst Krenek, and Kurt Weill. Small-scale works destined for theatrical performance were also produced in France by members of *Les Six* including Francis Poulenc and Darius Milhaud, and in the United States by Weill, Marc Blitzstein, Benjamin Britten, Leonard Bernstein, Gian Carlo Menotti, Stephen Sondheim and others.

In a wider sense, neoclassicism and neo-tonality embraced elements from traditional modal and tonal forms derived from popular and folk music as well as popular song and jazz. There were also close associations with the political left, which first equated artistic revolution with the possibility of political change but later, partly under ideological influences, turned away from avant-garde experimentation in favor of accessibility and a presentational form of theater meant to instruct or provoke as much as entertain. The best-known formulation of this is by Bertolt Brecht whose "epic theater" includes a major role for music and who coined the term *Songspiel*. The word was an intentional reference to the eighteenth-century *Singspiel*, the popular musical form used by Mozart to reach audiences outside the elite court circles that patronized the Italian opera. But it also suggested a reference to American popular music, particularly the jazz-influenced "blues" song, which they regarded as anti-romantic as well as anti-opera. The *Dreigroschenoper* or *Threepenny Opera* of Brecht and Weill was described as an "opera for actors" and consciously followed the English ballad opera tradition. Brecht, Weill, and members of their circle (notably Hanns Eisler) argued that the "confusion of sentiments" provoked by romantic music (e.g., in the Wagnerian music drama) was a way to dull the senses of the public and predispose them to passivity. On the other hand, discontinuity and fragmentation, interruption and distance would keep the audience aware of what was happening. The performers did not "become" the characters they were playing but presented themselves to the public as actors creating roles and dramatic situations for the public to ponder. This concept of "play" was intended to draw in the audience as a partner and participant and, often as not, the public was literally invited to make up its own mind.

Although music was important to Brecht and his concepts of theater, he does not appear to have envisaged a music theater in which music would participate in telling its stories. He characterized opera, with its vocal display, seductive virtuosity, spectacle, and romantic music, as "culinary"—literally "cooked up" with appropriate recipes. In opposition, therefore, to the culinary form of opera, he carefully chose the number form with its separate songs and ensembles, and strong influences from popular music and jazz. Brecht himself played the guitar and wrote or adapted music for his performances before he began working extensively with composers like Weill, Hans Eisler, and Paul Dessau. His first collaborations with Weill were of a similar type. The early version of *Mahagonny* (often referred to as the *Kleine Mahagonny* or *Mahagonny Songspiel*) consisted of a series of songs—sometimes inspired by the recitation of the texts Brecht himself gave—and the first production, set to music by Kurt Weill and directed by Brecht himself, was performed in a mock-up of a boxing ring. The *Dreigroschenoper,* based on John Gay's *The Beggar's Opera* transposed to Victorian England, was written as a play with songs. A third collaboration, the ill-fated *Happy End,* had an almost complete disjunction between songs and scenes. The collaboration virtually came to an end when Weill, disillusioned with the *Songspiel* form, set a full-scale version of *Mahagonny* in a manner that was too operatic, too culinary for Brecht. As is well known, Weill emigrated to the United States where he became an important composer for Broadway, thus providing a link between chamber opera and theater opera, between the politically oriented, jazz-influenced *Songspiel* and the "serious" musical, a startling change of career that has provoked much discussion. (See also Chapter 16.)[3]

Popular music; music in the musical

The history of popular music theater is poorly documented and poorly understood. Popular music theater has deep roots in the historical past and close connections with the various forms of song-and-dance shows, music halls, vaudevilles, and other entertainments. Performances intended for the lower and often illiterate classes were (and to some extent still are) of a very transient nature and much of their history is lost. We get a few glimpses into the popular forms of past eras from a handful of surviving works belonging to the English ballad opera (notably *The Beggar's Opera*), the German *Singspiel* (as taken up by Mozart, Beethoven, and Weber), and the French *opéra comique* and *opéra bouffe.* These forms evolved in the nineteenth century into the various kinds of operettas, comic operas, and musicals that continue to be performed and created today. All of these works have in common the use of spoken dramatic scenes alternating with songs and ensemble numbers. In the twentieth century, the development of the American musical comedy (now usually just plain "musical") is marked by the introduction of elements of jazz and also vernacular or jazz dance. These elements first appear in black musicals (*In Dahomey* and *Shuffle Along* of Sissle and Blake) and in the still operetta-ish works of Jerome Kern (*Show Boat*; *Roberta*) and continue in the musical theater of George and Ira Gershwin (notably the political trilogy of *Strike Up the Band, Of Thee I Sing,* and *Let 'em Eat Cake*), Rodgers and Hart (*Pal Joey*),

3. Ironically enough, four of the major Brecht/Weill theatrical collaborations have "American" settings.

Frank Loesser (*Guys and Dolls*), Leonard Bernstein (*West Side Story*), and Stephen Sondheim.

The musicals of the period between the two world wars maintained a close relationship with the popular music of the era, often serving as showcases for hit songs, even at the expense of musico-dramatic logic. For a long period, the traditional operetta and the new jazz-and-pop-song-inflected musical coexisted side by side. The later "reform" musicals of Rodgers and Hammerstein (*Carousel, Oklahoma!*) and much of the work of their successors are essentially updated, serious variations of operetta tradition as are the so-called Euromusicals of Andrew Lloyd Webber and others. Many of these works approach the condition of opera with musical scenes and even entire scores that are through-composed with little or no dialogue; they also make a good deal of use of trained, high singing voices and have taken on many of the other trappings of traditional opera (spectacle, historical subjects, big orchestral sound). One element that all the big musicals have in common is that they are extensively amplified for performance in large theaters.

In the latter half of the century, the Broadway musical—influenced by Weill and off-Broadway—began to show influences from contemporary theater. The so-called concept musical abandoned the traditional forms of realist theater, often relying heavily on dance and on strong conceptual design elements. Musically these works include a wide range of influences from rock, rhythm and blues, country music, and even rap and non-Western music. More recently, however, the Broadway musical seems to have largely regressed to revivals, revues with unoriginal scores (the so-called jukebox musical), and imitation old-fashioned musicals. (See also Chapter 15.)

The return of modernism; experimental music; serialism and anti-theater; electro-acoustics and computers

The notion of "modernity" in the arts was originally proposed in the early decades of the twentieth century at a time when the parallel notions of political and artistic revolutions were bound together in people's minds. Modernity meant youth and freshness as well as evolving or even revolutionary ideas. It also merged with notions of scientific and industrial progress. *The Iron Foundry* (*Zavod*) of Alexander Mosolov was an all-percussion piece from the ballet *Steel*. It is meant to represent modernity—technological and social progress—in both its means and its content (and, rather naively, it revives the old idea of mimesis in music). Later, under the influence of Stalinism, Mosolov's modernist work—like that of most of the early Soviet avant-garde—was denounced and a populist socialist doctrine (under the name of "socialist realism") was proposed.

When the notion of technical modernity and the unbroken faith in progress reappeared after World War II, one had the impression that once again everything had to change at whatever cost. As before, there was a sociopolitical connection. It was necessary to change habits and old traditions, to make things different from what they had been. The new "modernity," this new avant-gardism, was different from the earlier one in that it followed, did not precede, war and the holocaust. In Central and Eastern European terms, it appeared as a reaction to cultural totalitarianism. But it was almost equally powerful in Western Europe and the United States where it was fueled by a love of innovation (sometimes called *neophilia*) and was, in fact, connected to the political ideas of the New Left. The notion of radical and thoroughgoing change was allied to theories of perpetual experimentation in life and art—parallel to the notion of perpetual revolution that was popular in the Maoist political rhetoric of the time.

There is a rigidity in that part of the classical music business known as "the repertoire" that does not have the ability to deal with change. "Experimental music" is a pseudo-scientific category created in traditional middle-class society to permit the exploration of nontraditional art forms. There is a need to classify such work, to give it a place in the social order. Calling such work "experimental" places the unexpected and unforeseeable results of modern art in a safe place right next to the sciences and scientific research. The artists themselves seem to have been driven by the prestige (and the funds) that technical and scientific research and development gave to otherwise socially incomprehensible study and activity. The *atelier* or studio of a painter or a composer was transformed into a laboratory for experiments, the end results of which could not be foreseen and the rationale for which was therefore beyond criticism. Milton Babbitt wrote an article entitled "Who Cares If You Listen" in which he argued that the size of his audience was of no more concern to him than it was to a research scientist; he further proposed that government or university support for advanced work in music was as logical as it was for advanced work in physics. IRCAM (Institut de Récherche et Coordination Acoustique/Musique) was founded in 1969 by Pierre Boulez at the Pompidou Center in Paris on the precise model of a scientific research institution and much of the work accomplished there was concerned with acoustic matters and with the creation of programs for sound synthesis and manipulation. In its early phases, this meant the extreme application of formal mathematical theory (information theory, set theory) to music. It also meant the application of electro-acoustic technology (electronic music), the use of computers for structuring composition, and, eventually, the digital synthesis and manipulation of sound.

From this heroic period of scientism and technologism in music, with its emphasis on instrumental music and acoustic abstraction, only a few things emerged that were relevant to music-theater performance—mainly the development of programs for the live manipulation of sound that, along with the new microphone technologies, could be used in theatrical contexts. Otherwise, the split between a purely musical practice and the theater only grew wider. Boulez, in a well-known interview a few years before he founded IRCAM, proposed the destruction of all the opera houses. The music theater movement was partly an offshoot of modernism and partly a reaction to it.

There is another way to look at the notion of experimental music in music theater. Contemporary music theater is also sometimes regarded as experimental music theater and is itself an experimental art form par excellence because, among other things, it offers new perspectives on what music is. Most cultures do not have a strong concept of pure music as separate from other arts and other aspects of human social life; many, perhaps most, musical cultures are therefore more or less theatrical. To invent music theater as an artistic experiment is only a way of reinventing the oldest forms of musical practice. In this sense, every new work of nontraditional music theater becomes an experiment in how music is used and even defined in a performance context.

Not accidentally, the first composers to treat music theater in this way were associated with mid-century experimental music and had New World origins. The best known of these was John Cage whose work was dominated by radical ideas about sound, the perception of sound, and the nature of performance. Although he created only a few overtly music-theater works—*Music Walk* (1958) was one of the first musico-theatrical performances in the new mode—his long affiliation with choreographer Merce Cunningham and the modern dance world, his continuing interest in nonconventional performance situations, and his absorption of speech and noise into his work all had major implications for music theater. The Argentine composer Mauricio Kagel, working mostly in Germany, has created a series of performance situations that theatricalized the concert hall, and he has also worked in theaters with actors as well as singers and musicians. (See Chapter 8.) Cage and Kagel have inspired many others to avoid the institutionalized or clichéd implications of traditional narrative and storytelling in order to experiment with the theatrical-visual implications of "sound making"

Sondheim, miminalism, the return of tonality, crossovers and hybrids

Just as neoclassicism emerged in the wake of the experimental movements in the early years of the twentieth century, so did minimalism and a new tonalism appear in the later decades of the century in clear opposition to the experimental period that had preceded them. There is in fact a music-theater link from the old theater music through the influence of Kurt Weill on theater in New York. Weill's own American chamber opera work as well as his theater musicals; the political music theater of his American follower Marc Blitzstein; the early work of Blitzstein's close friend and colleague, Leonard Bernstein (both on Broadway and in chamber opera); and the music theater of composer/lyricist Stephen Sondheim are all in a direct line. Sondheim, a protégé of Oscar Hammerstein (the librettist of *Show Boat*—music by Jerome Kern—and all the later works of Richard Rodgers), also studied composition with the American serialist composer Milton Babbitt. He was the lyricist of Leonard Bernstein's *West Side Story* and a composer with a distinctive style of his own, influenced by Broadway, by jazz, by Brecht/Weill and Bernstein, and by many aspects of post-serialist modernism. Sondheim's characteristic use of repetition and variation moves far away from the old song forms, and his music has a great deal in common with minimalism. There is now also an entire post-Sondheim generation of composers writing a kind of off-Broadway of new music theater using a contemporary rock-and-jazz inflected language.

Unlike the other modernist styles, all of which originated in Europe, minimalism has an unusual history. It mixes traditional Asian reductionist styles with the complex patterns and rhythm-oriented traditions from Africa and transfers them to a European-based notation technique, the whole coming together in New York and California in the late 1960s and early 1970s, and influencing European music shortly thereafter (mostly outside of the traditional new-music centers). This multistyle became one of the most pregnant and successful new musical languages of the century. There are many parallels between the old neoclassicism on the one hand and minimalism and its neo-tonal allies on the other. Both started on the periphery of Central European musical culture; both started as serious, even avant-garde movements; both had strong music-theater roots; and both were accused of commercialism and other heinous crimes. These impressions are underlined by the fact that these Asian, African, and American cultural sources nourish also the stories themselves or the way the stories are told in such matters as time spans, ritualistic repetition, and gesture.

In Europe, some deadly serious battles were fought on the esthetic field in this period, and cultural ideologies were invoked to sustain official government support and defend the traditionally dominant European culture against the huge growth of popular music, the new minimalism, and other cultural trends. Anti-Americanism, the identification of popular music with the nonliterate layers of society, the equating of minimalism with commercial music plus a hodge-podge of leftovers from fascism and anti-communism all played a great role in this curious cultural war. Strangely enough, music-theater issues can be found in many of these "ideological" corner shops. The most famous was probably the attacks on Kurt Weill in America that began at the time of his death in 1950; similar attacks focused on the eclectic music of Leonard Bernstein and continued with the invasion of minimalism from America via Great Britain and the Netherlands.

Minimalism comes in two flavors—as "reductionism" and "repetitionism." It has roots in alternate theater and in New York performance art. The connection is most clearly seen in John Cage's reductionist conceptual performance pieces, many of which have a theatrical component. Cage's close associate, Morton Feldman, had a minimalist style of composing that was based on long durations and endless repetition with literally minimal change. Although no musical style would seem more untheatrical, he used it in his *Neither*, a setting of a text by Samuel Beckett who himself was very interested in music and the compositional structuring of text. When Beckett had told Feldman that he did not like his "words being set to music," Feldman replied that he very seldom used words and had written a lot of wordless pieces with voice.[4] *Neither* is minimalist music theater from an existentialist's point of view.

Philip Glass was music director of the Mabou Mines theater company (JoAnne Akalaitis, one of the company's innovative directors was, at the time, his wife). Glass has gone on to write a whole series of operas and music-theater works with Robert Wilson and others. Nearly all of the first group of American minimalists—La Monte Young, Terry Riley, Philip Glass, Steve Reich—emerged from the New York downtown music and performance art scene and most of them worked with their own performance ensembles. Robert Ashley developed a personal kind of storytelling and mixed media theater using minimalist elements of repetition, verbal recitation, and bits of improvisation derived from pop and blues as well as electronic and visual elements. Reich, who came late to music-theater performance, has evolved a kind of documentary music theater with visual elements by his partner, Beryl Korot, and music that is often literally derived from speech.

Among the second generation of composers associated with minimalism and music theater, the best known are John Adams (who has worked in more traditional media) and Paul Dresher (who has his own ensemble and has focused on music theater). The Adams collaborations with director Peter Sellars have tended to focus on recent historical events and characters (*Nixon in China; The Death of Klinghoffer, Doctor Atomic*). The composers affiliated with Bang on a Can in New York—Julia Wolfe, David Lang, and Michael Gordon—have developed a hard-edged, more complex form of

4. Wordless vocalism is characteristic of early minimalist works by Reich, Glass, and others.

minimalism, characteristics that have adapted well to music theater (*The Carbon Copy Building* based on an underground comic with music written collaboratively by all three).

Although minimalism has links with world music, it has also had a fruitful exchange with the more experimental side of jazz, pop, and so-called art rock, all "refusenik" music scenes that functioned outside both the classical and commercial music scenes in New York and elsewhere. Various forms of fusion and cross-over have produced a number of hybrid styles often featuring vocal elements, text, and theatrical settings (Brian Eno, Lou Reed, Laurie Anderson) on common harmonic writing. Minimalism entered Europe through the work of Louis Andriessen in Holland and a group of British composers including Michael Nyman and Gavin Bryars, all of whom have written operas and music-theater works with a European spin. In recent years, a distinctly Eastern European form of minimalism has developed in Poland, Hungary, and the Baltic countries (Henryk Gorecki, Arvo Pärt, recent work of Krzystof Penderecki). (See also Chapter 14.)

Further Reading

Babbitt, Milton. "Who Cares If You Listen?" *High Fidelity*, February 1958.

Babbitt, Milton. Charles Homer Haskins Lecture for 1991. From *The Life of Learning*, edited by Douglas Greenberg and Stanley N. Katz. New York, 1994. In this lecture, Babbitt points out that his own title for the *High Fidelity* article was "The Composer as Specialist" and that the title inserted by the editor did not represent his point of view as expressed in the now-notorious article.

Cage, John. *Silence* (1961); *A Year from Monday* (1968); *M* (1973); *Empty Words* (1979); *X* (1983); *Anarchy* (1988). Middletown, CT.

Salzman, Eric. *Twentieth-Century Music, An Introduction*, 4th ed. Englewood Cliffs, NJ, 2002.

part ii   Theater in Music Theater

chapter 4

Cultural Narratives and Performance Institutions

Wenn ich das Wort Kultur höre, entsichere ich meinen Browning. (When I hear the word culture, I reach for my gun.)

attributed to Reichsmarschall Hermann Göring or Reichsminister Joseph Goebbels (but actually from a play by Nazi playwright and poet laureate Hanns Johst performed for Hitler's birthday in 1933)

Wenn ich das Wort Kultur höre, übermannt mich der Schlaf. (When I hear the word culture, I'm overcome with sleep.)

Helmut Qualtinger, actor, writer, and cabaret performer

Narratives from inside and outside

Culture is the soil in which theatrical works are planted.

Unlike the visual or plastic arts, which produce objects that spring from their moment of creation, the performance arts must be constantly re-created and each re-creation puts them into new circumstances. There are social and class issues not only inside the narratives of *Don Giovanni*, *Fidelio*, and *Carmen* but also outside—in the societies that produced the works and that continue to support the production of old classics. The modern-day cult of director reinterpretations of the operatic classics is just one of the results of this situation.

The classic narrative of the origins of theater tells us that all theater was originally music theater that grew out of religious rituals and celebrations. This is certainly true of Western theater: Greco-Roman theater and the medieval mystery and miracle plays created theatrical forms in which known stories of religious significance were acted out with language, music, and physical movement. Parallels can be found in Asian theater; music and traditional subject matter persist in Indian theater and film and in other forms of South Asian theater and dance as well as in the various types of the so-called Chinese opera. Religious stories and forms of ritual (sacred texts, mythology, and traditional stories about the origins of life and society) are part of the early history of most theater.

It is probably more useful to think of these kinds of performances not as sources of information about cosmology or political history but rather as social activity. Performance arts might help bind up society at a certain stage of growth and complexity through the presentation of communal narratives and themes from the so-called collective memory. Or, at another stage, they might do the opposite and reinforce class differences by producing different art for different classes: popular art for the unwashed and uneducated, high art for the ruling classes, and eventually middle-class art for the *nouveaux riches*.

But society is not static and the retelling even of familiar stories changes as the culture changes. Old stories come to have different meanings in different contexts. Growth, increasing (or decreasing) wealth, and the development of new technologies change the physical and acoustic environments within which performance takes place. This may alter the style and even the meaning of familiar works. It might require different language or different performing forces. It might mean the introduction of masks or puppets, actual or metaphoric, of a more or less declamatory style of speaking, or new theater architecture, or even new technologies using stage machinery, elaborate costuming, and lighting. It may also require various kinds of vocal delivery and a larger-than-life physicality, all natural adjuncts to an epic music-theater performance style that flourishes in times of wealth. Or perhaps a homemade poor theater for hard times. History and mythology (the distinction is not always clear), fatalistic tragedy, and class distinctions are, not surprisingly, almost always favorite subject matter.

Opera, at least as much as any of the performing arts, is a representation of the society producing it. It is a baroque form, taken over by the bourgeoisie, which specialized in the representation of power and wealth. It has had a more uncomfortable "museum" role in socialist and free-market democracies where it has held its position as the most prestigious of the arts and, on account of its lavishness, the most suitable to show the cultural and economic power of the society. As is well known, adding music, text, and stage together is an expensive proposition that represents the power and wealth of those who invest in it. It is hardly surprising that the new music theater in its various manifestations appears as an alternative to grand or opera-house opera.

There are other alternatives. Not everything is a matter of serious, classical art; a lighter popular art also makes its appearance early in this evolution. Song-and-dance performances recapitulate popular themes. Stories or characters from contemporary life are associated with comedy, not tragedy, and the method of delivery is more likely to be a direct declamatory style and a lot of physicality mixed with more-or-less relevant song and dance. The differences are reflected not only in content but also in the way texts are structured and in the dramaturgical forms employed. These, in turn, reflect differences in the social status and education of the publics for which they were intended. Even so, the theater often mixes classes, and at various times, elements of comedy and tragedy have been intermingled or alternated in close proximity. The long history of arguments about comedy and tragedy and the legitimacy of mixing the two is, in part, a class issue and has implications for the history of music theater.

Structural models for an opera/music theater company

The organization of performance and performers into guilds and companies is, almost inevitably, a mirror of the structure of the society that produced it. For example, opera companies are, at their base, baroque institutions. Even when the standard repertoire system gives way to newer work, the stories and performer types generally remain stereotyped. Standardized singing voices and character types were typical of theater and opera companies from an early period and they largely remain so in opera to this day. Over a period of three hundred years there have been a few major changes, notably the disappearance of the *castrati* and the introduction of supported voice singing in the nineteenth century, both in response to social changes in the functioning of opera and the opera house. Nevertheless, the persistence of the old idea of a repertory company and the solidification of the repertoire has kept certain vocal character types dominant and impeded change. This connection between received story types, familiar character types, and standardized voices works well within the repertory company structure but not when faced with social change and the need for renovation.

In fact, other structural models for performance companies are available. One is the method typically used in film (but also well known in the theater), which involves the formation of a company for each individual project and the casting of roles through performer auditions. This requires the density of a large talent pool, something mostly to be found in large urban centers with high levels of performance activity and economic support.

Another model involves the creation of roles and pieces for specific performers but outside the historical structure of the repertory company. Although this has theatrical antecedents, it is closer to the structural model used by contemporary dance companies and musical ensembles. Productions conceived in this manner, particularly if small scale and economically viable, can run in small theaters for extended periods or tour to various locations. The latter option has been considerably helped by the creation of performance centers and festivals with a strong orientation to new work. This co-evolution of performance locales and institutions on the one hand and singer/performance artists on the other has had a major impact on the change of performance styles and vocal techniques (technology has also played a role here). New music and new music theater are no longer dependent on the old system of conservatory training and repertory companies (i.e., opera houses) that cast to vocal and character type, and this has opened the door to a wide range of vocal and performance styles and techniques. Thus does social and technological change interact with artistic change.

Storytelling

Linear, narrative storytelling was the leading characteristic of several large-scale performance media including the long narrative or epic poem (originally always sung or chanted to a musical accompaniment) and traditional theater and music theater including opera. The narrative form closest to opera after the high baroque was, somewhat surprisingly, the novel. The works of Samuel Richardson, Walter Scott, Goethe, Dumas, and Hugo had a strong influence on opera in the classic and romantic periods. In the nineteenth century, classic and contemporary drama—from Shakespeare to Beaumarchais to Schiller to Dumas and Sardou—also became a major source for opera librettos and one can say that with very few exceptions, romantic theater mostly survives in the form of romantic opera.

Operatic storytelling tends to select its subjects from a fairly limited stock of well-known stories. These function as metaphors and generate prototypical—even stereotypical—roles and characters. Setting types and stereotypes to music had many advantages. It generates vocal categories and stage characters that are suited to the repertory companies that dominated not only opera and musical theater but all forms of theater. Hence the *ingenue*, the young lovers, the elder statesman, the comic bass, the betrayed spouse, the artful villain, and so forth. As the genres of classical and historical tragedy give way to more recent folklore and contemporary plays, new prototypical characters emerge (Orlando, Othello) while others fade. Sometimes old ones from prototypically cautionary tales move up quickly through the social system (Don Giovanni, Faust). Although character and vocal types continue to evolve, the standardization of vocal types is a basic feature of the European or European-style opera house. In the early nineteenth century, after the disappearance of the *castrati*, the vocal techniques and types that dominate opera to this day—sopranos, mezzo-sopranos, tenors, baritones, and basses—appear in their "modern" forms.[1]

The use of typical and familiar stories is an inheritance from the religious or communal nature of music-theater performance. Such stories often have the character of moral instruction, sweetened, dramatized, or made emotional with music. Stories that are already known—in their general outlines if not always in their specifics of character and event—not only permit casting to type but make it easier for the public to follow the twists and turns of newer retellings and to appreciate the variations introduced by new creators and interpreters. Although old operas were rarely revived, new works based on old subjects were common and sometimes even the old librettos were used and reused. The modern idea that an opera is equivalent to its (original) musical score did not appear until quite late in the romantic period and is by no means dominant in the popular musical any more than it is in film. Just as *King Kong* could be filmed and refilmed, Rossini could do a remake of Paisiello's popular *Il Barbiere di Siviglia* and Jonathan Larson could make a rock musical out of *La Bohème*.

Casting to type led to the formation of standardized repertory companies in both theater and opera. Playwrights, librettists, and composers would have advance knowledge of the kinds of performers and voices they were writing for, and such companies could, by and large, adapt themselves to novelties coming from elsewhere. This was, in large part, already an international system in the eighteenth century and it has remained so until this day.

Although linear narrative continues to hold an important role in contemporary arts, its principal outlets are now film and television (not surprisingly, film—and to a lesser degree television—are now also major sources for operatic subject matter). As visual media gained in popularity and technical perfection in the twentieth century, the older live performance media have tended to "modernize" themselves by abandoning realism, returning to prototypical myths and moralities, favoring inner expression over clear narrative, experimenting with nonlinearity, and using stage action as a metaphor rather than as a simulation of reality. At the same time, they tend to accentuate the physicality of the performer, the nature of the performance medium, and even the performance concept itself as substitutes for storytelling, which may be reduced, merely alluded to, or abandoned altogether. This has led to a revival of the use of well-known classical myths but also the introduction of news stories from relatively recent times; in both cases, the assumption is that audiences already know the stories, at least in their

1. An operatic vocal type that is in the process of disappearing in our own day is the female alto.

general outlines, so that all the details do not have to be spelled out in realistic fashion.

Highbrow/lowbrow

Opera, popular theater, and music theater in all ages have been characterized by the mixture of highbrow and lowbrow culture—a dialectic, if you will, of high art and the vernacular, instruction and entertainment. This is partly an inheritance of the origins of music theater as a communal activity, partly a condition of the interaction of music and representational theater, or both. If, for example, opera (sung throughout) represents the highbrow form, the *Singspiel*, musical and comic opera (with songs and other set numbers alternating with spoken scenes) is the usual popular form. However *opera buffa,* with its more-or-less contemporary settings, stories about social mobility and gender, and patter recitative alternating with character numbers and melodic songs, also has roots in popular culture. Like popular dance, the popular forms of musical theater were upwardly mobile and came to influence highbrow opera and music theater. There are also works (Mozart's *Don Giovanni,* Beethoven's *Fidelio*, and Bizet's *Carmen*, for instance) that mix genres—serious operas that include elements from the *opera buffa* and *Singspiel.* Popular works that draw on the high-art tradition or serious works with popular elements occur in every period and style. In fact, the mixed genre testifies to the ability of opera and musical theater to cross class boundaries and plays an important role in periods of transition. Examples include works of Cavalli, Rameau, Mozart, Weber, Offenbach, Bizet, Gilbert and Sullivan, Schoenberg, Stravinsky, Les Six, Weill (with or without Brecht), Gershwin, Ellington, Sondheim, and Laurie Anderson.

The interweaving of entertainment and instruction is common in many of these works. The classic or historic narratives of early *opera seria* revolve around the conflicts of passion and duty, on the inevitability of fate, and on gender issues, combining "show" (elaborately beautiful décor, vocal virtuosity) with cautionary stories. The entertainment/instruction duality is even more obvious (although not always so coherent) in morality plays like the Mozart/Schikaneder *Zauberflöte,* Beethoven's *Fidelio*, and the satiric comedies of Offenbach and Gilbert and Sullivan. Operettas and musicals of the late nineteenth and early twentieth centuries are often said to lack a strong moral or instructional element but, on closer examination, it turns out that the instructional element is actually present but is often disguised, has become sentimentalized, or otherwise has lost its impact over time. In any case, the idea was revived by Brecht and his musical collaborators in their *Songspiele* and *Lehrstücke* (teaching pieces). In these works, a serious contemporary issue is presented in parable form, using storytelling rather than role playing and asking for active intellectual rather than emotional response from the audience. This is an attempt to intellectualize the emotional. Instead of evoking or trying to induce emotional involvement on the part of the spectator (that might render him or her incapable of acting in the real world), the piece asks for participation in a train of thought that might lead to action. This so-called epic theater was also called *Bewusstseinstheater* or "theater of consciousness," or, in Adorno's vocabulary, *Mündigkeit* or "coming of age." In such pieces, the use of popular music acts partly as a sweetener and partly as an alarm clock to wake people up, but it also serves to emphasize the presentational, anti-realistic, anti-romantic form.

What is popular art?

The question of "what is popular art?" cannot in fact be answered very easily as most of its history is lost and modern examples are highly tainted by commercialism and mass media. Popular performance arts have, no doubt, always existed in all cultures and periods, but until recently at least, they have been highly ephemeral. Unlike the arts of the wealthy and educated levels of society, popular arts of the past are poorly documented and most of their history has vanished. In their most basic manifestations, they are undoubtedly nothing more than communal activity—mostly singing and dancing. Only in later and more complex societies are they professionalized with a class of specialized performers distinct from the public they serve.

A great deal of what we know about the history of popular performance arts comes from the upward mobility of these art forms, which offer a stream of material to influence and inspire—not to say be appropriated by—the cultivated arts of the well-to-do. The best-known examples are in music and dance, which have a long history of being refreshed by influences welling up from below. It is amusing to contemplate the history of dance, much of which has peasant origins or comes from the fringes of Europe or beyond. Such songs and dances were described as "so indecent in its text, so repulsive in its movements, that even the most respectable people were inflamed by it" and so "sensuous and wild, most passionate and unbridled" that it seduced the young with a "sexual pantomime of unparalleled suggestiveness."[2] It is a shock to realize that these are early references to the *Sarabande* and *Chaconne*. The pattern has remained the same throughout the centuries; new songs and dances are denounced and banned as lascivious, and this causes them to spread like wildfire until they are eventually domesticated and rendered acceptable to the upper classes.

2. Quoted by Curt Sachs in his *World History of the Dance*, New York, 1937.

Such examples can be found in theater as well. *Commedia dell'arte* was a vulgar and *risqué* popular art that proved to be upwardly mobile and spun off into the comedies of Goldoni and the *opera buffa*. Legendary figures like Faust, Pulcinella, and Don Giovanni arose originally out of the popular imagination and later became subjects for high art treatment. Popular art tends to put its characters (even legendary or historical figures) into new and contemporary settings and tends to use linear forms—songs and dances—in simple, easily assimilated forms.

There is a point at which high art and popular art meet and, like the social climbing characters of an *opera buffa*, actually interbreed. Popular art is about big emotions, especially the erotic and the dangerous as well as the exotic, most of it at or near the surface. Highbrow art is about power and inheritance; it is multilevel, and when it takes up emotional themes like passion or evil, it tends to want to show their intellectual content and to insert a certain amount of layered emotional distance.

The *singspiel* and *opera buffa* expressed their themes of social climbing and interaction between classes through a new and popular simplification of musical style; in an age when Jean-Jacques Rousseau's theories about man in a state of nature were widely influential, the new simplicity essentially took over highbrow music. Operatic reform in the eighteenth century—from Pergolesi and Rousseau himself (he was a successful music-theater composer[3]) to Gluck and Mozart—was almost completely a matter of moving away from the complexities and "artificiality" of the baroque to notions about the natural, the simple, the authentic and true. Although these qualities are associated with "classicism" and "neoclassicism" in the higher arts, many of their musical practices were intentionally taken up from popular sources.

Rousseau himself looked inward and was concerned with feelings but the classical and back-to-nature movements of the eighteenth century were largely products of rationalism and the Enlightenment. By the end of the century, however, the expression of feelings, the appeal of folk art, and various strands of irrationalism, exoticism, and the supernatural began to dominate the new romantic movements. The so-called magic opera of the nineteenth century, from Weber to Wagner, drew on popular themes of eroticism, evil, danger, and individual action. Again, much of this welled up from the popular imagination, but in highbrow form, artists took these themes in the direction of transcendence and metaphysics.

---

3. Rousseau initiated two important musico-theatrical forms: the *opéra comique* with *Le Devin du Village* (1752; music by Rousseau himself) and the melodrama with *Pygmalion* (1770; music by Horace Coignet).

Social and class issues, some of them quite revolutionary, run right through this history. Pergolesi's *La serva padrona* of 1733 (the servant girl who seduces and marries her master), Mozart's *Le nozze di Figaro* of 1786 (the servants and their masters wear masks so they can change places) and the Lecocq *La Fille de Madame Angot* of 1872 (the fishwife's daughter and the market people of Les Halles dress up in costume to expose the game-playing aristocrats at a masked ball) were all huge hits that play with themes of class identity and mobility. To get their libretto past the censors, Mozart and his librettist, Lorenzo da Ponte, replaced Figaro's original soliloquy railing against the aristocracy with an aria about the unfaithfulness of women—but few in the audience would have been confused. Wagner, like many other radical nineteenth-century artists, started out as a social revolutionary (see George Bernard Shaw's *The Perfect Wagnerite* for an amusing explanation of how Wagner's *Ring* proposes and then eventually turns away from revolutionary motifs). All these themes—the return to the simple, authentic, and true; the social concerns; and the espousal of popular forms—come together in the music-theater reforms of the 1920s and 1930s in which the intellectual qualities of evil (now transmuted into injustice) and a popular eroticism combine with a certain emotional distance.

Kurt Weill wrote extensively about the popular roots of theater and music theater before and during his collaborations with Brecht and after his emigration to the United States, which was very important for his development. Curiously, it may be that European culture has become too differentiated to have one musico-theatrical art form for all social classes and Weill's own work—his own genre of musical theater, which he played a major role in creating—still has no fixed place in European performing institutions (his works appear in concert halls, small opera or theater companies, or in festivals). In this respect, the situation is quite different in America where the links between both the European and American Weill and the "serious" musical theater of Gershwin, Bernstein, Blitzstein, Sondheim, and the post-Sondheim generation are easy to trace and still linger. But even in America, it could be said that every social class, every social field, has its own music which might develop in musico-theatric form. Pop, rock, and rap concerts have already reached show dimensions with projections, videos, costumes, props, and role playing imposed on top of what was once merely a succession of songs.

How far can opera and music theater go in this direction? In the early 1960s, Hans-Klaus Metzger reproached Luigi Nono for having set the voices of tortured Algerians to music "for the amused applauding of the bourgeoisie." The 2006 production of *Ghaddafi: A Living Myth*—a "CNN opera" dealing with Libyan leader Colonel Muammar Qaddafi —at the English National Opera in the summer of 2006, split the public and critics precisely

Ghaddafi: A Living Myth as staged by the English National Opera (ENO) with Ramon Tikaram in the title role. With kind permission of the English National Opera. © 2006.

on the issue of what kinds of subject matter can and should be treated in the opera house. The opera house opened its doors to the British ethno-punk band, Asian Dub Foundation, and its musical head Steve Chandra Savale to join forces with its symphonic orchestra. The piece uses hip-hop or rap declamation with female dancing/singing choruses to tell the story. Some called it a radical shake-up of stuffy operatic conventions while others described it as patronizing and a desperate attempt to attract a new audience.

Changing roles

As "realistic" forms of storytelling passed from the epic poem to painting to the novel and the theater and then to the opera, they attracted a middle-class public with an appealing combination of passion, tragedy, scenic spectacle, vocal power, virtuosity, and emotive music. This reached its operatic peak in the spectacles of Meyerbeer, in the Wagnerian music drama, in the sentimental and exotic tragedies of Puccini, and the erotic fantasies of Debussy and the post-Wagnerians. Afterward, this kind of narrative passed into the realm of film (and, to a lesser degree, television) where music continues to play an important if largely unacknowledged role. Theater itself lost its commitment to "missing-fourth-wall" realism. The compact between author and public (and performer and public) to provide a linear narrative of character and motive was no longer in force.

What replaced it? Modernism (or avant-gardism) challenged conservatism; internalized emotions or abstraction replaced external representation. In music theater this produced an explosion of small forms beginning with *Erwartung* and *Die Glückliche Hand* of Schoenberg and *L'Histoire du Soldat* of Stravinsky and continuing with the chamber pieces and *Zeitoper* of the 1920s and 1930s. A series of new proposals was made about narrative and performance both in theory and in practice of which the Brechtian epic theater was the best known (but by no means the only one). The revival of a theater of masks and the notion of presentational theater were strong anti-realist (and anti-psychological) currents that inevitably involved the extensive use of visual presentation, mime, dance, new technologies, and, of course, music. Actors no longer had to become the characters they were assigned to play. Quite the contrary, the audience was expected to be aware at every point that they were witnessing a spectacle in which performers presented themselves before the public to tell stories, to put on identities or even masks, to sing ballads, to propose ideas and issues.

New technologies made their appearance at the same time as the traditional societies of Europe broke apart. World War II, the holocaust and the *shoah*, the forced emigration of millions of people, and the sheer level of destruction put artistic development on hold in the Old World even as new art emigrated with its practitioners to the New World. The Cold War marked a period of deep divisions. In Western Europe, innovation in art was connected to the destruction of the past and new commitment to leftist and communist ideology. Ironically, in Stalinist Eastern Europe, such innovation was regarded as formalist and subversive (and was, in fact, often a form of anti-Stalinist protest). And, even more remarkably, innovation and avant-garde experimentation were regarded in America as a symbol of liberalism, freedom, and anti-communism and even received government support as an anti-communist weapon in the Cold War!

New roles for the performer

Even the role of performers changed. The orchestra gradually sank into the opera house pit (and, in Bayreuth, vanished entirely under the stage) and then melted into the film or television sound track. No one would claim that because the orchestra in Wagner's Bayreuth is invisible it is therefore secondary or an afterthought. Similarly the film sound track plays an important if often unacknowledged role in structure of many (if not most) films.[4]

---

4. The story is told of an ex-director of silent films who was teaching a course in early film and insisted on showing everything without music except his own work, which he always showed with an added music track.

At the same time, instrumentalists reappeared on the stage and often came to play leading roles in new performance theater, roles quite equal in importance to those played by singers, actors, and dancers. The idea of asking instrumentalists to perform specific tasks or to appear on stage in certain ways has led to the notion of the *azione musicale* or *instrumentales Theater*, physical activity which becomes intrinsic to the performance of works by members of Fluxus, Cage, George Crumb, Mauricio Kagel, and others. One also finds increasingly that the singer/actor may be expected to play instruments (see a recent production of the Sondheim *Sweeney Todd* where the actors are also the orchestra or Rinde Eckert's *An Idiot Divine* where he speaks, sings, and plays various instruments) and instrumentalists may take physical, singing, or speaking roles.

The modern focus on the performer is a major cultural shift, which has taken place in all forms of performance from traditional live music, theater, and dance to various contemporary media, and it has changed the balance between creator and interpreter. There is nothing new in the idea of writers, choreographers, and composers creating works and roles for particular performers, and many performers and conductors in the past were also composers, often providing their own repertoire. But there has been a new emphasis on the performer/creator following the model of the artist-driven modern dance company or the jazz/pop groups whose repertoire is self-created. This tendency is also seen in the work of composers who perform and tour with their own ensembles. The movement away from strict adherence to a previously existing text or score and the return of improvisation are both a result and a cause of the changing relationship between creator and performer.

It is an easy and short step for performers, particularly vocalists of various kinds, to become the subject of their own performance, and in fact "performance art" (and sometimes the English word "performance" by itself) has been used to designate such pieces. The origins of performance art lie in the traditional actor's monologue and to a lesser degree the solo dance. However the concept has been extended into the realm of music with an admixture of language and other vocalizations, the employment of a wide variety of nonverbal sounds (singing, "extended voice," nonmusical sound, etc.), the use of audio and visual media to extend both the voice and physical presence of the performer, and a wide variety of instrumental, prerecorded, or electronic/computer accompaniments. Performers like Laurie Anderson, Pamela Z, Diamanda Galás, Kristin Norderval, and Maja Ratke create their own large-scale performance pieces, works in simple and direct or extended and exaggerated form, whose subject matter and principal characters are most often themselves.

The subject matter also changes roles

Concept art is a vaguely defined principle in which works of art are generated by their intellectual and formal conceptions or in which their formal structure—the *matériel sonore*—is the content, literally the subject matter, of the artistic action or activity. In a very real sense, the various forms of serialism were early applications of concept art in music. Computer music, dependent on the rigorous use of programs and templates, often belongs here as well. Much concept music, especially in physical performance situations, derives from ideas closely related to the visual arts. From here it is only a short step to installation art in which the spectator is confronted with visual and physical constructions in which sound may provide an important focus or may play only a supporting role. The composer Charlie Morrow built what he calls a "sound cube" for which various composers have created multidimensional sound sculptures that are experienced in "real" time in a space that is partly real and physical, partly virtual and psychoacoustic. A common feature of such installations is interactivity; that is, the physical presence and action of the spectator/auditor creates or alters the result in some more-or-less predetermined way.

Sound installation is related to another type of music-theater activity that should be mentioned here: "site-specific performance." While the physicality of site-specific art works—so-called earth works, for example—has had some musical counterparts (for example, Max Neuhaus's noise installation arising from below the street through a sidewalk grating in Times Square, New York), most site-specific music theater follows the lead of theatrical performances created for and growing out of designated locales of historic, architectural, social, geographic, or even environmental interest. The 2003 *6-Tage Oper Festival* in Düsseldorf, Germany, showed a series of works created for performance in a mental institution, on a farm, in a museum, and at a salon. Although none of these works was specifically interactive, the action of getting the public to the designated locations and the nontheatrical character of these locales had a major influence on the nature of the performance, the relationship of the performers to the public, and the piece to the environment. Still more complex are those site-specific performances—typically in an old mansion or abandoned factory with multiple spaces—in which the classic face-front single-action theatrical forms no longer apply and audience members have to choose from multiple possibilities which performers and which lines of action they will follow. (See also the various theatrical audience-performer paradigms illustrated in Chapter 7.)

More narrowly defined examples of conceptual music can be found in the work of John Cage, Mauricio Kagel, the composers associated with

Fluxus, Alvin Lucier, and many others. The classic examples of scenarios or recipes for activities that may produce sound can be found in La Monte Young's early sets of verbal instructions ("Hold...for a Long Time" [*Composition 1960*] or "Draw a straight line and follow it" [*Composition 1961*]). Kagel's *Pas de cinq* requires blindfolded actors to use canes to tap their way around a stage. Lucier's *Vespers* similarly asks performers to find their way in a space by using clicking sounds as a kind of sonar; his *Music for a Solo Performer* amplifies the electrical pulses produced by the brain of a performer attempting to go into a state of alpha sleep. There are many other examples.

Do sound installations and various forms of concept music constitute musical performance or, in any sense, music theater? The question is, of course, unanswerable. Music theater today exists on a continuum from traditional performance in a designated theater or opera space to sound-producing actions and activities, which may take place in nontraditional spaces or nontheatrical public sites.

Loudspeaker culture

The musical culture of microphones, loudspeakers, amplification, and recordings is now over a century old and it has gained ground rapidly in recent decades with the advent of digital reproduction. By far the vast majority of musical experiences of all types passes through loudspeakers, and the unmediated acoustic experience of music is now the exception rather than the rule. No aspect of musical life remains untouched by this. Even the performance of live classical music and opera in an acoustic environment cannot completely avoid the influence of recorded music. Often the performers actually try to imitate the sound of recorded music or, at the very least, they strive to imitate the seamlessness and repeatability of recordings (this has produced a far less idiosyncratic and personal style of performance than was the case in earlier generations). In the evolution of recorded music, engineers at first attempted to reproduce the effect of live performance in optimal sound conditions. Gradually, the situation has reversed itself and now the acoustic design of new concert halls and opera houses strives to duplicate the sound of high-quality recordings. Performers, musically literate or not, learn music by listening to recordings and try to reproduce them, consciously or unconsciously imitating their essential qualities. A vast enlargement of the familiar repertoire of music has been extended backward to include the earliest surviving music and lengthwise to include large samplings of the world's surviving musics. What was esoterica a few decades ago is now commonplace. The revival of early baroque, Renaissance, and medieval music, the old-instrument movement, the revival of early pop styles, and the rediscovery of relatively neglected composers like Vivaldi, Mahler, and Scott Joplin (to name only three) are all phenomena fueled by recordings. The widening horizons of pop music and the world music movement are also closely identified with electronic transmission and diffusion. It would be easy to extend this list almost *ad infinitum*.

Although all of this was well under way in the age of vinyl and tape, the switch to digital technology and the easy availability of high-quality and powerful computers has accelerated these developments and made them accessible on a wide scale.

Technology brings two obvious things to the cultural table: memory and distribution/diffusion. But it also brings flexibility and multiculturalism in the form of an egalitarianism (or at least the illusion of egalitarianism) in which a field recording made in an African rain forest has as much weight or significance as a Vienna State Opera recording. Also, the microphone functions like the camera in making the small large and turning the detail into the whole. This has a particularly strong impact in the transmission of the human voice. The spoken, whispered, or unprojected singing voice—normally not audible beyond the confines of a small room or intimate public gathering—can be transmitted over large distances in a performance space through recording. The idiosyncrasies of highly individual voices are emphasized and brought into focus.

The implications of all this are vast. The old idea—first proposed by Varèse and Cage—that any existing sound might be available for artistic use in composition has become a practical reality. And these technologies make sound manipulation and the creation of "new sounds" a relatively easy task. But the mere and unending availability of even the most banal sounds of a noise-polluted world has made the process of selection relevant again. In a curious way, this turns the old avant-garde paradigm upside down. Since everything is possible, it is no longer enough to discover something "new" but rather one must make something new by learning how to use it and discovering what it means. In many ways, the old abstract musical culture is not well set up to deal with this problem. It is striking how often even the purest of instrumental music concerts strive to find theatrical form in musical life today. In one way or another, music theater—with its multiple connections between proscenium and public, theater and street, interior and exterior culture—moves to the front lines as both a traditional and forward-looking place where these issues play themselves out.

Further Reading

Benjamin, Walter. *Selected Writings 1913–1938*, 3 Vols. Edited by Marcus Bullock and Michael W. Jennings. Cambridge, MA, 2004.

Sachs, Curt: *World History of the Dance*. New York, 1937.

Sheppard, W. Anthony. *Revealing Masks. Exotic Influences and Ritualized Performance in Modernist Music Theater*. Berkeley, CA, 2001.

Unamuno, Miguel de. *Tragic Sense of Life*. 1921; translated, New York, 1964.

Weill, Kurt. "The Future of Opera in America." *Modern Music* 4 (May–June 1937): 183–88; also "The Alchemy of Music." *Stage* (November 1936): 63–64.

entr'acte ii

A woman's earring, a diamond necklace, a knee, a yogi in meditation, drawing, a mahout looking after an elephant: the language of *Kathakali*

In trying to understand what music theater has been or could be (and what its universal underpinnings might be), it is worthwhile to look at ancient and non-Western forms that have survived relatively untouched by the current domination of Western forms. *Kathakali*[1] represents an ancient form of music theater based on the *Puranas* or Hindu religious scriptures and can provide us with a case study in the antiquity of music theater and its place in society. We will use it as one example of an alternate form of music theater in a non-Western (in this case, southern Indian or Dravidian) context.[2]

The very name *Kathakali* means acting out a story. Stories from the *Puranas* are mimed by the *Kathakali* actors in colorful, highly ornamented costumes with elaborate makeup or masks. The performances are a blend of mime, music, and dance, the last deriving from ancient ritual dance forms like *teyyam*, *tirayattam*, and *mudiyettu*. Theater forms like *kutiyattam* include the *hasta-mudras*—hand gestures and the movement of eyes, eyebrows, and other parts of the face according to a prescribed and recognized lexicon of meaning.

Dancing and singing has been always part of the ritual in the temples of Kerala. *Kutiyattam* is perhaps the best-known survivor of all the ancient forms of dramatic performance in India. It follows the *Natyasastra of Bharata*, a basic book that describes Indian dramaturgy. Each act is based on one of the stories (which are or were presumably already known to the public) and presents the thoughts and feelings of a character in a performance that might extend in time over many days. The pieces are presented in specially built temple-theatres (the *Kuthambalam*) with dry acoustics to facilitate comprehension and a single oil

1. Kathakali—a traditional Indian theater form—uses about 470 hand gestures ("Mudras"), which are listed in the *Hasthalakshana Deepika* or "Book of Hand Gestures." The significations of the gesture called *Vardhamanakam* are listed in the headline of this Entr'acte.
2. The Bollywood musical, probably the contemporary world's most prolific form of musical theater, is a modern invention and, in many ways, an Indian adaptation of the Hollywood musical.

lamp for light. Background music, mostly percussion, is provided by performers who come from families whose sole profession is the performance of such plays. This arrangement is reminiscent of European circus families who have trained and carried on their performance tradition for generations.

Besides *kathakali* and a martial art form (*kalari payattu*) mixed with performance, most Indian performance arts are solo or ensemble dance (*nagiar koothu, mohiniyattam, krishnanattam*). These are mostly based on the life stories of Krishna and others as they appear in the *Mahabharata* from which most Indian or Hindu performance art derives. These performance arts became widespread in the seventeenth and eighteenth centuries but nearly vanished in the early twentieth century due to the neglect of the ancient language of Sanskrit and the loss of traditional art sponsorship in the colonial period. Apparently these art forms were preserved in a few schools and institutions enabling them to resume in the postcolonial period.

In addition to theater, music theater, mime, and dance, another important stream of performing arts in the subcontinent is represented by puppet theater in all its forms. The use of heavy makeup, masks, and costumes in many types of Indian theater and dance creates a clear connection between live performance and puppetry, and Indian puppetry may even be said to create an ideal of movement for live human beings.

From all these traditions, a method has evolved that includes training schools and performances in the open air: fight scenes acted out in and around the audience and through the temple precinct; shadow dancing and puppetry behind a curtain; dancing in front of the curtain; and so on. A performance day might start at 8 P.M. and last till 5 A.M. while the complete performance might take up to eight nights. Although performers undergo an elaborate training, there are generally no rehearsals of particular pieces in the Western sense. The performers know the material and any possible variations would fall under the heading of permissible improvisation. The actors arrive about two hours before the performance to prepare their makeup and costumes. Only then do they learn what character or role they will play that evening. There are at least fifty popular roles out of a wider repertoire of as many as five hundred including stock characters. An important part of the art of the performer consists of his qualifications in knowing these roles.

Percussion dominates an instrumentarium of conch shells, hollow wooden cylinders, sticks, drums, a bronze gong of middle size, and bronze cymbals combined with the "background" vocals of singers who also play instruments. The plays themselves are written in verse. The forms, figures, stories, costumes—indeed everything in this theater—are restricted and well delineated. Even the eyes of the performers are strikingly defined, turned into a flaming red through the application of the juice of the chunda plant. This is music theater in a very ancient form.

One might ask from a Western view, what kind of progress or invention could be expected in such a tradition? The complexity and precision of an art that allows no inventions and few deviations, even for art's sake, would seem to occupy almost all the focus and attention of the performing artist. Nevertheless we do know that in traditional Asian performance arts, new paths and new ideas do appear from time to time and even gain entry into the standard repertory.

Further Reading

Venu, Gopal. *The Language of Kathakali*. Kairali, Kerala, India, 2000. A clear account of this traditional form of south Asian music theater.

chapter 5

Text

*GOLEM: Feefa, feega oow iggly? WB: If I submit then
I die. GOLEM: Oraasamay dodofelliu ferumptious?*

from *Shadowtime,* libretto by Charles Bernstein,
music by Brian Ferneyhough

Language and nonlanguage

The close association of music and language is a given in most societies
and most musical cultures but it has been easy to lose sight of this in the
long period dominated by the practice and the esthetics of abstract instrumental music. The question of whether there is such a thing as a "language"
or "languages" of music will not occupy us here; we are referring to the
synergy between spoken language, a medium of communication common
to every society, and that society's music. This is not just a music-theater
issue; it goes back to the fundamental role of intonation and rhythm in
the evolution and practice of music, and it is even an issue in instrumental
music where no vocal sounds or words occur. It is the derivation of musical
phrase and rhythm from words and from physical movement that gives
them "content," infuses them with associative power, and eventually allows
them to develop independently as pure music.

In the current view, a template exists in the human mind that frames
the underlying grammatical forms that are common to all languages (while,
of course, the actual sounds and the details of the rules employed vary

enormously). Although pitch is important in the basic structure of some spoken languages, there is usually a clear distinction between ordinary speech and the heightened intonation of language as used in public utterances, religious ritual (*tonus rectus*), and, eventually, recitation and theatrical/musical performance.

Any spoken, chanted, or sung text that consists of words—in isolation or in grammatical structures—obviously has roots in preexisting language or languages. Traditional theater is a storytelling medium that uses a heightened poetic or vernacular language to convey the interactions, sentiments, and desires of personages, their relationships to one another and to the course of events. Therefore, to state the obvious, theater texts are normally performed in the language of the locale where the performance takes place (exceptions to this rule are mostly connected with the continuing ritualistic use of dead languages like Latin or Sanskrit or the glossolalic fantasy languages known as "speaking in tongues" that evoke ancient mythic languages). If the original text is in another language, it is normally translated. This is true not only of spoken theater but also of music theater and, with some limited exceptions, opera. The best known of these exceptions, Italian opera in Italian, was originally able to spread outside the Italian peninsula because of the widespread emigration of Italian singers, musicians, composers, and librettists. They appeared first in Vienna, the capital of the multilingual Hapsburg Empire, which included a good portion of northern Italy. Italian was widely spoken and understood in Vienna, and with the establishment of an Italian opera, Italian musicians and singers came over the Alps in numbers to look for work. Afterward, Italian opera—or, in any event, opera in Italian—spread to other Austro-Hungarian centers, to the various German states, and eventually to Spain and Portugal, Russia, England, and even the New World. Its domination was successfully resisted only in France where Italian opera made inroads but where French opera had support from the royal court. It was because of this diffusion of Italian opera and Italian singers and musicians that Italian became the international language of music.[1]

The growth of nationalism in the late eighteenth and nineteenth centuries and the popularization of opera, operetta, and musical theater outside aristocratic precincts produced strong biases in favor of performances in the local language—original work produced locally and the translation of work from abroad. There has long been a close connection between music theater (including opera) as a popular art form and the formerly universal

---

1. Although Italian has lost ground, terms like *da capo* or *segue* are still used even by pop musicians, song writers, and studio arrangers.

practice of translation into the local vernacular. Even Wagner was trans-lated and performed in Italian in Italy and French in France!

Where opera has remained an imported, high-art phenomenon patron-ized largely by connoisseurs and the well-to-do segments of society, it is performed in its original languages. This has been reinforced by the exis-tence of a standard repertoire dominated by ultra-familiar "masterpieces" and by the standardization of vocal training everywhere (globalization has a long history in the world of opera). This has now extended even to works from Eastern European countries whose languages present major chal-lenges to Western performers.

The common practice of making opera librettos or synopses readily available, the growing prevalence of audio and video recordings, the increasing importance of international music festivals, the weakening of national styles, the introduction of assembly line methods in performance, the disappearance of the old locally based repertory companies, and the growth of a free-floating, jet-setting international corps of uniformly trained instrumentalists and singers (many of them from the Americas and Asia where all European opera was an exotic import) all contributed to the increasing practice of original language performance. And the introduc-tion of surtitles, now well established in most opera houses, has strongly reinforced this trend.

The arguments for original language performance have been strongly backed up by the formerly widespread (and still powerful) ideas about *Urtext* and textual fidelity that dominated critical thinking about music a generation ago. This view also has an esthetic component ("the sound of the language is part of the music") and to some degree an element of class distinction ("the educated consumer of opera should be able to under-stand foreign languages"). The notion that the music of language is equal in importance to its musical setting and at least as important as the meaning of the words requires an idealism that is inevitably in conflict with the reali-ties of actual performance. This argument is also weakened by the ubiquity of international casts of singers, many of whom have not fully mastered the languages in question (notably French) and whose styles of pronun-ciation in a single performance may diverge drastically and, on occasion, comically. The problem goes far beyond the mere question of having a good accent; it affects the styles of performance required and the detailed word-to-word meaning of the text, which, in turn, deeply affect the stage comportment and action of the performers, their musical phrasing, and other points of interpretation. The issue of surtitles is still more complex as they are a distraction from the stage and may defocus the audience's atten-tion. However they provide a solution to the dilemma posed by listening to an operatic or music-theater work in an incomprehensible language and therefore missing major dimensions of the work, dimensions that librettos and synopses scarcely begin to provide.

With the internationalization of performance (which began quite early in operatic history), the question of language became more and more important to composers and their audiences. A work like *Les Noces* of Stravinsky, with its typically Russian text sound, became widely known in a French translation. The issue of language was undoubtedly a factor in the long delay in the recognition of the work of Leoš Janáček who wrote in Czech but became known, outside of Bohemia and Moravia, in German translations. Composers sometimes adopted a widely used international idiom—French before World War II, English in more recent decades—as a way of transcending the language problem. Another language strategy involves the use of dead liturgical languages. The Stravinsky/Cocteau *Oedipus Rex*, described as an "opera-oratorio," uses a well-known story from Greek mythology, which is sung in a Latin translation while the narrator—originally Cocteau himself—explains the action of each scene in the local vernacular before it is shown. As an even more extreme example, the Philip Glass *Satyagraha*, an opera about Gandhi's early life in Africa, is in Sanskrit, a language that ceased to be spoken or understood even in its native India centuries before Gandhi was born. There are here a whole series of choices about language, subject matter, performance, presentation, and esthetics, which typify the neoclassical and presentational point of view.

Words in music—Storytelling, librettos, and dramaturgy

Traditionally music theater begins with the production of the *libretto*, often independently, sometimes in collaboration with the composer or with both the composer and the director. The *libretto*, a combination of book and lyrics, casts a long shadow on the history of music theater.[2]

The term *libretto* serves to differentiate the particular purpose of this kind of text from that of other functional texts such as filmscripts, dramatic

---

2. *Libretto* is a term owned by music theater and opera. The word means simply "small book" in Italian; the short length of text needed and the small-sized print made it easily portable so that it could be carried into the theater and read during the performances (ironically, the darkened theater came later with improvements in stage lighting). The librettist usually kept the right to print and sell his *libretto* as an extra source of income. As with many other ancient musical terms, the Italian word remains with us in reference to the text of an opera or a musical theater work that is set to music all the way through. "Book and lyrics" comes from the popular musical theater where the book refers to the spoken texts and the lyrics are the words of the songs. *Librettos* (Italian: *libretti*) also include information on the cast, setting, and stage directions.

(spoken) plays, *Hörspiele,* or any generic text with soliloquies or dialogues. The *libretto* is not a play. It lacks the good breeding or literary heritage that allows plays to be classifiable into tragedy and comedy. Sung text slows down the conversational exchange of words by an order of magnitude.[3] This problem is crucial for any setting of words to music, and every historical reform of opera has had, at least partly, to deal with this problem. Recitative, as typical as it is for opera, is often seen as a flaw or necessary evil. It must cover crucial moments in the understanding of a text-oriented narration and give background information about characters or actions. Mostly it is used to make a character's feelings and thoughts comprehensible before the performer sets out on a major musical expression of the same things.

The invention of recitative marks the beginning of the history of what we call opera. But why was recitative necessary in the first place? Spoken dialogue tends to sound profane and banal when it interrupts a thoughtfully crafted musical structure. An even bigger problem is that performers must adopt a completely different tessitura or vocal range when they switch from sung to spoken language (or vice versa). There is a tension in singing—as if singing were another state of being that is lost in normal or even theatrical speech. As a result, singers are sometimes forced into very artificial styles of speaking that may have been acceptable in the past but sound irredeemably artificial to modern audiences. These problems are particularly evident with supported-voice vibrato singing of the traditional operatic type and with head-voice singing in general. Pop singing and some theater styles are closer to the speaking voice so the distance between song and speech is not as great, but such voices must generally be amplified for this to work properly.

Above all, the pacing of the language in a libretto must deal with temporality. Music theater—like music itself—deals with the passage of time, real or perceived, in a perceptual process. All this goes well beyond the temporal aspects of normal speech. The polyphonic structure of music allows or even requires that texts be presented simultaneously in the form of choruses, duets, or other ensembles. In the Mozart/Da Ponte *Don Giovanni* Donna Anna's phrase parallels Don Giovanni's verbally as well as musically:

Donna Anna: Come furia disperata ti saprò perseguitar[4]
Don Giovanni: Questa furia disperata mi vuol far precipitar[5]

3. An amusing example of this is the Philip Glass setting of the dialogue track from the Jean Cocteau film *Beauty and the Beast,* which is meant to be performed simultaneously with a projection of the film. Even though the dialogue is rather sparse and laconic and Glass's setting is syllabic and swift, the performers have to scramble just to keep up.
4. "Like a desperate fury, I will find a way to track you down."
5. "This desperate fury wants to cause my downfall."

This example shows how different internal points can become audible in parallel texts. Many variations of this technique can be imagined and most of them have been realized at one time or another. These are methods of writing that are closely linked to musical composition and would make no sense in a spoken exchange. Parallel consonances sung by two opponents might be just a pleasant musical commodity, but an attentive composer would use them to symbolize a harmonious relationship; even opponents may show congruencies on a psychologically deeper level. Musical polyphony can offer parallelism, antagonism, or just the typical synchronism of two or more characters speaking clearly. It becomes apparent that the harmonic system with its voicings is eminently suited to make perceptible many hidden layers of human communication, behavior, and intention.

Over a period of two centuries or more, tonal-harmonic music developed a communicative system of rhetorical figures, the so-called *topoi*, which allowed some semantic qualities to the musical discourse (see also Chapter 19). The *topoi* or "figures," originally part of Greek rhetoric, played an important role in music theory in the seventeenth century and continued to be influential well afterward. The idea was that emotions or gestures could be described in music by the use of meta-musical significations for musical figures. For example, scales moving upward would indicate ascent while a descending musical figure might symbolize humiliation. A specific action or intention by a singer/actor in an opera might be accompanied by a contradicting musical figure, which would add extra meaning to the action or to what is being said. In a well known example in Mozart's *Don Giovanni,* Mozart uses a snide, laughing figure to accompany the assurances of our eponymous hero; even today, audiences get the message that our hero is stretching the truth. (Another example from *Don Giovanni* is given in Chapter 19.) In general, however, it is difficult to say how well these figures are understood, particularly when the works in question travel to geographically and culturally distant places. Sound symbols are a subset of such figures and some of them—hunting horns, militaristic trumpets and drums—are still well understood today.[6] A good libretto was one that offered the composer the possibilities of combining gestures or expressions with musical motives.

Although we have some classical examples in which the music contradicts what is being said, in most cases (especially in romantic music) the

6. A famous punning example comes from *Le nozze di Figaro*. Figaro, telling us about the unfaithfulness of women, adds the words "you know what happens next" and the instrumental response is a horn call. In Italian, horns signify cuckold.

music is written in a way that reinforces or doubles the meaning of the words and the stage action. The usual sequence is that we first hear things and then want to find the source. For example, bird watchers—even those who are not musically experienced—learn to identify songs by tracing the sound to the singer. This connection between what we hear and what we see is quite natural; it is very satisfying to us and may in fact have evolved for various reasons of security, finding food, and so on. However in modern theater and music theater, this "natural" relationship may be intentionally broken for artistic purposes. Modern compositional concepts may be based on a combination of contradictory elements, reflecting the need to find new ways of combining elements rather than merely arranging and rearranging them in known combinations. In such works, the audience may never get "to see what they hear" or "hear what they see." The quality of surprise or alienation that results is intended to work as an irritant or a spark to ignite new insights, new cognitions, or recognitions.

Musicologists and music lovers often underestimate the importance of the libretto in traditional opera for many reasons—among them, the complex relationships between music and text, the over-familiarity of many repertory works, and the fact that repertoire operas are (in most places) in foreign languages. Since the text was typically conceived first (before the musical composition), most historical milestones in all forms of sung theater were rooted in the libretto rather than in the music. Whatever our modern views of these old librettos might be, the early success of many classic and romantic operas rested on the stage-worthiness of the libretto as viewed by its contemporaries. Franz Schubert had very little luck with his operatic work due to his insignificant libretti. Even Beethoven, who had a strong subject taken from a popular play of the time, had libretto trouble, which caused him to undertake extensive revisions in his only opera (originally called *Leonore*, later *Fidelio*). On the other hand, Verdi and Puccini took care to base most of their work on popular or successful plays that had proven their theatricality before even a note was added.

From the very first conception of opera in Florence, to the development of French opera as a serious art form, to the reforms of Gluck and his librettist Calzabigi, to the triumph of the Italian *opera buffa*, to the revolutionary attitudes of Mozart and Beethoven, to the nationalization of non-Italian libretti in the early nineteenth century, to the Wagnerian music drama, to Italian *verismo*, to the Russian and Czech national opera based on Slavic languages, to the expressionist works of the early twentieth century, to the ideological *Songspiel* and *Lehrstueck* of the 1920s and 1930s, to the romantic and modern *Literatur-Oper* settings of preexisting literary works, it was the libretto that led to new types of opera and music theater and which determined the first success or failure of new work.

The synopsis: subject matter in music theater

Getting to know the synopsis of a theater piece is a common starting point even for the general public. But what if there is no story? Many new pieces do not rely on narrative but claim to represent a whole world. This is the artist's "anti-world" that carries the claim to improve the existing one. This is an environment that, like a zoo or an aquarium, is created to show a utopian version of the world. Perhaps the disillusionment of failed social revolutions induced artists to abandon the idea that art could actually change anything in reality. Instead, art could create an ideal world that would last just as long as the performance. The protagonists would distract the spectator from projecting himself into such a world. Or there would be no human protagonists at all. No more Aristotelian mimesis of a real world but utopia instead!

When traditional storytelling is abandoned, an essential aspect of theater is done away with. The purpose of eliminating narration is not to replace it with anything else; that would be impossible. Narration is simply erased as a generating or determining force. Confusingly, narrative stories may be present, but they are often just one or more elements along with or beneath the real message. But they are not the dominant carrier any longer. It is very difficult to discuss whether art has to be "understandable." Incomprehensibility is often simply the blurring of the line between intention and pretension, between the magic of not telling everything (leaving room for the spectator's fantasy) and a failure to communicate.

As music theater tends to become a laboratory for various experiments in terms of topics, issues, formal composition, synesthetic try-outs, and ideologically loaded messages or manifestos, it is obvious that narrative will also become the subject of such experiments. In story-oriented pieces, conceptually dominated by narration—whether linear or, in more modern fashion, nonlinear—the abbreviated story, the actions of the protagonists, the setting, and the intentions of the characters all combine to design a handy image. Such pieces, being in the tradition of opera and theater rather than visual art or dance, tend to focus on specific problems in human society and life without postulating a utopian anti-world environment. If we look at such pieces that have been performed in the last few years, we find a rich set of themes dealing with the conflicts of inter-human relationship, still the predominant subject of theater. The dynamics of the performance recreates the drama by acting out the situation. But where do the conflicts arise from? Disabilities or illness make for a well-known thematic complex. Family is another, a smaller society within the larger. Sex and crime are possible ingredients (not to be confused with sexuality and violence).

In the *verismo* tradition of opera, realistic accounts are acted out, while in modernism they are transferred into a world of metaphors—fairy tales as well as tales in which actors play animals that present us with caricatures of human behavior. These metaphors for human behavior are various and popular for many reasons. Illness and physical disability, or mental and psychological uneasiness are made less specific, becoming more accessible to an audience. The use of metaphoric performance roles as told through a fairy-tale setting—and especially when sweetened or underlined by music—may stimulate an interest in a subject without resorting to mere voyeurism,

When there are no such metaphors, the story might be drawn from actual documents that deal with social problems. This is the domain of the found text (as in *The True Last Words of Dutch Schultz*; see Chapter 17) or what the French call *faits divers*, the newspaper story taken from the police blotter. We find here tales concerning illegal immigration, globalization, the media, alienation, social striving, consumerism, television, and the world of shopping.

Literature and the news

A great deal of contemporary opera and music theater is in fact based on preexisting material. From the found text to the literary text may not always be a great distance. Debussy set Maeterlinck word for word and Berg put entire scenes from Büchner's *Woyzeck* into music without change. In the so-called *Literaturoper* the composer adapts the text into a libretto and then sets the writer's exact words, thus doing away with the need for an actual librettist. Maeterlinck, Poe, Büchner, Lenz, Kafka, Joyce, and others have been pressed into service in this manner.

In some cases, the subject matter may be as important as authorship. Both print literature and the dramatic or spoken theater may provide material. As already mentioned, well-known plays that have been turned into successful musical theater or operatic material include the sources of nearly all the major Verdi and Puccini operas; more recently, Chekhov, Tony Kushner, and Arthur Miller have been used in this manner by Peter Eötvös (*Three Sisters; Angels in America*) and William Bolcom (*A View from the Bridge*). Film has now become a major source for material.[7] Early films were often adaptations from the theater, and several silent film classics have been adapted into opera or music theater; the new version, in effect, adds the sound track. Modern theater production often strives to achieve

---

7. The recent hit *The Producers* is a movie musical made from a stage musical that was made from a film.

cinematic continuity and flow; nevertheless the transfer from film back to the theater is not always simple. Most typical film genres—the Western, crime thriller, horror film, science fiction—adapt themselves into music theater or opera only with difficulty, and there are often major problems with rights. Some recent examples of music theater or operatic adaptations from film are Michael Obst's *Solaris* (1995) after Andrei Tarkovsky, Olga Neuwirth's *Lost Highway* (2003) after David Lynch, and the William Bolcom/Arnold Weinstein *A Wedding* (2005) after Robert Altman.

A common practice in film that has had some resonance in music theater is the remake. A classic example is Peter Brook's *La Tragédie de Carmen* (1983) which created a music-theater version of the Bizet opera by going back to the original Prosper Merimée novel, using cut-down arrangements of the score by Benjamin Constant, and casting actors and theater singers rather than big-voiced opera singers. Other examples are the Viennese productions of *La Traviata* by Totales Theater in 1994 and *The Butterfly Equation* after Puccini by ZOON Music Theater. Another approach to the remake problem is offered by Henri Pousseur's *Votre Faust* with a text by Michel Butor and a score that refers to and quotes historical treatments of the subject, literary and musical. Some of the prototypical figures of classical opera like Faust, Figaro, Don Giovanni, and others have been the subject of latter-day treatments, and other popular figures of literary mythology like Dracula/Nosferatu and Frankenstein have appeared in multiple interpretations.

Material for new music theater has been taken from recent history, current events, and mass media. These works, sometimes referred to as "CNN Operas," actually treat events from many decades with a wide variety of subjects and personalities, political, scientific, artistic, mediatic, and otherwise. Among the public figures who have made major and more or less successful appearances in this latter-day *Zeitoper* we can list Albert Einstein, Robert Oppenheimer, Richard Nixon, Chairman Mao, Patty Hearst, Jacqueline Kennedy Onassis, Marilyn Monroe, Malcolm X, Colonel Qaddafi, and the television host Jerry Springer.

Does the piece sell the problem or vice versa?

Although there is a temptation to seize on current events and political issues, most of the more successful uses of contemporary material (and almost all the ones that outlast the events that gave them birth) are more like meditations on a theme than immediate, dramatized reactions. Theater reactions to current events always involve some necessary time lag. In terms of speed, theater cannot outpace television although it can be faster than film. Many pieces carved out from dramatic events come to seem absurdly speculative

with the passage of time. A more general reflection on events or a treatment of the inner psychological layers is usually more successful. A certain
necessary distance from the immediacy of the events prevents a topical
theater or music-theater event from becoming a weak imitation of television news. A spectacular subject will attract media attention but is rarely
sufficient to save a piece that is artistically deficient. Independent theater
never can function as a moral institution, desirable as that might seem to
author, composer, or producer. Addressing the problems of the world is
more likely to appeal to voyeurism than to solving anything. An art work or
production that succeeds in simply grasping, keeping, and conveying the
problems of living together in the world so that they remain present in the
collective consciousness may be more than enough.

In the early days, serious and tragic subjects were almost always set in
Italian (even by non-Italian composers), and the more successful of these
works made the rounds of the international opera houses that were prolifer-
ating all around Europe and its outposts. These stories, performed by vocal
virtuosi, among whom the *castrati* were predominant, generally involved
the complicated love lives of legendary figures, demigods, or great historical
figures. The main action in many of these works seems calculated simply to
show the regent's wealth, power, or wisdom. Tragic stories (including those
that were given deus ex machina happy endings) can be considered allego-
ries of fate and predestination and, as such, were viewed as supportive of
the status quo.

Comedies, with more contemporary stories about sexual intrigues, interaction between the classes, and social climbing, often revolve around the
clever servant or clown character (Scapin, Figaro, Pulcinella) who lives by
his wits; they were, almost by definition, more subversive and therefore
more popular with a larger public. Although often in Italian or based on
Italian models, they were also among the first to be performed in local
vernaculars and they employ a simplified, popular musical style, which
contributed enormously to their success and had a major influence on
the course of European music. Like minimalism today, the new style was
fought bitterly by the proponents of the old order, notably in France where
the traditional baroque opera of Lully was challenged by the popularity of
the new Italian comic opera (this controversy was known as the *Querelle*
or *Guerre des bouffons*). Jean-Jacques Rousseau, who was a composer as
well as a writer and *philosophe*, defended the Italians and the use of the
Italian language although his own great success, *Le devin du village*, was
in French. Rousseau's ideas about "natural man" and his espousal of the
simpler Italian style then coming into vogue were enormously influential and are astonishingly parallel to the "back to nature" movements and
the triumphs of folk music and minimalism in recent decades. The *opere*

buffe of Pergolesi, Piccini, and Mozart and the neoclassicism of Gluck (a composer who worked in Italian, German, and French and firmly brought neoclassicism into *opera seria*) diffused the new style throughout Europe. Listening to baroque opera sung by *castrati* wearing bejeweled and feathered costumes with hour after hour of *da capo* arias filled with endless spidery ornaments was an acquired, aristocratic taste. The new classicism, which cut across class lines by purveying simple dramatic stories or deliciously comic intrigues, contributed to a sharp rise in the popularity of opera and music theater.

As Rousseau famously argued, the new, lighter, classical style was closely connected with the character of the Italian language. The lyrical qualities of Italian, due largely to its mellifluous vowels, are well known. But Italian is also highly rhythmic and typically organized in quick, short, symmetrical phrases that allow for patter songs, lively dialogue, and speedy stage action. French lacks the internal rhythmic element and tends toward long, highly organized asymmetry while German, although very rhythmic, has major tendencies toward long phrases and complex grammatical structures. Even so, Rousseau managed to write a hugely successful popular opera in French. And it was a German composer from Bohemia (Gluck) who brought full-blown classicism to France, and classicism flowered, operatically and otherwise, in Vienna—first in Italian but then afterward also in German.

By the end of the eighteenth century, traditional storytelling in the opera began to change under the influence of the emerging romantic movement and the folklore revival in literature and the theater. A very high percentage of the major operas of the nineteenth century were musical settings of plays, adaptations of popular material, or in some cases both. Almost all the major operas of Verdi and Puccini were taken from well-known (and mostly contemporary) plays while the works of Weber and Wagner had folkloric sources. Opera drew on its source material in exactly the same manner as early cinema.

After the triumph of film and other mass media in popular culture, grand opera and operetta declined as popular storytelling forms, and in both spoken and musical theater, other values came to the fore. It could be argued that the commercial theater has continued to support the notion that popular music-theater works tell old-fashioned stories; see, for example, *West Side Story* and *Rent,* which transpose Shakespeare and *La Bohème* to the slums of New York and which combine elements of comedy and tragedy, high art, and popular theater. Nevertheless, in general, the traditions of linear narrative and role playing gave way in twentieth-century theater to new kinds of nonlinear narrative. If the old opera was closely allied to the novel and the spoken theater, new music theater and a good deal of modern and postmodern opera incorporates or assimilates elements from the visual arts and the condition of contemporary dance. Physical and visual elements come to play an increasingly important role in new work. Actors and singers are no longer always required to invest their stage personalities with the characters they are "pretending" to inhabit or to convince the public that they have "become" these characters. Similarly, the role playing required of all the participants—creators, directors, performers, and public as well—also changes as the act and activity of performance becomes itself a principal narrative.

This change in attitude about stories is also connected to a change of position with regard to the protagonists of such stories. The tragedy of the individual hero (or anti-hero), beloved of romantic opera, gives way to the anonymous (and symbolic or representative) protagonist, and the now dysfunctional narrative tale is replaced by a theater of images, also strongly imbued with symbolic or representative values. Brecht staged the original *Mahagonny Songspiel* in a boxing arena (presumably the working-man's preferred form of theater) and there has been a profusion of music-theater pieces in recent years dealing with sports.[8] With the disappearance of operatic heroes and heroines, there is a diminishing lack of interest in the singers who can sing heroically (i.e., highest and loudest), and low or undifferentiated voices gain ground. Hence, in Udo Zimmermann's *Weisse Rose*, described as "scenes for two singers and 15 instruments" (version of 1988), only an opposition between female and male voices is specified. In the Robert Wilson/Tom Waits *The Black Rider* no vocal types are prescribed at all; the psychology of the tessitura has disappeared. Many solo vocal performers (Robert Ashley, Laurie Anderson, Mikel Rouse, Pamela Z, David Moss, and others) simply use their own voices—not always trained—and their individual vocal idiosyncrasies as the basis for their performances.

Reciting stories melodramatically

In a literal sense, telling stories to a musical accompaniment is the oldest form of musico-theatrical declamation and it has periodically been revived in one form or another as a new idea.

Whether recited, spoken in rhythm, or intoned, these kinds of recitations are found in all cultures. The invention of recitative and opera in the late Renaissance and early Baroque period in Europe was based on the supposed revival of ancient Greco-Roman practice in the form of the so-called *stile rappresentativo*, vocal intonation accompanied by appropriate chords. The practice of reciting poetry or performing theatrical

---

8. Benedict Mason's *Playing Away* (1994), Moritz Eggert's *In der Tiefe des Raums* (2005), and Enjott Schneider's *Nullvier* (2004) are all football operas.

scenes or entire works to a fully composed accompaniment was popular in the eighteenth century under the name *melodrama* (the original meaning of that much-abused term) and can be found in the works of composers as varied as Jean-Jacques Rousseau, Georg Benda, Beethoven, Berlioz, Richard Strauss, Stravinsky, and Cage. Around the turn of the twentieth century, there was a new interest in the development of intermediate forms of speech-song, notably in the declamatory vocal style used by Debussy in *Pélléas et Mélisande* and Schoenberg's use of *Sprechgesang* in the last section of his *Gurrelieder* and *Pierrot Lunaire*. The latter work was written for a *diseuse* or monologist, a type of performer/reciter popular in cabaret, music hall, and vaudeville who reappeared in the latter part of the century as the protagonist of "performance art" performance. As with so many other things, it was John Cage who seems to have set the style with his *Indeterminacy: New Aspect of Form in Instrument and Electronic Music* of 1958, which, in spite of its long and intentionally preposterous title, consists of a set of ninety small anecdotes accompanied by piano and electronic sounds, each slowly recited or gabbled through to fit a predetermined one-minute sound space. Many of the so-called New Monologists were actors (Spalding Gray, Eric Bogosian), but a whole new style of music-theater performance also developed out of the recitation of stories that were spoken informally or intoned ritualistically to the accompaniment of repeated musical patterns or fragments (Laurie Anderson, Robert Ashley, and others). In the Steve Reich/Beryl Korot video opera *The Cave*, the musical score is actually generated from the rhythm and pitch of the talking heads that appear in the video. It is not only the language but the voice itself—with every gradation between singing and speaking, screaming and squeaking—that counts, and all of it is transmitted and transformed electronically through distortion, multiplication, or an amplification of intimacy. The recitation itself and the accompaniments separate out into equal bands or streams that may or may not interact (mostly on the rhythmic level) but otherwise remain independent.[9]

It is undoubtedly not a coincidence that these performance styles and techniques appeared at the same moment that rap began its rise in popular music, a fact that also suggests that rap has a still unrealized role to play in music theater. With rap artists, not only the text content counts but also the virtuosity of the rhymes, the speed of the speech, and the sound of the voice itself. It should also be noted that the DJs and turntablists who sample and alter existing recorded music to create performance collages are not very

9. These ideas had a predecessor in the work of Leoš Janáček, who owned a chronometer that was able to measure durations of speech fragments, which he would then use in his operas.

distant *confrères* of the performance artists who process themselves and the world around us in real time.

Can music itself tell stories?

There is another question that needs to be asked here: can music itself tell stories? The Wagnerian notion—at least as important for Wagner as his concept of Total Theater—is that music can track a story and shape the rhythm and sentiment of a narration with great precision, almost as if we could know what the character was saying from the music alone. This principle is dependent on the continuous stream of music that issues forth from both Wagnerian singers and the Wagner orchestra, a stream that is itself dependent on the avoidance or long postponement of resolution (and resolution is, in turn, a concept based on the idea of expectation as created by traditional romantic tonality and key structure[10]). This basic idea, if not its actual musical realization, was carried forward by Schoenberg and Berg and became the stock-in-trade of modernist opera even long after keys, tonality, expectation, resolution, and nonresolution ceased to be important. It is found, enlarged to monumental proportions of size, complexity, and difficulty, in Bernd Alois Zimmermann's *Die Soldaten* dating from the late 1950s, and it even informs some surprising operatic work by pure modernists such as Helmut Lachenmann (*Das Mädchen mit den Schwefelhölzern*) and Brian Ferneyhough (*Shadow Time*). The association of familiar stories ("The Little Match Girl" and "The Golem" in these two cases) with the unfamiliar and highly abstract languages of these composers has the odd effect of suggesting something extra-musical in the music but without any clarity as to what that might be. It as if there were metaphors in these scores for something left unsaid, something about shades of *angst* and anxiety perhaps. In the end, it may be that these scores belong to the history of opera rather than the narrower (or perhaps wider) world of music theater.

There are other possible answers. One is that music does not and cannot tell stories. Another is that it tells different kinds of stories. Neither of these answers precludes theater music. Quite the contrary; the traditional role of music in theater is to physicalize the moment, sweeten it, make it more amusing or even more thought-provoking. Almost all the anti-Wagner movements of twentieth-century music theater draw on popular musics, closed forms, rhythmic clarity, irony, and alienation. Stravinskyian neoclassicism

10. It is typical of the structure of the German language that the "resolution" of long sentences is suspended by the delay of the arrival of the verb to the very end, a normal feature of German grammar that fits Wagner's musical technique very well.

and the Brechtian *Verfremdungseffekt* are the best known But there are more recent examples that show the influence of minimalism, separating the streams of verbal recitation and musical accompaniment into independent bands of sound based on extended repetition with or without variation and only occasional rhythmic intersection. This form, which actually arose as a kind of Cage-inspired performance art, is, in fact, the neoclassicism of our day.

No sense or non-sense? From no story to no text at all

As the importance of linear narrative and character recede, the use of fragmented and nonlinear texts has gained ground. The issues of text become at once simpler and more complex. Found or documentary texts have been used as the basis for music-theater works, often without a conventional scenario. A typical strategy uses so-called *macaronic* texts, fragments from various languages, overlaid on one another like palimpsests. There is a complicated cat-and-mouse game between meaning and comprehension with a musical setting (itself often polyvalent) imposed on top of the whole thing. Perhaps the most extreme example is Zimmermann's *Requiem für einen jungen Dichter,* an oratorio in form rather than a purely scenic work but closely allied to the composer's monumental *Die Soldaten* (1965). This work uses sacred and liturgical sources as well as texts from James Joyce, Vladimir Mayakovsky, Kurt Schwitters, Albert Camus, Ludwig Wittgenstein, Joseph Goebbels, Hitler, Chamberlain, and many others; the plurality of styles is itself the style of the work.

Fragmentation of language is found in many works of the period. In *Le Marteau Sans Maître,* the Boulez setting of texts by René Char, makes it impossible to grasp the actual words (which, in any case, do not aspire to "meaning" in the traditional sense). In Berio's *Omaggio a Joyce,* the use of electronic and tape techniques serves as an audio microscope that fragments Joyce's words—already difficult to understand in the conventional sense—into phonemes. Cage's *Aria* consists of fragments in various musical, textual, and vocal styles, which can be ordered and performed aleatorically with one of his independent electronic works. Pieces like this exist on the border between literature, theater performance, and experimental music.

In such works, the signification of words and texts may play a role but one not much greater than the value of the texts as pure sound. Inevitably, in such contexts, the communication of anything but the sound of the text becomes chancy. Not surprisingly, composers, following the example of *concrète* poetry, have used arbitrary sequences (for example, counting in numbers as in the Philip Glass/Robert Wilson *Einstein on the Beach*) or pure sound syllables mimicking the quality of language as pure sound (the classic example is the *Ursonate* of Kurt Schwitters, which has been performed as a piece of music, as the score for a dance work, and as a recorded CD). Invented or fantasy-language is used in works such as the György Ligeti *Aventures* and the music theater of Georges Aperghis and Guy Reibel's *Rabelais ou la naissance du verbe. The Ten Qualities*, a choral work by Eric Salzman (it also appears as part of his *Nude Paper Sermon*), is based on nonverbal, nonmusical vocal and body sounds, arranged according to their normally emotive effect (and affect) but performed on cue in a purely musical fashion; what appear to be dramatic reactions are in fact organized as purely musical sounds. In such examples, music and text can be said to merge.

Another work in this category is Giorgio Battistelli's *Teorema* (after Pier Paolo Pasolini) in which the protagonists are mute. Battistelli, a student of Stockhausen and Kagel, is very active in the creation of music theater. His earlier *Experimentum mundi* for actor, five natural female voices, sixteen craftsmen, and a percussionist (1981) also has no actual singing but is based instead on the sounds of working craftsmen. (See Chapter 10.) In this theatricalization of traditional activity, there are no individual heroic protagonists who sing dramatic arias to express their individual tragedies; the voice is merely one acoustic element among others and subtext is more important than any actual text.

This kind of theatricalization has been extended into the concert situation, formerly the exclusive domain of abstract and instrumental music. George Crumb (*Echoes of Time and the River*, 1967; *Lux Aeterna*, 1971) and George Lopez (*Schatten vergessener Ahnen*, 1994) ask performers to make processions, to move on stage, and even to wear masks. Concert works have been composed with the idea that a stage director as well as a music director will be needed. Terminology such as "instrumental theater" or *azione teatrale* ("theater action") suggests that there can be a musical theater with only instrumentalists or that instrumentalists can be actors in their own musical dramas. The end of the line might be reached with *Séraphin—Versuch eines Theaters für Instrumente/Stimmen/...* (1993–1996) by German composer Wolfgang Rihm. This piece, referring to the theatrical theories of Antonin Artaud, takes the view that neither text nor stage action is necessary as the activity of the performers already is action. The notion of abstract theater crops up from time to time. Boris Blacher wrote an *Abstrakte Oper Nr. 1* with a text by the composer Werner Egk but no narrative. But why isn't there an *Abstrakte Oper Nr. 2*?

In general, the theoretical basis for turning concert music into dramatic action rests with the Brechtian notion that actors do not turn themselves into characters but present themselves to us as players with whom we have an unwritten agreement: to accept them as representing the roles they are asked to play. In the same way, instrumentalists—particularly in new and appropriately designated work or as improvisers creating a performance—ask us to accept a performance role that is constantly redefined as it unrolls. In such circumstances, any performance may be considered an *azione teatrale,* particularly when there is any perceived danger of failure or lack of success. For example, an improvisation that could succeed or fall flat or a piece that structures some kind of competition between musicians or one that invites some unforeseen element of audience participation becomes willy-nilly an *azione teatrale*.

It should be added that the mere abandonment of storytelling and the substitution of quasi-rituals—imagined or borrowed from somewhere—do not in themselves create new forms of music theater. The story as a driving force is what creates the swift passage of time in the music/theater combination. The elimination of traditional models in the course of experimentation with fragments, collages, and abstraction puts the issues of duration and time span back onto center stage. Whereas abstraction in painting and in dance seems to be acceptable simply in terms of sheer physicality—of the object or of the human body—the lack of anything being abstracted presents a problem for theater in any form. When the theater is simply what it is, without referring, presenting, or re-presenting anything, the passage of time can become ponderous, a real challenge for the writer, composer, director, performer, and public.

Further Reading

Bernstein, Charles. Libretto to *Shadowtime* by Brian Ferneyhough. Los Angeles, 2005.

chapter 6

Visual Strategies

*In giving equal weight to "music" and "theater," I was
trying to remove the dividing line that exists between the
terms "opera" and "theater."*

Walter Felsenstein, 1957

The appearance of the stage director: Movement and rhythm; staging and choreography

Although we normally distinguish between staging (stage direction, blocking for actors and singers) and choreography (which involves dance and dancers), this distinction is not old. Or, to put it more precisely, choreography was a well-defined art long before stage direction emerged in the theater or opera. The figure of the stage director appeared late in the game, much later even than the conductor/music director. Stage direction is essentially a twentieth-century invention. Until recently, actors and singers were expected more or less to stage themselves. At the Bayreuth *Festspiele* of 1874, the only one that took place in Wagner's lifetime, the composer himself directed the performers on the stage, and when the festival was revived after his death in 1883, Cosima Wagner took over this job by trying to re-create Richard's directions from memory. In most cases, the writer, librettist, or most often stage manager moved the cast around, more like a traffic policeman than what we now think of as a stage director. Even today there is a confusion in some European languages between the terms for stage director (*metteur en scène* in French; Regisseur in German) and stage manager (*régisseur* in French).

On the other hand, dance has been a major element in music theater and opera from its earliest origins. Theatrical dance is prominent in those Renaissance spectacles that preceded opera and often included a participatory element: the aristocratic sponsors who also provided the core of the audience were expected to take part and show their dancing skills in public (there were aristocratic singers in early Florentine opera as well). Most of the instrumental music in the early Florentine, Mantuan, and Venetian operas of Monteverdi and others is meant to accompany dance. This theatrical model was brought to France by Lully (who was from Florence) and it remained very important in French opera, which produced an enormous amount of dance music for the stage including such hybrid forms as *comédie-ballet* and *opéra-ballet*. While Italian opera quickly settled out into a formula of extended recitatives broken by rhythmic arias, French vocal setting tended to be virtually through-composed and rhythmically flexible while the dance numbers, mostly instrumental, constituted suites of set pieces with strong rhythmic structures. The distinction is not only between vocal and instrumental settings; it also reflects the dominant influence of language on vocal music (French is the least dependent of all the European languages on the tonic accent). By contrast, dance settings, mostly instrumental, have roots in folk dance and are driven by their rhythmic organization. Dance rhythms had an important influence on the growth of orchestral music (in and out of the theater) and the eventual evolution of classical style out of the late baroque.

Long before the nineteenth century, the participation in musical and operatic performance by amateurs, aristocratic, talented or otherwise, came to an end. Opera singing and ballet dancing *en pointe* became highly developed, professionalized, and marketable skills. They existed side by side in the major opera houses—often in the same works—but only occasionally was there any actual interaction. Romantic ballet is a feature of many major operas, especially in works produced in Paris, but it usually occurs in very defined dance segments that can often be removed from the operas without much damage. The subject of major dance interludes in opera was, often as not, sex pure and simple (the Walpurgis Night in Gounod's *Faust*; the *Venusberg* ballet that Wagner added to his *Tannhäuser* for the Paris production of 1861; the orgy scene and "Dance around the Golden Calf" in Schoenberg's *Moses und Aron* are some examples).

Two parallel developments in the twentieth century changed the relationship of dance to music and altered the treatment of singers on the operatic stage. One was the emergence of modern dance, which produced dancers and choreographers who were relatively free of the constraints of romantic ballet (starting with the elimination of dancing *en pointe*). Many of these choreographers absorbed influences from popular dance styles (jazz and folk dance), merging them with the emerging vocabularies of modern dance. A number of these choreographers (George Balanchine, Agnes de Mille, Jerome Robbins, Michael Bennett) were able to combine—often with surprising ease—the worlds of formal dance (ballet), musical theater, and more experimental performance arts. Dance is often an important element in chamber opera, and sometimes characters are both danced and sung simultaneously by two different performers (the animals in the Stravinsky *Renard*; Anna I and Anna II in the Weill/Brecht *Die Sieben Todsünden*). Collaborations between composers and choreographers often produced new methods of integrating physical movement and sound. The works of John Cage with Merce Cunningham represent a double lifetime of exploring this relationship, which evolved from tight integration to parallel but independent tracks. Dance regained much of the ground it had lost as an equal partner in music theater although not necessarily in traditional opera.

The emergence of the modern dance choreographer also paved the way for a new type of stage direction that is usually designated as "musical staging." This kind of movement, available to actors and singers with little or no formal dance training, was made usable by modern dance's espousal of "natural" movement, often closer to the everyday than the more artificial physicality of traditional ballet or even folk dance. The exploration of this area—also related to traditional mime and clown movement—became part of new music theater from early in the twentieth century and continues to be a source of physical realization and visualization. As a result, many choreographers also became stage directors, particularly in musicals and music theater (Rhoda Levine, Bob Fosse, Twyla Tharp, Graciela Daniele, and Martha Clarke are examples).

The other development was the appearance of the modern stage director, not only as a re-creator and re-interpreter of existing work but also as a creative force. As suggested above, the stage director—*metteur en scène, Regisseur*—is surprisingly absent from the history of theater before the appearance of influential theoreticians like Gordon Craig, Constantin Stanislavsky, Vsevolod Meyerhold, and Bertolt Brecht in the early twentieth century. Although the innovations of these men are usually connected with the history of spoken theater, all of them seem to have been fascinated by the precise layout of time inherent in musical settings and based much of their work on opera and musical theater in various forms.[1] Also, the growing

---

1. Like film directors who cut scenes to "dummy scores," some of these pioneering directors were known to stage scenes to music which they later eliminated.

prestige of film directors, many originally from the theater, helped their stage *confrères* to stake equivalent claims as *auteurs*. The modern operatic stage director has become notorious for applying conceptual thinking to rethinking the classics of the repertoire. More significantly perhaps, stage directors have become virtual partners in the creation of new work. Robert Wilson (*Einstein on the Beach;* music by Philip Glass), Peter Brook (*Marat/Sade;* music by Richard Peaslee), Martha Clarke (*The Garden of Earthly Delights*; music by Richard Peaslee), Julie Taymor (*The Transposed Heads, Juan Darien, Grendel;* music by Elliot Goldenthal), Peter Sellars (*Nixon in China, The Death of Klinghoffer;* music by John Adams) have all created operas and music theater pieces by bringing together writers, composers, choreographers, and performers to realize their conceptions. Music theater in France has been particularly characterized by what we might call "director-driven" work as opposed to the more common case elsewhere of "composer-driven" music theater.

Many directors and director/choreographers have also formed ensembles on the model of small contemporary theater or dance companies and created work with small troupes of performers. With the work of certain dance- and movement-oriented artists—Pina Bausch (*Tanztheater Wuppertal*), Jan Fabre (a visual artist who also functions as a playwright and choreographer), Meredith Monk (*The House* as well as Meredith Monk and Vocal Ensemble), and others—the term *dance theater* has sometimes been used in a way that is parallel to the term *music theater*. The Meredith Monk case is exceptional because she functions as her own composer (as well as lead performer). A similar case is that of Mauricio Kagel whose activity as a stage director is inseparable from his creative work as a composer. The parallel is with the choreographer who both creates and directs his or her work and it often becomes impossible to tell where creation leaves off and direction begins. In these situations, stage directors and choreographers have become the *auteurs* of music-theater works, and composers have, of necessity, turned themselves into directors. In many of these cases, the *auteur* concept extends from the creative side into the management and financial aspects of running a company. Such central *auteur* figures play a vital role in driving new music theater forward.

Image, light, design, and color

Text, in the traditional form of lyrics and librettos, has receded in importance in inverse proportion to the increase in the creative role of stage directors and choreographers. On the other hand, the elements of design (including set, visuals, light, costumes, and even makeup), once considered to be peripheral adjuncts to the libretto and the score, have become important parts of the stage director's conceptualization along with physical movement. The notion of performance works in which color and light would be orchestrated along with music was first proposed early in the twentieth century by the Russian composer Alexander Scriabin, the American eccentric visionary John J. Becker and others. In the 1930s and then again in the 1960s, a modernist interpretation of the idea of a *Gesamtkunstwerk* reappeared in the form of multimedia or mixed media performance genres, which integrated film and other forms of projection into live performance. Although large-scale mixed media performance did not maintain its initial levels of size and intensity, many of the techniques that were developed found their way into music theater and operatic performances at various levels. Just as director/choreographers have increased the importance of dance and dance/mime in new music theater, a new generation of designer/directors has done the same with visual elements used in ways that far exceed the once secondary category of "design."

One of the first and perhaps still best known of these is Robert Wilson who creates visual "story boards" instead of librettos as the basis for his work. The Belgian Jan Fabre, even more a conceptual artist than Wilson, has created a whole series of performance works—live and using various media—which often led to his being described as a dramatist, playwright, stage director, and choreographer (although all these are obviously merely aspects of his "*auteur*-ity"). Other examples of stage directors whose background is in the visual arts and design include Julie Taymor, Achim Freyer, and Christoph Marthaler. The tendency toward visualization and abstraction of theatrical work has had considerable resonance in opera direction in Central Europe, raising design and its related technologies of set, light, and color to the first plane in music theater and multimedia performance.

New technology as a performance strategy

Almost from the first introduction of each new technology we can find examples of performance works making use of it. Film was used in opera in the 1920s and 1930s, musical films were staples of the early sound era, and various forms of projection were the mainstay of experimental forms of theater and music theater in the 1930s, again in the 1960s, and with the aid of new technologies, continue to be so. The title character of Maurizio Squillante's *The Wings of Daedalus* (Ascoli Piceno, 2003) is transformed into a cyborg whose movements are controlled by motors and a computer; Squillante's work also uses virtual reality and holograms. In Pauline Vaillancourt's *L'Enfant des Glaces* (Montréal 2000), Zack Settel's computer-derived score is linked to the light and color scheme of the design and to the singing and speaking of the performers. In her performance works,

Pamela Z wears a "body synth," a synthesizer that uses her physical movements to trigger musical, visual, and other responses. In many sound installations, the movements of the spectators play a similar role in determining what is actually seen and heard.

The complexity of this borderless subject makes it impossible to be comprehensive about all the possibilities that have been realized in recent decades. Wireless microphones, general amplification, computer-controlled light boards, projection devices, sound-processing programs, cue-in of CD tracks or video, and laptop computers have all become quite standard technologies in theaters and performance spaces and more advanced techniques—multispeaker-systems, head-phoned audiences, 3-D projections, interactive systems, technologically intense projects—are increasingly common. One result is that a lot of rehearsal time is now devoted to fixing technical problems. The more complex setups demand substantial rehearsal time on their own, and there is a history of stalled, interrupted, or abandoned performances because of technical breakdown. The contemporary music theater director, author, or composer has to be also a technician or must be sure of having adequate technical help to get through these problems.

When new technologies became available in earlier decades, laboratories, universities, radio stations, and corporations supported an artistic approach to the new machines and the technology often became a principal theme of new work. It gave a modernist, even sci-fi, impression of up-to-date artistry. Although the available technologies are now more advanced by several orders of magnitude, they have become so widespread that there is hardly any way to make the technology appear as a theme without the work appearing retrograde or unduly commercial.

In short, the technology now has to be a well-integrated part of a theatrical whole, without standing out on its own. When institutions like IRCAM (Institut de Recherche et Coordination Acoustique/Musique) in Paris or STEIM (Studio for Electro-Instrumental Music) in Amsterdam research individual solutions for technical problems, they provide the hidden intelligence behind mostly naturalistic, traditional staging. In computer sciences, the terms *extended*, *virtual*, and *reality* usually imply outcomes meant to be watched on a computer screen. But such extensions can also be realized in a physical theater as well. For example, the Canadian group 4D Art of Michel Lemieux and Victor Pilon, has produced very successful and convincing work in the theater with hyperreal holographic projections that make it difficult to tell the real actors from the virtual ones. Effects that look only possible on film are used in live performances to blur the borders between the real and the virtual. Although the performances use a highly virtuosic style of visual effects, they often make extensive use of music as well. The

4D Art: Michel Lemieux and Victor Pilon. Live holographic projected images of "virtual" actors on stage with actual actors.

results are so striking that the spectator's first questions are invariably about how it all works technically. The "reality impact" of live performances like these reaches the point at which we have to ask what such virtuosity delivers in the way of intellectual or esthetic insight or content. At the moment that we are presented with new and highly developed technologies, they become the very subject matter of our perceptions. It remains to be seen whether, as was the case with earlier technologies, these new ones will reach the point of transparency. Will the medium continue to be the message, or, as with older technologies, will it just become a possible choice of medium for the transmission of other kinds of messages?

Further Reading

Craig, Edward Gordon. *Craig on Theatre*. London, 1988.
Stanislavsky, Constantin. *Stanislavsky on the Art of the Stage*. Translated by David Margarshack. London, 1961.

chapter 7

Space

SMYSLOV (pleasantly): Well, Dr. Floyd, I hope that you
don't think I'm too inquisitive, but perhaps you can clear
up the mystery about what's been going on up there.

Stanley Kubrick and Arthur C. Clarke: *2001: A Space Odyssey*

What is a theater?

Any space that permits actors and singers to be seen and heard by large
numbers of spectators might serve as a theater, but traditional theaters
define a visual space and an audience point-of-view (and point-of-listening),
usually with a fixed set or backdrop that serves, among other things, to help
project sound. Early theaters were out-of-doors and since they depended
on natural light, performances took place during the day. Such performances depend heavily on the physicality of the performers, amplified
mainly by costumes, makeup, and, often as not, masks. This is typical of
Greco-Roman theater and also of most Asian forms.

The closed-in theater with artificial lighting developed in Europe in the
Renaissance. This type of theater gives better control of what is seen and
heard in terms of both design and also in the way theater space is used.
Such theaters could make use of more complex spaces as well as movable
scenery. A whole art of design and support technology, now mostly obsolete, developed around this, a veritable machinery of illusions that was an
important part of baroque opera. The illusions were aided and abetted by

the *théâtre à l'italienne*, which introduced the proscenium arch to frame complex stage pictures and scenic transformations and, not so incidentally, hide the machinery that made them possible. Scene designers and machinists were superstars of the baroque and were sometimes better known than the composers and writers of the works they were presumably illustrating. Designers did not return to a similar position until the twentieth century with the development of modern lighting as well as the theories of Gordon Craig, the popular designs of Joseph Urban, and the artist commissions given by Sergei Diaghilev for his ballet and opera productions (see also Chapter 6 on the subject of the designer/director).

Time and space

The structure of Italian theaters was a reflection of the structure of Italian society and created a complex and shifting relationship between the public and the works being performed. The private boxes, generally sold or rented by the season, provided the main source of revenue for the performances, and the impresarios were under pressure to produce star vehicles and lengthy performances that could be either followed in their entirety or sampled for their highlights.[1] The result was the production of long, multi-hour operas or bills in which ballets were performed during the intervals and *opera buffa* comedies followed the featured *opera seria*. This richness of opera bills continued throughout the nineteenth century even as the economic base of opera performance shifted from the sale and subscription of boxes to the aristocracy to a more mixed strategy based on selling seats for individual performances to the new middle-class audience. The length of the Wagner music dramas and the construction of his specially designed *Festspielhaus* were actually the culmination of traditional large-scale operatic performance although with added features borrowed from the church and the classroom (among other things, the doors are locked as the lights go down so that latecomers are not allowed in and seated customers cannot escape).

Only with the twentieth-century breakaway from traditional theaters and opera houses did all this begin to change in earnest. The cabaret- and folk-influenced forms of works like *Pierrot Lunaire* and *L'Histoire du Soldat* and the chamber opera movements of the 1920s began to turn the one-act music-theater work, produced in small theaters, music halls, or even non-performance spaces, into a new standard model. Even full-scale works

---

1. Social rubbernecking, romance, and the gambling rooms—the so-called *ridotto*—attached to Venetian opera houses and perhaps elsewhere, also provided some major distractions.

tended to become more tightly organized with fewer act divisions, fewer intermissions, and a more economical use of theatrical time. This tendency, which is widespread in performance arts, has been explained in various ways. In general, the mass media (film and TV), in terms of both style and competition for attention, have influenced the evolution of shorter, tighter, faster-moving forms in live performance.

Theater as space

Theater, musical or otherwise, is space. In principle, this is not a simple, unitary space but is split into the performance area (the stage) and the public area (the auditorium). How the space is further divided and how it is used exactly remains in the hands of the designer and the stage director. In this area, we reach a watershed between music theater and more traditional opera-like productions.

Although the number of variations is potentially unlimited, some basic stages can be represented by the shapes of letters, showing the layout of the space as viewed from above. The two most common contemporary types are the proscenium (which might be represented by the letter H) and the related black box (a square or cube divided into two square or quadrilateral blocks). More ancient types have the form of the letter O (theater in the round) or C (the amphitheater); in both of these, the audience, mostly on the ground level, sits around the stage with stair-like tribunes descending. The letter T describes a thrust stage, where the actors actually penetrate the center of the auditorium.

Here are sketches showing some of the more radical recent designs.

In traditional opera, there is a chain of creators starting with an author (usually a playwright, novelist, or story writer) and a librettist. The composer, next in line, eventually hands over score and libretto to the stage director and his design team. Only then do the singers become involved along with another team of coaches, accompanists, and music directors. (This is, in many respects, similar to the traditional Hollywood team system.)

On the other hand, the author of a work of music theater may, in the process of giving philosophical and visible form to his piece, act not only as composer but also as author, stage director, and, on occasion, choreographer and designer. In Heiner Goebbels's formulation, the "staging of a music" ("Composition as *mise-en-scène*") may be an important or even essential part of the underlying concept. The composer of new music theater may control the musical performance but is also likely to have ideas about text and staging. This goes at least as far back as Wagner, who thought of himself as a poet as well as a composer and who not only designed his sets and costumes but also staged his works in his own theater, which he

The stage above or beneath the audience: in the design above, the audience watches the actors standing on a grid or glass surface, while in the lower design, the audience walks around a narrow balcony looking down on the actors on the ground floor (the so-called Raaijmakers-Stage).

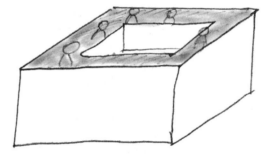

also designed. This is a full-blown *auteur* concept, and many composers since have attempted to follow in this path with more or less success.[2]

The space occupied by the public plays a role as well. This space is usually static and the traditional perspectives of opera seating depend on the cost of the ticket. The various sectors of the auditorium reflect the social status of the visitors: loge or box seats, *parquet* or orchestra, first and second balconies, standing places, and so on. The tendency to overthrow this socially determined layout is strong in contemporary opera and theater. Nevertheless, in the traditionally stratified seating plan, the frontal perspective is more or less the same for everyone, and the stage is viewed in its totality from almost all seats. In nontraditional performance locales, the view may vary. In *The Fall of Mussolini* (1995) by Dick Raaijmakers, performed in an old factory building, the audience looks down on the factory floor where the action takes place. In Nader Mashayekhi's *Malakut* (1997), the view is from underneath. (See figures above.) Other angles might be employed as well, but unless the public is asked to move or the

2. Composers who, like choreographers and bandleaders, create their works through a process of improvisation with an ensemble belong in this category. This process, formerly restricted to popular musicians, has become far more common in recent decades, particularly with composers who have organized their own performing ensembles (see Chapter 20).

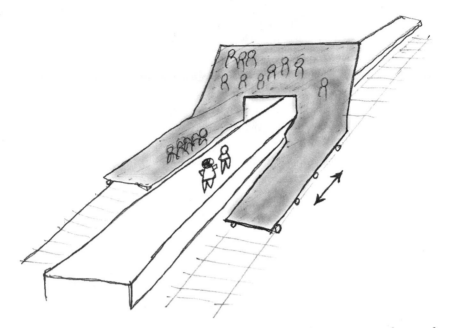

Stage designed for Zimmermann's *Die Soldaten* by Robert Innes-Hopkins and David Pountney; the "tribune," which holds about 1000 spectators, travels on wheels along a 120 × 3 m (394 × 10 ft) stage.

The "everywhere"-stage. Actors mix with audience, amplified either through sound, light, or costume.

performance space is drastically altered during the performance (see top figure above), the fundamental relationship of the public toward a fixed stage usually remains uniform and unchanging.

The performing area itself can be used in many different ways. The proscenium stage in particular lends itself to various kinds of play with space illusion, either in size or in "atmosphere." Using light and smoke

("smoke and mirrors" is the popular expression), a virtually infinite horizon can be created. The unstructured backgrounds of Robert Wilson's stages are of this type: are we looking at a far-off horizon, a colored wall, or just space? In Heiner Goebbels's *Max Black* there is a moment when a large door at the back of the stage opens and the audience can see outside, but curiously, this moment of "reality" seems more staged than the actual play. Something similar happens in his *Eraritjaritjaka—museé des phrases* when the windows open on a child's scrawl drawing of a house and we seem to see the inside of the apartment that we have just been watching in a video projection (live or taped; we never really know). These illusory moments illuminate what theater does to our spatial perception in connection with the illusion of being elsewhere. This "elsewhereness" becomes a new reality, and the reality outside appears to be another stage or perhaps another video projection. Goebbels and his performer, André Wilms, are playing with our experience of space as we orient ourselves in everyday life—our expectation, for example, of what we will find when we enter or leave a building.

Many music-theater artists, after having tried various seating arrangements for the audience, have returned to the proscenium theater in preference to multilevel stages or arena-style theater.[3] The argument is made that music theater should be "more primitive" than spoken theater, but there is a good question as to whether the proscenium theater is, in fact, a more primitive arrangement (the Greeks used the arena theater). The proscenium certainly works better for the notion of theater as a "machine of illusions" and also for the projection of sound in a forward and uniform direction. The presentation of stage pictures in a proscenium theater to an audience sitting in fixed, raked rows is exactly parallel to the way that projected film works in the cinema where the aim is also to create relatively uniform perspective for the entire audience.

In addition to the spatial illusions so beloved of theater artists, there is also the use of images as metaphors for the ideas of the piece. For example, a large open space or the ambience of the ocean might suggest the loneliness of the protagonist. Or the suggested atmosphere of a room, a street, or a forest might help define the existential condition of the protagonist—the conflict or the problem to be solved—through the metaphor of the space that he or she inhabits.

Theater outside theaters; participatory theater

The traditional uses of space in theater mostly deny the theater's own architectural identity. In contrast, the black box theater that appeared during

3. Cf. Mauricio Kagel, *Tamtam* (Munich, 1975), 93.

the last decades of the twentieth century provides uniform and neutral conditions for a stage director to create his piece without any specific reference to the physicality of the actual space where the transaction is taking place. At an opposite extreme, there are directors and artists who look for characteristic locations with an authentic and exciting aura within which performance can occur. Sometimes the actual and unconventional route that the public has to take just to arrive at the performance venue becomes part of the experience.

Such notions may be relevant or extraneous. The production of *Mr. Emmet Takes a Walk* by Peter Maxwell Davies (libretto by David Pountey) by *Freies Musiktheater NRW* in a subway station was at least an amusing idea. On the other hand, *Doodgoed*, a "farmer's opera" by the Dutch company, *Muziektheater Struweel* (2004), is a piece about farm life that is played in a working barn so that the mooing and other random animal sounds become part of the sound of the piece. *Armada von Duldgedalzen* was produced by the *6-Tage Oper Düsseldorf* (2005) using a small Tyrolian village as its "theater." Different scenes are played simultaneously in different houses and other venues while, according to a predetermined scheme, heavy trucks drive through the village honking their horns and thus becoming part of the score. The audience walks around in groups watching the village becoming an opera theater.

Works that attempt to use nontheatrical spaces are typically concerned with the effort to bring audiences to those spaces for historic, social, or other reasons. Even the unconventional use of designated theatrical spaces can sometimes be used in a similar way. The Serban/Swados *Greek Trilogy*, at La Mama in New York in the 1960s, created a performance mode in which the audience, led by the performers, moved through various physical spaces and in which the performer/spectator roles were constantly in play and thus, in effect, constantly being reevaluated. For his *Verkommenes Ufer*[4] Heiner Goebbels asked people in public places—streets, train stations, small cafes, and public transport—to read a text that he gave them, and this recorded sound material was then played back as part of the performance of the piece. In this case, the ambient sound in each recording became a piece of "reality" transferred into an artificial container.

It might be possible to go out, involve bystanders, and perform music theater in a "real" environment thus avoiding altogether the "artificial" environment of a theater. But by using a theatrical space instead and bringing artificially recorded fragments indoors, the artist can achieve things that the site-specific performance may not be able to offer, notably control and

---

4. This title has been translated as "Wasteland Waterfront" and "Squalid Shore."

protection. Working in a theater permits the artists to achieve the form intended and to control the audience's perceptions and, to some degree, their reactions. It also protects the performers and the public from interruption or interference. This is perhaps a more serious matter than is sometimes thought. In a performance, both audience and actors suspend the necessity of self-defense and may ignore the possibility of danger. There are also some rules, not always written down but well understood, about how to behave in a theater, and these rules help the seated, immobilized audience let go their normal tensions and concentrate attention on the piece.

The "real" space

The "real" theatrical space is the performance center otherwise known as the stage, however defined but always clearly distinguishable. This space can then stand in for some another place as defined by the performance and within which the performance takes place. Or it can be an actual physical prop—a chair, a bed, a table—on which or next to which an action takes place. Or the stage can just be a stage, as in some forms of "instrumental theater," where the space is the actual concert hall itself.

Landscapes—"Textscapes"

So far we are talking about only the visible aspects of space in theater. But semantic space and virtual space are two concepts that have gained importance in recent years. Text itself can be composed in a spatial manner: trailing white space, distances between the paragraphs, breaks in words, dots, signs—the whole arsenal of graphic notation and concrete poetry may inspire the composer to find corresponding ideas for musical settings.

Such a text, considered as "landscape" (*fide* Heiner Goebbels) creates spaces of meaning, of different historical times, of geographies, or of abstract viewpoints. There are terms such as *intertextuality* that deal with space in a metaphorical manner.

Finally there is the notion of actual physical distance, which seems always to have played a more important role in (music) theater than (psychological) closeness. Even though the problems of closeness are more obvious in everyday life (parents/children, danger, friends or lovers breaking up), distance is always easier to interpret as conflict or a problem to be solved. Distance may mean loneliness or abandonment or remoteness from home or from unreachable goals. Concepts like god and ghosts or even the Brechtian idea of alienation are connected with the idea of distance (the alienation effect is often referred to as a "distancing technique," which prevents the audience from getting too drawn into the illusion of theater).

Where the metaphor of distance has provided the conflict, the metaphor of closeness might offer the climactic moment in which the conflict of distance is resolved.

Movement in space

The static space inhabited by most audiences and the sense of distance created by stagecraft are connected by movement. In a sense, musical performance "moves" sound into and around the space, and the sound sources themselves can be physically moved. The use of technology can take the form of stereo, surround sound, moving sound projections, or multiple sound sources that can project and move synthesized, recorded, or amplified sound "objects." The reverse situation occurs with sound installations that require the visitor to move in order to experience change.

Manos Tsangaris, who studied with Kagel, has developed what he calls a "universal" music theater, which contains a variety of artistic expressions. Many of his works explore performance space from a miniature model on up to life size (as in his 1993 *winzig* in which invisible performers make objects appear in a theatrical space). He has also worked with multiple spaces or rooms from which composed sounds emanate, interfering with each other either acoustically or in the memory of the visitor. Georg Nussbaumer makes music theatrical installations of a similar nature although more bizarre and more oriented to the specific architecture of a given site. Michael Hirsch explores "semantic space" in *The quiet room* (2000).

The possibilities of creating "sound objects" in motion, of moving audiences from one sound space to another, and the combination of these with a concept or a text provide new kinds of theatrical material. Instead of the total-theater ambitions and obsessions with the re-creation of naturalistic effects that previous generations prized so highly, we might look to the interpretation of conditions and events as the next step forward.

Musical space

These considerations on space finally must include some of the particularity of music. If you don't want to look at something, you can close your eyes or turn your back, but closing your ears is a lot more difficult and turning your back doesn't help much.

An art gallery or museum can present hundreds of images simultaneously but nothing like that is possible with music. Music and music theater can present multiple musical lines at once (difficult in spoken theater with its verbal/semantic elements) but the phenomenon of polyphony must be based on some principles of synchronization that allow heterogeneous elements to be combined. Although there have been some attempted exceptions (Charles Ives's idea of multiple marching bands being the best known), music generally creates—and is created from—a single audible space. The multiplication of heterogeneous, nonsynchronized sound sources not only loses the main meaning and focus of music but it also tends to create an undifferentiated sound-mass whose meaning is either chaos or poor acoustical insulation, neither of which work very well theatrically.

Music theater in the opera

In new music theater, the economics of "poor theater" are more than likely to dominate the creation of new work. In contrast, contemporary opera occupies only a small marginal space inside the world of opera, but this space is nevertheless filled with works of a certain size. Anyone working in the opera must respond not only to architectural demands but also to the expectations that come with the idea of opera. Since the time of Satie, Weill, and even Kagel, opera has changed. The tolerance for what can be shown on an opera stage has been stretched considerably, often to the accompaniment of protests from the less open-minded. The weight of comparing every new production with the well-known masterpieces from four hundred years of history makes the production of new work in the opera house a difficult and often frustrating experience. This weight is felt at every premiere in every opera house of the world, but it is absent in those places where new music theater is the focus of creation and production. Certain composers, like Berio, have actually used the resulting tension and dynamic as part of their conceptions. But this has also led many observers to conclude that new music theater cannot flourish even in a sympathetic opera house environment but may need its own generic space or spaces to grow.

Further Reading

Ebrahimian, Babak A. *Sculpting Space in the Theater: Conversations with the Top Set, Light and Costume Designers.* New York, 2006.
Wilson, Edwin. *The Theater Experience.* New York, 1991, rev. 2005.

A theater of warm bodies?

If the first part of this book was devoted to the voice and after that to sound and music, it makes sense to conclude any discussion of the physical aspects of music theater with something about the human body and how it functions in this art. It has been said that the voice is the only part of a performance that is not visual (this assumes that the sense of smell—presumably weak in human beings—cannot play much of a role in the performance arts). Voice is, of course, essential to most theatrical activities, and the way the voice is used obviously distinguishes music theater and opera from other sorts of theater.

Theatrical performance can hardly be imagined without some kind of treatment of the human body. The physicality of performance is measured by its relationship with the human body. If there is an empty stage—literally no body—it takes its significance from the absence or negation of the body.

In evolutionary terms, we are creatures of the day, and this accounts for the fact that we are visually oriented beings, voyeurs, eye-ballers. We like to look at things and watch what happens. This voyeurism might be one of the basic reasons that we prefer to have a theater presented before our very eyes rather than just imagine a story in the mind. The voyeuristic aspect becomes even more predominant in watching unusual or even forbidden scenes. Although many taboos have nearly lost their power in a society that continually strives for new shocks and excitements, we are still impressed with physical extremes. This is not necessarily as new an idea as it might appear. Both Roman and Elizabethan tragedy dealt with such matters as rage, lust, rape, incest, murder, mutilation, assassination, and other extremes that showed or implied violation of the body in ways that could not be seen in ordinary life without putting the spectator in danger or in harm's way. In the twentieth century, artists like Antoine Artaud (Théâtre de la cruauté), the Viennese Aktionismus group in the 1960s, the Spanish/Catalan theater group La Fura dels Baus, and others consciously searched for experiences on the edge. The artists in Aktionismus were well known for their use of the body as a sculptural medium, especially with regard to taboos, sado-masochism, hedonism, pain, and death. Performance art has also been closely associated with the body, often the performer's own body. This has been particularly true of female performance artists like Carolee Schneeman, Annie Sprinkle, Karen Finley, Diamanda Galás, and Elke Krystufek but also male performers like Vito Acconci, Rudolf Schwarzkogler, Günter Brus, Matthew Barney, and others. This work, on the borders between visual art, performance art, exhibition, installation, and theater, is about artists exposing or otherwise dealing with their own bodies—often breaking taboos—as a kind of narcissistic solo theater.

Hermann Nitsch, part of the above-mentioned *Aktionismus* group, began organizing performances in his *Orgien Mysterien Theater* as early as 1969, performances that often lasted six days and mixed mysticism and Wagnerian gigantomaniac ideas with archaic notions of the intensification of existence. These ritualistic events, which dealt with blood, wine, red colors, and white clothing, intentionally recalled or modeled themselves on human and animal sacrifice, evoking the imagery and theatricality of religion by creating modern rituals intended not merely to be watched but also to be participated in by a group of people believing in a noumismatic or transcendental experience.

In this sense, theater stops being role playing and becomes the scene for action. All that is required is that the action be attended to. We have theaters of war, of action, of events. In all of these theaters, performances take place that are defined as "acts." Light is shed, acts follow, attention is paid. Stockhausen's *Originale* was created under the influence of Cage's ideas, Kagel's concepts of instrumental theater, and the Fluxus happenings, all of which use their participants as "originals." David Tudor, Nam June Paik, and Mary Bauermeister were not playing roles; they were playing themselves. Kagel's concept of instrumental theater, where the musicians themselves are the only actors, and the Fluxus happenings, where no roles are played, suggest that there are now two opposing directions to travel. In one, the world becomes a huge Wagnerian stage in which the creators merely throw a frame around some portion of it so that time can be measured out in acts—the acts of an opera perhaps or some merger of the acts of willing or unwilling role players. In the other, the performer becomes the creator, acting on his or her own body. Is there any common ground between the two? In both cases there is a sense of distance. In the one, it is the distance between the role playing of the participants and a historic or imagined reality. In the other, the distance is between the conscious "self" and the physical body that is its subject matter.

Although many of these performers and performances are not text or music driven, the physicality of making sound is important. The intense but amateurish relationship that many visual artists have with music belongs here. Bodies without sound are like cold bodies. This is obvious in dance and in film where the presence of music is usually required and its absence is always notable and even fraught. The sound of the voice in traditional opera has become rather detached and "out of body," as if the performer were playing on an instrument that happened to be situated within his or her own body. This is in contrast to the sound-making potential of the performer in performance art, which is always both body and mind connected. This is true of a performer like Meredith Monk who physicalizes all of her music for herself and her vocal ensemble as well as in her dance-theater and music-theater work. It is characteristic of the Cage *Europeras* which treat the phenomenon of operatic performance on a stage as a series of acts or events physically performed by opera singers who play opera singers singing actual old opera or causing old operatic recordings to play with and against the live performers. It is most obviously evident in the work of Diamanda Galás where the classic physical entrapment and suffering of the operatic prima donna—sometimes actually singing fragments of old opera—is expressed in terms of violence being enacted on the singer as she is in the very act of singing. It might be said that almost all conscious experiences lead to an audible reaction: commentary, laughter, a cry, a sob, mourning, mumbling, shouting. It is the body that speaks through the voice. We want to SEE the voice and HEAR the body!

Further Reading

Warr, Tracey, and Amelia Jones. *The Artist's Body*. New York, 2005.

part iii Putting It All Together: *La Mise en Scène*

chapter 8

The American Eccentrics

*Is it a man? No. To tell you the truth, I never have
thought about what it is.*

Marcel Duchamp on his painting "Nude
Descending a Staircase"

Harry Partch and "corporeality"

Harry Partch constituted a California school of composition all by himself.
He was self-taught and largely self-invented in all aspects of his life and
creative work, which included his own musical instruments (which he
built himself), his own tuning system (a form of just intonation based on
an underlying division of the octave into forty-three tones), his own style
of vocalism and approach to setting language, his own view of how music
should function in society, his own performing ensembles, and his own
myth-derived and highly ritualistic music theater. Much of Partch's work
was concerned with his ideas about theater, about singing, and about declamation from his early settings of hobo graffiti to the theater and dance works
of his later years: *Oedipus* (1950, rev. 1952–54 and 1967), *The Bewitched*
(1955), *Delusion of the Fury: A Ritual of Dream and Delusion* (1965–66),
and *Revelation in the Courthouse Park* (1960). Partch's work was created
almost entirely outside of the world of professional music. He himself
trained the singers, actors, instrumentalists, and dancers, mostly students
and amateurs, to perform his work, and this training activity itself helped

create and spread the Partch mystique, which has not entirely vanished decades after his death.

Revelation in the Courthouse Park is his major work. It is based on the *Bacchae* of Euripides, set partly in ancient Greece and partly in the central square of a small middle-American town in the 1950s. Dionysius becomes Dion, a pop singer; King Pentheus turns into Sonny, mayor of the town; and Agave becomes Mom. Some of the smaller roles use rhythmic speech while others are sung in Partch speech/song that occasionally takes melodic flight. There are big ensembles, notably the central section entitled "Heavenly Daze." However, any resemblance to a conventional operatic ensemble is remote as this is the maximum moment of clash and splatter between tempered and microtonal tuning systems. There is a chorus of female bacchantes, an ensemble of Partch instruments, and an American-style marching band with baton twirlers, tumblers, gymnasts, clog dancers, and the like. The Partch ensemble is contrasted in every possible way with the marching band, which is tuned in equal temperament. The Partch instruments—all carefully tuned to his specifications—consists of kitharas, harmonic canons, double bass, crychord, adapted guitars, adapted viola, chromolodeons, bloboy, spoils of war, diamond marimba, boo, the huge marimba eroica (two players for three notes!), cloud chamber bowls, cone gongs, bass marimba, and drone devils, all instruments invented or adapted by the composer.

Delusion of the Fury combines elements taken from a Japanese Noh play and an African folk legend. There is no libretto and the narratives are conveyed through dance and mime. There are three principals, an ensemble of dancer/mime/actors, and eighteen or twenty musicians who perform on some three dozen Partch instruments and also serve as the chorus. The instruments also form the set and the instrumentalists wear costumes whose character is specified by the composer.

Partch's musico-dramatic ideas were based on concepts that he designated "monophony" and "corporeality," both distantly derived from what he understood to be Greek and non-Western practice. Monophony refers not only to the solo voice, which derives its melodic and tonal shape from the rhythms and tonal shape of speech, but also to his concept of harmony as an expansion of the pure ratios inherent in the overtones. Corporeality is a more complex notion. On the largest scale, it represents his vision of total theater incorporating language, music, song, dance, mime, and so forth. In detail, it refers to the expression of emotions and feelings, which is simultaneously both unfettered and ritualized.

Partch set up his idea of corporeality to oppose what he called "abstraction," which he thought dominated both popular and high arts in Western culture. It was the evil of abstraction that kept the arts separate and

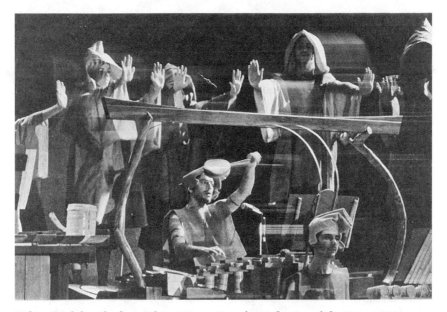

"Chorus of the Shadows" from Harry Partch's *Delusion of the Fury*, University of California at Los Angeles production (1969); shows instruments closely integrated into the production including Bass Marimba (ends of bars and square resonators visible on the left), Belly Drum (the round object sitting on the end of the Bass Marimba), Quadrangularis Reversum (the large instrument with the Tori bar that surrounds the performer), Waving Drum (being held aloft and "waved"), and a few of the tubes of the Bamboo Marimba or Boo in the right foreground. Photo: Ted Tourtelot from the Harry Partch Archive, San Diego, California.

specialized and produced such pure and artificial phenomena as equal temperament, *bel canto* singing, dodecophony, and pop music! For Partch, abstraction meant the law, the rules of bourgeois society, the sublimation of feeling to proper behavior, and a straitjacket for the artist.

Revelation is, in fact, a piece that actually dramatizes the conflict between corporeality and abstraction. The choice of subject itself; the transposition to mid-century small-town America; the evocation of the Elvis Presley phenomenon (there actually was a 1960s pop singer who used the name Dion); the physicality of gymnasts/tumblers and their contrast with the followers of Dion/Dionysius; the contrasts between spoken, intoned, and sung language; and notably, the dialectic between the tempered marching-band music and the microtonal music of the (nonmobile) Partch instruments. Curiously enough, there are no hints of rock 'n' roll in Dion's music, which adheres quite strictly to corporeality and not to abstraction!

Performances of Partch's works have been limited by the need to use his original instruments. Partch himself produced *Revelation* in 1961 at the University of Illinois using student performers. The only other full production was at the American Music Theater Festival in 1987 with a mixed professional/student cast that was directed by musicians who had worked with Partch; this performance was also recorded. *Delusion of the Fury* was performed and recorded in audio and video form in 1969 and 1971 in Southern California. In spite of the limitations, the influence of this music, spread by an army of Partch disciples, has been widespread in America. The instruments are now in the possession of the percussion ensemble NewBand; many of them have been reproduced and new work has been composed for them. NewBand has been engaged in the systematic production and reproduction of Partch's major work including, most recently, the first performances of the revised version of *Oedipus* in Montclair, New Jersey, and a new production of *Delusion of the Fury*, at the Japan Society in New York City.

Partch's influence can also be found in the work of other composers with California and West Coast connections, notably that of his contemporary Lou Harrison and, in the next generation, Roger Reynolds and Pauline Oliveros. There is also a connection between Partch and the ideas of John Cage; these two California composers were aware of each other's work.

De-semiotization

Marcel Duchamp proposed the idea of random music in 1913, and the actions of the dadaists in the 1920s were already theater (if not music theater). When Duchamp moved to New York and met Cage, the two became friendly and often played chess together. In 1968 in Toronto and then again on the opening night of the Electric Ear series at New York's Electric Circus, the Duchamp-Cage chess board was wired up and the moves of the two players triggered other events, sonic and otherwise.

The line of connection that takes us from Duchamp and the dadaists to Cage and, in Europe, from Mauricio Kagel to Heiner Goebbels provides us with a history of the search not for nonsense (as has been claimed) as much as for "new sense." As with the physicist's experiment in which particles of matter are shot into other particles in order to find or create new forms of matter, the work is about probabilities in controlled conditions with results that cannot be predicted. What actually happens (still continuing this metaphorical analogy with quantum physics) is the hyper-fragmentation of the material.

On the artists' side, there is a conscious aim to accomplish the "de-semiotization" of the complex connection between the different arts; that is, to take apart the cause-and-effect relationship. When, in the early 1920s, Arnold Schoenberg was influenced by Kandinsky's theory of art, he

Reunion; a chess game between Marcel Duchamp and John Cage played on a board designed by Lowell Cross wired to trigger other events operated by David Tudor, Gordon Mumma, and David Behrman; the onlooker is Alexina "Teeny" Duchamp (Toronto, 1968). Photo: Shigeko Kubuta. With kind permission of the Cage Trust.

imagined music theater as polymorphous play, a game made up of lights, colors, shapes, words, sounds. These esthetic games (they derive also from Scriabin's synesthetic ideas) do not require—indeed, they negate—the production of meaning. The interaction is nothing more than the sum of the elements, no "semiotization" intended.

In the early days of the history of modernism, the discovery of abstraction was exciting, new, and liberating. Dadaism, automatic writing, surrealism, collage-techniques, found footage, the *objet trouvé* were all connected with this freedom from meaning. Not surprisingly, all this was also loaded with ideology and, secondarily, with the allure of the ordinary, of everyday life. For Cage, this meant the liberation of will, an abandonment of intention, of desire, of ego (this is where Cage's vaunted Zen Buddhism kicks in). But it was also a liberation from the dramatic, the climactic catastrophes that were the stuff of romantic art, above all of romantic opera (the end of the Wagner *Ring* can serve as the classic example but there are many others). The real catastrophes of World War I were enough to devalue the catastrophes of romanticism in the eyes and ears of the dadaists just as the catastrophes of World War II accomplished the same thing for Cage and his confrères. The ideas of Antonin Artaud (*Le théâtre et son double*) as well as the works of Kurt Schwitters and Duchamp are probably as important an influence as the more opaque influence of Zen Buddhism.

"De-semiotization" has been recognized as a liberation from the compulsion of the civilizing process to produce sense and meaning in its artistic work.[1] The theoretical statements and the music-theater art attached to it have been around for some decades now and the result is a widespread assumption that contemporary music theater, in its experimental forms at least, doesn't have to make any sense. The paradox inherent in this is summed up by the dictum "it doesn't mean anything so it must be art." Officially supported high-brow culture still deals with the nonsensical moment in art as a marker of artistic quality, excellence, and elitism (i.e., a class marker) while the naive, simplistic, easy, and direct is simply dumped (or left to the popular arts as another class marker).

Other tendencies have become noticeable. For example, information overload and hyper-fragmentation are a consequence of the media presence in every corner of our lives. Paradoxically, this makes the desire for continuous, protected narration appealing, and it has survived in film, in the popular musical, and, to some extent, in the more conventional forms of new opera. Between the equivocal revival of long-gone operatic traditions and the reload of powerful narration lies a possible reconciliation or "friendly takeover" of the stalled, institutionalized opera houses (whose post-bourgeois audiences look mostly like any collection of tourists anywhere in the world) by the anti-bourgeois, anti-operatic music theater. Waging war against traditional grand opera may, in any case, be hopeless and the composition of new grand operas (even by composers as impressive and as original as Olivier Messiaen or Elliott Carter) may only testify to a missing historical consciousness. What remains are the safe areas of festivals and the various forms of alternate theater, those "off" platforms that still keep on trying to renovate and re-innovate.

Cage and Kagel

John Cage, through his works and the musico-philosophical views behind them, opened up new thinking about music, sound, and theater. One of Cage's favorite aphorisms was that theater is another word for life. We do not have to do something new or different but merely perceive, look, and listen differently. Is this only a question of definition? How many people must change their ideas about how to look at things for a generalized new

---

1. This might be compared to the psychoanalytical methods that are intended to free one's mind from oppressive elements of our culture. But this idea exceeds the scope of this book.

culture to evolve? The perceived failure of modernism and the conservatism of most forms of postmodernism show us that no single philosophy
has the power to change society. So we cannot speak of widely changed
attitudes toward theater and theatricality that have been brought about
through the work or thought of Cage, Weill, Kagel, or any other composer.
Nevertheless, their ideas about their intentions demand our attention.

As Michael Nyman has pointed out, Cage implicitly says that theatricality
is inherent in experimental music. In Cage's own words, "With theater our
life is complete. There is no backdrop. Theater is the most complex form
of art in my experience...let it be together, not hold it together." One
could read those statements as implying that theater is the missing half of
life. The connection between life and theater—either through imitation
and close relationship, or as a pretext to abscond from present reality—is
beyond discussion. But we cannot read this as an answer to the old discussion about "art IN life" versus "life IN art" because we must also ask about
the difference between these two, their opposition. This dialectically placed
opposition and complementarity has itself become a close relationship in
contemporary art, which is derived from modernism and which unburdens
art from its romantic, larger-than-life symbolism, as well as its obligations
to be exemplary and to mean something. When theater does not have these
heavy duties to perform, it becomes anti-sensational, more like everyday
life. Instead of dramatic or traumatic moments of epiphany, insight, or
greater truth, we have simply the time-flux that carries our lives forward in
security, democracy, steady consumption, and growth.

Cage was born in southern California, studied with Henry Cowell and
Arnold Schoenberg in New York and Los Angeles, and began his career in
Seattle and San Francisco where he met and began working with Merce
Cunningham. He formed a percussion ensemble, invented the prepared
piano, and wrote music for a variable speed turntable, and recorded
frequency tones. After a brief stop in Chicago (where he worked at László
Moholy-Nagy's "New Bauhaus"), he moved to New York in the early 1940s,
working mostly in the modern dance world and composing his major cycles
for prepared piano but also works for percussion and voice.

Cage's interest in percussion, in mechanical reproduction, and in the
prepared piano were not only an extension of the idea that any sound could
become part of a musical discourse but also of wider notions about the
negation of individual will and psychology as well as the traditional notions
of form, composer choice, and even history. His famous statement was that
he wanted to create music that was "free of individual taste and memory
(psychology) and also of the literature and tradition of the art."

In 1952, at Black Mountain College, Cage made the first "happening"
based on a lecture punctuated with silences that he read from the top of

a ladder while disparate activities—dancing by Merce Cunningham, an exhibition of paintings and playing of recordings by Robert Rauschenberg, reading of poetry by Charles Olson and Mary C. Richards, and the piano playing of David Tudor—all took place inside chance-determined periods of time within the overall time-frame of the lecture.

The "let it be together, not hold it together" of Cage was anchored in the tradition of dadaism or surrealistic nonsense. Society, thirty years earlier, had already set up not a new world but new corner shops. As it turned out, artists were happy to help with this enterprise. Instead of responding to the proposed revolution, the targeted traditional institutions (and classes of society) set up shop, selling ideas from the avant-garde as a stock in trade that actually acquired and gained market value over the years.

Cage never set out to create new forms of theater, but actual physical theaters were the frame for much of his early work. This was mostly, but not exclusively, music for solo dance. However *Four Walls* of 1944 was a "dance play" by Merce Cunningham with spoken parts, character roles, and keyboard accompaniment. Cage's early percussion ensemble music was too costly and unwieldy for the modest requirements of new dance, which led him to invent the prepared piano as a one-man percussion ensemble, originally for use in dance accompaniment but afterward as an important solo instrument for which he composed large-scale cycles of pieces. A commission from the CBS Radio Workshop in 1942 led to a collaboration with poet Kenneth Patchen and a "sound score" (percussion ensemble plus sound effects, both acoustic and recorded) for a surrealist radio play entitled *The City Wears a Slouch Hat*. Many of Cage's later performances and performance pieces have strong theatrical aspects. His *Theatre Piece* of 1960 was much like the Black Mountain "happening," that is, made up of actions and activities organized on aleatory or chance principles (this was the model for Stockhausen's *Originale* of 1961; see Chapter 9). Many Cage pieces, although not literally intended for the theater, have the characteristics of "music as theater." Large-scale performance pieces—probably the best known are the *Roaratorio* based on James Joyce's *Finnegan's Wake*, commissioned by IRCAM (Institut de Recherche et Coordination Acoustique/Musique) in 1979, and the several editions of the *Europeras*, starting in 1987 in Frankfurt—became characteristic of Cage's later work.

Cage's ambiance in the United States was originally almost entirely outside of the traditional musical world and his work, which helped to create the alternate or "downtown" music scene, was influential among painters, writers, choreographers, and what came to be known as performance artists. The two composers most closely associated with Cage,

Earle Brown and Morton Feldman, were both influenced by him and influenced him as well, especially in areas of open form and aleatory (or chance music). Cage had a major and direct influence on performance groups like Fluxus in New York (George Maciunas, Nam June Paik, La Monte Young, and others), ONCE in Ann Arbor (Robert Ashley, Gordon Mumma, Roger Reynolds), and Sonic Arts in New York (Ashley, Mumma, David Behrman, and Alvin Lucier), all of whom played a role in changing the notion of musical performance from its classical definitions. Cage began visiting Europe in the 1950s—originally at the invitation of Pierre Boulez[2]—and had a major effect on the turn of the European avant-garde away from a strictly determined serialism and toward the development of *azione musicale* or, to use the German term, *instrumentales Theater*.

Of the composers associated with Darmstadt (the Darmstadt *Ferienkurse* were the center of new music activity in Europe; see Chapter 9), the most highly developed conceptual and theatrical ideas came from a composer who was also from the New World, although a very different America from that of Cage. Mauricio Kagel was born and raised in Buenos Aires where he studied music and also philosophy and literature. After having cofounded the *Cinématèque* of Buenos Aires, he became chorusmaster at the *Teatro Colòn* and directed the *Colòn Chamber Opera*. By the late 1950s and early 1960s, he was established in Cologne, Germany, and at Darmstadt as the leading figure in Central European music theater after World War II. He is historically linked to the notion of *instrumentales Theater*, which may be his invention. At least that was his claim in September 1958 at the Düsseldorf Gallery 22 when German musicologist Heinz-Klaus Metzger used this term in reference to the John Cage *Music Walk* (the Polish composer Boguslaw Schäffer also used this term at about the same time or shortly thereafter). Whoever deserves the credit, the phenomenon was obviously new and innovative enough that there was a felt need for new terminology and the use of the term shows the link between Cage and Kagel.

Kagel's *Staatstheater* (1967–1970) is a monumental collection of actions and instrumental theater compositions—or perhaps one should say "prescriptions." Kagel sees himself as a critic of society and his notion is that the state, in representing society, acts as if it were in a theater. Kagel looks at the inhabitants of both the state (*Staat*) and the State Theater (*Staatstheater*) at the same time, mirroring details of behavior in the one or the other to have them become the material of his musico-theatrical piece. There is a charming,

---

2. Boulez, who became a champion of aleatory or chance elements in musical form, nevertheless ultimately rejected Cage's ideas and his music.

John Cage: *Europeras I & II*. Scenes from the Frankfurt Opera production, 1988. Photo: Mara Eggert. With kind permission of the Frankfurt Opera.

melancholic humor in these and other Kagel pieces, which look at tiny spots of our real lives rather than proposing revolutions or utopian worlds. When the entrance of Tosca onto the stage becomes the content of a new piece of Kagel, we find a fresh approach to modernist fragmentation, which becomes a bit of technique, an artistic method, or even an ideology. There is something humble, almost naive, in this alternative approach and its success speaks of the communicative capabilities of the author with wider audiences.

Cage did something similar—at least from a formal point of view—some twenty years later. In his early work, Cage showed very little interest in European music whose principal characteristics—personality, directionality, narrative, rhythmic unity, and so forth—were directly antithetical to his vision of a very different kind of music and musical culture. On the other hand, the *Europeras*, which were commissioned in 1987 by Heinz-Klaus Metzger for the Frankfurt Opera and the Almeida Theater in London, are Cage's commentary on traditional European culture from the very end of his life. They are based on elements from repertory operas including even lighting, program booklets, décors, properties, costumes, and stage action as well as the music, fragmented and reorganized using computer randomization programs. There is no role playing here; there are no plots, no dramaturgical narratives. There is no succession of elements and nothing is synchronized or placed in an intentionally close relationship. There is nothing held together or that could hold together. The more alien, the more separate the elements of the piece can be, the more useful the dialogue between them.

Under the influence

The influence of Cage has been so wide-ranging that almost any performance event, whether ruled by chance or by the strong exercise of will, can be attributed to his influence. The direct Cage line of influence on his colleagues and on groups like Fluxus and Sonic Arts has already been mentioned. The Polish composer Bogusław Schäffer used the term *instrumental theater* and created a series of stage works and theatrical actions in the 1960s and early 1970s. A number of North American composers— Charlie Morrow, Wendy Chambers, Robert Moran, and others—have taken the "happening" event concept out of the private art sphere and into the public square. The Canadian composer R. Murray Schafer has organized large-scale performances out-of-doors and in natural settings. *The Princess of the Stars* (1981) requires that the performers and audience travel to the appropriate locale, a lake at dawn. *The Enchanted Forest* (1993) for singers, actors, dancers, movers, and an orchestra of recorders, pennywhistles, didgeridoos, and ten to sixteen drummers is intended to be performed by a mixed ensemble of professionals and amateurs, adults and children, and is directed to take place in a forest adjacent to meadows or open fields.

Tom Johnson provides us with some good examples of how the search for new ideas in music has been linked to a theatralization of the music itself. In a loose way, this approach comes from Cage and Kagel. Cage's *Europeras* form a quasi-traditional link to operatic history by regarding classical opera repertoire as "material" or a dramaturgical mine. This goes back to the idea that music can be structured in other ways than merely by following inner musical conditions. Chance has been one important element in this development but decisions taken in the moment of the performance by the performers themselves, also not under the composer's direct control, may play a psycho-emotional rather than purely musical role. Another possibility here is ultra-mathematical rationality as in the music of Yannis Xenakis and Milton Babbitt. These various methodologies—chance, performer choice, and mathematical determination—have a lot in common, above all in removing the composer's will, personality, or biography from the compositional process.

This might at first glance seem paradoxical. Isn't art the expression of an individual's emotions and feelings? Johnson's reply is, not necessarily. This composer, who covered the emergence and development of minimal music and other new-music trends in New York as the music critic for the *Village Voice* from 1971 to 1982, moved to Paris in 1983. His best-known work at the time was *The Four Note Opera* of 1972—a piece literally and entirely made out of only four different pitches. This work has since been staged up to a hundred times, an exceptional success that makes it sort of a repertory piece in new music theater, a genre that, normally, continuously reinvents itself. How could this happen? The composer himself has explained that he wanted to "find the music, not to compose it." This protest against the romantic and expressionist musical past might seem naive but it is true that music has always been the child of an uneasy marriage between mathematics and something only slightly less abstract (feelings? emotions? trains of thought?). The mathematical part conveys an outsider point of view that many recent artists have wished to introduce to their work. The key words in Johnson's work are "minimalism" and "self-similar melodies" as well as "truth and interpretation." Johnson's view of minimalism is not only a reductive one but also one in which the dimensions of the work are determined by a generative formula or rule that "creates" the piece itself.

The titles of his instrumental pieces are self-explanatory: *Composition with Ascending Chromatic Scales in Twelve Tempos, All Beginning Simultaneously, the Piano Playing the Low Notes, the Clarinet the Middle Notes, and the Violin the High Notes* (1993); *Composition with Descending Chromatic Scales in Eight-Voice Canon Played in Three Ways, Separated by Two Piano Interludes which Bring the Music Back up to Its Starting Position* (1993), and, astonishingly, *Chord Catalogue* (1986) in which all of the 8,178 chords possible in one octave are notated to be playable on any keyboard in a period of approximately two hours. These titles might seem to suggest works like the Bach *Art of Fugue* or Eric Satie's *Vexations*, but the actual acoustic results of these conceptual calculations are not in any kind of meaningful relationship to its methods—quite like the hard-core serialism of earlier decades. The inhuman and unyielding musical grid that imposes itself on the performers becomes a kind of music theater when it encounters the humanity of musicians trying—and sometimes failing—to live up to these prescriptions. Indeed, another instrumental piece by Johnson is entitled *Failing, a Very Difficult Piece for Solo String Bass* (1975). In this work, which is still very often played, the musician becomes a partner in a performance project and has to talk about his own playing and its difficulties. *The Four Note Opera* works in a similar way with singers who sing about what they do. Strangely enough—perhaps because it in fact is a perfect little "meta-opera"—the work has been programmed quite often by small opera companies.[3] The singers explain not only how the music is constructed but also their feelings about having to carry the stereotypes of classical opera—for example, the soprano as *prima donna*; the carping contralto eager to take the soprano down a peg or two; the arrogant tenor, disgruntled at having less music to sing than the baritone. This adds the obviously inevitable or necessary action to a music that is constructed systematically out of only four notes.

In his book *Self-Similar Melodies,* Johnson investigates the precise mathematics of the musical "rows" that are discussed. Perhaps it is the very hopelessness of attempts by human beings to function like a Swiss watch that provide the wit and irony of these pieces. Another piece, entitled *Riemannoper* (1988), brings us to the extreme opposite point of view from Cage, Nono, and Goebbels who strictly ban the "doubling" of sense between the acoustic, the visual, and the dramatic. In Johnson's piece, dictionary articles from Hugo Riemann's famous 1882 reference work provide the texts. The article about *Aria* is sung as an aria, one about *recitativo* is in form of a recitative and so forth. *Nine Bells* is less theatrical but highly visual. The bells are hung in a space as a kind of installation and played by someone running through the space so that, according to the composer's instructions, "the sound of the performer's feet should be part of the music." This is close to Mauricio Kagel on the surface but it intentionally operates in another galaxy as a kind of theater that does not indulge in social criticism. The success of these works with the audience is one of mutual understanding, a sort of thankfulness that one can deal with high-brow culture without its intricate side effects.

Nothing new is said, but the old performance ritual is stripped of its tedious and momentous pretentiousness. For someone who doesn't find autobiographical music a problem, there may be a point that is reached in this repetitious, closed world where the lack of a way out becomes crushing. Up until that point is reached, Johnson's work is refreshing.

3. Opera about opera—whether "meta-opera" or simply "backstage opera"—goes back at least as far as the eighteenth century and there are well-known examples by Salieri, Mozart, Cimarosa, Donizetti, and Richard Strauss not to mention, in another vein, Berio, Kagel, and Cage.

This page and opposite: scenes from three different productions of Tom Johnson's *Riemannoper*, opera in two acts for baritone, tenor, primadonna, primadonna assoluta, and piano; text directly from the Riemann Music Lexicon. Above: Landestheater of Linz, Austria, 2006. Photo: Christian Brachwitz.

Above: Staatstheater Braunschweig, Germany. Photo: Thomas Ammerpohl; below, premiere, Krefeld Theater, Germany, 2000, directed by Aurelia Eggers. Photo: A. Eggers.

Further Reading

Cage, John. *Silence* (1961); *A Year From Monday: New Lectures and Writings* (1969); *Writings '67–'72* (1973); *Empty Words: Writings '73–'78* (1979); *X* (1983). Middletown, CT.

DeLio, Thomas. *The Music of Morton Feldman*. Westport, CT, 1996.

Friedman, Ken, ed. *The Fluxus Reader*. New York, 1998.

Johnson, Tom. *Imaginary Music*. Paris, 1974. The "text" of this volume consists of 104 drawings with music notation symbols, many of which have been reprinted in magazines and as program covers.

Johnson, Tom. *Self-Similar Melodies*. Paris, 1996.

Johnson, Tom. *The Voice of New Music*. Eindhoven, The Netherlands, 1991. This collection of Johnson's *Village Voice* articles written between 1971 and 1982 is available online as a free download (www.editions75.com/English/booksenglish.html).

Nyman, Michael. *Experimental Music: Cage and Beyond*. London, 1974.

Partch, Harry. *Genesis of a Music*. New York, 1949; 2nd ed., 1974. More information on the Harry Partch instruments can also be found at www.HarryPartch.com.

Ruhe, Harry. *Fluxus, the Most Radical and Experimental Art Movement of the Sixties*. Amsterdam, 1979.

Thomson, Virgil. *Selected Writings*, 1924–1984. New York, 2002.

Young, La Monte, and Jackson MacLow, eds. *An Anthology*. New York, 1963.

chapter 9

Music Theater as Musiktheater

I once had a conversation with Stockhausen, where he said: "You know, Morty, we don't live in heaven but here on earth." He began to hit the table and said: "A sound exists like that or like that or like that." He was convinced that he was showing me reality and that time would be something he could manipulate at his discretion. To be honest this way of dealing with time is boring to me. I am not a watch-maker.

Morton Feldman, quoted in *Münchener Biennale* 6, 1999, catalogue, p. 47

Musiktheater

For almost a half century now, one can find, in the biographies of composers from Europe and beyond, the familiar line "attended the Darmstadt summer course...." In one way or another, this credit served to legitimize composers of contemporary music far more than any university or conservatory degree. Music theater was, at least in the beginning, not on the agenda.

Why was this so? A little history will help us track it down.

Opera was originally Italian, operetta reached its peak in Paris and Vienna, and experimental ideas as well as popular musicals came from America. But the new music theater was invented in Germany. The word *Musiktheater*—from which the English term *music theater* was intentionally derived[1]—was strongly connected originally to Kurt Weill and the new

---

1. One of the authors (ES) used the term in an article in the *New York Times* in the 1960s. Whether this term had ever been used before (or had ever previously appeared in print), it had, at the time, the quality of a fresh coinage.

chamber opera (or *Zeitoper*) of the period after World War I. It is worth pointing out that this word is typically German in that it forms a new noun by connecting two existing forms. This is more than merely a play with words; language gives an insight into the mechanics of the mind. *Musik-theater* connects its constituent elements in an unpretentious manner: one even might feel the Brechtian attitude behind it. In opera, the music, text, and action are merged, whereas *Musiktheater* keeps the elements apart even as it brings them together.

After World War II, music theater came back. This new new music theater was not a rewind to something that Weill, Brecht, Hindemith, or Schoenberg had already achieved in the 1920s or 1930s. The first nonconventional works of the Darmstadteers were called "instrumental theater" or *musikalisches Theater*. In English, these terms may have quite different meanings. When a Broadway producer advertises his latest show as "music theater" (no one calls Broadway shows musical comedies any more), he does not mean to imply that it is a show in the style of Stockhausen.

New music as morality play

The reference to Kurt Weill reminds us that the Berlin melting pot between the wars was a lively place where ideas from abroad—Paris, Moscow, Italy, and New York—were absorbed and turned into new visions and utopias. The explosive mixture of exorbitant wealth, high unemployment and inflation, social upheavals resulting from the introduction of aggressive industrial mass production, the huge growth of the cities, and the parallel growth of mass culture are just some of the ingredients that fueled Berlin culture but eventually helped nationalist politics triumph over all other systems and ideologies. The huge gaps between rich and poor produced a lot of inspiration in the arts. Social themes vied with experimentation and new forms imported from abroad such as jazz.

All that changed when the Nazis came to power. Jewish artists were deprived of their ability to work, and both social and artistic modernism were proscribed. Many of the major artists emigrated; those who did not were silenced or murdered in the camps. After World War II, everything changed again. Composers whose work was celebrated by the regime—Richard Strauss, Werner Egk, and Carl Orff were three of the best known—were afterward regarded as suspect and found themselves demoted in the history books. Orff, who had unparalleled success with his oratorio *Carmina Burana* (based on medieval German texts) and a series of (minimalist *avant la lettre*) operatic and theatrical works, was regarded as a kind of musical propagandist for the "strength through joy" youth philosophy of the Nazis. Strauss continued to write period pieces for the protected, parallel world of the opera house, seemingly in blissful ignorance of the violent, changing world outside.

It is difficult to imagine the almost total destruction of Germany and German life, cultural and otherwise, brought about by World War II. Twelve years under Nazi rule had cut off all avant-garde activities and silenced intellectual and artistic life. Many artists and intellectuals—a good number of them (perhaps the majority) of Jewish background—were gone, never to return, and large areas of cultural life were simply decimated. Much the same applied as well to Austria, which had been incorporated into the Third Reich early on.

Reconstruction was therefore not only a physical and economic task but a cultural one as well. With its traditions of intellectual and artistic endeavor, its organizational abilities and its work ethic, Germany was able to orchestrate a revival in a remarkably short period of time. The nearly complete destruction of the old order was, in one sense, a gift. It offered a clean slate and a huge potential for the new. And a dramatic turn toward the new was exactly what was needed for Germany and the Germans to make a clean break with their recent and totally discredited past.

The Darmstadt *Ferienkurse* or Summer Course in Contemporary Music was established after World War II.[2] It was, in its origins, simply designed to provide information and knowledge—historical, theoretical, and otherwise—of the evolution of contemporary music in the preceding quarter century that had been denied to an entire generation by Nazi cultural policy and the war. Darmstadt, which had been largely destroyed, was to symbolize cultural rebirth and become the pole or anti-pole for what would define contemporary music—not just in Germany but throughout Europe for the next forty or fifty years.

By 1950, Darmstadt had already captured the attention of younger composers due to the presence of Ernst Krenek, Edgard Varèse, and Theodor W. Adorno. The last-named, a Jewish refugee from Nazism, had returned to the land of the Holocaust, no longer a composer but a major theoretician and critic. Adorno was able to restate what he had said before the war in an objective and reflective manner but now with tremendous authority: that naive, instinctive, esthetic behavior only led to pseudo-historical myths and lies. Between this trauma and the resulting deep mistrust of, on the one hand, any strong statements of deadly and aggressive

---

2. It is one of history's little ironies (and a well-kept secret) that the Music Officer running the Music and Theater Branch for the U.S. Military Occupation was a German-speaking American composer and critic named Everett Helm who was able to convince the American occupation authorities to support and fund a center for new music.

ideological power and, on the other, the unrevivable historical influences of competing religious influences, Adorno saw a new role for art as the bearer of an admonitory, uncorrupted, and unconditional—one almost could say scientific—truth. This was certainly a new and stirring concept: new music as the bearer of a new morality!

An essential element in the dynamics of the new music scene in Germany after 1945 was the fact that merely intuitive, naive behavior would no longer be sufficient or even desirable. The German tendency to be less spontaneous, less instinctive—now reinforced for historical and political reasons—meant that German art had to be more careful, more analytical. At the same time, the history of German nationalism gone bad meant that the new Germany had to be more open, more interested in other cultures.

What was clear was that theater had no place in this concept. Theater was the preferred medium for the Nazi program, which was staged in the form of countless party meetings, parades, Olympic games, self representation, and architectonic absurdities, all at the service of the Thousand-Year Reich that was to start up at any moment. For Adorno and the avant-garde, theater in any guise was not pure and could not respond to the objective and transparent approach to musical thinking and composition that was now needed.

The year 1951 was decisive for Darmstadt. Arnold Schoenberg, the remaining authoritative figure from the old avant-garde (Berg died before the war; Webern had died in 1945, shot in error by an American GI), was invited to teach at the Summer Course but he was very ill and could not attend. It would have been a remarkable vindication for him but he died only three days after the Darmstadt session opened. His substitute was his former student, Adorno. Ironically, Adorno, for all his importance in this historical moment, was no champion of the new serialism that was hatching, the model for which was not Schoenberg but Webern. Nietzsche had said "God is dead"; Boulez's 1952 obituary of Schoenberg was entitled "Schoenberg is dead."

Messiaen's structural experiments in the late 1940s and Webern's highly personal, refined, and abstract version of dodecaphony were what fascinated young composers as they discovered unknown and forbidden musical territory with its unrevealed potential for the future. Twenty-three-year-old Karlheinz Stockhausen started off his career with these experiences, meeting with Messiaen and Pierre Boulez and diving into serialism, essentially a mathematical extension of the idea of twelve-tone music. Music-theater issues were not part of the "summer of '51" any more than the intuitive judgment of the listening public was brought into consideration. Compositional methods became more important than audible results. Even the ideological aspects were obscured by the emphasis on hermetic theory. And Adorno, whether he intended it or not, set up the classic rift in new music as it was then understood: Schoenberg versus Stravinsky or, as it was translated, dodecaphony versus neoclassicism.

Not all the younger composers went along with the program. In 1951, Hans Werner Henze, already a Darmstadt alumnus, was composing an opera. Henze was interested in "film, graphic work and literature of Jean Cocteau, jazz, the modern opera of Weill and Milhaud, in brief, all those beautiful and interesting things of which we had been deprived under the fascist regime."[3] But these were all the things in which Darmstadt had no interest. When Henze realized that his predilections for the beautiful, the lyric, and the elegant put him in direct conflict with the Darmstadt serialists, he went into exile in Italy (where he continues to live), becoming one of the most successful contemporary opera composers (*Boulevard Solitude*, 1952; *König Hirsch*, 1956; *Der Prinz von Homburg*, 1960; *Elegy for Young Lovers*, 1961; *Der junge Lord*, 1965; *The Bassarids*, 1966; *The English Cat*, 1983; and others). Henze is strongly connected to the opera world and represents a Germany that has been and continues to provide a platform for the realization of ideas and concepts that other countries do not undertake. Although he is best known for work that uses the standard operatic and symphonic apparatus, his involvement in left politics after 1968 also led him to compose small-scale, *engagé* works of music theater like *El Cimmaron* (1970), *Der langwierige Weg in die Wohnung der Natascha Ungeheuer* (1971), *La Cubana* (a "vaudeville," 1974), and *We Come to the River* (1976). He also composed two radio operas (*Ein Landarzt*, after Kafka, 1951, and *The End of a World*, 1953) and an opera for television in 1973. In 1988, Henze founded the Munich Biennale "for New Music Theatre," a festival devoted to new opera and music theater, one of the few such institutions anywhere; he remained its artistic director until 1996.

For a short period, serious contemporary music had an important role to play in society. When John Cage appeared, he was called both a charlatan and a liberator. The first rock 'n' roll groups turned up in Germany at just about the same time and were also eagerly denounced. The first decade or two of pioneering avant-gardism established a reference point against which anything else could only be a mere alternative.

The human voice is back

In the mid-1950s, the composers associated with Darmstadt began to show an interest in the voice—always, however, from their particular

3. *Reclam Opernlexikon*, 351.

and hermetic point of view. There was Stockhausen's electronic collage *Gesang der Jünglinge* ("Chant of the young man in the fire"; 1956) which uses a fragment of biblical text, a boy's voice, and an enormous number of tape splices to create a milestone piece of electro-acoustic composition. *Le Marteau sans maître* (1954) of Boulez sets a very obscure René Char poem in a highly coloristic manner in which the voice functions largely as a member of the instrumental ensemble; almost nothing of the text is comprehensible at any level. This is all obviously still very far from theatrical representation.

The first breaks with doctrinaire serialism came from the active and influential Italian contingent. Nono's *Epitaphs after Garcia Lorca* of 1951 and his *Canto Sospeso* of 1955 introduced both solo and choral voices into the toolbox of the serialists. Berio's *Omaggio a Joyce* (1958) and *Visage* (1961) were electronic studio pieces using the voice of Cathy Berberian. Operatic and music-theater works were shortly to follow (see Chapter 10—The Italians).

When Mauricio Kagel came to Germany from Argentina in 1957, he brought an interest in the intersection of music with speech. One of his early works, written in Argentina, was *Palimpsestos* (1950), and his first German work was *Anagrama* (1957–58) performed at Darmstadt in 1960; shortly thereafter, Kagel taught a course at Darmstadt entitled "Word and Voice." His later work involved both actors and musicians and often requires action from the musicians themselves (see Chapter 8).

Questions of text, language, and speech were in the air at that time. There was a revival of interest in the work of dadaists like Tristan Tzara and Kurt Schwitters and in the James Joyce language of the unconscious. The French structuralists were inspired by research on how language works. Poets like Hans G Helms, Arno Schmidt, Franz Mon, and others were again exploring the borders between literary language, performance, and the visual arts; the so-called *concrète* poetry inhabited a no-man's-land between language and music.

Oddly enough, there is no precise equivalent for the word "sound" in German. The expression in vogue was "the musical material," a term that is scientific sounding enough but does not necessarily suggest the possibility of incorporating "nonmusical" sound into the musical body.[4] When John Cage, the enigmatic figure out of the Wild West, introduced notions of coincidence or chance and their musical equivalents, "noise" and "nothingness,"

4. The way in which the word "material" has been used was more abstract or metaphorical than concrete: only in a later, postmodern sense do we discover that recorded sound, synthesized sound, everyday sound, and noise of any sort are unmetaphoric material ready for use.

Stockhausen's "craftmanship of the composer" quickly began to weaken. The aim of objectivity in art was a chimera and the quest for it was leading nowhere. Silence and noise, electronically stored sound, and the possibilities of sound manipulation with electronic devices had shown how open, unlimited, and unclassifiable these notions of sound (or "the musical material") actually were. The reference to something precise and objective in the music, along with all the accompanying social and moral implications, started to disappear.

When abstract, instrumental music began to lose its absolute primacy and composers started again to write for the voice, they discovered the theatrical potential. Ideologically, there was no way to push back into tradition, or to reinvent opera, or to invent a new German music theater (the way Nono was inventing a new Italian music theater; see Chapter 10). Kagel, who was, like Cage, from the New World, did not feel obligated to deal with the German and European struggles between tradition and innovation. There was just one direction: straight ahead. And, as Henze said, who knows where "ahead" is?

The return of the voice brought with it a Pandora's Box of emotional issues. After the war, the Germans had had enough of emotions and feelings, but by the 1960s, the human factor and the expressive gesture were back. The voice cannot be treated just like any other instrument. Its use immediately implies all the problems and characteristics of the human psyche.

There were a great number of ghosts to be exorcised. Traditions are, in many places, holy rituals, bearing the codes of self-identity. To question tradition is to question people's identity, perhaps even their existence. Even the structure of concert halls and opera houses, the very way they are built, responds to the traditions of how they are used. Kagel said, "What repels us is not the music, but the bourgeois concert hall."[5] Kagel dealt directly with those rituals, habits, and procedural traditions in music: the concert as a social event caricatured in a theater. Berio actually stated the need to perform his works in the opera house for them to have their revolutionary meaning. Boulez, on the other hand, founded a major institute for electronic music and a performing ensemble without blowing up the opera houses as he had once proposed. These are different strategies with, as will be seen, different consequences.

The singing voice actually does not need words to produce strong emotional impressions. This fact is well demonstrated by the popularity—in opera and also in pop music—of singing in a foreign language. It is also demonstrated by the paradoxical case of works in which nothing

5. Cited in *Musik-Konzepte*, vol. 124 (Berlin, 1975): 67.

semantically intelligible is said, but we seem to understand something quite precise nonetheless. The idea of a *vocalise*—the traditional term for a text-less vocal piece—goes at least as far back as the early twentieth century, but the notion of composing a text out of nonsense syllables as if it were part of the musical scoring is relatively recent. The *Aventures* and *Nouvelles aventures* (1962–65) of Ligeti are good examples (see below). In the Boulez *Marteau sans maître* (1952–54; rev. 1957) the voice functions as a pure instrument (there is a text but it is incomprehensible whether the words are understood or not). Kagel typically uses either the singing voice purely as an instrument or a speaking voice to communicate a text. In his *Sur scène* (1960), a narrator talks extensively about "today's music business" and the singing voice is not used. The sound of the narrator is, in effect, a speaking voice in quotation marks. This makes coherent Kagel's concept of instrumental theater; it is the instruments that speak and act while a speaking voice gives us reality in the form of quotes.

In contrast, the reappearance of the voice in new music also meant a rediscovery of the link between music and text (language, speech). Kagel, in his *Anagrama*, explored many methods of using a single text, the famous palindrome *"In girum imus nocte et consumimur igni"* ("we circle in the night and are consumed by fire"). He systematically treats this one line so that an entire work for speaking chorus, voice, and instruments results. The notion of music and speech (or language; the German word *Sprache* is the same for both) could now, with the aid of linguistics and phonology, be researched scientifically in musical form. Here are some of the methods used:

- speech as sonic material for composition (Berio: *Sequenza III*; Kagel: *Anagrama*; Ligeti: *Aventures*)
- invented vocal sounds as the compositional material (Dieter Schnebel: *Maulwerke*; *":!(Madrasha 2); Glossolalie*)
- speech treated as or transferred into musical sound (Stockhausen: *Gesang der Junglinge*; Ligeti: *Clocks and Clouds*; Herbert Eimert: *Epitaph für Aikichi Kuboyama*, an electronic piece that uses speech sounds mixed with a live voice; Berio: *Thema—Omaggio a Joyce*)
- speech as the result of composition (the classic example is the *Ursonate* of Schwitters; also Hans G Helms: *"Hörspiel" Fa:m' Ahniesgwow* and Berio's *Cries of London*)

The easiest way to manage speech is to record it in order to manipulate it in an electronic studio as sonic "material," and that was the most common way that voice and language reentered the new-music scene. Music theater came to Germany in the wake of Cage's arrival in the 1950s, in the form of

meta-theater built on existing structures. Cage belonged to another generation, came from another continent, and brought with him chance and coincidence as well as his special mix of Eastern fatalistic philosophy, humor,
and let-the-buyer-beware put-on.

The preoccupation with chance and coincidence provided some totally
new viewpoints, differing from the forbidding hermetics of serialism and
the nationalist-elitist attitude inherent in the Schoenberg/Webern heritage.[6] Indeed, the entire notational fixation of the heritage of Western
music was challenged. To the Europeans who were trying to rebuild their
national identities after the war, the approach of extra-European cultures
was a distinct provocation. Non-Western cultures were much less obsessed
with leaving traces and accumulating documentation through notation and
archives. Improvisation played a much greater role, as did oral transmission.
And, with the arrival of Cage, Cage-ian philosophy, and Cage-ian theatrics,
there was something else, something even more terrifying: a transgression
of the boundaries of notation that also meant a loss of control that up to
then had been the absolute point of reference for the serious composer.
The equal-tempered piano with its division of the octave in twelve, the
structural necessities of the cadence, and the rules of sonata and fugue,
everything that is canonized and written in the secret book of music-as-
magic, was now at risk. This secret book was also a way to insulate music
from the rest of the world and from the other arts. What Virgil Thomson
once called "The State of Music"[7] is an isolated domain, preoccupied with
its own well-being and endlessly self-reflective.

These conditions (which have been challenged but still remain strong)
have had various consequences. One of the most obvious is the split between
"classical music" and the large public which, aided and abetted by the mass
media, simply created its own music. Another was the complete disappearance of improvisation, which, in the not too distant past, was a major feature
of European music (Bach, Handel, Mozart, Beethoven, and Liszt were all
composers who made their reputations as improvisers in much the same
way that a jazz artist does today). Another result was the split between the
world of theater and opera—even classical and romantic opera could not
be fitted into the control box—and new music. Equally damaging was the
split with the other arts—visual, literary, and performing—which were all
evolving quickly and without the constraints of control, order, or even (in
many cases) notation. Cage might seem to have arrived from an alien planet

---

6. In the summer of 1921, Schoenberg had told his student and friend Josef
    Rufer that "with this discovery [i.e., of the twelve-tone method], the domi-
    nance of German music is assured for another hundred years."
7. See his amusing and still instructive book of this title.

but he was actually stepping into a closed room that needed fresh air from (to quote Stefan George as set by Schoenberg in 1908) "other planets." With Cage as the catalyst, healthy curiosity allied to the new freedoms of improvisation and chance pushed composers toward music theater.

Curiously, jazz hardly figures in this discussion at all, possibly because jazz as an improvisational art—and especially in its more advanced forms— was still surprisingly little known or understood in serious European artistic circles at the time. Adorno had famously dismissed jazz as a serious art form and that judgment was taken seriously in Germany. When a certain flavor of jazz appears in Zimmermann's *Die Soldaten*, it may represent depraved society. Or it may be there (along with everything else in that work) just because it exists. Is it Zimmermann's response to the out-of-tune piano and simple-minded polka in Berg's *Wozzeck*? Or did Zimmermann just have a taste for the forbidden art?[8] Zimmermann's *magnum opus* is a piece of total theater, megalomaniacal, even unperformable in some respects. It includes all possible means of projection, reproduction, and presentation and it is also post-stylistic. In 1966, the city of Cologne offered its Grand Prix in the arts to both Zimmermann and Stockhausen. Stockhausen, rather than be associated with Zimmermann and his work, refused to accept the joint award. In his defense, Zimmermann cited Cage and Kagel as composers who turned their backs on the idea of a fixed style, preferring the "authenticity of a music that was more than style." This was a conflict of historical size and significance and it resonates today when many of these issues are being revisited.

The hesitations and difficulties about working in the theater were legion. For the purists, the theater was seen to have roots in the messy spectacles of circus and fair. Music theater is the court clown in the history of music, only slightly redeemed by the serious side of the history of opera. Imitation, caricature, and admonishment are key features of music theater that are not hidden behind the wordless esthetics of music which, as the great estheticians and philosophers have long told us, is what causes music to rise above even its sister arts to occupy the highest seat in the pantheon. Finally, music theater is not the work of isolated geniuses but demands teamwork, a feature that may appeal or repel depending on the artist's ego and politics.

Originale

In 1961 Stockhausen premiered his *Musikalisches Theater* (his term) under the title *Originale*. As in English, an "original" is someone who

---

8. Zimmermann had earlier written a jazz-inflected trumpet concerto under the later discarded name of "Darky's Darkness"!

steps out from the ordinary to show his individuality. Stockhausen was going to show himself as both a team player and as an original! This was his response to the Cage *Theater Piece* performed in New York the year before and which he consciously mimicked, even to the point of inviting some of the original Cage performers (among them David Tudor and Nam June Paik) as participants in *his* piece. Cage had a participating poet and so Stockhausen had to have one as well (Hans G Helms who, along with Cage, was a major influence), as well as a painter, cameraman, coat check girl, newspaper seller, child, and some people who would simply play "themselves." Stockhausen's riposte to Cage consisted of taking all the imaginable parameters of theatrical action (or, at any rate, what Stockhausen understood as theatrical action) and organizing them according to the principles of serial composition. He writes in the program note: "Characters, occupations, events of life (nothing is "as if"… "nothing is intended; everything is composed, everything intends)—tighten in one space, one time: Theater."

This is the traditional question about the difference between life and art in a new and up-front guise. Artaud tried to reinterpret the old idea of catharsis with a more modern notion of a theater that would cleanse the soul through a traumatic situation. A shock—even if only a theatrical one—might lead to a new point of view, a change of mind or soul. In the Brecht/Weill version, it is assumed that it is not the individual who creates the behaviors, traditions, and rituals that condition and dominate, but society. The individual is then a witness; the theatrical event, always understood as a theatrical event (and not an imitation of life), is meant to provoke the viewer to testify.

On the other hand, Stockhausen—the anti-Brecht—would like to have us believe that a represented situation, which manipulates our feelings and intellect, is simply truth and life and nothing else. Life = art = world = me. And for Stockhausen (see his foreword to *Originale*), "me = musical theater." What sort of theater is it that pretends not to be theater, but only life? What Stockhausen is denying here is the necessary condition that theater creates a different reality—but a reality nevertheless.

Originale has a structural score, which describes eighteen scenes with a staff or row for every actor indicating his or her appearance on stage. The music is in fact borrowed from the composer's other compositions, including *Kontakte, Zyklus, Gruppen, Gesang,* and *Carré,* but it also includes two tapes with the voice of Stockhausen himself. The score asks for a composer (!), director, pianist/percussionist, and violinist as well as "actions" from a singer, poet, painter, a woman named Edith Sommer, cameraman, light and sound technicians, wardrobe lady, newspaper vendor, child, and six actors/actresses. Dogs or monkeys were brought on the stage and fed and members of the audience received fruits as well (but only "if they ask"). The seven parts include "structures," that is, possible actions. The accurate notation of time on a ruler-like layout marking the seconds makes the actors function like instruments; in fact, Stockhausen called the work a "time piece," referring to his writings on time.[9]

There is an obvious contradiction in saying that "nothing was intended" and then specifying this level of control. Asking the pianist to dress in a religious costume or asking all performers to move their heads in slow motion is "intention" *par excellence*.

In all these attempts to control time and prescribe actions, there is finally a large amount of the uncontrollable. Stockhausen tells us that he changed entries and durations in an improvisational manner during the performances, that Nam June Paik never repeated a single one of his actions, and that other performers refused to perform some of the required actions. There was also a street singer who came, very ill and pale, only to the first performance, impatiently waiting for his appearance in the final scene. He was well received and generously tipped by the audience but it is difficult to avoid the sense that he was being patronized in a rather ugly way.

The piece itself got off to a bad start when the Arts Council of the city of Cologne did not approve and withdrew its support leaving the composer to finance the twelve performances on his own. The New York performance of 1965 (with a cast that included Alvin Lucier, James Tenney, Allan Ginsberg, Charlotte Moorman, Allan Kaprow, and, again, Nam June Paik) was strongly protested by many New York artists and composers (mostly from the Fluxus group) who regarded it as an attempt by Stockhausen to poach on their territory in more ways than one!

After these experiences, it took Stockhausen a long time to get back to music theater—sixteen years to be precise and then another twenty-five years to complete his cycle of *Licht* ("Light"), still unperformed as a cycle at this writing. In the interim, his interest in voice was apparently aroused by the innovations and radical techniques of Roy Hart (see Chapter 17), and the solo part in his *Momente* (originally 1964 but there are several later versions) was intended for Hart. This huge concept piece for solo voice, choirs, and instruments, uses found texts from the Bible, New Guinea, William Blake, letters from friends, fairy tales, invented words and nonsense syllables, screaming, laughing, breathing, whispering, and so on. Like *Originale*, *Momente* shows the influence of Cage's aleatory or chance techniques and also espouses the Cagian esthetic position that any kind of sound might turn into music. Typically, however, the range and the

---

9. Again, this is Stockhausen responding to Cage, who specified that the actions in his work take place during a designated period or length of time, often indicated by the arms of a conductor imitating the hands of a large clock.

open-form aspects of the work are actually organized in complex and rigorous ways according to the composer's "moment form" theories.

In the 1970s, Stockhausen began a series of instrumental works that use lighting, costumes, mime, and other aspects of ritual. As planned, *Licht* consists of seven full-evening works, one for each day of the week, combining elements from both German and non-Western cultures in a music-theater setting. Like *Momente*, these works are notable for, among other things, the composer's continuing attempt to control scenic realizations with some of the same techniques and methods that he had previously applied to musical performance.

Ligeti

György Ligeti was born in a Hungarian community in Transylvania, Romania; he studied and worked in Hungary as a very solidly trained musician, theorist, and composer with a lot of curiosity. During the anti-communist revolt of 1956 and subsequent Soviet invasion, he escaped to Vienna. He went to Darmstadt and worked in the electronic music studios of West German Radio in Cologne before settling in Vienna where he became involved with the serialist and post-serialist movements of the time. Although, like other new-music composers from Eastern Europe, he was first known for large-scale instrumental pieces written in densities and planes of sound, he also wrote for the voice, making imaginative use of invented texts and sounds.

Stanley Kubrick's use—without the composer's permission—of his *Atmospheres, Requiem, Piano Piece,* and *Lux Aeterna* in the film *2001*—made his music world famous. Like Kagel, Ligeti came out of another place, another culture and language. Turning away from the serial cul-de-sac, he directly explored the electronic medium, using vocal sounds. His *Articulation* of 1958 was, like the Stockhausen *Gesang* or the Berio *Omaggio,* a key work. Ligeti's *Aventures,* designated as a "Mimodrama," and its sequel, *Nouvelles aventures,* have no intelligible text but use nonsense syllables attached to expressive vocal gestures. The instruments—flute/piccolo, horn, percussion, piano/celesta/harpsichord, cello, and bass—act as glue to keep the vocal actions together.

The invisible becomes visible. The indication in the score *zum Publikum* ("toward the audience") is telling the performer how to communicate something to the audience that literally "makes no sense." This piece has the form of human communication without the verbal content. In effect, what musicians call the expression becomes an essential and theatrical part of both the gesture and the sound, and in the end, it is difficult to decide what can be understood from these very suggestive but literally unintelligible messages. The necessity of having to move and behave in a certain emotional manner creates—in the gestures, theatrical and otherwise, as well as in the sound—a true invisible theater.

The fact that Ligeti uses natural timing for those actions throughout makes these gestures, and indeed the whole piece, very suggestive. This is in contrast to other experiments with time by other composers, especially those of Stockhausen and Berio, which tend to remain experimental in character. The notion of time as a primordial subject of interest was back, and once again, time was seen as a key to the problems of form in avant-garde composition. But time is not an arrow on paper. Most of the concepts of time in that period treat it as if it were a sort of dough to be squeezed, expanded, combined, layered, and so on. Zimmermann, whose collages deal with multiple musical styles, had his own theory of time, regarding it as a sphere where past, present, and future are all equally distant from each other. This concept, close to postmodernism, is very realistic and direct but lacks the innovative approach of Stockhausen. Time is historical. Theater (including music theater) always deals with "historical time," even in a narrative that is telling or retelling the history of something dramatic that happened earlier and elsewhere. But with *Originale, Aventures*, or a piece like *Sur Scène* of Kagel, there is no story or narration so there is no question about "retelling" the past. Everything we see and hear is present and takes place in the present. With no historical or geographical distance to be evoked, the theater comes closer to the audience and this closeness has a more and more direct impact. For many modernists, the Golden Age can be found not in some glamorous view of the past but in the possibilities of the present and that hopeful future that always seems to lie just around the corner.

Time is a tempting object for philosophical or pseudo-philosophical speculations, most of which do not work for the simple reason that the visible and audible reality of the moment is inevitably their major enemy. Talking, singing, and acting not only create their own timing but also have a natural, inherent timing in reference to everyday life. This reference is lacking in pure music; if no story is told, there is no past and also no flow from past to present. The grammar of storytelling is nearly always in the past imperfect, and it is much more difficult to tell a story in the present tense.[10] A lot of new music theater is, in fact, not interested in telling a story. The lack of narrative became a hallmark of modernism in music theater. Such pieces have no historical space at all. This kind of modernist theater and music theater lives only in the present and this can be refreshing

---

10. Film scripts are written in the present tense as they must describe what the viewer sees and hears at every given moment.

and unpretentious (see many of Kagel's works). There is no pretense to narrative or historical time in these pieces but only the actual passage (and the perception by the audience) of performance time.[11]

The invisible theater of Ligeti's *Aventures* and *Nouvelles aventures* is invisible only as a coherent theatrical text of the kind that can be read like a libretto. The musical texture of these works is dense and focuses attention on the music, on the sound-making itself and therefore on the moment. Ligeti has composed a musical composition, not a theater with music. As in *Neither*, Feldman's setting of Beckett, there are no waits for the scenery to be moved. These pieces work very well as audio recordings while some true music-theater pieces do not make good CDs without major alterations.

In 1978, Ligeti used a vastly expanded version of this invented verbal and vocal language in setting a play by the Belgian writer Michel de Ghelderode. *Le grand macabre* is a Rabelaisian black comedy set in Breughelland where political corruption, human folly, and the grotesque reign of death compete with one another. Originally written in the 1970s in the shadow of the old communist regimes of Eastern Europe, it was revised in the 1990s by the composer and has been widely performed in the more adventurous precincts of operaland. In this piece, narrative time in the past imperfect makes a reappearance.[12]

Dieter Schnebel

Starting in the late 1950s, Dieter Schnebel proposed various projects in which "visible music" was a major concern. The music has to be imagined; what we see is the theatricality of music making. Schnebel, who in 1969 wrote a profound book on the works of Mauricio Kagel, had the notion here of a genuine music theater expressed in the forms and gestures of making music. At the point where electronic devices start to take over the actual production of sound, the role of the live musician becomes that of an actor. A good example of this is Schnebel's *visible music I* (1961–1962) for a conductor and an instrumentalist. The composer writes: "Watching how someone performs music has long been appreciated and was even necessary in some cases. Some *crescendos* are better experienced from the *espressivo* face of the musician than from what comes to the ears. In other cases, it would better to close your

11. It is characteristic of the return to opera and chamber opera in the 1980s that the old storytelling in the past imperfect has come back again.
12. Although this work is often referred to as music theater, it can scarcely be mounted—given its size and performing forces—except by large opera companies. Ligeti has, however, used elements from the work to make shorter, more practical excerpts for concert or semi-theatrical performance.

eyes and just listen."[13] What we see in *visible music I* is a conductor who dances in a manner that is a little more exaggerated than that of a real conductor but nevertheless suggests musical structures and expressions. In the even more radical *nostalgie* (1962) for conductor only, all we hear is the conductor's breathing. There is a strong aspect of dance in this and these are matters that, forty years later, are being explored, in a theoretical as well as a practical way, in contemporary dance. This is a theater about music, a study about the conductor in tails, still with us today but on the threshold of disappearing.

There is a real question behind this would-be irony: what do we actually get to see when the absurd side of musical performance is made obvious? The grimace of an operatic diva caught with her mouth open in a still photograph is certainly ridiculous. In fact, there is not much else to see since when we turn the microscope onto music, what we get is a specialized form of self-reflective theater. Schnebel created a number of other pieces in this vein for pianist and even for the public. In 1951, he noted that a performance of the Boulez *Polyphonie X* produces a sort of collective gymnastic exhibition on the part of the ensemble.[14] The closeness of the deadly serious to the ridiculous in art music, particularly of the avant-garde variety, has often been observed.[15] It produces a kind of involuntary theatricality that breaks the concentration on sound by calling attention to the earnest physical and visual exertions of the performers. Newer media, like video and film, are probably best suited to the study of such performance by-products; in fact, Schnebel proposed making a film out of *nostalgie*.

A subform of music theater that might be mentioned here is related to Schnebel's idea for music that is intended only to be read. His *MO-NO* of 1969 is a book with suggestive designs that incorporate musical symbols. This is close to the scores of Bussotti and other sorts of graphic notation but without the need to be actually realized in sound. It also suggests the graphic work of Gerhard Rühm and other visual artists who use musical paper and musical symbols in an "artistic" way to suggest a music, a kind of music theater without actors or actual sound.

13. Dieter Schnebel, *Denkbare Musik, Schriften 1952–1972* (Cologne, 1972): 269.
14. Ironically, as the music and the musical style become more familiar to the performers (and audiences), the need for extraordinary physical activity diminishes notably.
15. And has been parodied on a number of occasions in various media. See, for example, Peter Ustinov's BBC interviews in which he plays contemporary composers, one of whom is an electronic music composer by the name of Bruno Heinz Ja-Ja.

The disintegration of Darmstadt

By this time, music theater had become a true no man's land between the arts.[16] *Verfransung der Künste* ("fraying of the arts") was Adorno's way of summing up the whole business. His view was that work in this genre always could be booked into the opera house, the concert hall, dance theater, or performance art space or put into the category of audio-art or given some other label that was seemingly more precise than "music theater."

In 1962 the Austrian composer Friedrich Cerha was busy with the completion of the last act of Alban Berg's *Lulu*. Cerha had founded, together with Kurt Schwertsik, an ensemble for contemporary music called *Die Reihe* (referring to the rows of the serialists). He had also worked on a large symphonic cycle and a "stage-piece" entitled *Netzwerk* (1962–67), which presented the idea of the world as a net; by looking at the small events inside a mass, it would be possible to establish the complexity of the mass as if it were an organism. Astonishingly, the century of "the masses" and mass culture had not yet produced music theater occupied with this phenomenon.

A phrase from Dieter Schnebel throws light on the attitudes of those days. When asked if he would work on the esthetic level of pop music, he answered that avant-garde music should be made accessible to all levels of society. "We [the composers] have to step down from the pedestal, but without intentionally falling behind in our potential" (i.e., without falling back into the trap of writing simple music—popular, tonal, emotional, etc. like that preferred by Nazis—and thus dropping out of the avant-garde into the mainstream). Schnebel pointed to the systems of communication that would have to be opened up so that, just as there was an audience for rock or pop or folk music, there could be a popular public for serial music that would seriously discombobulate all those specialists in the modern music listening public!

The idea that music theater could be a means to open up and reach a large public was striking. If we ask the same question today, we see that there are publics for commercialized mass music of all sort. What was formerly known as pop music is divided into many specific categories, one of which is now contemporary avant-garde music! Music theater drops out of this scheme nearly completely. It is too theatrical for the concert hall and for most music festivals, and, with certain exceptions, it does not fit inside

16. Carla Henius, *grande dame* of experimental music theater in Germany, has pointed out that the small Opera Studio, the pool for all "crazy experimenting," was the first item to be cut for financial reasons as an unprofitable appendix of the larger state theaters (Carla Henius, *Schnebel, Nono, Schönberg oder Die wirkliche und die erdachte Musik* [Berlin, 1993]).

either the opera house or the spoken theater. The "happening" has been streamlined or has disappeared.

To get an idea of what the unknown land of the future might look like, we might turn to an operatic music-theater version of a Kafka novel. Roman Haubenstock-Ramati, from the Polish city of Krakow via Tel Aviv and Paris, was commissioned by the Berlin Opera to set Kafka's *Amerika,* and the work was premiered by Bruno Maderna to a largely negative reception. Haubenstock-Ramati was known as an innovator of musical notation from which he drew mobile forms. Working with tape and electronics in Paris, he had a wide background for creating his vision of Kafka's novel. An immense orchestra is extended with four-track tape containing various recordings of music. In some parts of the score, the notion of "sound-mass" is present (as in the work of Xenakis or Penderecki) where a continous sound-stream is manipulated by the composer through the medium of live, individual musicians. The sense of mass and the struggle of the individual within that mass is a recurring theme in Eastern European music of that time; it is also found in early Ligeti and in the work of Witold Lutoslawski. Although most of the works of this type were written for concert performance, there is an element of the theater in much of it.

In the same year as Haubenstock-Ramati's *Amerika,* Ligeti came out with his *Nouvelles aventures,* a rare example of a sequel in contemporary music theater. The two *Aventures* are often staged together and continue to be performed. Like Kagel in Buenos Aires, Aribert Reimann, a composer of the next generation, actually worked in the opera as a coach and *répétiteur* in the Berlin *Städtische Oper.* With *A Dreamplay,* after Strindberg (1964), he entered the opera scene, a place where Henze was the leading figure. Reimann's major later contribution was the widely discussed *Lear* (1976–78). Although he was classified as a follower of Webern, he officially abandoned serialism after 1967.

The *Weisse Rose* of Udo Zimmermann has a notable history. This story about a young brother and sister who opposed the Nazi regime in Germany during World War II and were executed in 1942, had its premiere in Dresden, East Germany, in 1967. Twenty years later, 1986, at the *opera stabile* of Hamburg, the composer presented a considerably reduced version for the two protagonists and a small instrumental ensemble. This has permitted the piece to be much more widely heard and it serves as a remarkable example of how large-scale operas may be stripped of excessive orchestral or casting demands and brought back to their music–theater roots. The *Weisse Rose* has also provided an important example of how music theater can treat history by allowing reflection on a not-so-distant past without the ponderous apparatus of the "me-music-theaters" (see also the so-called CNN operas discussed in Chapter 14).

1968: "Your Faust"; arte povera

The year 1968 was a watershed. The events in Paris, the hopes and utopian ideas about freedom and liberty, however vague they might now seem, had deep meaning for a whole generation. Even new music was affected by the implied obligation to develop new styles and new techniques for musical creation. Until that point, everything and everyone was positioned in relation to Darmstadt. Now even those who had been part of the system felt growing doubts about it.

Kagel, who occupied an ambiguous area among media, theater, and composition "with objects" (as he says), was neither a hard-core serialist nor even a hard-core composer restricted to working the world of music; he demonstrated his ironic, musically structured visions on the stage, in texts, in concepts, as film, as "pure" music...in short, anywhere.

In 1960, the Belgian writer Michel Butor published an article concerning *"La musique, art réaliste. Les paroles et la musique"* in the Parisian journal *Esprit*.[17] The article was read by the young Belgian composer Henri Pousseur, a composer who had been close to the Darmstadt esthetic but now questioned the musical spectrum of the atonal-serial world.[18] Pousseur, like Henze, turned to Schoenberg's polar opposite, Igor Stravinsky, a composer whose work had been rejected by Adorno and who could hardly be accepted by the Germans as one of their own. Pousseur became the famous "first dissident" and the Butor-Pousseur collaboration—most notably in the opera/music–theater work *Votre Faust*—became an issue for nearly ten years (we can call the controversy the *"Votre-Faust*-complex"). Pousseur worked with Butor on an "electronic play" that marked a major break in the composer's work; this was a ballet entitled *Electra* with an electronic score, directed and choreographed by Sylvano Bussotti and performed in 1964/65 by the National Ballet of Canada. *Repons*, from same year, also with a text by Butor, was already a quasi-musico-theatrical collaboration. There is a Cageian element here; the musicians throw dice in order to construct the score. This mobile element found a new form in the music theater of *Votre Faust* (1961–68), subtitled "Variable Fantasy in the genre of opera," which incorporates, in collage form, earlier settings of the Faust story. The public (as the title indicates, this Faust belongs to us, the public) votes on whether the young composer Henri should go with Maggy (Butor's names for Heinrich Faust and Gretchen or Marguerite). In spite of the obvious potential here, no one seemed ready to deal with these new ideas. After the premiere

17. *Esprit* 1 (1960): 138–56.
18. Pousseur is, of course, Belgian, not German, but he was a major figure on the Darmstadt scene and in the Darmstadt sphere of influence so his defection had its biggest impact in the German sphere of influence.

at the Piccola Scala, Luciano Berio, apparently in a rebuke to Pousseur for having abandoned the Darmstadt ideals, wrote a fervent letter to the composer about how bad he had found the libretto and calling the idea of public participation "a lottery where there was nothing to win." It is ironic that Berio could not accept these early "postmodernist" concepts, particularly since Berio himself employed techniques of quotation and collage only a year later in his *Sinfonia*!

In any case, Pousseur continued to defend his librettist and eventually things changed and not only in the music of outsiders like Pousseur, Berio, Kagel, or Ligeti. The quest for a new identity and a new sound to represent a new morality turned from pure instrumental music to "instrumental theater" and even to music theater itself as a way of refreshing the musical body politic. Innovation in sound did not succeed in changing the world, and, indeed, quite the opposite was true. The world outside was changing and the insular world of new music could not help being affected.

Votre Faust, composed through most of the decade, actually appeared just on the edge of the 1968 uprisings. By the end of the decade, Darmstadt was also in flux. Boulez ended his teaching there, and after a hiatus, Stockhausen returned to present collective ensemble pieces in the spirit of the times. Kagel's efforts to promote his instrumental theater had been less successful than anticipated and so had the notion of extending the ordinary concert with action, lighting, sets and costumes, projections, and film.

This period is extremely interesting to examine from our quite distant vantage point. Social and political engagement on various levels produced a series of new and different obligations as the Vietnam war, the political climate, and the affirmation of conformist national politics created major disillusionment. In this ambience, we find the *arte povera* movement. The view of poverty as a reduction to essentials combined with its implied or overt critique of consumer society had a big impact in many fields. The nonestablished and the noninstitutionalized were now celebrated, but they were also the improvisational and the imperfect and they were lacking in professional tools and the necessary financial support. The end result of a lack of means was not so much a sociopolitical attitude as it was a personal esthetic like that found in the work of Kagel, Hespos (Hans Joachim Hespos), or Schnebel.

The *arte povera* idea, which had much in common with the simplest small-scale music theater, had many ramifications. It was, of course, a way to make art on the cheap and thus to opt out of the big-time funding game. It also produced a taste for the rough, the unfinished, the nonpolished as being somehow more real, more authentic, and also an associated suspicion of technique and traditional skills; these are tastes that remain influential today.[19] It was also connected with the "refusenik" attitudes of the time. An example is the "anti-opera" label which Roman Haubenstock-Ramati gave to his *Comedy* (after the Samuel Beckett play of the same name; 1969). Kagel described his *Staatstheater* of 1967–70 as the "negation of opera" (see Chapter 8); not surprisingly, it created a major scandal when it was performed in an opera house for an opera house public.

After 1968

In the early 1970s, Dieter Schnebel inaugurated multimedia performances of what he called "psychoanalytical" music. *Maulwerke-für Artikulation-sorgane und Reproduktionsgeräte* ("Mouthworks for Organs of Articulation and Reproductive Devices"), which he worked on between 1968 and 1974, belonged to the laboratory variety of music theater; the title itself has a clinical scent. The compositional setup is something like "if I do this, let's see what will happen." However, instead of electronic generators and tape recorders, the new obsession was with a microscopic view of the creation of speech and a back-and-forth interplay between analytical decomposition and compositional re-synthesis. Schnebel used the living vocal performer for his research into the human mouth (the German word *Maul* actually refers to the muzzle of an animal) and its capability to create communicative sounds. The effect is something like the opening of the skull of a genius after his death to examine his brain for evidence of his intellectual gifts.

Just exactly what does this microscopic music theater consist of? Schnebel looked into the human *Maul*, observing its complex and excessive movements and choreographing its movements and positions. In the end, he obtains a sound—not really a fixed sound but something more like a movement or an action that will produce some kind of sound. The listener (actually also the viewer) is a participant in an experimental moment but one in which the results are to be expected. The narration is the setup.

In 1976, Henze came out with his *We Come to the River*, the last in a series of politically *engagé* works that were the result of the composer's political turn to the left and his subsequent sojourn in Cuba. The work, with a libretto by English playwright Edward Bond and subtitled "Actions for Music," was premiered at the Royal Opera House, Covent Garden, in London. It uses three stages with simultaneous acting, singing, and onstage

19. For example, the return to acoustic music in both pop and non-pop was as much the result of a taste for simplicity and "back to basics" as it was a post-modern nostalgia for the past.

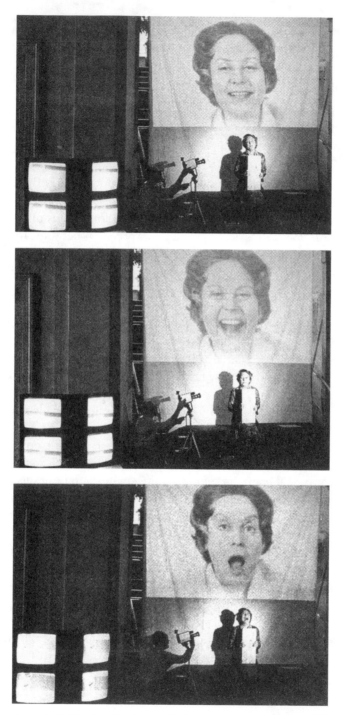

Dieter Schnebel: *Maulwerke-für Artikulationsorgane und Reproduktionsgeräte*; images from the premiere with Carla Henius, Staatstheater Braunschweig, 1977. Photos: Jürgen Peters.

orchestral performance. After this piece, Henze turned to writing children's opera and the treatment of more purely esthetic subjects.

This period also produced the terms *opera impura* and *musica impura*—the source was Pablo Neruda's *poesie impure*[20]—which Henze happily applied to his own work. It was a late but clear statement against the notion of music as "art for art's sake" and a revival of the old dream of music becoming language.[21] The musical/historical precedents were John Gay's *Beggar's Opera* and perhaps the Gilbert and Sullivan operettas that satirized Victorian society. But Henze's anti-war message is quite different and creates an atmosphere intended to seriously overwhelm the spectator. The musical language, based on twelve-tone motives, is intertwined with tonal but harmonically deformed references: marches and patriotic songs that evoke the self-affirming business of war and militarism.

In Austria in the mid-1970s, Kurt Schwertsik renounced atonality and serialism and demonstrated his version of a Maoist message in *The long way to the great wall* (1975). The satiric and ironic intent gains strength by being expressed in tonal music, as if tonality were itself ironic and the whole compositional style was a unified self-irony In 1966, Schwertsik, Heinz Karl (HK) Gruber, and Otto M. Zykan formed the group *MOB art & tone ART*, rejecting all nontonal concepts. Gruber adopted his vocal technique from the Berlin singer/actor Ernst Busch, a technique whose basic rule is "speak the text as accurately as possible on the notated pitches." This was a kind of gruff extended voice technique, a pop version of *Sprechstimme* that was related to the vocal styles of Bob Dylan and Tom Waits. Gruber called himself a *chansonnier* and wrote a popular work, *Frankenstein!!*, with a *chansonnier* (i.e., himself) as its leading character. This homemade radical leftism in art—also found in England in the work of the former Stockhausen disciple Cornelius Cardew and in the music of Frederic Rzewski —had little impact on the academic scene and was far from the

20. "Let [this] be the poetry we search for: worn with the hand's obligations, as by acids, steeped in sweat and in smoke, smelling of lilies and urine, spattered diversely by the trades that we love by, inside the law or beyond it. A poetry impure as the clothing we wear, or our bodies, soup-stained, soiled with our shameful behavior, our wrinkles and vigils and dreams, observations and prophecies, declarations of loathing and love, idylls and beasts, the shocks of encounter, political loyalties, denials and doubts, affirmation and taxes" (Pablo Neruda, "Para una poesia sin pureza," from *Caballo verde para la poesia* [Madrid, 1935]; translated by Ben Belitt from *Selected Poems of Pablo Neruda* [New York, 1961]).

21. See Hans Werner Henze, *Musik als Sprache Melos* 39, Mainz, [1972]; reprinted as "Musica impura—Musik als Sprache" in *Music and Politics: Collected Writings 1953–1981*, translated by Peter Labanyi (Ithaca, NY, 1982).

crude and dangerous actionism prevalent in the visual arts. Nevertheless, these composers had a certain influence, particularly in the Netherlands, Britain, and the United States where new forms of neo-tonality were brewing (see Chapters 12, 14, and 15). In 1966, Otto M. Zykan had a hit with *Singers Nähmaschine ist die beste* ("The Singer Sewing Machine is the best") although, in the end, he was more concerned with Austrian politics and with his research on the commercial as a field of art than with global revolutions.

The Munich-based Josef Anton Riedl[22] oscillated between film, the visual arts in general, and a correlation of movement between music, gesture, and image. In his *Klangleuchtlabyrinth* ("Sound-Light-Labyrinth"; 1976), Riedl portrayed an eccentric who had reinvented a whole new instrumentarium and who did not accept such things as "genres" or "artforms" (supposedly inspired by Pierre Schaeffer but seemingly closer to Harry Partch). In 1967, he founded his own multimedia ensemble, *Musik/Film/Dia/Licht-Galerie* in Munich and realized light-projects like *Olympia-street* (1972) or *sound-light-odour-theater* (1973). Riedl worked with fragments of phrases from magazines, composed a *Paper Music* for sounds made with paper, and worked in film and also in his own electro-acoustic laboratory. Hardly a single one of his pieces has a definite form and each performance reshapes and adapts the basic idea. Riedl also organized the Munich *Klang-Aktionen* ("Sound Actions") which, in its long history, initiated various projects to reach young audiences and to bring new composers to Munich. Munich became particularly important as a major music theater center in the late 1980s when Henze founded the Munich Biennale for New Music Theater (see below).

The 1970s were seemingly preoccupied with light and color. Stockhausen, after a series of multicultural and mystical group experiences, decided to dedicate the next quarter century of his life to a project called *Licht* (or "Light") in which every day of the week would have its own opera. The first day was *Donnerstag*—Thursday—and the first company to produce this very Germanic piece was *La Scala* in Milan, Italy. Thereafter, Stockhausen had great difficulty in revealing the significance of this project in his own country and the whole cycle has never been staged in a German theater.[23] Twenty-five years later, the ultimate Stockhausen concept of "ME = Theater" was revealed, when he communicated his interpretation of the 9/11 attacks in New York as "the greatest work of art imaginable."

22. Riedl's exact birth date is not known, even to Riedl himself, as he was given false documents during the war to hide his Jewish origins and protect him from deportation; after the war, no relatives were left who might have known the correct date.
23. Since this was written, theaters in Dresden and Essen have announced their intentions to stage the entire cycle.

In the early 1980s, another German eccentric appeared on the music-theater stage. Hans-Joachim Hespos created pieces in an invented genre that he called "scenes," endowing them with fancy titles. Various combinations of performers and musicians are involved in *Fulaar* for "things in a room" (1989); or *Black Beauty* for snare drum (with snares on), actress with cross-fantasy—coq dream/dancer/craziness, worker, a man for various tasks; "opportunity piano," *Klüpfel*, light technician, and lighting assistant (1993). Also *spot*—"Fragment of a departure into whole theatre" (1979); *itzo -h u x*—"a satirical opera spectacle" for singers, actors, musicians, listeners, madonnas, bodybuilder, go-go girls, things, no chorus (!) and orchestra, (1980/81); *za' khani* (1984); *a r a*—"StageACTIONS for Mezzo-soprano, 3 percussionists on special steel plates, sound artist with assistant, actors, picture-light-room-processes, voice track" (1985/86); *Nachtvorstellung*—A SilenceFictionimagination (1986); and the "chamber music/speech theater" *Zeitwasser* for "two guides, Madame Feudel, 2 *Sprechgeschwoof*, audience (plus three musical instruments)" (1994). As might be expected, the academic music scene did not know where to put this man and his work. This reinforces the assumption that the humorous, the strange, the absurd, the ironic, and the caricatural form a sort of contemporary *buffa* in a *seria* world of high-brow music that cannot be called anything else but tragic. When this theatrical music disintegrates before our eyes and ears, something awkward and amusing turns up. Comedy is popular; it takes down the mighty and gives courage to the oppressed (*opera seria* is about the status quo; *opera buffa* is about change and outwitting the class structure). But humor can be difficult. It changes from mile to mile and minute to minute; like music, it can be fragile, subject to breakdown and a source of unhappy misunderstandings.

A lot of this is packed into those forms of music theater that often play the clown's role—music theater as the music with the red nose. There is a relationship between the means of a production (large orchestra, chorus, singers, etc.) and the importance of the work for the public and for the critics. Size matters; it even affects the musical style employed. For a time, music theater followed the poor theater model and *arte povera* is usually (but not always) tragic. By the late 1980s, the unwritten motto seems to have become "small but intelligent and witty."[24] The operatic point of reference

24. Carla Henius, long-term *Intendantin* of small music-theater productions in Germany, writes: "What we (…) never allowed were "Alibi-Productions."… The basic pattern of such pieces is a small ensemble with few instruments, two or three singers with only easy roles, no chorus, nearly no set design, easy to learn, easily transferable to many venues, and a big, 'idealistic' and politically correct story: for example Hiroshima or the last hours of the [anti-Nazi] Scholl sisters" (Carla Henius, *Schnebel, Nono, Schoenberg*, 52–53).

for anti-opera was now the grown-up, lumbering, elephantine grand opera. The music-theater audience was not looking for a poor man's opera; it was looking for an experience that could not be found in the opera house. Most contemporary composers take themselves too seriously to be really funny, but there are exceptions. At the very least, the concept of playfulness— very strong in Cage's work, in late Fluxus and much performance art but also found in works like those of Vinko Globokar, Ladislaw Kupkovic, and Dieter de la Motte—became a sign of innovation. Kupkovic, who was born in Slovakia, invented the *Wandelkonzert* where the audience has to wander around the concert hall (see Chapter 22). De la Motte's playfully interactive musico-theatrical performances were actually aimed at entertaining audiences during the most deadly serious period of new music.

Out of the East

As we have seen with the example of Udo Zimmermann's *Weisse Rose*, there was some artistic exchange in the past between the two Germanys. However, East Germany was an independent country with its own culture and dynamic. Composers in the East were under ideological pressure—overt or covert—to prove that communist society and communist art were superior to those of their Western counterparts. Some theater artists from East Germany (DDR = *Deutsche Demokratische Republik*) became very influential in the West, notably a group of stage directors including Harry Kupfer and Frank Castorf. This was less evident with composers.

Hanns Eisler (1898–1962), probably the best known of the East German composers (he wrote the country's national anthem), was originally a student of Arnold Schoenberg and Anton Webern and the composer of modernist works that show the influence of his teachers. In 1926, he joined the Communist Party and began to compose political theater in collaboration with Brecht and Ernst Busch. In exile in the United States, he taught at the New School and in southern California where he resumed his collaboration with Brecht; he also wrote theater and film music as well as a book on film music composition with Adorno. Under pressure from Senator Joseph McCarthy and the infamous House Un-American Activities Committee, Eisler returned to what had become the *Deutsche Demokratische Republik* where he devoted himself to music for film, television, cabaret, theater, and public events. His output was remarkable and included music for thirty-eight stage works—including scores for his old collaborator Bertolt Brecht and the Berliner Ensemble—as well as forty-two film scores; even his concert music was often derived from his stage and film work. His return was not an unmitigated success as he was attacked for continuing to employ formalist (i.e., twelve-tone) methods, even in his theatrical and other popular work.

After Eisler, the music-theater composer most closely identified with Brecht and the Berliner Ensemble, was Paul Dessau (1894–1979). Dessau came from the world of opera and operetta but he also had an important role in prewar German film. "The cinema, the place for the entertainment of the masses," he wrote at the time, "is much more obliged to do something for the people's education than opera, which still only reaches a relatively small amount of people and can only be visited in a few large cities. The most modern, actual and lively art form, the 'living image,' should be accompanied by the most modern and lively musical language."[25] The implication was that theater would be overthrown by film, something that did not happen exactly as predicted. In any case, Dessau, like many of his colleagues, was able to survive in exile in Hollywood by writing film music. Back in East Berlin after the war, he began to write scene music for Brecht and also works of music theater and opera. *Das Verhör des Lukullus* ("The Trial of Lucullus") was originally a radio play and first given by Brecht to be set to music in 1947 by the American composer Roger Sessions. The Dessau setting, made in 1949 and produced two years later, was attacked as "formalistic and alien to the people" and it was rewritten by both Brecht and Dessau as *Die Verurteilung des Lukullus* ("The Condemnation of Lucullus"). Dessau had better luck inside this politically organized art system with his cantatas and scene music. His scores for contemporary dance pieces (written for his wife, the well-known choreographer Ruth Berghaus) and his collaborations with leading writers like Peter Weiss and Heiner Müller were followed by more music theater in the operatic genre: *Puntila* (1966; based on Brecht), *Lanzelot* (1969; text by Heinrich Müller), *Einstein* (1971–73), and *Leonce und Lena* (1978/79; after Büchner). It is one of the ironies of the times that Dessau struggled to produce a politically correct communist style while at the same time maintaining close friendships with Luigi Nono and Hans Werner Henze, who supported communist ideology but who composed in totally divergent styles that were unacceptable in the communist countries.

The most successful composer to emerge from this world of workers' songs, popular theater music, and socialist realism was undoubtedly Siegfried Matthus. Matthus, who studied with Eisler, was summoned to become the resident composer at the famous Berlin *Komische Oper* by its director Walter Felsenstein. He has been extremely prolific and is still, it is claimed, one of the most-performed composers in Germany.

25. Dessau, *Reichsfilmblatt* 27, no. 10 (1928).

His works include *The Last Shot* (1966/67), the black comedy *Another Spoonful of Poison, Darling?* (1971), the mythological *Omphale* (1972–74), *Mario and the Magician* (1974; one of at least three operatic treatments of the Thomas Mann story), *Judith* (1982–84; based on the Old Testament), *The Tune of Love and Death by the Cornet Christoph Rilke* (an "opera vision" with libretto by the composer after Rainer Maria Rilke; 1983/84), *Mirabeau* (1987–88; written for the 200th anniversary of Bastille Day); *Desdemona and Her Sisters* (1991), *Farinelli or The Power of Singing* (1995–97), *Crown Prince Frederick* (1999), and *The Never-Ending Story* (2003; based on a best-selling book—also movie and TV series—by Michael Ende).

Works like the *Cornet* of 1983–84 were a personal triumph for Matthus whose lyric style, forged in the old East Germany, easily merged into the more harmonically softened tendencies of the 1980s.

This sounds like pages turning. In fact, only a few years after this musical success, the Wall fell and Eastern European communism became officially a closed case.

After the Fall

The *Wende* or "turning point" that marked the end of communism in 1989 also initiated a period when experimentation was vanishing as well. The fear that audiences were abandoning the concert halls and a growing belief in the necessity of "music management" produced many attempts to take contemporary composition out of its specialized precincts and integrate it into general musical life. Inevitably, the result was a pluralistic, postmodern esthetic that flourished in a musical scene that had previously been dominated by experimentalism. Music theater provided a potentially open form (or forum) for this widening esthetic. Good examples may be found in the program of the Munich Biennale, which came into being at just at this time (see below). The ever-increasing use of the term *postmodern* (sometimes used in a positive way, sometimes as a pejorative) revived the old discussion about what is modern and "progressive" and what is conservative and popular. The participants in this doctrinal debate—sometimes worthy of a medieval ecclesiastical council—are the surviving believers in hard-core avant-garde doctrine and those who write operas about sporting events or compose for TV, film, or the so-called *Euromusical*. Enjott Schneider fulfilled a commission from the German football club Schalke 04 with his opera *Nullvier: Keiner kommt an Gott vorbei*; 2004). This work, which lasts over three hours and requires 136 participants including full symphonic orchestra, choir, and soloists, has been a success. The musical style is a *mélange* of rock, pop, and classical ambient moments, more *Euromusical* than avant-garde opera. Hardly any other German composer could represent more clearly the postmodern loss of esthetic orientation than Schneider, but he is by no means alone. The tendency to follow the emotional impacts of a narration (a technique learned from motion picture sound tracks) and the discovery that *collage* does not have to sound like Bernd Alois Zimmermann, has produced new genres of eclectic, "quotational" styles in which the whole mighty arsenal of twentieth-century music can be encountered. Among a number of possible examples we will cite Jörg Widmann, whose *The Face in the Mirror* is an opera about cloning and the Austrian Johannes Maria Staud, whose *Berenice* is based on Edgar Allan Poe. These are composers who know how to arrange modernist skills to fit well into the contemporary musical systems of opera and concert.

But this kind of postmodernism is not the whole story. Frankfurt, geographically a center of Germany, has always been also an intellectual point of reference. This is true from Goethe to Adorno to the Mousonturm and TAT theaters; it also includes techno-movements and the electronic music scene, with the retrospective but by no means conservative work of the electronic music-theater group *TEXTxtnd*, which has realized a series of works based on the biographies of figures such as Eisler, Adorno, and Marx.

One of the problems with new music is that different and innovative positions do not always integrate very well with the existing concert/opera/theater system. But sometimes they do. Good examples might be found in the works of Iris ter Schiphorst, whose background is in electronic music and who has worked on music-theater pieces with her partner, Helmut Oehring. Oehring, the child of deaf/mute parents, developed special techniques of gestural communication into musical/theatrical pieces. This mix of electric/electronic instruments, deaf performers, and new media provided a fresh approach to the genre in the late 1990s. *Anna's Wake*, a 3-D opera for tape, voice, and 16 mm film (1993); *D'Amato System* (music by Oehring; performed at the 1994 Munich Biennale); *Effi Briest* (composed with Helmut Oehring in 2001) for vocalist, soprano, an undefined voice, a deaf/mute performer, eighteen instruments, and live electronics; and *Erlaube, Fremdling, dass ich dich berühre* ["Allow me, stranger, to touch you"] for mime, two instrumental ensembles, video, and CD (2004) are examples of an innovative theater that deals with social concerns of contemporary life.

Heiner Goebbels, also from Frankfurt, has a background in sociology and in art rock as well as in theater and film music. In the 1980s, he began to create a series of audio plays based on texts by Heiner Müller as well as staged concerts, all of which took him directly to music theater as his natural form. A series of widely performed music-theater works has led to his recent trilogy of pieces for the French (Alsatian) actor André Wilms (including *Max Black* and *Eraritjaritjaka–museé des phrases*), which have been widely performed by Wilms in both French and German. Goebbels has been active since 1994 as a teacher in both theatrical and musical institutions, and since 1999, he has been a professor in the Institute for Applied Theatre Studies at the Justus Liebig University in Giessen, Germany. This institute, virtually created for him, includes a fully equipped stage plus audio and video studios. It is notable that to an important extent, the research and artistic practice of new music theater may be passing from the world of music to the theater world and often involves musical creators who are not exclusively composers. This sometimes produces very different views about who a composer is and what he or she does. Goebbels, for example, makes free use of other composers' music in some of his works. This is not quotation *à la* Pousseur or George Rochberg but outright appropriation similar to what some stage or film directors do in compiling their own music for a production.[26] In 2002, Goebbels published a book under the title *Komposition als Inszenierung* or "Composition as Mise-en-Scène." For more on Goebbels, see the section devoted to *Max Black* in Chapter 18.

The step out from the post-political but experimental to the post-experimental can be illustrated by the theater work of Peter Ruzicka. Ruzicka is an attorney with classical training as a composer, musician, and musicologist. In his *OUTSIDE—INSIDE*, "a model for musical theater" (1972), there is a singer and two actors plus a small ensemble, including electric guitar, which plays along with playback of an orchestral recording. In contrast, his *Celan: Music theater in seven sketches* (1999) is actually an operatic-sized work that is, in effect, a psychogram of the poet Celan at three stages of his life (as a young boy, as a thirty-year-old, and at the end of his life). It was premiered at the Semper Opera in Dresden. Ruzicka's musical style is based on the idea of a musically interrupted communication; the *"canto"*—as he designates the main lines of a work—which disintegrates, is interrupted or fades into silence. The drift here is away from contemporary sources, away from Ligeti, Henze, and Stockhausen, and toward Mahler, Webern, or even Haydn (Ruzicka actually wrote an orchestral piece that is based on what he calls a Haydn "sound field"—that is, a fragment from a score of Haydn). When Henze retired as artistic director of the Munich Biennale, he asked Ruzicka to replace him in what is one of the most influential adminstrative/artistic positions in the European music-theater scene.

26. The classic example is Kubrick's *2001* in which the director threw out a specially composed score and used instead the dummy hodge-podge score—made out of music of Ligeti, Richard and Johann Strauss, and others—to which he had originally cut the film!

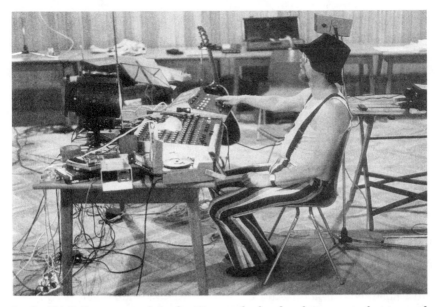

In the K&K Experimental Studio Vienna, the borders between technician and performer were blurred as in *Moritaten zwischen Eisprung und Todessprung* (1982). Photo: Michael Leischner.

Activity in the German-speaking world outside of Germany has followed along the same general lines as in Germany. Groups like the Viennese *K&K Experimentalstudio* of Dieter Kaufmann and Gunda Koenig, founded in 1975, have followed a path of experimentation with electronic sound and synesthetic devices like the "moviophone" (something like what we would call a data-glove, i.e., a device with photoelectric cells to control electronic sound manipulation). There was also experimentation with the audience along the lines of creating a relaxed concert environment or encouraging reflection about everyday issues. The group created about twenty-five projects in total.

One of Kaufmann's students, Klaus Karlbauer, founded the media-theater group *MOOP*, which explores the possibilities of combining narrative with film and electronic music (including dance music) in a theatrical environment. The *Klangtheater* of composer Thomas Pernes is another example of this. *ZOON* music theater, directed by Thomas Desi, reworks existing operatic material with new media and electronic means in "opera decompositions," thus staging the music rather than the theater.

In the mid-1990s, the dusty Viennese State Operas enlarged their scope of activity by opening new venues and presenting opera in off-theater locations. This was not only a question of "old wine in new bottles" as there were also some festival premieres as part of the program. In its *Symposion* project, the group *Netzzeit* offered a selection of wines—real wines not figurative ones—to an audience that consumed them lying on their collective sides while listening to contemporary music, thus creating an imaginary theater of the inebriated (or perhaps "new wine in old bottles"). Recently the group has proposed a concept for a festival, including a music-theater laboratory.

This might be the place to put a difficult-to-classify artist like the Austrian Georg Nussbaumer, who calls himself a "*gesamtkunst* artist," describing his work as "using musical instruments, various organic and inorganic materials, machines, appliances and ideas." His primary medium is a group that he calls the "symphoid," which he describes as an ensemble for music and its derivatives.

Nussbaumer's appearances are a mixture of exposition/installation and performance in a quasi-ritualistic flux that is reminiscent of Harry Partch, Fluxus, and the Happenings but more introverted. In this polystylistic ocean, it gets more and more difficult to describe approaches and style. Although local attributes in new music and music theater have prevailed up to a point, globalization, Euro-ization, bureaucratization, and networking have taken their toll in flattening the national profiles of artists without really changing certain cultural habits or rituals in the various countries. The next step might be for Europe to learn and understand how to deal esthetically with the art world of Eastern countries—in Europe and beyond—where self-identity alternates, not to say vacillates, between old-fashioned

Georg Nussbaumer: Tristan "Swimming and silence!" Photo: Georg Nussbaumer.

nationalism and the overwhelming acceptance of Western domination. Two composers from Rumania might illustrate the point: Adriana Hölszky and Violeta Dinescu, who came to Germany in 1976 and 1982, respectively, and have realized their music theatrical works mainly there and not in their economically and ideologically still fragile homelands.

The Munich Biennale

Getting a clear separation between music theater and opera was still on the agenda of many composers. When Henze founded the Munich Biennale, a major part of the idea was to institutionalize a small-sized lyricism that, if nothing else, gave new music theater something like a business model for reaching the public. The Biennale's own presentation of its history and objectives makes it clear that knowledge and local interests worked together in a unique way to create an institutional form for music theater. Henze himself wrote that "the whole story started with a query from the departmental head of the (Munich) cultural office...whether I...would be interested in considering the creation of some sort of civic music festival in Munich. After a period of time, I suggested organizing something that had been lacking up until that point, something that also did not exist anywhere else in the world[27] and yet was an urgent necessity—namely, a place where the young generation of composers interested in theater...could realize their ideas." The first International Festival of New Music Theater, which took place in 1988, was notable for its production of Adriana Hölszky's *Bremer Freiheit* or "Bremen Freedom," an opera based on Rainer Werner Fassbinder's drama about Geesche Gottfried who was convicted of murder and hanged in Bremen in 1831. Hölszky is from Bucharest but has lived in Germany since 1976. This was her first music-theater piece and as a result of its appearance at the Biennale, it has now been performed more than forty times at state theaters in Stuttgart and Bremen and at festivals in Vienna, Wiesbaden, and Helsinki. Gerd Kühr's *Stallerhof,* based on a play by Franz Xaver Kroetz, provides a similar success story. Detlev Glanert's first opera, *Leyla and Medjnun,* opened the festival; it is based on an ancient Persian fairy tale about poetic love, insanity, and death. Mark-Anthony Turnage's *Greek* (see Chapter 12) rounded out the series of premieres; this work has been performed over sixty times in Germany, Great Britain, Italy, the Netherlands, Australia, and the United States.[28]

27. In fact, the American Music Theater Festival had been founded in Philadelphia in 1983.
28. For more on the Munich Biennale see the Biennale's Web site: www.muenchenerbiennale.de/site_en/index.htm.

A multitude of group and collaborative efforts have evolved in the context of festivals where new work is regularly shown. In Germany at least, the festival is still the most important factor that keeps the performing arts creative, and, for a while at least, festivals will likely remain the places where things happen. In addition to the now quite official Munich Biennale, there are the "Dresdner Days for Contemporary Music," which, since 1995, have included a competition for multimedia and music-theater projects. There are also smaller initiatives, sometimes the part-time occupation of people inside the big opera business, sometimes put together by the composers themselves, sometimes the work of younger theater artists motivated to create their own productive environments. Examples are the *6-Tage-Oper* in Duesseldorf and *Zeitgenössische Oper Berlin.*

Some of the smaller opera theaters in Germany are also looking toward music theater. Andreas Breitscheid, composer and director of the Stuttgart Opera, is persuaded that contemporary music theater can become part of a system like the classical opera subscription season. In 2002, Bielefeld, under Roland Quitt, grouped three freshly written pieces on a single theme—the myth of Orpheus under the rubric *Orfeo*—into a series of performances, thus finding a new formula that stands between the festival idea and the theater/opera season. This also parallels similar work by theaters and smaller opera companies in other countries (the *Chatelet* in Paris, Almeida in London, Center for Contemporary Opera in New York, and *Piccolo Regio Torino* are other examples).

Further Reading

Darmstädter Beiträge zur Neuen Musik, edited by Internationales Musikinstitut Darmstadt. Between 1958 and 1994, twenty volumes on New Music appeared.

Dessau, Paul. *Reichsfilmblatt*, No. 43, 1928.

Henius, Carla. *Schnebel, Nono, Schönberg oder Die wirkliche und die erdachte Musik.* Hamburg, 1993.

Henze, Hans Werner. Entry in *Reclam Opernlexikon*, p. 351. Berlin, 2004.

Henze, Hans Werner, ed. *Neues Musik Theater.* Munich, 1999. About the first Munich Biennale.

Henze, Hans Werner. *Vier Stunden auf Henzes neuem Weg.* Conversation between Henze and Hans-Klaus Jungheinrich in Melos 39, IV, 1972. Reprinted as "Musica impura—Musik als Sprache" in *Musik und Politik*, 1976.

Kagel, Mauricio. Cited in *Musik-Konzepte*, vol. 124, p. 67. Berlin, 1975. The "Musik Konzepte," Edition Text+kritik, Munich (German only), has included volumes on composers, such as Kagel, Stockhausen, Ligeti, and

others as well as a special edition on Darmstadt 1999, including many
documents.

Klüppelholz, Werner. *Mauricio Kagel 1970–1980*. Cologne, 1981.

Schnebel, Dieter. *Denkbare Musik, Schriften 1952–1972*. Cologne, 1972.

Schnebel, Dieter. *Mo-No*. Cologne, 1969.

Schnebel, Dieter, and Mauricio Kagel. *Musik, Theater, Film*. Cologne, 1970.

Trimmel, Gerald, and Armgard Schiffer-Ekhart. *Das K&K Experimentalstudio*.
Vienna, 1996.

chapter 10

From the Homeland: Teatro Musicale

*Nella cabina Dio ti vede, Stalin no. (God sees you in the
polling-booth, not Stalin.)*

Giovannino Guareschi: *Don Camillo e Peppone*

Verismo, futurismo, and *fascismo*

Italy is, of course, the home of opera; Italian is the original language of
opera and was long the international language of music. The operatic form
of music theater—what the Italians call *opera lirica*—started there about
four hundred years ago, and the old Italian opera, although somewhat moribund but often updated, is still the primary classical musical activity of
the country. The Italian scene is marked by extensive government support
of the large operatic institutions and a few festivals, but there is a lack
of support for smaller initiatives. The strong and continuing tradition of
popular music has had some impact on contemporary opera and new music
theater in the peninsula.

The still-performed works of *realismo, verismo,* and *neorealismo,* the last
great acknowledged flourishing of *opera lirica,* are, in their way, the Italian
version of northern expressionism. The more abstract arts of modernism
also had their Italian counterpart in *futurismo.* The futurists of the first
years of the twentieth century, like other early modernists, were responding
to the lure of discovery, the fading of romanticism, the explosion of science
and technological innovation, the growing impact of the New World on

the Old, and the rise of mass media and its associated political movements. There was also an element of violence and *machismo,* which ultimately had consequences. In contrast with modernism in Western Europe (but more like futurism in Russia), Italian futurism had political and revolutionary connections almost from the start. The movement, which exalted speed, technology, violence, and a definitive break with the past, quickly became part of the youth cult of nascent fascism and was patronized by *Il Duce* himself. Thus, modern art in Italy was more political and more immediately successful than anywhere else. The exploitation of the arts for ideology and the first general use of mass media for political purposes was an integral part of the history of fascism that led directly to the alliance with Nazi Germany and the disaster of World War II. Those in opposition suffered persecution, exile, or worse. The Italian Renaissance (which invented *opera lirica*), the *risorgimento* (which produced *verismo*), and Italian Fascism (which nurtured *futurismo*) all came crashing down in 1944–45. After World War II, the futurists paid a heavy price for being collaborators. Art had lost its innocence; a whole generation of creative artists was stigmatized as tainted by fascism and was effectively written out of the history of modern art for decades.[1]

In 1946, Luigi Dallapiccola, who had suffered internal exile rather than collaborate with the previous regime, said that the Italian musician, once the most endowed and sophisticated in the world, now lacked everything.[2] Even a superficial impression of the Italian situation for many years thereafter would seem to confirm this. The next generation of Italian composers had to go abroad to establish their careers and participate in the new avant-garde movements coming out of Germany and France.

The weight of tradition

One major reason for the success of the old baroque/classic/romantic/post-romantic opera in Italy over a period of four hundred years has been, no doubt, the musicality of the language. Italian words are rich in vowels, end on vowels, and have a rolling, iambic rhythm in which the accented syllable comes just before the end. At the next level, there is also an aggregate of tonic accents, which create rhetorical and musically suggestive qualities. Also to be considered is the traditionally strong moral-religious system based on family life and campanilismo or localism (also the source of the domination of *mafia* and *camorra* families in certain times and places). This medieval

1. The Russian futurists were written out of history by Stalin and the Stalinists but, partly because of this, they were able to keep their reputation relatively intact either in exile or in revisionist art history.
2. Fearn, Raymond. *Italian Opera since 1945* (Amsterdam, 1997).

canon of localism (city states, primacy of the family, protectionism, connections, corruption and racketeering, feudal pressure on population, toleration mixed with quiet opposition to invaders and foreign rule), the long history of Roman Catholic domination of the *terra santa*, the conservation of local culture and local dialects along with the recognition of the literary tradition of the Florentine language all helped to keep Italian culture alive over the centuries long before there was a central Italian state. The quality of beauty inherent in agricultural, gastronomic, and artistic activity; the typically voluble, outgoing, and theatrical personality of Italians; and a fatalistic and aristocratic view of life combined with a comic, underdog sensibility are all ingredients of what opera still represents as a spectacle of life.

As a result of long periods of peace, the consumption of resources from colonialism, and the management of trade in the Mediterranean, the means were present in several parts of Italy to allow the *opera lirica* to expand into the great baroque/romantic machine that it became. Although opera began as an aristocratic and humanistic court entertainment, the first real opera houses in the larger cities (Venice, Rome, Naples) were frequented by the public, and by the early nineteenth century, they were found all over the peninsula, many of them named simply *il teatro*. Along with the improvised *commedia dell'arte*, opera was *the* theater of the Italians, and, as already suggested, it doesn't take much to switch from speaking into singing in Italian. When opera spread all over Europe, it did so as an elevated court or aristocratic entertainment, mostly in a foreign language. Only in Italy was it a popular pastime that appealed to all segments of the population.

Opera became a truly popular art form in the eighteenth century with the rise of the *opera buffa,* but not long into the nineteenth century, seriously tragic operas came to dominate popular taste; *opera seria,* now in a newly romantic form, again became the norm. This is a history of bravado and bravura, of the *bel canto* soprano or tenor exhausting their vocal abilities on the everlasting stories of tragic passion, illicit trysts, betrayals, and abandonment. There is occasionally some political spice as when a chorus from Verdi's *Nabucco* is taken up by supporters of the *risorgimento* or when a regal assassination in a *Ballo in maschera* leads the Bourbon censors to force a Swedish king to be transformed into the Governor of Boston (was anyone deceived by this?). Sex and violence, generally of the illicit or illegal type, occasionally stirred up trouble, but the high art status of opera permits things to take place on (or nearly on) stage that would be banned in less exalted surroundings. Oddly enough, sex and religion are often mixed up together; examples would include Verdi's *La Forza del Destino* and *Don Carlo*, Puccini's *Tosca,* and the strange *Tosca Amore Disperato* of 2003 with costumes by Giorgio Armani and music by songwriter Lucio Dalla, which mixes hip-hop, funk, rap, Italian pop, dance, and a lot of video to produce a remake in which nuns and priests dance in sexy underwear and a black angel saves Tosca.

The easy mixture of the sacred and the profane, of pastime and political, is typical of the history of Italian opera. It marks out the degree to which music has the shine of the metaphysical and how singing can create the ambiance of ritual. In sharper, more ideological work outside of Italy, "the people" may be directed to rise up against an alleged enemy *en masse*. This is the dark side of Wagner. Scriabin in his *Prometheus*, Op. 60 of 1909/10, proclaims his intention to "save mankind." Twentieth-century operas, of a modernist persuasion, dramatize the coming of calamity and the gloominess of the future. In *verismo*, religion often becomes part of an exotic plot and politics provides material for thrillers, not ideological manifestos.

Dallapiccola, Nono, and Berio

Luigi Dallapiccola, born in Istria but active most of his life in Florence, was cut off from official new-musical life during the fascist and wartime periods. He was, in effect, an internal exile, without an official position as a composer, supporting himself mainly as a pianist and piano teacher. He had been interned in Austria during World War I and ironically, the later Italian-German alliance made it easy for him to visit Vienna in the 1930s and 1940s where he met Berg and Webern. As a result, he adopted a modified form of the twelve-tone method, one of the very few Italian composers to do so. During the German occupation of Italy in World War II, he went into hiding with his Jewish wife. Although he already had a catalogue of major works, he emerged as Italy's leading composer only after the war. His personal use of the twelve-tone method, his obsession with themes of oppression and liberty, and his caustic irony about Italy after the war constitute a political as well as artistic statement. The freedom motif is only suggested in his early opera *Volo di notte* (1940), based on a novel by Antoine de Saint-Exupéry, but it is explicit in his *Canti di prigionia* ("Prison Songs") of 1938–41, a work that is the homologue of Messiaen's *Quatuor pour la fin du temps*, composed in a German prisoner-of-war camp. The *Canti di prigionia* was a preparation for Dallapiccola's opera *Il prigioniero* ("The Prisoner," 1944–48), based on a story about a prisoner of the Spanish Inquisition but, in fact, a clear manifesto against fascism.[3] Dallapiccola uses twelve-tone technique in an individual manner to symbolize the human condition: liberty and hope in the original form of the row, loss of liberty

---

3. Other anti-fascist dramatic works of the time include Karl Amadeus Hartmann's *Simplicissimus*, Wladimir Vogel's *Thyl Claes*, and the Arnold Schoenberg *Ode to Napoleon*.

and despair with the "inversion" or upside-down form. The libretto for the work was put together by the composer himself from existing texts.

In these respects and others, Dallapiccola laid the groundwork for the younger generation of Italians whose work was otherwise a clear break with the Italian past. About ten years after *Il prigioniero*, Luigi Nono, a young composer from Venice active in Germany—and associated with serialism as Dallapiccola was with dodecaphony—assembled texts written from prison by partisans and other opponents of totalitarian regimes, many of them awaiting execution. This was the basis of his *Il Canto sospeso* or "The Interrupted Song" of 1956. Nono's politics were far more rooted in leftist politics than Dallapiccola's and we can see the influence of Antonio Gramsci. Gramsci, one of the founders of the Italian Communist Party, was a philosopher who had demonstrated that even under totalitarian oppression, autonomous thinking is possible and had notably articulated a connection between the political and the private as activities of a single person.

In spite of the influence of figures like Gramsci and Dallapiccola and the political wars between the Communist Party and its left allies on the one side and the Christian Democrats and Catholic Church on the other, there is a lack of ideological rigidity in Italian life that has been often depicted in various forms. This is nowhere more evident than in the formerly very popular series of films about Don Camillo and Peppone after the equally popular stories of Giovannino Guareschi. The ambiguous and amusing relationship between the Catholic priest and the communist mayor of a small Italian village provides insights into the visible part of Italian society (the invisible part is aristocratic society that quietly survived all the wars and revolutions). One could say that both protagonists have similar intentions but play out their roles by pretending to follow predetermined and not quite believable scripts written by others. Both play these roles knowing what is expected of them but also knowing what their publics will let them get away with. There is, in both men, a mixture of predetermination, individuality, and improvisation that is quite typically Italian.

The Italian musical scene quickly developed a Don Camillo-like situation between the "communist mayor," Luigi Nono (he actually ran for mayor of Venice on the communist ticket and a real mayor later served as his librettist), and the "high priest" of new music in Italy, Luciano Berio. Both men started their careers in the ambiance of Darmstadt serialism and were involved with the innovations of electronic or electro-acoustic music but both turned fairly early in their careers to new vocal and theatrical forms. In Nono's *Intolleranza 1960*, a fugitive from a hostile homeland suffering from injustice and cruelty follows, like Jesus on his way to the cross, a series of "stations" on his journey, a form that was inspired by Sartre's theater of "situations" in opposition to psychological theater. Berio's *Passaggio* (1963) deals with the destiny of a woman who, under similar circumstances, also passes from station to station in another *via crucis*. The text of *Passaggio* is by Edoardo Sanguineti, a poet who experimented with new forms, mixing a left political *engagement* with an Italian Catholic sensibility. Nono was able to work with a writer of similar calibre only later in his career; the philosopher and former mayor of Venice, Massimo Cacciari, was the author of the text of Nono's *Prometeo* (1984). Twenty years later, after the upheavals of the 1960s, the Vietnam War, and the Red Brigades, both composers discovered a profoundly musical subject: listening. Berio's *Un re in ascolto* and Nono's *Prometeo—Tragedia dell'ascolto* appeared in 1984. (For more on Nono see the section below on his *A floresta é jovem e cheija de vida*.)

Luciano Berio was born in 1924 in Liguria, the son and grandson of musicians. He studied at the Milan Conservatory, began his career as a *répétiteur* in provincial Italian opera houses, and studied with Dallapiccola, not in Italy but at the Berkshire Music Center in Tanglewood, Massachusetts. In 1955, with Bruno Maderna, he opened the *Studio di fonologia* at Italian Radio in Milan. His early vocal and theatrical performance works were written for and highly influenced by the abilities of his first wife, the American singer (of Armenian background) Cathy Berberian. She recorded the texts from *Ulysses* and the highly emotive sounds that were transformed electronically by Berio to form his *Thema (Omaggio a Joyce)* of 1968 and *Visage* of 1961. Besides *Passaggio*, Berio's *Laborinthus II* and *Recital I (for Cathy)* of 1972, also with texts by Sanguineti, as well as his *Circles* (1960; texts by e e cummings) were all also written for Berberian. Later operas are *Una vera storia* (1982; text by Italo Calvino) and the aforementioned *Un Re in ascolto* (1979–1984; text again by Italo Calvino).

Although there are political subtexts in many of Berio's compositions, the surface of his work is largely about language and form. An opera called *Opera,* a recital entitled *Recital,* and a *Sinfonia* that incorporates a rewrite of a movement from a Mahler symphony all suggest meta-dramas about the events themselves and, by extension, about how music and musical performance function in society. Berio himself pointed out that these works all require the classical concert or operatic houses and performance situations for their maximum effectiveness. The artfulness and playfulness of much of his work and its acceptance in the mainsteam of classical music also suggest many parallels to Stravinskyian neoclassicism, itself a measure of the distance that he had come from Darmstadt serialism.

Politics, improvisation, and the turn from serialism

Luigi Nono was inspired musically by the Austro-German avant-garde (Schoenberg in particular) and combined modernist conceptions with rigorously leftist political convictions.[4] These two facets of Nono's thinking have to inform any examination of his work. His aim was to give meaning to his music through its social function. He was influenced by the theatrical ideas of Vsevolod Emilevich Meyerhold, Erwin Piscator, and Bertolt Brecht; he cited Kurt Weill and identified with theatrical innovations such as those of Josef Svoboda, whose *Lanterna Magika* used an innovative combination of film and live theater.[5]

As a fervent idealist supporting changes in society, Nono believed that music could be a medium to articulate such claims and help organize revolutionary projects. On the occasion of the premieres of several of his work, he wrote about his convictions, his opposition to traditional opera, and his ideas about new music theater. His theatrical works are still of interest and these writings help to clarify his motivations in creating avant-garde music theater.

According to Nono, opera has the following characteristics:

- It has a fixed separation into two levels of audience and stage, which reminded him of the Christian churches where the priests are largely separated from the believers who follow the service from a distance.
- There is a simplistic relation between the visual and the acoustic, expressed in the formula "I see what I hear and I hear what I see." This "doubling" has been much criticized in modernist circles elsewhere. Cage, admittedly from a very different point of view, spoke about a "useful dialogue" in which heterogeneous elements would lead the way.
- Opera is organized in a hierarchy in which every element of the performance is a decoration of the singing and the sung text.

4. Nono was from a well-known artistic family in Venice. His grandfather, also Luigi Nono, was a successful realist academic painter in Venice. He was married to Arnold Schoenberg's daughter Nuria who was brought up and educated in Southern California; this alliance gave him a connection to the second Viennese school but also to the United States. When his opera *Intolleranza* had its American premiere in Boston, he was refused a visa to attend on the grounds that he was a communist. According to Nono himself, when asked by the American consul in Venice whether he had ever been a member of the Communist Party, he answered "Yes" upon which the consul suggested that he change the answer to "no." "How can I do that?" was Nono's reply. "I ran for mayor of Venice on the Communist Party ticket!" Only after editorials in the *New York Times* and intervention from the Kennedy administration was he allowed to attend.

5. Svoboda's *Lanterna Magika* production 1958, shown at the Brussels World's Fair of that year, has no spoken text and comes close to music theater in many ways.

- The accompaniment of the voices by the orchestra is comparable to the relationship in film between the foreground dialogue and the background music. For Nono, the cinema is an industrialized version of traditional opera.
- The perspective in opera is focused on the visual and the acoustic.

The various elements in music theater stand in one or more of three different relationships with one another: accompaniment (or decoration), complementation, and confrontation, the last being the one that (together with many other modernists) he distinctly preferred. When disjointed material is mixed, a dadaist interpretation is possible but there is another, more Brechtian, choice that involves breaking the theatrical illusion to throw a new light of realism and truth on a supposedly known subject. Nono quotes Giulio Carlo Argan:[6] "Brecht yes, Ionesco no."

Schoenberg's twelve-tone method set up a democracy of pitches; the twelve pitches in an equal-tempered octave were no longer hierarchical but were all of equal weight. It was now thought that this theory could be applied to all the parameters and domains of music and theater as well. Nineteenth-century romanticism, which reached its twin peaks in Wagner's bigger-than-life music drama and the rallies of the Nazi period, had to be abandoned. The antithesis, a truly scientific approach, would bring purity, objectivity, and avoidance of the weight of inherited tradition. And democracy as well.

The classical bourgeois theater never questioned its traditions—the architecture of theaters and operas, the seating of the audience, the placement and form of the stage. The canonical traditions of musical as well as literary forms were expected to remain as they had been defined by the great masters. In many ways, post-Renaissance art had become a huge system of expectations, based on knowledge, points of reference, and repetition. For Nono, the temporal dimension in music held a similar rigidity. The duration of a traditional symphony and its movements, of a three-act opera, or of an instrumental piece remain within expectations. Whenever these basic parameters have been subject to modification, there has been scandal, revolution, or at least a reform movement that has had to fight its way to acceptance.[7]

---

6. In the magazine *Avanti!* (May 1961) with the title "Intolleranza 1960 and the theater of [the] avant-garde."
7. The extraordinary lengths of Robert Wilson's earlier works including *Einstein on the Beach* with Philip Glass are now part of the early history of minimalism. Most current works are well within the normal expectations of theater and opera audiences.

The alternative, based on the new esthetics of fragmentation and experimentation, demanded the creation of works that defocused, deconcentrated, and decentralized our theatrical perceptions. In an analogy to atheism, anarchism, and communism, the vertical top-down hierarchies of bourgeois society were to be replaced by horizontal structures. The new spatial orientation goes back to Albert Einstein as if changes in time-space relations in physics had directly influenced time-space relationships in music. Instead of the Newtonian physics of rigid and static states, Einsteinian physics is based on movement and point of view. The theatrical analogy for Nono was the so-called dynamic symbolism of Meyerhold, Tairov, and other Russian artists. New music theater had to be based on the decentralization of space, sound, stage, and all the other elements; above all, this meant new ways of using the stage and it meant movement. Whether Nono was right or wrong in these assumptions, they underlie the theoretical and practical possibilities for change that are the basis for his music-theater work.

In view of the preceding, it is ironic that the best known of Nono's music-theater works is *Intolleranza*—originally *Intolleranza 1960*—which is now almost invariably described as an opera and has always been performed in opera houses. Nono described it as a "scenic action" from—as its original title tells us—the year 1960; the idea was that whenever the piece would be performed, the title would change to include the year of performance. Before 1960, Nono was closely associated with the Darmstadt group of serial and electronic music composers in Germany. He saw himself in a historic line from Schoenberg[8]—to whom *Intolleranza* is dedicated— and the Russians. *Intolleranza* was apparently the first of his works to be performed in Italy and it was one of the works in which the composer discovered music theater as a medium for sociopolitical engagement.

Intolleranza equates the struggle against fascism in World War II with the class warfare of the postwar period. Nono had come to see music theater as a means of communication for the fight against fascism and capitalism and for a world without terror or torture. *La Fabbrica Illuminata* of 1964 mixes factory noises and electronic sounds with the live setting of texts about a so-called model factory in northern Italy. Nono's idea of an *engagé* theater was influenced by Jean-Paul Sartre's "theater of situations," a theater of conscience that would wake up the audience by communicating the terrifying facts of present-day reality.[9] In all this, we are very close to the concept of the *moritat,* a sort of medieval morality in which a drawn or

8. Especially the Schoenberg of *Die glückliche Hand*.
9. Sartre and some of the workers from the actual *fabbrica illuminata* were present at the work's premiere at La Fenice during the Venice Biennale of 1965.

Luigi Nono: *Intolleranza 1960*. From the premiere at the Teatro La Fenice, Venice, April 12–13, 1961. Set by Josef Svoboda, décor, costumes, and projections by Emilio Vedova; stage direction by Vaclav Kaslic. Photo from the Archivio Camera photo Venezia, courtesy of AAF, Fondazione Cassa di Risparmio di Modena.

painted tableau is shown while a storyteller makes comments. It is no coincidence that Brecht called the famous *Mackiemesser*—"Mack the Knife" from the Threepenny Opera a *Moritat*.

A similar setup was chosen by Nono for *A floresta é jovem e cheja de vida* ("The Forest is young and full of life") in 1965/66. *Intolleranza 1960* is a screed against fascism, *La Fabbrica Illuminata* is a piece for and of the workers, and both pieces are more or less conventionally scored. What makes *A Floresta* different is the lack of a score and also the subject. It is dedicated to the Vietnamese Liberation Army and is Nono's most anti-imperialist and military work. The sound-images of *A floresta* come from the bombs, bombers, missiles, guns, and helicopters of the Vietnam War. We know—from the sound of the piece as well as from the performers' accounts of working with the composer[10]—that the musical esthetic of the piece was intended to be metallic and cold. The entire forty minutes of the work is dominated by the sounds of five copper plates played by five percussionists, noisy and abstract music that suggests synthesized electronic sounds. Only the clarinet allows for some

10. Nono's publisher, Casa Ricordi, conducted interviews with the performers about thirty years after the premiere.

human breathing in the piece, which ends in a breathy and trembling clarinet fluttertongue.

In addition to the live clarinet, the work also uses a number of sound sources including recorded fragments from William O. Smith, an American clarinetist who had developed a catalogue of multiphonics and other special sounds that were new at the time. Vocal sounds were provided by members of the Living Theater, the New York–based performance group that had been founded in 1947 by Julian Beck and Judith Malina. Malina had been a student of Erwin Piscator, one of the major figures of twentieth-century radical theater; Nono had met with Piscator whom he admired for his leftist politics and technically inventive theater esthetic. Piscator, one of the founders of the so-called epic theater with Brecht, had developed the "Piscator Stage," a set in the form of a segment of a sphere that can be unfolded and rotated to show multiple levels and simultaneous action;[11] he also used projections and animated film showing texts and political slogans.[12]

The voices of the Living Theater performers along with Smith's clarinet were recorded and manipulated in various ways, often sounding synthetic or unrecognizably distorted. Metallic and synthesized sounds produced at the electronic music studios of Italian radio were also used. The librettist, Giovanni Pirelli, provided a collection of various texts from military, communist, and documentary sources. As in several other pieces by Nono (and other works of the period), language is autopsied—that is, analyzed into its musical and semantic elements—to create a sound vocabulary at the limits of comprehensibility and of an almost mystical intensity. No score was ever written for this piece, which was "composed" in rehearsal with live performers (a soprano, three actresses and an actor, a live clarinetist, and five percussionists) between 1965 and 1966. A conductor led the ensemble, which was surrounded by some ten loudspeakers. While *Intolleranza 1960* had been a "scenic action," this new piece had more of an oratorio character or, as it has been characterized, a "listening theater." There are no characters playing defined roles and telling a story.

No score was ever written for this piece for several reasons, and aside from the principle of a group or ensemble effort, popular at the time, none of them appears to be ideological. A musical work might be created by an

11. A similar stage concept is used in Bernd Alois Zimmermann's *Die Soldaten*, which dates from the same period as *Intolleranza*.
12. During World War II, Piscator went into exile in New York City where he directed the Dramatic Workshop at the New School for Social Research and was one of the founders of the Studio Theater; he later returned to Germany.

improvising performer working alone or (in the manner of a jazz ensemble) with an improvisational group. A work without a score might also result from the desire to propagate a theater of the ephemeral, an event that takes place at a particular time and place and can never be repeated. A Cage-style chance operation might produce a work in performance that would be different every time it took place. Or, as is the normal procedure with dance companies, work can be created through collaboration with performers in a rehearsal process.

The case of *A Floresta* is most similar to the last named. The electronic means, the difficulties of notation, and the uniqueness of the performance space all coalesced to generate a transcription of what had been found in the rehearsal process rather than an autonomous composition that could be attributed to a single creative artist or even repeated on future occasions. The recording that was made produced a fixed version of a score that had been created only in the singers' minds. When asked to redo the piece, Nono said that he preferred to create something new. He considered the recording to be perhaps 10 percent of what was in the live performance. Ironically, in 1998, some years after Nono's death, the "Editorial Committee for the Works of Luigi Nono" reconstructed a score in which the clash of cultural systems and changing times became apparent. It is not clear what the value might be of a performance based on a reconstructed score based on a recording that reflects only 10 percent of what the composer said the piece ought to be.

More important than the committee-constructed score are the participants' accounts of how Nono worked with the singers and actors on a daily basis over an extended period. Nono insisted that the performers had to know the texts intimately and draw artistic inspiration from these sources. He gave them tasks such as "choose a low note or a very high one," and "make a crescendo to maximum forte and hold as long as possible." He wanted a purity—if not a harsh relentlessness—of sound with high tension and dramatic expression. Liliana Poli, one of the singers, described herself as being an instrument (in the sense perhaps of being a tool rather than a musical instrument) in the compositional process. Nono defined the signification of phrase, expressive modalities, and the region of the sound but always avoided specific tonal intervals. Whatever was then created became definitive for the performance. Nono, who controlled the audio setup for the recording, may have used some "lead sheets" but nothing else.

In one important sense, this compositional moment was a major turning point away from the controlling influence of serialism, not only in Nono's music but in new European music in general. Not long ago, a three-hundred-page book appeared in print analyzing the compositional structure and methods of *Il Canto Sospeso,* Nono's 1956 setting of letters from World War II resisters.[13] This monument to our script-oriented and collectionist culture could hardly have been undertaken if Nono had not written out the score. In *A Floresta* we find the same compositional mind improvising and creating together with his performers, abandoning all notation and compositional documentation. Four decades after its premiere in Venice, nothing similar has been written about *A floresta é jovem e cheja de vida* although one might imagine that a piece about the Vietnam War would be as relevant today as one about World War II resistance. (For more on the issues of improvisation and collective composition see Chapter 20.)

Sylvano Bussotti and *La Passion selon Sade*

Sylvano Bussotti is a composer who does not fit in easily in the standard histories of twentieth-century music but in fact provides the most direct connection between the great tradition of Italian opera and postwar experimental music. Bussotti, a kind of one-man latter-day *camerata,* was born in Florence, the birthplace of opera, where he studied piano with Dallapiccola. Like his compatriot, Jean-Baptiste Lully, he spent formative time in Paris. He was influenced by the serialists, by Cage, and also by developments in the art world; his uncle and his brother were painters and he himself cultivated design and stagecraft as well as composition. He actually taught the history of music theater at the Academy of Fine Arts in L'Aquila and has served as artistic director for major Italian opera theaters and festivals. He describes his own theatrical work as *fra luna e laser*—"between moon and laser"—and his music as "sound-sign" or "designed sound." He designs sets, costumes, and scores with equal facility. It might have been the French structuralist Roland Barthes who said that a manuscript of Bussotti is already a total opera, beginning in the graphic apparatus, which transports the idea of the work. The opera of Bussotti is not a product but an operation.

The music theaters of Berio, Nono, or Kagel are theatrical in the way that they use performance space in musical ways. The core of Bussotti's music theater is more in the activity of approaching and conceiving, more in the moment of realization than in the actual result. This idea that process and method are more important than results comes from the influence of Cage and perhaps Umberto Eco's "open work" theory but also from the idea that music could become more like a science through research, investigation, experiment, and laboratory work. Like higher mathematics or advanced physics, the work of high-brow musicians would hardly be

13. Laurent Feneyrou, *Il canto Sospeso de Luigi Nono.*

understandable by the ordinary public.[14] But when it comes to words and theatrical performance, this point of view holds up much less well. Avantgarde music in a theater space is "open" in a different sense: open in being unveiled, exposed. Not surprisingly, landmark music theater pieces are almost always scandalous.

Bussotti's *Passion selon Sade* is one of those truly original theatrical inventions that cannot be placed in any category except "new music theater." First performed in Palermo in 1965 by Cathy Berberian, it is described as a *mystère de chambre avec tableaux vivants* for female voice mime, narrator, and eleven instruments. Even its title was considered *risqué*. In Italy the word "passion" had to be written with an exclamation mark (presumably to avoid any blasphemous connotations of the word) while in France "Sade" became an asterisk! The idea of a "passion play" is present in other works of the time (*Intolleranza, Passaggio*; see above) but with Bussotti, we are close to a surrealist version of Artaud's *théâtre de la cruauté*. This is partly due to the work's aristocratic attitude, partly due to its sixteenth-century text (based on Louis Labé), but also largely because of its structure, which has the character of a densely confused collage in which the eleven musicians as well as the other performers play major roles. We are far away from the concerns of real life. It was Ferruccio Busoni who, half a century earlier, had proposed that music theater could become a counterpoint to the reality of life. In this vision, bodies would behave differently and the "supernatural" as well as the "unnatural"—with all the factual evidence and all the feelings and sentiments attached thereunto—would become the subject matter of the new opera. Is it the *italianità* in these sentences of Busoni that suggests Bussotti's approach or is it the scientism of the twentieth century that is uncomfortable admitting that art may have nonscientific qualities?

An illustration from the score shows Bussotti's very original approach to music via design (or "de-sign"); it also shows how close this is to some scores of Kagel. There is one major difference between these works. Kagel's subject is the theater action itself while Bussotti's is sexuality and, more specifically, operatic sexuality. As is well known, sex has always played a major role in opera. But when sexuality becomes an explicit subject in twentieth-century art, it usually involves unveiling and disenchantment. What is striking about Bussotti's work is the discrepancy between its visual and its acoustic appearance. A complex and abstract score seems

14. Milton Babbitt has written the classic statements of this point of view ("Who Cares If You Listen?" *High Fidelity* vol. 8, no. 2 (February [1958]), 38–40, 126–27; reprinted several times. It should be added that Babbitt has not written for the theater since he abandoned his Broadway song-writing career early in his life.

Cathy Berberian in Sylvano Bussotti's *La Passion selon Sade*.

to clash with a voluptuous subject and elaborate design, suggesting the difficulty of any direct comparison between musical/acoustic art and visual art. Bussotti not only writes, composes, and designs his works but he also stages and choreographs them. The driving virtuosity of his talents has also been employed in staging the work of many other composers, past and

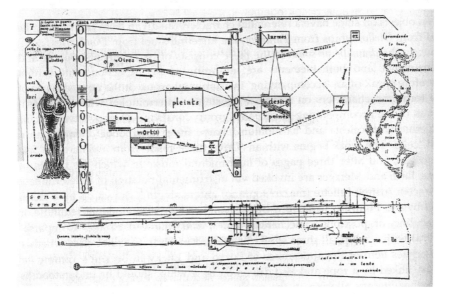

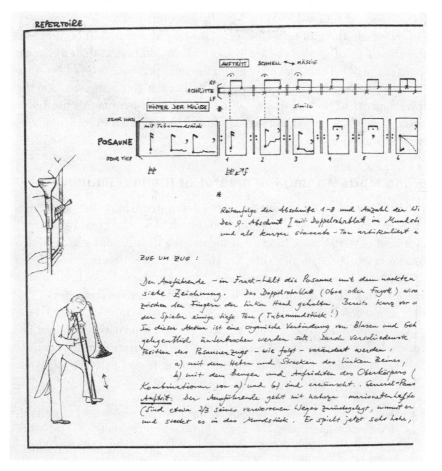

Above: From the score of Sylvano Bussotti's *La Passion selon Sade*, p. 7; below: From the score of Mauricio Kagel's *Staatstheater*, "REPERTOIRE". © 1971. With kind permission of Universal Edition A.G., Wien/UE 15197.

present, typically mixing dance with music theater and opera, creating a form that has been dubbed "Bussottioperaballet." *La Passion selon Sade* remains his best-known work, a remarkable opus that simultaneously deals with the operatic heritage of his native country, a personal synthesis of the arts (hence a contribution to the developing form of music theater), as well issues of human sexuality and social anarchy that were coming to the surface at the time.

The confrontation between new, experimental work and the weight of tradition has often led—not always intentionally—to one form or another of collage technique. *Collage* was logically also used as the name of a journal of new music and the visual arts, founded in 1963 at the New Music Festival of Palermo. Bussotti became involved with this festival, which was intended to make a counterpoint to the northern concentration of the avant-garde. Its polystylistic nature, a characteristic of Italian art in general, reflects the rich presence of earlier centuries, which even in everyday Italian life creates its own idea of renewal and avant-gardism. Compared to Germany, where virtually everything of value had been destroyed and had to be replaced, the Italian avant-garde appears as more of an addition to than a replacement of the old. This dialogue between the omnipresent good-old-but-dead past and the bad-but-alive present resulted in a high creative tension that forced artists to find their way out of a seeming dilemma. All the Italian composers of the period had to deal with this and it was a spur to originality and innovation.

Bruno Maderna and the theater of the imagination

Bruno Maderna, another Venetian, was a major figure in postwar new music both as a composer and conductor, and if he had not died relatively young, he might have had time to shape his ideas of a theater of the imagination. Maderna studied with the Venetian composer Gian Francesco Malipiero (as did Nono) and started out as a neoclassicist in the mode of his teacher.[15] He also studied conducting with Hermann Scherchen (perhaps the leading new music conductor of an older generation), made his conducting debut in Germany in 1950, and quickly developed an international career as a conductor of new music.[16] In 1955, with Luciano Berio, he founded the *Studio di fonologia* or electronic music studio at Italian Radio in Milan. His

15. Malipiero was an important figure in Italian music who was involved in the movement to force a major break with the nineteenth century and who himself created both instrumental and theatrical works, almost all now forgotten.
16. As has been the case with Boulez, Maderna's flourishing career as an interpreter of other people's work nearly overwhelmed his own.

Musica su due dimensioni (1958) is an early example of the combination of electronic and instrumental music.

Maderna did not always differentiate between instrumental and theatrical music. Like Nono in *Intolleranza*, Bussotti in *La Passion selon Sade,* and Stockhausen in *Originale*, he mixed previously composed instrumental music into his theater pieces, sometimes sacrificing internal narrative coherence but giving a larger coherence to his own work. His *Don Perlimpin* (1962; after Lorca) was composed as a radio opera. This was literally a "theater of the imagination"—we might call it a "virtual opera"—as the work had to create its visual form purely in sound. The collage technique has a clear function here; it serves as the musical *décor* for the listener and enables the composer to costume the characters of the play. Also, the instrumentalists play roles, a concept that was more deeply explored in the complex around *Hyperion* (1964), where the protagonist is a flute player who never says a word. *Hyperion*, described as a *lirica in forma di spettacolo* ("*opera in the form of theater*"), was written for flutist Severino Gazzeloni who has to spend the first ten minutes of the piece unpacking various flutes and, when he attempts to begin to play, is confronted by the loud sounds of phonemes taped from several languages by Hans G Helms.[17] There is a question as to what the definitive form of *Hyperion* actually is. Maderna gave stage director Virginio Puecher some existing compositions along with sketches and tapes saying: "This could be material for an opera, but you are the one who will have to give it a form." A later realization of the piece was undertaken by Hungarian conductor-composer Peter Eötvös, who incorporated new arrangements of those compositions that Maderna had intended to go into *Hyperion*.

Another radiophonic opera is the witty *From A to Z* (1969), quite abstract in its play with words and punctuation. His last work, *Satyricon* (1973), was another return to the past and not only in subject matter; Puccini, Tchaikovsky, Wagner, Gluck, and military marches are all commingled and again there is no "definitive" version. When Maderna wrote that *Satyricon* portrays a society "which, in many ways, is neither better nor worse than ours," he comes close to Bussotti and also to Busoni's vision of an alternate reality. "Whoever belongs seriously to a political party, whether Right or Left, has a precise idea of the society in which he lives, and I believe it would be difficult to find an image as close to our own reality as that given by Petronius in his description of Roman decadence...my aim is to make

17. Helms is a German poet who had realized, a few years earlier, a radio *Hörspiel*—the term means *earplay* but might also be translated as *soundscape*—in which some eight layers of text were mixed down into a single sound-band.

for the theater a political act and it was for this reason I was drawn to this text."[18]

These remarks are a long way from the idealism and utopianism that marked the early adventures of the new music scene; quite the contrary, they suggest pessimism and political resignation. The great hopes of 1968 for radical change were dashed and the avant-garde itself had essentially disappeared or become mainstream. Maderna died in 1973 in Darmstadt, the new music center to which he and his colleagues owed a lot but to which they had also contributed so much (Maderna was the founder and conductor of the Darmstadt International Chamber Ensemble). By 1973, Darmstadt had become merely a hothouse. All the major figures had decamped except for Stockhausen, and even he would leave shortly after protests from younger composers. Openness had failed as had other concepts of community life and human relationships. The Maoist notion of perpetual revolution was replaced by the melancholy realization that everything had already been invented or already happened. A better world (or maybe only a different world) could exist only in the imagination. Music, theater, lights, costumes, and the like would inspire only dreams.

Satyricon was, in effect, Maderna's mid-life crisis. Berio's mid-life piece was *Opera,* a theater about theater, or, more precisely, a meta-opera about opera. Nono, speaking about his *Al gran sole carico d'amore* of 1975—with its texts from the Paris Commune and the early Russian revolution—said he had been out looking for "other loves."

The 1968 generation

In the *Atomtod* (1965) of Giacomo Manzoni, society is either vanishing in the deadly glow of atomic radiation or, for those who can afford it, surviving in hidden bunkers. Manzoni's collaborators were Josef Svoboda, the great Czech designer and, as director, Virginio Puecher. This apocalyptic piece, a true sibling of Zimmerman's *Die Soldaten* (see Chapter 9), is a melange of media and musical styles. This collage, a huge landfill of cultural junk, is an ambitious work of strong *engagement* about the present and the future. With *Per Massimiliano Robespierre* (1975), again with Puechner's staging and a collage of texts from Büchner, Rolland, Anouilh, France, Marx, Schopenhauer, and Nietzsche, Manzoni created a piece that looks back into the eye of the revolutions of the past with another eye on an uncertain present. He still uses open form but it has lost its immediacy, and in dealing with the present and future, it sometimes suggests something more like aimless wandering than a directed search. The music is refined. Knowledge

18. Fearn, *Italian Opera,* 139.

and skill have grown; there is more certainty and more esthetic autonomy to carry these nonnarrative, wandering, and undramatic statements about theater and history. The old themes of 1968 have become obsolete but the "new loves" are not yet completely embraced. Time has not been kind to these ambitious works, which remain peripheral to a world that obviously did not want to be changed for the better. Here are a few others:

- Niccolò Castiglioni with *Attraverso lo specchio* (1961), a radiophonic opera based on Lewis Carroll's *Through the Looking Glass* as rewritten by Alberto Ca'Zorzi.
- Franco Evangelisti, the most Germanic of the Italians and the founder of an experimental music group, *Nuove Consonanze*; his somewhat uncharacteristic music theater piece, *Die Schachtel* ("The Box") of 1963, uses mime.
- Franco Donatoni, a *protégé* of Maderna, battled for a lifetime with Darmstadtian self-consciousness and with illness. His *Alfred, Alfred* (1995) is a twenty-five-minute piece based on words overheard in a hospital in Melbourne, Australia, where he found himself in a diabetic coma in 1992; despite this setting, the piece is meant to be *buffa*, somehow light and a truly individual step toward music theater.
- Egisto Macchi, whose *Anno Domini* appeared in Palermo in 1962, was cofounder of the Roman *Compagnia del Teatro musicale* together with
- Domenico Guaccero, also a Roman composer (originally from the Abruzzo), active as a teacher and politically engaged with the left. His work is characterized by graphic notation and a search for new theatrical forms. In 1978, he founded *Intermedia*, a performance group that included singers, mimes, dancers, and actors with a strong improvisational approach. Somewhat later he also founded an "Institute of the Voice" to study new approaches to the vocal instrument.

One of the principal issues that all of these composers faced was where their music could be performed. With the exception of two or three festivals of new music—the Venice Biennale, the Palermo Festival, and the more conservative Festival of Two Worlds in Spoleto—and the patronage of Italian radio (hence the numbers of radiophonic pieces), the number of places where new music theater and opera could be performed in Italy was quite limited. Nono accepted that *Intolleranza* and *La Fabbrica Illuminata* would have to be performed at La Fenice if he wanted them to be heard in Italy at all. Maderna imagined an ideal theater with fantastic spaces but the reality was that the virtual theater of radio transmission had to serve instead. Luciano Berio, who had entrée to La Scala as well as to opera houses and festivals elsewhere, actually preferred the traditional proscenium situation.

Operagoers and the opera house itself serve as active elements in his conceptions, and the resulting uproar and scandal became part of the piece itself. This is difficult to imagine in today's opera houses where such provocations have lost their ideological underpinnings and "class struggle" has become an abandoned term, a mere historic reference.

The audience itself has changed. In many of the famous houses, there is now a high percentage of visitors from elsewhere. Opera is part of the intelligent tourist's sight-seeing tour but new opera rarely fits into the eclectic touristic arrangements in houses like La Scala or the rebuilt La Fenice. New music theater in Italy was and is closely related to the programming in the traditional houses of Milano, Bergamo, Venice, Florence, Palermo, and elsewhere. The large orchestral apparatus of Berio's *Passaggio* is needed to realize its provocative concept. "*Passaggio* is an opera because it can only be performed in an opera-house; it needs that medium, that frame. Its subject is the opera-house itself…to be correctly understood, it must imply the experience of opera." The quotation is from the composer himself,[19] and what he is saying is that this "new music theater" is actually theater about theater or opera about opera. Berio's commission for Santa Fe is called *Opera* just as Kagel's piece for the Hamburg State Opera in 1971 is called *Staatsoper*.

The post-1968 generation

The events of 1968 were a watershed in Europe. The generation of composers born between 1920 and 1930 were passing through their midlife crisis almost at the very moment that the new generation arrived on the scene. Germany, the most destroyed and the most willing to shed its past, was the homeland of a promising and radical avant-garde, determined to restart history under different circumstances and with different visions from those of the past. The battle against the shadows of the past was complicated by the fact that many of those who were guilty of the catastrophe of World War II were not only still alive but were often the very ones in charge of the reconstruction. Inevitably, this created an atmosphere of mistrust and revolt. The promise of 1968 and its failure to overthrow a conformist society and its corrupt governments led to resignation and indifference on the part of the masses and the extreme radicalization of terrorist groups like the RAF in Germany and the Red Brigades in Italy.

Darmstadt, the mecca of modern music for all true believers, began to lose its attractiveness and status. Development and wealth arrived, even in a place "with only one xylophone." Italy was no longer a third-world country. The former Darmstadteers came home and became mainstream,

19. Fearn, *Italian Opera*, 91; Berio, *Two Interviews*, 159–60.

professors in new academies that they had founded or in newly renovated old ones. Popular music and mass media tightened their grip on the former new-music audience, especially on the left with its residual tendency to identify with pop and folk music. Postwar pioneerism was over, political activism in the arts outdated. Even Nono, new music's best-known communist, abandoned the subject. The Wall fell, the communist governments of Eastern Europe collapsed, and the Italian Communist Party, the leading front in the battle for political change in Western Europe for most of the twentieth century, closed its doors.

The modernist phase of provocations and scandals was over in new music and in the music theater world as well. Opera, that supposedly outdated form, showed strange signs of life as even opera-hating modernist composers began to write "operas" again. In Italy, composers of instrumental music like Aldo Clementi and Azio Corghi began to write for the opera. Bussotti made a new career as a director of operas in the big houses. And younger composers appeared on the opera stage with new ideas about what to do inside the old opera. Three of them will be discussed here: Salvatore Sciarrino, Lorenzo Ferrero, and Giorgio Battistelli.

The breathing voice: Salvatore Sciarrino

Of these three, Sciarrino is the most music-oriented and the most radical in his extreme emphasis on timbre and sound. The fragile and muted sounds of his work hover on the narrow threshold between the barely audible and silence. Despite such fragility, which lacks the broad brush of most typically dramatic scores, theater has been part of Sciarrino's work from the beginning of his career. The theme and subject of his *Amore e Psiche*, an "opera in one act" of 1972, suggest a Bussottian neoclassicism rather than other avant-garde models. In his very detailed scores, suspended between the mythic and the surreal, he has made the voice again the center of attention. After *Aspern* (a *"singspiel"* of 1978), *Cailles en sarcophage*, (1980; subtitled "acts for a museum of obsessions"), and *Vanitas* (1981; subtitled "Still life in one act"), he wrote a *Lohengrin* (1982–84; an "invisible action"). In this last named, there is a reference to Donatoni's *Alfred-Alfred* (1995) in which the hospital is a real place where the distorted mind fantasizes into a dream world. In Sciarrino's work, time is not only fragmented or static but runs backward; the love scene between Elsa and Lohengrin occurs before the swan arrives with our hero in tow. In Sciarrino's theater the subject is the fragility of perception or the incertitude of what we think we perceive. *Perseo e Andromeda* (1990), an opera in one act and again with a classical reference, uses computer sound programs that were created for insertion into his musical sound world. His statement was: "Only a new thought can make use of new means, not a scientific or commercial hybrid."[20] This is difficult to understand without some knowledge of the history of electronic music, which began as an amalgam of scientific research and esthetics in the electronic music studios of radio stations, universities, and a few large corporations but was later adapted to the creation of electronic instruments (synthesizers, samplers) for pop music. Whereas electronic music (and its offspring, sound processing and modification) was compromised in the world of instrumental music, its use in opera and music theater is still a subject of discussion and experimentation.

Sciarrino re-introduced the voice as primary. For some composers, the voice had become a "problem" and they tended to treat it as if it were only one sound among many or perhaps merely unavoidable noise issuing from warm bodies on stage or just simply a strange instrument producing those enigmatic sounds known as "speech." Another quotation from Sciarrino clarifies this: "An *opera lirica*, in the precise meaning of the term, implies two characteristic properties of the voice: the intonation of an intelligible text, and the specific humanity of the sound."[21] Despite the fact that these words sound like a manifesto, Sciarrino has no real conceptual answers. After all, he argues, the voice (he means the classical operatic voice) is limited in its range, limited in its technical aspects, and not subject to innovation or change; the voice is coded in its intervals and in its expressive variety and tends to fall into clichés, which Sciarrino calls "exhausted by banality." His aim is to find a way to put the traditional Italian operatic voice back at the center of interest in his sung drama without resorting to cliché.

His next piece, *Luci mie traditrici* (1997–98), is a full-length *opera lirica* based on a historical subject: the composer Gesualdo who murdered his wife and her lover. Sciarrino quotes or mixes in compositions by Gesualdo, often nearly imperceptibly or in a highly distorted form, a use of history that has become a typical Italian trait in recent music theater. At one point Sciarrino also substitutes a madrigal by Claude le Jeune instead of the expected Gesualdo. Everything in this piece is pared to the bone—narrative, instrumental sound, the lines of the protagonists and their actions. The chamber orchestra plays mostly in the upper, overtone-like registers and always softly. The score indicates, as a musical action, the actual breathing of one of the characters! Like the composers that the Germans call "deniers" (see Chapter 19), Sciarrino wants to assert his music against the banality of everyday life or the reality of physical appearance. For him, music and music theater are the places where his adventures take place, a remarkably romantic view for postmodern artist! Two more recent works that continue in this line are *Infinito nero* (1998) and a *Macbeth* (2002).

20. Sciarrino, 1991, cited in Fearn, *Italian Opera*, 213.
21. Fearn, *Italian Opera,* 213.

Here are three excerpts from the score of *Luci mie traditrici*:

- The first excerpt, from page 41 of the score, shows not only the complexity of the writing for the voice (second bar, baritone) but also the suggestion of madrigal technique. This is accompanied by solo strings with short high pianissimo passages and cello and bass glissandi in their highest registers.

From Salvatore Sciarrino: *Luci mei traditrici*, p. 41. With kind permission of BMG PUBLICATIONS s.r.l.

- From page 50: part of the madrigalesque instrumental *Intermezzo I*, where the saxophones have to play a "false unison." Both examples show the transformation from a Renaissance original into the distorted and somewhat psychologicalized world of a twentieth-century music-theater piece.

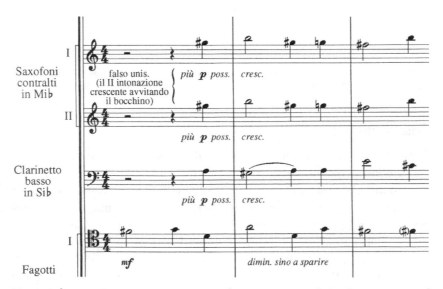

From Salvatore Sciarrino: *Luci mei traditrici*, p. 50. With kind permission of BMG PUBLICATIONS s.r.l.

- Finally, here is a measure of the intricate flute part, which interacts with the notated breathing of the "servant" (*Un servo*), sounds that are on the edge of the barely perceptible.

From Salvatore Sciarrino: *Luci mei traditrici*, p. 121. With kind permission of BMG PUBLICATIONS s.r.l.

Postmodern opera

Lorenzo Ferrero was involved at the beginning of his career with the experimental music-theater scene, working with the German group *Musik-Dia-Licht-Film-Galerie* in the early 1970s. His later works, however, are more dedicated to operatic traditions of dramatic writing, both in music and text. His *Rimbaud, ou le fils du soleil* (1978) is "quasi un melodrama in tre atti" ("almost a melodrama in three acts"). His next work, *Marylin* (1980, described as "scenes of the 1950s") is clearly an opera, and his publisher, Ricordi (the traditional publisher of Italian opera), has presented the young composer as "neo-tonal" and "neo-romantic." *Marylin* is a story not about the contradictions in Italian society but about the dream of a better life in America, a theme that recurs also in his bandit opera *Salvatore Giuliano*. The mixture of styles and the theme itself suggest an Italian version of postmodernism. Ferrero's 1984 *opera buffa Mare Nostro* is a piece of "theater about theater" (or art about art), which has a roster of quotations that runs from classical and romantic European music to jazz, pop, and contemporary sources. The center of the action is a magic machine called the *Leitmotif* that is nothing but a ticking clockwork mechanism. The issue of values does not even arise nor is any latent cultural background necessary; everything works through the arbitrary differences of styles.

In Ferrero's style of narrative and operatic dramaturgy, the broad brush and the staccato of Italian *opera buffa* are back in play. The list of Ferrero's works and performance pieces is impressive: *La figlia del Mago* (children's opera, 1981), *Night* (1985), *Salvatore Giuliano* (1986), *La fuga di Foscolo* (1986), *Charlotte Corday* (1989), *Le bleu-blanc-rouge et le noir* (marionette opera, 1989), *La Nascita di Orfeo* (1996), *Storie di neve* (1997), and *The Conquest* (2005), which includes rock voices. Ferrero began as a young composer in new music theater but in the end he went over completely into opera. Even his efforts to mix in elements from music or musical theater into opera did not ultimately succeed, at least in part because of the rigid structure and routine of opera. In the early 1980s, he became Sylvano Bussotti's assistant at the Puccini Festival in Torre del Lago, Italy.

Mastering the new music theater

Giorgio Battistelli, originally a percussionist, studied with Kagel and Stockhausen in Germany and worked in Paris where he was influenced by Aphergis and Bussotti. The work that made him well known grew directly out of his ability to think about and hear music from a percussionist's point of view. *Experimentum Mundi* had its origins in the rhythmic tapping of the shoemaker at work. Craftsmen of all sorts—originally all from his hometown near Rome—were instructed to do what they do. The score asks for 10 kg of flour, 30 kg of eggs, 70 kg of bricks, and 50 kg of sand as raw materials. There is an end result to the performance: shoes are made, knives are sharpened, a wall one meter high goes up, and the pasta is ready to eat. All those activities produce rhythms and sounds that not only reproduce a traditional soundscape of human life but also connect to many ideological, historical, and sociological ideas.

The score of *Experimentum Mundi*—the title comes from Marxist philosopher Ernst Bloch's last book—instructs the craftsmen who cannot not read music to accomplish certain phases of their work within a given time span or to do a certain number of actions. The difference between this

Giorgio Battistelli: *Experimentum Mundi* in performance. Photo: Giorgo Battistelli.

and a Cage-ian happening comes from the composed and musical structure of these actions, which carefully defines what both artisans and artists have to do. The score gives minute instructions about the sizes of the saws and nails that have to be used. The time-frame is equally strict; all the actions have to be completed in one hour.

There are other layers in the piece that transform the activity and help prevent the exposure of the craftsmen to sheer voyeurism or turning them into sort of a living wax museum. These additional elements are provided by two magicians (originally played by Bussotti and the composer himself), a narrator who reads the articles on arts and crafts from the eighteenth-century French *Encyclopédie,* and some female voices reciting names.

Experimentum Mundi is very close to other conceptual art pieces of relatively recent vintage. For example, visual artist Michelangelo Pistoletto's theater piece *Anno Uno—Anno Bianco* (1989) uses villagers from Corniglia in Liguria on the Genoese coast who reconstruct their village on stage and become both the architecture and the society but also speak and sing. Pistoletto said, referring to performances of The Zoo, a group that *he* created in the 1960s, "...you don't really know who is the viewer. *Is* it the caged animal, the prisoner, or the people on the other side of the barricade, or yourself? There is always the other...." This also applies to some extent to Battistelli's piece. It could even be asked whether the craftsmen on the stage are also watching the audience in the same way that the audience watches them

After the success of *Experimentum Mundi*, Battistelli has never stopped producing music theater and opera on a vast field of subjects:

- *Aphrodite* (1983), using antique costumes
- *Auf den Marmorklippen* after Ernst Jünger (2000–2001)
- *Begleitmusik zu einer Dichtspielszene* (1994), which is a pun on Schoenberg's "*Begleitmusik zu einer Lichtspielszene*," and includes video and scenes "ad libitum"
- *Chanson de geste* (1990) using audio tapes and two interactive video screens
- *The Cenci* after Artaud (1997), an ambitious and important work using live electronics and voice amplification
- *Le combat d'Hector et d'Achille* (1989)
- *The Embalmer*, a "*Monodramma giocoso da camera*" (2001–02)
- *La scoperta della lentezza* (1996), based on Sten Nadolny's novel "The Discovery of Slowness"
- *Lady Frankenstein* (1993)
- *Giacomo mio, salviamoci!* (1997–98)
- *Impressions d'Afrique* (1999–2000)
- *Jules Verne* (1987)
- *Kepler's Dream* (1989–90)
- *El otoño del patriarca* after Gabriel García Márquez (2003)
- *Prova d'orchestra* ("Orchestra rehearsal")(1994–95), based on the script of Federico Fellini's movie
- *Richard III* after Shakespeare (2004)
- *Teorema* (1991–92) after Pier Paolo Pasolini, a rare example of an opera without singing (although Robert Wilson has one without music)
- "*Experimentum Mundi Remix*" (2004) including much of the composer's impressive music theater catalogue

Here is Cristina Cimagalli's comment about his work: "Invisible yet strong threads connect Battistelli's work to the influences of the historic and post-war *avant-gardes*. From a distillation of this musical heritage—too hastily forgotten by many today—Battistelli has developed an approach that is as distant from a restorational aesthetic as it is from all technological fetishism."[22]

This is very close to Sciarrino's statement against the "scientific-commercial hybrids." We would have to go through his prolific output, piece by piece, to be certain. Apparently, technology—even new media

22. www.ricordi.it/composers/b/giorgio-battistelli/giorgio-battistelli-1/view?set_language=en.

and electronic/digital software—has become art's beloved enemy, the monkey on the back of that barely surviving species, the "serious artist." The ambiguous relationship between artist and technology consists in this simple contradiction: the artist hates technology but he can no longer live without it. Sciarrino knows this but he does not want to fall into either the trap of using commercial software (producing commercial results) or the pitfall of becoming a computer researcher in order to find his own individual programming solutions. The job of the artist is to create ideas that, one way or another, then must be realized.

An Italian postscript

The Italian scene, which had been widely influenced by the German esthetics of avant-gardism, changed when Darmstadt lost its allure and when economic prosperity and a new generation arrived on the scene. Neo-tonality and neo-romanticism signaled the return of operatic form and style.

Nevertheless, some organizations and centers devoted to new music theater in Italy have persisted. Two places that do *teatro musicale* in small spaces are the Scatola Sonora (connected to a conservatory in Alessandria) and the Piccolo Regio Laboratorio (part of the Royal Opera in Torino). The Torino prospectus speaks of composers who still "believe in the necessity to write music for the stage" while Laboratorio suggests a continuation of the idea of experimentation.

The language about "research concerning the relationship between music, theater and gesture" is also a way of putting art work in a box (*scatola* literally means "box") to sell it to audiences amidst media and information overkill. This particular box has been around for many years and it remains as difficult as ever to open it up. It also suggests a policy of containment regarding the financial demands and requirements of such projects. Berio's *Passaggio* employs only one singer but uses a large orchestra and requires the space of an opera house as its playground. Creating big conceptions for large forces can be a dangerous and costly experiment for younger composers. Better to open up studio theaters, lofts, and smaller spaces previously reserved for meetings or chamber music. Composers and producers could develop an art, handy and small, that could be carried around or toured in various ways.

Of course, it is hardly the producers' fault if they find themselves in a highly confusing and chaotic situation where everything can be criticized ideologically or esthetically. There is no rule of thumb here, not even in music theater. The world of opera (and this includes chamber opera) is quite consistent in its conservatism, which is historical but also applies to means and even terminology (which comes mostly from the archives of musicology and criticism). The problem of commissioning or programming music theater is that there are no such traditional, inherited rules and so it is constantly necessary to react and to orient one's policies according to the tendencies and issues of the moment. A little something of everything often seems to work best in these situations. The program of the sixth edition of the Torino Laboratorio shows a whole panorama of different elements: a piece by Mauricio Kagel followed by the work of a young Italian composer; an "oriental" piece about the role of the woman in Islamic culture; the "Ghost Opera" of Tan Dun (which is for instruments only); a music-theater piece with jazz and one with marionettes; a Lolita piece that includes dance.

What is notable is not only the confusion of elements but also the decision not to speak of genre ("What is music theater?") but to focus instead on the exploratory or experimental aspects in the manner of a research project. The results are unknown and the needed platforms and spaces are missing, but this is just part of what a music theater laboratory should be. It is not easy to program music theater when the demands are so different in each piece. But this is exactly why the Torino Laboratorio is so valuable.

In 1985, Roberto Paci Dalò founded the association *Giardini Pensili* as a vehicle for his various ambitions and creations, notably in music theater. His work, presented in various festivals, covers a very wide field of interests, sometimes with a political background, always with a sociological as well as artistic point of view. Incredibly prolific, Paci Dalò is a network artist who, through an indefatigable policy of collaboration, has been able to place his various work (music theater, radio art, installations, architecture, soundscapes, writings, and stagings) in many contexts, not so much in the operatic or post-operatic world but rather in the world of the visual arts. Being also a performer, his extraordinary activity is also linked to a multi-instrumentalist's experience of music.

Although Fausto Romitelli was not a typical opera composer either, he projected his compositional ideas—often inspired by the world of rock and techno, mass media and mass communications—in theatrical or multimedia form. Romitelli, who died at the age of forty-one leaving behind an unfinished body of work, was obsessed with the idea of performance as a drug that works not only on the mind but inside the body. Acoustic impact can work on the body like a drug in terms of loudness, pumping beats or particular frequencies. About his *Audiodrome* of 2003 (which was inspired by Marshall McLuhan's famous dictum "the medium is the message"). Romitelli said: "Perception of the world is created by the channels of transmission: what we see and hear is not simply reproduced, but elaborated and recreated by an electronic medium that overlays and replaces the real experience."[23]

A third composer who belongs to this group but whose aims are quite different is Maurizio Squillante. Squillante has been trained mainly in New York (he studied sound engineering at the Institute of Audio Research) and this leaves him less obligated to Old World traditions than his colleagues, trained in Europe. Squillante's work can be described as a contemporary form of multimedia that revives operatic tradition with the most advanced stage and musical technology. Two pieces, *The Wings of Dedalus* (2003) and *Alexander* (2006/7), are the fruit of this elaborated program. Squillante and his co-author Sebastiano Fusco, found in the ancient myth of the flying Dedalus an example of human transformation into a machine. The protagonist of *Dedalus*—a woman—is transformed into a cyborg whose movements are controlled by motors and a computer. All this takes place in an ambiance of virtual reality through video projections and the eventual transformation of the cyborg Dedalus into pure energy. *Alexander* uses holographic techniques. Both Romitelli and Squillante show interest in the body from a psycho-physiological point of view—Squillante even uses hypnosis in working with the performers—which suggests a new kind of alienation resulting from an unsentimental and parascientific view of the body and the senses.

A scene from *The Wings of Daedalus* by Maurizio Squillante with Pauline Vaillancourt as a cyborg Daedelus. Photo: Rosella Gori.

23. www.ricordi.it/composers/r/fausto-romitelli/fausto-romitelli-1.

Further Reading

Argan, Giulio Carlo. "Intolleranza 1960 and the Theater of [the] Avant-garde."
 Avanti!, May 1961.
Berio, Luciano. *Two Interviews*. Translated and Edited by D. Osmond-Smith.
 New York and London, 1985, pp. 159–60.
Fearn, Raymond. *Italian Opera since 1945*. Amsterdam, 1997.
Feneyrou, Laurent. *Il canto Sospeso de Luigi Nono*. Paris, 2002.
Gentilucci, Armando. *Oltre l'avanguardia un invito al molteplice*. Milan, 1980.
Schlömp, Tilman. *Gian Francesco Malipieros Musiktheater-Trilogie
 "L'Orfeide."* Frankfurt am Main, 1999.
Teatro Musicale Italiano nel Secondo Dopoguerra. Articles by Simonetta
 Sargenti, Umberto Eco, Sylvano Bussotti, Giacomo Manzoni, Adriano Bassi,
 Piero Santi, Enrico Girardi, Lorenzo Ferrero in *Civiltà Musicale*, no. 4
 (1990). Milan, Florence.

chapter 11

Théâtre Musical

*L'opéra mort ou vif et si le divorce entre la création lyrique
et l'opéra était le symptôme de la mauvaise santé, non
de la création, mais de l'opéra lui-même? (Opera, dead
or alive, and what if the separation between music theatre
creation and the opera was the symptom of the poor
health, but not of creative forces, but of the opera itself?)*

Michel Rostain and Marie-Noel Rio, 1982

Avignon

Although French opera has an independent tradition that goes back to the
seventeenth century and Paris dominated both opera and operetta throughout
much of the nineteenth century, the once thriving French operatic and
musical theater culture largely disintegrated in the twentieth century. Unlike
Italy, where popular support for traditional opera never disappeared, French
cultural life after World War II centered on film, theater, literature, dance,
and, in music, on jazz and experimental music. The latter included *musique
concrète*, based on the manipulation of recorded sounds on tape and founded
by two French composer/sound engineers, Pierre Schaeffer and Pierre Henry,
and serialism as established by the students of René Leibowitz (a pupil of
Schoenberg) and the innovative Olivier Messiaen. Pierre Boulez, who studied
with both Leibowitz and Messiaen, and was one of the early major figures
of the Darmstadt group, was music director of the famous Renaud-Barrault
company at whose theater he established his famous *Domaine musicale*
concerts in the 1950s. Although Boulez began his career in the theater and
has spent a major part of his career conducting opera, he is the only one of the
hardliners from the Darmstadt inner circle who has never written an operatic

or music theater work. When, after years outside of France, he returned at the invitation of Georges Pompidou, François Mitterand's Minister of Culture, he founded the IRCAM institute[1] and became the virtual cultural czar in French new musical life. In great part because of Boulez's influence, the government, the major source of arts funding in France, was slow to recognize the sociocultural value of music theater. Eventually, two or three theatrical institutions were established that specialized in music theater as an art form: Pierre Barrat's Atelier du Rhin in Colmar, Alsace; the Atelier de théâtre et musique (ATEM) of Georges Aperghis in the Paris suburbs; and the Atélier Lyrique Experimental (later known as Un Théâtre pour la musique) of Michel Rostain, first in Vincennes just outside of Paris, and later at the Scène nationale de Quimper in Brittany.

Given the initial antipathy of the French new-music establishment to opera and music theater, it is not perhaps surprising that music theater in France has been strongly associated with theatrical life and has been, in great part, a stage director's art. Of the three directors mentioned above, only Aperghis has worked as a composer, although mostly in a theater milieu. Rostain, a stage director and writer, worked on a number of occasions with Aperghis as well as with other composers of varying backgrounds (including jazz and flamenco musicians as well as one of the authors [ES] of this book); he has also published and edited programmatic texts on the subject of music theater.

For many years, the major outlet for new music theater in France was the "fringe" festival at Avignon, a center for new and alternative performance arts. Avignon was founded as an outlet for experimental theater just after World War II and, to a great extent, has remained fundamentally a theater festival. In 1967, however, festival director Jean Vilar decided to introduce new music, not in the form of conventional modern music concerts (which had little appeal to the young and hip Avignon audience) but in the form of new music theater. The Italian composer Girolamo Arrigo was commissioned to compose *Orden* on a libretto by Pierre Bourgeade. The production, directed by the Argentinian/French stage director Jorge Lavelli, was very successful and moved from Avignon to Paris. Lavelli worked with percussionist and conductor Diego Masson to create a *décor* of car wreckage that served as the musical instruments used in the production. This use of unusual sounds (a kind of live *musique concrète*); the process of creating a piece over a period of weeks as a collective improvisation; the introduction

---

1. *Institut de recherche et de coordination acoustique/musique*, whose very name has served as a model for the notion that new music is a form of scientific research, worthy of government subsidy and insulated from the musical marketplace.

of chance and variability as well as the undesigned and unintentional; liberation from conventional genres and forms as well as notions of collaboration and community—all contributed to the anti-authoritarian character of these performances and became the hallmark of works produced at Avignon.

In the early 1970s, the well-known film composer Antoine Duhamel (he wrote scores for Godard, Truffaut, Rohmer, Jacques Rivette, Barbet Schroeder, and others) entered the music-theater no-man's-land of Avignon with his *Opéra des Oiseaux* and *Ubu à l'opéra* (based on the famous *Ubu Roi* of Alfred Jarry). Duhamel, who studied with Messiaen and Leibowitz, has spoken about the differences between the speed of production and role of music in film and how music functions in the theater.[2]

Among other pieces produced at Avignon were *On veut la lumière… Allons y* and *Les fêtes de la faim* by Claude Prey, a very prolific composer of music theater and the creator of a style that he called "variable realism." In 1976, the opera-studio of the Lyon Opera under Louis Erlo commissioned Prey's *Young Libertad*, based (more or less) on poetry of Walt Whitman, which mixes the world of Broadway, social psychology, and a Romeo and Juliet story. The creation of the piece with twelve young singers became a group experience. In 1981, five singers commissioned *L'escalier de Chambord*, a musico-theatrical piece inspired by the double-helix form of the stairs in the *Château de Chambord* where the piece was premiered. Each of the five singers tells a fable or story and each of them has his or her musical system. Prey was one of the most performed living composers of music theater in the early 1980s although virtually forgotten today.

Another figure to be cited here is Michel Puig. Despite his studies with René Leibowitz, his music was more influenced by contemporary jazz and by abstract, *tachist* painting and sculpture than by musical modernism. His world was a theatrical one and by the late 1980s he had created and staged over twenty pieces. In pieces like *Stigmates* (1961) or *Les Urbanistes* (1963), described as an *opéra bouffe*, he worked with a mix of music, stage, and film. His long list of works, many using film or tape, include *Provisoires Agglomérats* (1966), *Les Portes du soleil* (1970), *La Chasse au Snark* (1971; after Lewis Carroll), *Isaac* (1973), *Sa Négresse Jésus* (1973/74), *Nuits sans Nuit* (1974), *Fragments pour Che Guevara* (1975), *Miroir* (1975), *Le Rêve du Papillon* (1976), *Visite à Locus Solus* (1976), *Les Loups* (1977), *Graal Filibuste* (1977/78), *Monet ou la Passion de la Réalité* (1979), *Divagation-Mallarmé* (1981), *Vertiges Exquis* (1981), *Phèdre-Opéra* (1981/1994), *La Véranda* (1982), *L'esprit Léger* (1982), *Sur Quatorze phrases de Marcel Proust choisies par Claude Malric* (1984/1992), *Sortir du Temps* (1985/86), *Les Moments Heureux d'une Révolution* (1988), *La Liberté* (1989), *Un*

2. Maurice Cury, *Visite à Antoine Duhamel* (Paris, 2005).

visage, une Voix (1991), *La Table du Petit Déjeuner*, (1993), and *La Caverne* (2000). In 1972, he founded the music theater group *Le Théâtre des Ulis* where he inevitably became the director of his own works.

Maurice Ohana was a Casablanca-born member of the Zodiaque group formed to resist "artistic tyranny" (i.e., of serialism). His *Syllabaire pour Phédre* and much of his other work employ a musical language based on traditional Spanish and North African music that included microtones and later electronics.

In contrast to Ohana, Jean-Yves Bosseur studied with Stockhausen and Henri Pousseur. Bosseur's idea of music theater was that of an experimental research collective with performers and creators working closely together. This concept of interdisciplinary work by open-minded and forward-looking artists, programmers, and directors was widespread at the time and led to the creation of performing ensembles, mostly in the theater. But lacking public support and funding, this approach never really achieved the institutional status that would have allowed its work to continue.

Avignon, from its founding in 1947 and through its turn toward music theater after 1967, produced well over one hundred new pieces of *théâtre musical*[3] almost none of which resembled any of the others in structure or approach. In the revolutionary spirit of the time, music theater seemed like an alternative to the dust of classic operatic pathos as well as a way to get out from under the ideological hermeticism of serialism. It was also a useful term to describe a way of working. The collective, the collaborative, and the interdisciplinary were fresh ideas of the time which, after the political wreckage of the Sixties, kept on glowing for a long time in the performance arts. But there were also some big misunderstandings in this gathering of the disciplines. For example, the babble of artistic languages, dominated by theater and dance, and the notions of the collective, group rehearsal, and improvisation brought many problems for classically trained musicians and composers who lacked the theatrical sense of a chaotic, improvisational, and time-consuming art form. Sometimes, unable to confront the secular problems of organization and physical involvement, and unwilling to give up their traditional control, they abandoned the nascent art form, leaving it largely to performing musicians from the adjacent (but often unconnected) worlds of jazz and pop. Another problem was Avignon's singularity. In a discussion from 1982, the then-director of the festival, Bernard Faivre d'Arcier, pointed out that the festival alone could not carry the responsibilities and

3. Not including those music-theater pieces that were presented in theatricalized concerts organized under the name *Musiques Eclatés*, which could be translated as "Exploding Musics," "Sparkling Music," or, perhaps more idiomatically, "Dynamic Music."

the risks without collaborators and co-producers from elsewhere in France and Europe.[4] Although Avignon was by far the world's most prolific center for new music theater and related multimedia—or, as the festival itself would say, works of *théâtre musique performance danse vidéo*—only a few things have survived from this hotbed of performance activity.[5]

Xenakis and the Philips Pavillion; *musique concrète*

Iannis Xenakis utilized extra-musical means, most notably from mathematics, to structure sound and music. In his largely instrumental music, the extra-musical actions, gestures, and texts come to serve as a set of rules, structuring principles, or compositional tools to organize the infinite possibilities of freedom in sound. Although Xenakis did not work in theater per se, he collaborated with the architect Le Corbusier and composer Edgard Varèse in developing the famous Philips Pavillion at the Brussels World's Fair of 1958, using the same compositional criteria he had used in his *Metastasis* for sixty-one instruments. In designing this structure—which held Le Corbusier's visual projections as well as Varèse's *Poème électronique*—Xenakis came close to a form of music theater that deals with mathematical, stochastic ideas and architectural space as its "story" or "text." His methods intentionally evoked a theater of nature, populated with the "singing of the cicada, the noise of raindrops on a circus tent, calls of a political manifestation, sounds of objects thrown in street fights."[6]

In the early 1970s, Michel Guy, then director of the Paris Autumn Festival, commissioned Xenakis to write an opera. "[N]ot interested," was Xenakis's response, "but I can create an automated, abstract spectacle with lights, lasers, and electronic flashes." The work that resulted, *Polytope de Cluny*, was installed in the Roman ruins of Cluny on the Boulevard Saint-Michel in Paris in 1972 and ran until January of 1974. The score was an 8-track electroacoustique tape that accompanied a computer-controlled light show made up of white flashes and four hundred mirrors that reflected colored beams. The result was a merger of the popular *son et lumière* spectacle and a sophisticated, computer-driven multi-media event. This installation, visited by tens of thousands, turned Xenakis from a purveyor of obscure, mathematically derived and esoteric works of art into a "successful" and well-known artist.

Extra-musical means and materials of quite a different sort were developed at *Radiodiffusion française* by Pierre Schaeffer. Schaeffer had the idea

4. Michel Rostain and Marie-Noel Rio, *L'opéra mort ou vif* (Paris, 1982).
5. Avignon also hosted important works from elsewhere including some notable premieres (e.g., the Robert Wilson/Philip Glass *Einstein on the Beach*, which started its career at Avignon in 1976).
6. Iannis Xenakis, *Musique, Architecture* (Tournai, Belgium, 1971).

of editing and manipulating tape recordings of recorded sounds and organizing them as musical compositions. Some of his tape pieces, developed as music for radio plays from the late 1940s, constitute not only the first works of *musique concrète* but are generally accounted as the beginning of electro-acoustic music. Schaeffer organized the *Groupe de recherche de musique concrète,* later renamed *Groupe de recherches musicales,* in the 1950s, where many of the major composers of the day worked on tape and electronic music. In 1953, Schaeffer collaborated with Pierre Henry on *Orphée,* considered the first electronic opera. Henry, who was one of the first composers to combine live performance with tape and electronically altered sound, also collaborated extensively with choreographer Maurice Béjart. The basic principle of *musique concréte,* that any sound that can be recorded is potential material for musical composition, was actually anticipated by Cage's use of phonograph records and even radio broadcasts in the 1940s. It turned into a useful tool for theater as well as music theater, blurring the previously existing line between scene music and sound effects. The advent of digital recording, editing, and playback in the 1980s revived interest in recorded sound as part of the composer's tool kit with a particular impact on theater and music theater.

Georges Aperghis

The years of experimentation known as the Sixties (actually the late 1960s and 1970s) had a very social side. "Music theater in the streets" was one of the ideas of the time that for various cultural, educational, and ideological reasons (above all, faith in the democratization of contemporary art) attempted to reach new audiences. The French traditions of mime, clowning, and street spectacle were extended to opera starting in the 1970s when the city of Paris supported the artistic and musical social work projects of Georges Aperghis and his ATEM (Atelier Théâtre et Musique) group, and continuing as recently as 2004 with *"opéra dans les rues"* (which included Tom Johnson's *"Four Note Opera,"* an abridged version of Wagner's *Ring,* and a squeezed *Carmaine* for four singers and brass ensemble).

Georges Aperghis, born in Athens and self-taught as a composer, has lived and worked in Paris since 1963. Inspired by such unorthodox figures as Pierre Henry, Pierre Schaeffer, and Iannis Xenakis (all three badly treated by the French new-music establishment of the day), Aperghis discovered music theater about 1971 when he wrote *La Tragique histoire du nécromancien Hiéronimo et de son miroir,* a piece that includes two female voices that sing and speak as well as a lute and a cello. Text, music, and scene come together to create the musical dramaturgy of the piece; something extra-musical drives the music just as something extra-theatrical seems to drive the theater. In 1976, a generous government subsidy permitted the foundation of ATEM in the outskirts of Paris.[7] Aperghis was able to create a laboratory for theatrical and musical work with musicians and actors, an ideal situation that has rarely existed before or afterward.[8] A series of works was created experimentally through improvisation and ensemble rehearsal as well as by more traditional processes of composition; Aperghis himself liked to quote his friend, the French theater director Antoine Vitez, in saying that he wanted "to make music from everything," a music/theater aphorism related to both *musique concréte* and to the Cage esthetic.

Aperghis left ATEM in 1991 having created an impressive catalogue of works. Some of them are listed below.

- *Histoire de loups*, opera after Sigmund Freud (1976)
- *La Bouteille à la mer*, for soprano, six actors and four instrumentalists (1976)
- *Fragments, journal d'un Opéra* (1978)
- *Récitations* for solo voice (1978), his best-known work; "voice-theater" in the form of a catalogue of vocal virtuosity
- *De la Nature de la gravité*, a *"spectacle musical"* after Leonardo da Vinci (1980)
- *Fidélité* (1982) for "she-harp-player, observed by a man"
- *Le Corps à corps* (1982), an equally witty piece for a percussionist and his zarb[9]
- *Le Rire physiologique* (1983) for baritone and pianist
- *Jojo* (1991), music theater on texts by the composer and Philippe Minyana

Excerpt from the score to Georges Aperghis, *Le Corps à corps* (1982).

7. As part of a forward-looking policy to better integrate the suburbs into urban life, a policy that was later abandoned.
8. Quog Music Theater, founded by one of the authors in New York (1970–1981), was a similar if much less well-funded effort.
9. The Zarb, or Tonbak, is a Persian or Iranian goblet drum.

There are also many instrumental pieces that are built on playful allusions to music making, to social situations, and even to mini-dramas in which the theatrical impact comes as a side effect of the music making. More recent work includes *Die Hamletmaschine* or *Machinations*, the result of an invitation to work at IRCAM; it is a multimedia theater based on an enigmatic text of Heiner Müller and set for women who manipulate objects in light-desks projected onto a screen over their heads and produce vocal sounds that are supported and treated by a computer. *Dark Side* is a piece based on the *Oresteia* of Aeschylus. The Opéra de Lille premiered his *Avis de tempête* ("Storm Warning") in 2004.

The musical results of the merging of language and music in Aperghis's work has involved a fragmentation of syntax and meaning and the use of fantasy-speech. Aperghis is a composer who is fascinated by the possibilities of the human mouth (not only the voice!) to generate sound. Speech, language, and text are just some possibilities among others. The gestures of the physical body as it creates sound and the social ritual within which all this happens are essential ingredients (elements such as notation and the historical situation are secondary).

The tradition of structural modernism rejected the performer's critique or intervention on any level, a kind of post-romantic egocentrism and a theoretical and intellectual selfishness that goes a long way to explain the gulf between the composer and a society that made music theater an oxymoron for decades. Aperghis, on the other hand, not only wants to make music out of everything but also music theater out of everything and with everyone as well. Not that this is such an easy task in a world that accepts the category of sober and serious composers of music as something quite distinct from songwriters, movie composers, and the like. The drama of overcoming obstacles to create a new music theater of everything and everyone is the musico-dramatic subtext of Aperghis's work.

Although Aperghis is a somewhat isolated and unique figure in French musical life, his work is not without influence. Perhaps the liveliest of his disciples is Richard Dubelski, a percussionist and mime who creates music theater in a rehearsal process working with both amateurs and professionals. A recent work is a series of vaudeville or music-hall sketches for actors and instrumentalists based on *The Ten Commandments*.

Récitations of Georges Aperghis with Pauline Vaillancourt, Montréal (1989).
Photo: Daniel Kiefer.

Lyon and Quimper

In 1982 the composers Pierre-Alain Jaffrennou and James Giroudon founded GRAME as both a festival and *atelier* in Lyon under the title *Musiques en Scène* ("Stage music"). Jaffrennou, a trained mathematician who studied electro-acoustic music with Pierre Schaeffer, established the GRAME laboratory for musical data research; his colleague was responsible for the music theater festival.

In 1992, GRAME became an annual "multidisciplinary showcase for musical creation," and in 2002 a biennial festival. International projects in collaboration with partners in Europe, North America, and China and programs supported by the European Commission complete a network whose local bases are the Ministry of Culture, the Rhône-Alpes region, and the City of Lyon. Behind all this lies the declared belief in the creation and production of new art by the French state. The creation of art as part of any civilized culture has here the same value as any other economic sector. Unlike other countries, France has shown, with initiatives like this, the persistence of a belief in a consistent and creative cultural system. Whether this shows a realistic attitude toward shifting global conditions or not, it still functions as a reference for the culturally interested.

Michel Rostain, who has been referred to in these pages as a stage director, librettist, and writer on music theater themes, founded the *Atelier Lyrique Experimental* (later known as *Un Théâtre pour la musique*) in Vincennes just outside of Paris. This company was incorporated into the *Scène nationale de Quimper* (*Théâtre du Cornouaille*) in Brittany, France, when Rostain took over as director there in the 1990s, and, more recently, Rostain has established a Centre de Création Musicale at the Quimper theater. These closely related organizations, all essentially creations of Rostain, have been active in creating and producing new music theater, working with Aperghis, Dubelski, Bernard Cavanna, Eric Salzman, the French jazz composer Gérard Marais, Pierre-Alain Jaffrennou, and Susumu Yoshida. The last-named is a Japanese composer who studied with Messiaen and lives and works mostly in France. He has written a trilogy of music-theater works for Rostain's wife, Martine-Joseph Thomas, under the collective title of *Chamanes* (Shamans), an earlier opera entitled *Les Portes d'Enfer* (The Gates of Hell), and the more recent *Sumidagawa: La Rivière Sumida*, based on the same fifteenth-century Japanese Noh play as Benjamin Britten's *Curlew River*; all these works have been staged by Rostain. They employ an evocative use of language set against musical scores dominated by a delicate use of percussion and a stagecraft that blends traditional Japanese elements with contemporary music-theater forms. This mixture of Eastern and Western ideas about theater has been attempted on a number of occasions, mostly by westerners (Partch, Britten, Brecht/Weill), but the idea has never really caught on. Its current revival is perhaps due to the impact of so-called world music and the new and growing prominence of non-Western composers working in an increasingly globalized culture.[10]

From the point of view of the history of new music theater, it is of great interest to see how the labels have changed over time. "Stage music" and "mixed music" have replaced the old terminology of *atelier expérimental* and *théâtre musical*. The concepts behind these projects mix elements from the Avignon years, from the IRCAM doctrines, and from ATEM. The aim is the creation, production, and distribution of the so-called mixed musics with composers-in-residence, scientific research on computer-assisted composition, and educational activities. GRAME gives about twenty world premieres each season of mixed works, music theater, public events, and audio installations. The Quimper program is only slightly less ambitious with a variety of productions, performances, and creations. Whether all this makes Lyon and Quimper way stations for an international movement, these are ambitious programs for the creation of new work with a strong music-theater character.

Pascal Dusapin and Bernard Cavanna

Although the Paris Opera was once Europe's leading opera house (even Wagner worked very hard to get his work produced there), it has long since lost that position, and in general, opera has lost its preeminent position in French intellectual life. As a result, large-scale institutional opera has not provided a home for new work of operatic dimensions (let alone for new music theater). There are, however, some exceptions, notably the Messaien *Saint François d'Assise* at the Opéra Bastille in Paris conducted by Pierre Boulez and directed by Peter Sellars, and a number of new productions at the Théâtre du Chatelet, also in Paris. Outside of the French capital, the operas of Marseille and Lyon have also produced contemporary work.

Pascal Dusapin was one of the few students of Iannis Xenakis; he also studied with the Italian composer Franco Donatoni (see Chapter 10). He

10. Probably the best-known Asian composer working in this vein is the Chinese composer (resident in New York) Tan Dun, well-known for his film scores. His large-scale operas (*Marco Polo*, 1996; *Peony Pavilion*, 1998; *Tea, A Mirror of Soul*, 2002; and *The First Emperor*, 2006) have been widely produced. His *Ghost Opera* for string quartet, pipa, water, metal, stones, and paper is an instrumental work meant to evoke the shamanistic ghost operas of Chinese peasant cultures in which spirits of the past and future communicate with the living.

has composed a number of pieces for the stage, all designated as operas: *Roméo et Juliette* (1988), *Medeamaterial* (1991), *La Melancholia* (*Opéra-torio*) (1991), *To Be Sung* (1993), and *Perelà, Uomo di fumo* (2001). Another work, *Faustus, The Last Night,* had its premiere at the Berlin Staatsoper Unter den Linden and the Lyon Opera in 2006; it is based on Christopher Marlowe (rather than Goethe) and has the unusual feature—for a French opera—of being in English. He has also been commissioned to write another opera for the Aix en Provence Festival for 2008.

Bernard Cavanna, a self-taught composer who has worked extensively in the theater, for the dance, and also for film, wrote an opera, *La Confession impudique* ("The Indecent Confession" 1992; rev. 1998) based on a some-what *risqué* novel by the Japanese writer Junichiro Tanizaki, and *Messe pour un jour ordinaire* (1994), which mixes the text of the Catholic Mass with the wry comments of a young female drug addict just released from jail. Most recently he wrote a companion piece for Mozart's unfinished *Zaïde* entitled *Zaïde Actualités* with a libretto by Michel Rostain.

Does the work of these composers suggest a turn away from the *théâtre musical* and back toward the opera, so long discredited and neglected in French intellectual life? Or does this simply mark the return of a music-driven music theater, operatic or otherwise?

Québec

In considering French music theater, we need also to look at the *scène québécoise,* which has been very active artistically and is interesting because of its geographical position—that is, dangerously close to the United States, nostalgically far from France. In the francophone world, Québec has been a principal source for major new work in the popular musical theater. The rock operas, *Starmania* (1979; music by the French composer Michel Berger) and *Notre Dame de Paris* (1998; music by the Franco-Italian composer Riccardo Cocciante), both by the Montréal lyricist Luc Plamondon are two well-known and widely performed examples.

In 1990, the singer and performer Pauline Vaillancourt, in collaboration with Joseph St.-Gelais and Renald Tremblay, founded the Montreal-based group Chants Libres. Not surprisingly, the center of this project has been the voice, especially the voice of Pauline Vaillancourt, who has performed extensively in France and elsewhere in Europe, working with Georges Aperghis, Michel Rostain, Maurizio Squillante, and many others. In her various roles as performer, artistic director, and more recently, as librettist, stage designer and/or director, she has been responsible for many premieres. *Chant Libres* is a very good example of the type of music theater discussed earlier in which the human voice and a particular performer become the creative focus. In recent years, the group has also shown a notable interest in electronic media in connection with live performance. *L'enfant des glaces* (2000) was created in collaboration with the American composer Zack Settel who, at IRCAM in Paris and at the University of Montréal, has done considerable research on the use of live interactive electro-acoustic systems. Other productions include *Manuscrit trouvé à Saragosse* (2001) by José Evangelista and Alexis Nouss (based on a 1965 film by Wojciech Has); *Paca-mambo* (2002) by Zack Settel and Wajdi Mouawad; and *L'Archange* (2005), described as an *opér'installation*, based on a text by Alexis Nouss with music by Louis Dufort and staged in a huge video installation by Alain Pelletier consisting of about forty monitors arranged in the form of an arena. Other productions of *Chant Libres* include *Ne blâmez jamais les bédouins* (1991), music by Alain Thibault; *Il suffit d'un peu d'air* (1992) by Claude Ballif and Renald Tremblay; *La princesse blanche* (1994) by Bruce Mather and Renald Tremblay; *Chants du capricorne* (1995), a stage setting of a much earlier work by the Italian Giacinto Scelsi; *Le vampire et la nymphomane* (1996) by Serge Provost and Claude Gauvreau; *Yo soy la desintegracion* (1997; based on the life and work of Frida Kahlo) by Jean Piché and Yan Muckle; and *Lulu, le chant souterrain* (2000) by Alain Thibault and Yan Muckle.

Claude Vivier, who was born in Montreal and studied in Europe with Gottfried Michael Koenig, Stockhausen, and Paul Méfano, was recognized as a major figure only after his tragic early death in 1983 in Paris. His musical ideas were dominated by preoccupations about death, love, childhood, and immortality, all archetypical operatic themes. He rejected traditional opera and his *Kopernikus*, subtitled *rituel de mort*, and composed three years before his death, belongs to a theatrical oratorio tradition, where pieces like Schoenberg's *Moses and Aaron*, Honegger's *Jeanne d'Arc au bûcher,* and Stravinsky's *Oedipus rex* can be found. The work uses French and German texts plus an imaginary tonal language of his own invention. A series of tableaux depict the passage from life to death in the presence of such arche-typical figures as "the mother," Lewis Carroll, Merlin, Mozart, the Queen of the Night, Tristan and Isolde, and Copernicus. Like a dream and vision, its mixture of the new ideas and archaisms make it a truly original concept.

Further Reading

Cury, Maurice. *Visite à Antoine Duhamel*. Paris, 2005.

Rostain, Michel, and Marie-Noel Rio. *L'opéra mort ou vif*. Paris, 1982.

Xenakis, Yannis. *Musique, Architecture*. Tournai, Belgium, 1971.

Xenakis, Yannis. *Musiques formelles*. 1962; later revised, expanded, and translated into *Formalized Music: Thought and Mathematics in Composition* in 1971.

chapter 12

Music Theater in Northern Europe

Come, pray. let's begin. O Gad: there's a flat note! there's
art! how surprisingly the key changes! O law! there's a
double relish!
I swear, sir, you have the sweetest little linger in England!
ha! that stroke's new; I tremble, every inch of me; now
ladies, look to your hearts—softly, gentlemen—remember
the echo—captain, you play the wrong tune—O law! my
teeth! for God's sake, captain, mind your cittern—Now the
fuga, bases! again, again! lord!
Mr. Humdrum, you come in three bars too soon.

The conductor, Sir Symphony, from Thomas Southerne's play
The Maid's Last Prayer (1693)

Great Britain

The history of music theater in Britain has to begin with Benjamin Britten,
a composer better known for his operas but whose work includes several
pieces in the line of Stravinskyian chamber opera and Brecht/Weill music
theater. From 1939 to 1942, Britten emigrated to the United States, where
he was in contact with the music theater movement that had emerged
in New York (see Chapter 15). Aside from incidental music, Britten's
first major theater piece was a chamber opera or operetta based on the
American folk tale of *Paul Bunyan* (1941; libretto by W.H. Auden) that,
in its use of folk songs, blues, and gospel hymns, owes something to the
populist modes of the day. One year after his first major operatic success
(*Peter Grimes* in 1945), he wrote *The Rape of Lucretia*, a Stravinskyian
chamber opera with characters designated as "Male Chorus" and "Female
Chorus" to tell us what we are watching and provide Brechtian distance
while guiding us through a certain kind of morality play. Although this work
had its premiere at Glyndebourne in England in 1946, it played the Ziegfeld
Theater on Broadway only three years later. In 1948, he made a version of

John Gay's *Beggar's Opera,* and a year later he wrote *Let's Make an Opera,* intended for performance by and for children. He continued throughout his life to be occupied with chamber opera (*The Turn of the Screw,* after Henry James, 1954) and music theater parables (*Noye's Fludde,* 1957; *Curlew River,* 1964, based on a Noh play; *The Burning Fiery Furnace,* 1966). Finally, in 1970, he wrote an opera for television (*Owen Wingrave,* also based on Henry James, 1970).

Although Britten paved the way, it remained for the next generation of British composers to establish the idea of an alternative music theater in Britain. In 1967, Peter Maxwell Davies, Harrison Birtwistle, and the pianist, composer, and polymath Stephen Pruslin founded the *Pierrot Players,* modeled on the instrumentation and the esthetic of Schoenberg's *Pierrot Lunaire.*[1] This group, which later metamorphosed into *The Fires of London,* was specifically organized to produce and perform new music-theater works. Some of Davies' best-known works were produced for this ensemble including *Revelation and Fall* (1968), *Eight Songs for a Mad King* (1969; written for Roy Hart; see Chapter 17), *Vasalii Icones* (based on the sixteenth-century anatomical art of Vesalius; 1969), *L'homme armé* (looking even further back to the early Renaissance; 1971), and *Miss Donnithorne's Maggot* (1974). Later music-theater or operatic works by Davies include *Blind Man's Buff* (a masque; 1972); *The Martyrdom of St. Magnus* (1976); *Salome* (actually a ballet; 1978); *The Lighthouse* (his most often performed work; 1979), *The Rainbow* (1981); *Resurrection* (1988); and *Mr. Emmet Takes a Walk* (2000).

There is a big range here, from the *Eight Songs*—in which the mad King George III converses with his birds (represented by instrumentalists inside bird cages) in a vocal technique extended in all directions—to chamber operas based on true stories from far-flung outposts of civilization. Miss Donnithorne was a Dickensian character from Australia who sat in her wedding dress for a quarter century waiting for a bridgegroom who never showed. *The Lighthouse* is a tale of lighthouse keepers off the British coast who mysteriously disappeared in raging tempests of both natural and human origins. Davies, who studied with Petrassi in Rome and with Babbitt and Sessions at Princeton, mixes a latter-day serialism with elements taken from early music (*Taverner* uses music by the historical John Taverner; *Mr. Emmet Takes a Walk* has quotes from Bach and Schumann) and various kinds of popular music (sea chanties in *The Lighthouse;* American pop music in *Mavis in Las Vegas* [1995]; foxtrots in *Vesalii Icones* [inspired by anatomical drawings but also, as with Nono and Berio, by the Stations of

1. Davies and Birtwistle were both from Manchester, England, where they formed a a new music group with Alexander Goehr and others. Davies and Pruslin were also students together at Princeton in the United States.

the Cross], and Scottish or Orkney folk music in more recent music [he has lived in the Orkneys for many years]).

In addition to his interest in remote settings, another theme that runs through much of Davies' work is madness—most obviously in the characters of George III and Miss Donnithorne but also in *The Lighthouse* and elsewhere. Even the foxtrots do not always really belong to the light music category but often rather serve to suggest the hysteria and violence of modern life. Unlike Nono and Berio or even Britten, Davies has largely avoided any overt treatment of political themes, but the issues of identity and the individual in society are nearly always present in his work.

The case of Davies' one-time colleague, Harrison Birtwistle, is more difficult as this composer's dramatic sense is far more rarified. Birtwistle's music, although generally described as in the serialist mode, is more sculptural and closer to Varèse, Messiaen, and even certain works of Stravinsky than it is to Boulez and Babbitt. He composes in blocks of sound that reappear in different guises and shapes as though they were literally in space and being viewed from different angles. This is not in and of itself a dramatic method but, nevertheless, Birtwistle has produced a whole catalogue of music-theater works. The piece that first made his reputation, *Punch and Judy* (1966–67), was written for the *Pierrot Players* and premiered at Aldeburgh. The work, although cartoonish in some respects, was considered extremely violent (Punch murders Judy at least four times), and Benjamin Britten, the founder of the festival and Britain's premier composer of dramatic works since Purcell, walked out. A series of music-theater pieces with much more pastoral subjects followed including *Down by the Greenwood Side* ("a dramatic pastoral drawing on mummer's play and folk ballad traditions" with a text by Michael Nyman; 1968–69); *Orpheus* (1974–77); *Bow Down* with a text by the poet Tony Harrison (1977); *The Mask of Orpheus* (1973–84); *Gawain* (1991); *The Second Mrs. Kong* (1994); and *The Last Supper* (1999). The use of familiar and even mythic subjects allows him to cut back on the need for narrative and he tends to present the material in a sequence of ritualistic *tableaux vivants* in the manner pioneered by Stravinsky.[2]

Although both Davies and Birtwistle have connections to European modernism and postmodernism, the major English composer to carry on

---

2. He has also written several works for chamber ensemble that use theatrical or ritualistic form: *Tragoedia* (1965), *Secret Theatre* (1984), and *Ritual Fragment* (1992). In *Secret Theatre,* members of the larger ensemble stand up and become soloists, and the solos and tutti (Birtwistle calls them *cantus* and *continuum*) are in a constant struggle to take the lead. In *Ritual Fragment,* the players line up in a semicircle and pass around the melodic line.

the techniques and esthetics of serialism is Brian Ferneyhough. Most of his career as a composer and as a teacher has been outside of Britain. He has taught at Darmstadt since 1976 and directed its composition program from 1984 to 1994. He has been a composition professor at the University of California at San Diego and at Stanford University since 1987. He has also taught at IRCAM in Paris since 1993 and at a long list of other festivals and schools. Ferneyhough's music has a fearsome reputation for abstraction and difficulty, challenging both performers and listeners alike. Even though he had previously stated that he would never write an opera, when the Munich Biennale—the contemporary opera festival founded by Hans Werner Henze—approached him about the possibility, he accepted, taking on a subject that was perhaps suitable to his esthetic: the ideas of Walter Benjamin stemming from his famous remark that philosophy is about representation. This sounds like a direct challenge to a highly abstract composer like Ferneyhough and indeed the issue of what music can possibly be "about" is the hidden dramatic theme of the work. The work, which has a text by American poet Charles Bernstein, is actually a collection of six independent pieces headed by a "realistic" scene that more or less takes place at the moment of Benjamin's death on the Spanish border as he was in flight from the German occupation of France. After that we follow him (or perhaps only his ideas) into the next world. The sections that follow are a guitar concerto; a motet full of number symbolism; a solo by a speaking pianist dressed as Liberace in a Las Vegas bar (presumably representing Hades); a meeting in the next world between Benjamin, Karl Marx, Hitler, and Pope Pius XII; *tableaux vivants* "representing the Angel of History as Melancholia" (after Dürer) set as a contrapuntal weaving of poetry and music; and finally, "Stele for Failed Time," which introduces electronics as well as the composer's own voice speaking a language that he invented. The idea that music can transcend time truly takes music and music theater into a metaphysical dimension.

Both Davies and Birtwistle started out by challenging the very conservative and bourgeois classical music establishment in Britain but both came to have a very high degree of acceptance from the powers that be.[3] Ferneyhough is a classic example of a prophet without much honor in his own country (*Shadowtime* has yet to be produced in Britain) although he is a fixture in the serious academic modern music establishments in Europe

---

3. Among many recent British operatic works we might mention *Powder Her Face* of Thomas Adès, premiered at the Almeida Theatre, and several works for children written by Oliver Knussen (1952–) with Maurice Sendak, the illustrator of children's books: *Max and the Maximonsters* (1980), *Where the Wild Things Are* (1979–83), and *Higglety Pigglety Pop!* (1984/1990).

and America. But a truly alternate musical culture requires a "downtown" scene, connections among the avant-garde, pop music, and the visual arts, and perhaps some politics as well.

Cornelius Cardew, the most politically radical of all the British composers, started out as a choirboy at Canterbury Cathedral, became Stockhausen's assistant (and ghost writer) in Cologne, turned against Stockhausen (he wrote a work entitled *Stockhausen Serves Imperialism* in 1974), and, under the influence of both Cage and Chairman Mao, founded the infamous Scratch Orchestra, a musical thumb in the face of the staid British classical music establishment. He also took to composing simple agitprop songs for British workers more or less in the spirit (if not quite the manner) of Hanns Eisler.

In a country where the split between the classical music establishment and everything else (pop music, band music, amateur music making) had been total, the Scratch Orchestra was truly thumbing its nose at the musical establishment and its aggressive populism, and its very amateurishness influenced and nurtured a whole generation of young musicians outside the system. Among them was the pop musician and producer Brian Eno. Eno, who was completely self-taught in music and whose main instrument was a studio mixing board, provided a link between the avant-garde and the pop world in Britain. Another figure who came out of this colorful "grey" world was the composer Gavin Bryars, who started out as a jazz bassist; was influenced by Cage, Cardew, and the American minimalists; and released his first work as a composer on Eno's Obscure label in 1969. Although one might imagine that Bryars would have been a good candidate to write music-theater, his three major stage works are indubitably operas and just barely unconventional enough to be included here: *Medea*, adapted from Euripides in both ancient Greek and the local vernacular (with Robert Wilson; staged in Lyon and Paris in 1984); *Doctor Ox's Experiment* after Jules Verne (text by Blake Morrison; directed by Canadian film director Atom Egoyan at the English National Opera, 1998); and *G* based on the life of Johannes Gutenberg (libretto by Blake Morrison; commissioned by the Mainz Opera for Gutenberg's 600th anniversary). There are elements of jazz and also of pulse minimalism in these works as well as a preoccupation with the contradiction between extended time in the universe of minimalism (and of Robert Wilson) and "realistic" time as it might pass (or seem to pass) in a *verismo* opera.

Michael Nyman, first known as a critic and musicologist, became the best known of all these composers thanks to his film scores for Peter Greenaway (eleven films between 1976 and 1991), Jane Campion (*The Piano*, 1992), Volker Schlöndorff (*The Ogre*, 1999), Neil Jordan (*The End of the Affair*, 1999) and Michael Winterbottom (*Wonderland*, 1999, and *The Claim*,

2000). In 1968, Nyman was commissioned by Birtwistle, then the music director of the National Theatre in London, to produce arrangements of Venetian songs for a production of a Goldoni play; the Michael Nyman Band grew out of this. His first music-theater work, *The Man Who Mistook His Wife for a Hat* (1986) is taken from a case study by neurologist and author Oliver Sacks about a voice teacher with an affliction of the brain that leaves music as his only contact with reality. The centerpiece of the work is an actual Schumann song performed onstage by the title character, and the entire piece leads up to and away from this "real" or diegetic moment.

Nyman has subsequently written two operas, *Facing Goya* (Compostela, Spain, 2000) and *Man and Boy: Dada,* about the dada artist Kurt Schwitters in London during World War II after all his work had been destroyed in Germany (performed 2004). Nyman has also written extensively for dramatic performances, silent films, and the dance. It is typical of his kind of minimalism[4] that it has a European cultural and even historical context. One of his first pieces for the Michael Nyman Band was based on Leporello's aria from Mozart's *Don Giovanni*, his score for Greenaway's film *The Draftsman's Contract* is a take on seventeenth-century English music, and the music for *The Piano* evokes romantic piano music in contemporary minimalist form. All these historical reference points lend his music a context that has helped give it profile and made it popular with audiences.

Mark-Anthony Turnage, who studied with Oliver Knussen and Gunther Schuller, came to prominence with *Greek*, an opera based on a Steven Berkoff reworking of the Oedipus story and commissioned by Hans Werner Henze for his Munich Biennale in 1988. This piece, which has had many productions, has a striking level of rawness and brutality that is unexpected in a British work. Turnage was later Composer-in-Association to the English National Opera and advisor to its Contemporary Opera Studio, a residency that culminated in his setting of the Sean O'Casey World War I play *The Silver Tassie* (1990; premiered by the English National Opera). Although his reputation is that of a composer of strong and even violent music, his work actually alternates between high levels of intensity and a lyric quality, both intermingled with strong jazz influences.

Andrew Toovey was born in London, and studied with (among others) Morton Feldman. His 1991 setting of the infamous *Ubu Roi* by Alfred Jarry has a sort of arch and clownish expressionism that suits the bizarre nature of the subject (the title role is sung in an intense and wide-ranging baritone who often drifts upward into falsetto). His second opera *The Juniper Tree*, a grim Grimm Brothers subject (also treated by Philip Glass with Robert

---

4. He is said to have been the first to apply the term to music although that honor may actually belong to Tom Johnson.

Moran and the writer Arthur Yorincks), was produced at the Munich Biennale in 1997 and also performed at the Almeida Theatre in London. Toovey's melodramatic alternation of high dissonance, jagged leaps, and modal lyricism creates a dramatic dialectic that approaches the melodramatic.

British performing institutions

The performance situation for opera and new music theater in Great Britain is an uneasy amalgam of European and American models. The American or Broadway musical has its principal opposite number in London's West End, which has produced musicals like *Oliver* (based on Dickens's *Oliver Twist*), the collected works of Andrew Lloyd Webber (including *Evita, Cats, Starlight Express, Phantom of the Opera, Sunset Boulevard*, and others), and the Euromusicals of Alain Boubil and Claude-Michel Schoenberg, which were first produced in London, not in France. Broadway and the West End have a long history of exchange going back to the nineteenth century, and in recent years London has also had a lively "fringe"—equivalent to the New York off- and off-off-Broadway movement—that has flourished in the renovated warehouse and industrial district in the eastern part of London, particularly in the dock areas of the Thames.[5] The notion of turning Broadway musicals into serious music theater is probably not one that could have gone very far, even in New York, but unconventional revivals of New York musicals have been a notable part of the London musical scene in recent decades and these have sometimes made their way successfully back to New York. An outstanding example was the National Theatre's production of the Rodgers and Hammerstein *Carousel*, which took this essentially serious and social subject back to its origins, a drama by the Hungarian writer Ferenc Molnár. Some of Stephen Sondheim's controversial works have been more successful in London productions than they ever were in New York. Notable examples include *Assassins* (a musical about the assassination attempts, successful and otherwise, on American presidents), *Sweeney Todd* (based on the Victorian story of a barber who revenges himself on society by turning its leading citizens into meat pies) in a production in which the actors also form the orchestra,[6] and a couple of sophisticated revues of Sondheim's work.

5. The Edinburgh Festival "fringe" is, of course, along with the Avignon Festival, the model for this sort of thing (there is now even a New York Fringe Festival, a sign, no doubt, of the decay of off- and off-off-Broadway).
6. Now also, with some changes, a musical film by Tim Burton, a rare and successful example of a serious musical theater work transferred to film using nonconventional singing voices that fit neither the operatic nor the traditional musical theater types.

The *Pierrot Players* of the 1960s, although active for only a few years (their successor, the *Fires of London*, was more of a concert organization), provided a model for music theater in an alternate mode and there have been a number of smaller opera companies and music-theater ensembles that followed. After a promising start, the English National Opera's Contemporary Opera Studio did not succeed in developing a viable new works program and, with one or two notable exceptions, the lively London theater and music scene has not developed a strong creative music-theater component. The result is that the Munich Biennale and the film industry have sometimes been better patrons for new British opera and music theater than local musical institutions.

The major exception has been the music theater and opera program of the Almeida Theatre, founded in the early 1970s by the Lebanese director Pierre Audi and later directed by Jonathan Reekie. Almeida introduced several of Giorgio Battistelli's works, including world premieres of *The Cenci* (1997) and *The Embalmers* (2002), as well as works by the South African composer Kevin Volans, Thomas Adès (*Powder Her Face*, premiered at the Almeida Theatre, London, 1995), the Alaskan composer John Luther Adams (*Earth and the Great Weather*; 2000), the Danish composer Per Nørgård (*Nuit des Hommes* with Jacob Schokking, 2000), Alexander Goehr, Nyman, Birtwistle, Aperghis, and others. In 1988, Audi became director of the Netherlands Opera and immediately introduced a program that included the Feldman/Beckett *Neither*, *Marco Polo* by Tan Dun, *Kopernikus* of Claude Vivier; the Andriessen/Greenaway *Rosa* (1994) and *Writing to Vermeer* (1999), the Philip Glass/Robert Wilson *Monsters of Grace*, the Birtwistle *Punch and Judy,* and others. The Almeida has, in the meanwhile, continued its policy of encouraging new work and, together with the Genesis Foundation and the Aldeburgh Festival, has announced a commissioning program for new work. Aldeburgh, which was founded by Benjamin Britten and is now directed by Jonathan Reekie, has announced the Jerwood Opera Writing Programme, with Giorgio Battistelli as artistic advisor, "designed for composers, writers and directors who want to widen horizons and equip themselves to create contemporary work combining music, theatre and text."

The Netherlands

In 1969, four young Dutch composers—Ton de Leeuw, Peter Schat, Jan van Vlijmen, and Louis Andriessen—collaborated on *Reconstruction*, a "morality opera" that was political not only in its content but also in its very notion of composer collaboration. Schat became known afterward for large-scale multimedia and theatrical works also with strong political implications. His later opera *Symposion* (1982–94) has been described as lyric and neo-romantic.

Andriessen, the best known and most influential of this group, started his career in the ambience of serialism but quickly broke away, incorporating popular and political elements, influences from jazz, Stravinsky, and minimalism, and a certain amount of exchange with alternate and anti-establishment currents in the United States and Great Britain (a number of younger British composers have studied with him.[7]) Theater has played an important part in Andriessen's work and thought and he has a long list of works designated as music theater or opera including *Mattheux passie* (1976), *Orpheus* (1977), *George Sand* (1980), *Doctor Nero* (1984), *De Materie* (created with Robert Wilson for the Netherlands Opera; 1984–88), *M is for Man, Music, Mozart* (1991), and a sort of sequel *M is Muziek, Monoloog en Moord* (1993), *Rosa* (with Peter Greenaway; 1993–94), *Odysseus' Women* (after Homer; 1995), *Oldenbarneveveldt* (1998), *Writing to Vermeer* (with Peter Greenaway; 1997–99) as well as music for dance and scores for films by Peter Greenaway and Hal Hartley.

Some of these works are far from conventional dramatic pieces. *De Materie*, for example, is a large-scale music-theater work on texts that include the Dutch Declaration of Independence and a shipbuilding treatise as well as letters from a medieval mystic, the Dutch painter Piet Mondrian, and Marie Curie. Sections of this piece may be performed separately and the only through line is the composer's deep involvement in "the material" and the way he conceptualizes in his hard-edged minimalist style. *Rosa*, subtitled "a horse drama" and "Death of a Composer," is a surrealist account of the death of an imaginary Latin American composer who writes scores for Hollywood westerns; Andriessen's score evokes Hollywood, Broadway, jazz, Bach, Brahms, and a lot more.

Writing to Vermeer is another large-scale opera written with Greenaway, this time dealing with artistic, social, and political history. In spite of all the references, Andriessen's style is not historical and his allusions to jazz, Ives, Stravinsky, and minimalism are well digested. His approach to repetition and process is, as he likes to say, not sunny and optimistic like that of the American minimalists but reflective, philosophical, and even fatalistic, a kind of pan-European philosophical approach to a musical style of writing.

Perhaps the most unconventional of all the Dutch composers working in music theater and related genres is Dick Raaijmakers, who studied piano at

---

7. The British percussion group Icebreaker, named for the Amsterdam new music center Ijsbreker Café, typically performs music by Andriessen, Gavin Bryars, Bang on a Can composers from New York, as well as some of the younger British pupils of Andriessen.

the Royal Conservatory in the Hague but has been involved for most of his life with electro-acoustic or electronic music. Raaijmakers's work has been characterized by his gradual adoption of visual media and theatrical techniques and his involvement in the philosophical implications of performance including chance, open form, and accident, or to use the terminology he prefers, risk and instability, falling and breakdown. Many of his works are closer to installations—he tends to call them "versions" or "operations" and they are often in unconventional spaces like abandoned industrial buildings—in which he uses electronic sounds, film, and other media as well as percussion and theatrical action to create multimedia meditations on a particular subject (old Laurel and Hardy movies, a ping-pong game, or the fall of Mussolini are examples).

Denmark

A major music-theater work to emerge from Denmark is the *Nuit des hommes* of Per Nørgård with a libretto by Jacob Schokking, a Dutch writer and director active in Denmark. The work was premiered in 1996 at the Musikteatret Albertslund near Copenhagen; it has subsequently been seen in many other places including the Almeida Theatre in London. The work, based on the poetry and war experiences of Guillaume Apollinaire, uses a male and a female soloist playing three roles each, and chorus with string quartet, percussion, and electronic keyboards. A major feature is the use of projections using fragments of the poetry—in the original French and in translation—and images of the performers. *Nuit des hommes,* which the composer describes as "an opera of sorts," is a theatrical work with a powerful social theme that does not preach but by treating its texts in multi-layered and complex ways, achieves a subtle and nontraditional balance of words and music.

More institutions

In 1992 at the *Theatre de la Monnaie (De Munt)* in Brussels, Lukas Pairon, then director of the Antwerp, Belgium, improvisational music-theater group Walpurgis, and Dragan Klaic, originally from Zagreb, Croatia, and then director of the Netherlands Theatre Institute in Amsterdam, founded the Conference on Small-scale Opera and New Music-Theatre (later shortened to NewOp), an annual meeting of directors, composers, librettists, and performers involved in the field. Subsequent meetings took place in Colmar (Alsace, France), Cambridge (England), Toronto, Copenhagen, Montréal, Oslo, Vienna, and Barcelona. The meetings, which involved seminars, lectures, workshops, and performances of new work, helped create a network—mainly north European—and encouraged international collaboration in the field.

Another Antwerp institution that has produced music-theater works and promoted international collaborations is *Muziektheater Transparant*. In Brussels, *De Munt* or the Théâtre Royal de la Monnaie, the main opera theater of Belgium, has a history of presenting new work especially under the former direction of Gerard Mortier and his successor Bernard Foucourolle. Mortier left Brussels to become the director of the Salzburg Festival where he introduced a policy of new work (notably the Messaien *Saint François d'Assise* staged by Peters Sellars and conducted by Pierre Boulez); more recently, he became the director of the Paris Opéra and then moved across the Atlantic to the New York City Opera.

The appearance of progressive opera directors like Pierre Audi and Mortier considerably altered the European landscape and helped shift the focus away from music theater and again toward the opera house. What is still exceedingly rare, an opera house devoted to new work, can be found in Denmark. As its original name suggests, Copenhagen's *Den Anden Opera* or "The Other Opera" was oriented toward chamber opera, but under its new name, PLEX—described as "Copenhagen's Musictheater"—it has a wider reach that includes a variety of collaborations between artists in different media. Other institutions such as the Munich Biennale and New York's Center for Contemporary Opera are producing entities but do not have their own theaters and tend to hover between contemporary opera and various forms of music theater.

Further Reading

Adlington, Robert. *De Staat*. Aldershot, Hants, UK, 2004.

Andriessen, Louis. *The Art of Stealing Time*. Edited by Mirjam Zegers. Translated by Clare Yates. Todmorden, UK, 2002.

Andriessen, Louis, and Elmer Schonberger. *The Apollonian Clockwork: On Stravinsky*. Edited by Jeff Hamburg. Oxford, 1989.

Cardew, Cornelius. *Stockhausen Serves Imperialism and Other Articles*. London, 1974.

Cross, Jonathan. *Harrison Birtwistle: Man, Mind, Music*. Ithaca, NY, 2000.

Griffiths, Paul. *New Sounds, New Personalities: British Composers of the 1980s*. London, 1985.

McGregor, Richard. *Perspectives on Peter Maxwell Davies*. Brookfield, VT, 2000.

Pruslin, Stephen, ed. *Peter Maxwell Davies: Studies from Two Decades*. London, 1979.

Seabrook, Mike, and Paul Griffiths. *Max: The Life and Music of Peter Maxwell Davies*. London, 1994.

Smith, Carolyn J. *Peter Maxwell Davies*. Westport, CT, 1995.

Tamm, Eric. *Briano Eno: His Music and the Vertical Color of Sound*. New York, 1995.

Trochimczyk, Maja, ed. *The Music of Louis Andriessen*. London, 2002.

Warburton, Thomas. Review of *Harrison Birtwhistle: Man, Mind, Music* by Jonathan Cross. *Music Theory Spectrum*, vol. 26, no. 1. Berkeley, CA, 2004.

entr'acte iv
The art form that never happened

This is a true story. A music-theater piece performed at an important Viennese contemporary music series that was intended to propose a new *Gesamtkunstwerk* seems only to have provoked a series of dramatic misunderstandings.

The specially adapted stage and auditorium of this unique hall were designed to satisfy the weirdest fantasies of a stage director or composer but had never been used until the very evening in question.

The piece was *Medea*, and it was subtitled "a Media Performance for Female Voice alone." The project included a large bank of video monitors all conceived, programmed, connected, and controlled—with much effort—by a promising and gifted video artist. One of the most prominent German performers of contemporary music theater, with extended voice capabilities and strong stage presence, had been engaged and had worked hard to learn thoroughly the demanding but convincing score. The composer had tweaked the pedals of the piano and the positions of the loudspeakers of the intricate electronic setup to perfection.

There was a large drop to be hung at the back of the stage with the motto "WE ARE YOUNG" emblazoned on it. Here was the first hint of trouble. After three attempts by the composer to get the house crew to hang it properly, the chief technician told him, in a dry, obscene tone of voice, "Do it yourself!" and the crew left for their lunch break.

The musical composition and the stage and performance arrangements were not the only innovative aspects of the evening. The three-hundred-seat auditorium had been set up so that the public would be seated around a pool where lighted underwater monitors spread a shimmering, bluish light and sound. The audience could dip their feet into the well-tempered water, which was heated to 27° Celsius (81° Fahrenheit). This same pampered audience was to be served an exquisite three-course dinner while they enjoyed the fabulous paintings and video art that surrounded them as well as the texts of a famous poet whose verses had been set to music for performance by the diva of extended vocal virtuosity. The performance was, in fact, brilliant. Never, in all the history of this great musical and operatic city had such a piece or such a performance been heard or seen...by the three people who were in the hall. Out of three hundred seats, only three tickets had been sold to this avant-garde music theater extravaganza—to the composer's mother and two of her old friends.

Was there at least a critique or review or story in the newspaper to document this remarkable event? Alas, the press did not take notice. No critic was present because no critic had been invited because no newspaper cared to write about it if there was even any newspaper that had the space for such a review, always assuming that there were still newspapers being published that still reviewed concerts and performance spectacles in this venerable city of concerts and performance spectacles. It turned out that all the employees of the public relations office of this innovative new music hall were either on holiday, ill, on pregnancy leave, absent without notice, or otherwise occupied with managing another, more important concert by a famous semi-nude violinist. When the composer asked for the recording of his premiere, he was given a minidisk that proved to be completely blank. The sound engineer explained, with a smile, that the recording was apparently made from a dead channel. He of course blamed the composer for his presumption in having written the piece at all.

There was warm applause from five actively clapping hands—one hand was in a cast, which brought up the old Zen question: what is the sound of one hand clapping? The backstage crew thought that the singer had given the performance of a lifetime. But none of this was enough to appease her anger and frustration. She gave the public a truly operatic bow and rushed out to find a taxi to the airport. The doorman was busy playing solitaire on his computer and ignored her pleas for help in getting a taxi or, at the very least, a phone book. The composer never heard from her again but it is believed that she did eventually find her way back to Germany.

The director of the venue was not present at any time in his bright new neon "new music space." When one of the audience members wrote to inquire as to why so little effort had been expended to spread the word about such a ground-breaking piece and outstanding performance, he eventually replied, explaining that it was a matter of one single performance only and that it was difficult to do publicity or public relations for a piece that was in no known category and which therefore, by definition, no one would be interested in. The public, he went on to say, only perceives what it already knows and does not perceive what it does not already know. Shortly after releasing these deep thoughts, he resigned in order to become the director of a large German opera house.

chapter 13

Downtown

*When you're alone, and life is making you lonely You can
always go Downtown You can forget all your troubles;
forget all your cares, and go Downtown—everything's
waiting for you*

from *"Downtown"* by Tony Hatch

New York: Off-Broadway

The history of music-theater creation and performance follows quite
different scenarios in the Old World and the New. In New York City, there
were two major streams of creation and performance, one connected with
the growth of the off- and off-off-Broadway theater and the other with the
development of the loft and gallery culture (and closely related activity
in the dance), all in lower Manhattan and in recent years in the nearby
borough of Brooklyn. As a result, while "uptown" has come to signify the
domain of traditional culture (Broadway, Lincoln Center), "downtown" has
become virtually a category of alternate visual and performing arts.

  One of the defining events in the history of the off-Broadway theater
in post–World War II New York was the eight-year run, starting in 1952,
of the Marc Blitzstein translation of the Weill/Brecht *Three-Penny Opera*,
at the Theater de Lys (now the Lucille Lortel) on Christopher Street in
Greenwich Village. However, important as this was, one must also cite
the presence in New York of an exile theater community from Central
Europe dating from the 1930s, much of it centered in Greenwich Village,

an early outpost of "downtown" and home of The New School (originally New School for Social Research), which was a center for the exile community. This community included Erwin Piscator, founder of the New School Dramatic Workshop and the Studio Theatre, plus various imported and indigenous Brechtians (including, for brief periods, Brecht himself). This created a direct line between Central European art between the wars and postwar New York.

Also starting in the 1930s, there was a series of attempts to produce small-scale opera and serious popular music theater that were widespread enough to merit being called a movement. During the Depression, the Roosevelt administration subsidized the arts through the Works Progress Administration (WPA) and some of this money was available to small theaters and music theater projects. The range of these works was very wide, extending from opera to serious musical to experimental agitprop with avant-garde theater techniques using music, action/movement, projections, film, and animations. The Living Newspaper, sponsored by the Newspaper Guild, produced docudramas in the 1930s on such subjects as *Power* and *Oil*, which were written and produced not by individual artists but by collectives.

It was against this background and tradition that ensembles like *The Living Theater* and the *Open Theater* appeared on the downtown scene in the 1950s. These constituted a new and experimental theater that made some radical proposals using documentary subjects or social issues in an unconventional performance style and milieu. These projects were often created, developed, or brought to production through an elaborate rehearsal process in which the actors participated as creators, working alongside stage directors, choreographers, designers, and composers and developing the piece out of the physical attributes and talents of the individual participants rather than out of a set of predetermined ideas about music, subject, sound, and form. The proscenium was generally abandoned in favor of a black box and an elastic situation in which performers moved into the audience or in which the audience became, in some way, involved in the action. A production that originated in this way and had a wide influence was the Living Theater's *Happiness Now*, which toured around the world to suitable excitement and outrage.

This radical environmental theater was a product of (or merged with) other artistic and political trends of the time. It was highly physical, decidedly nonliterary, and interested in the dynamics of the performer/audience relationship. Many productions used sources from ancient myth and legend as though it were possible to reinvent theater all over again from its "original" origins in ancient Greece or, pushing further back, in the African and Asian sources that were presumed to be behind even Greek mythology. Language was less important than emotive sound, music, and physical movement. Although these developments properly belong to the history of theater, this was, in fact, a theater that was rapidly approaching the condition of music theater. A well-known example, several times revived (and already mentioned here), was the La Mama theater's *Greek Trilogy* of André Serban and composer Elizabeth Swados. This production was developed over a period of years in the late 1960s as three separate pieces that were eventually put together in trilogy form in 1971. The public was required to move from space to space as the action—dependent on physicality and sound as much as on language and traditional ideas of music—unfolded in and around the spectators.

Richard Schechner's *Dionysius in '69* was a somewhat similar production, also based on Greek tragedy, created for, by, and with the Performance Group (which later became the Wooster Group) that he had founded two years before. Daniel Nagrin's *The Peloponnesian War* (1967–68), a full-evening, one-person dance theater work with music by Archie Shepp and Eric Salzman, was premiered at the State University of New York and at the Free Music Store in New York City. With its strong anti-Vietnam War motifs, the work was designed to tour and reach a popular, young audience. The music was on two unsynchronized open-reel tapes, the costumes were packed in a box, and any student could be taught to run the lighting plot; as a result, the work was performed dozens of times in the period throughout the country. Although these works and performances were notably nonverbal and nonliterary and often lacked conventionally spoken or sung texts, they had strongly political subtexts connected to the fast-developing political and anti-war movements of the time.

The inheritance of The Living Theater, Open Theater, and the Performance Group continues in the contemporary work of a number of theater ensembles in the United States and elsewhere. The best-known American groups, Richard Foreman's Ontological-Hysteric Theater (created by its director/writer), Mabou Mines (a collective of creative directors formed by Lee Breuer, JoAnne Akalaitis, and Ruth Maleczech), and The Wooster Group (now directed by Kate Valk) do complex, *engagé* work in radical forms, often with strong musical scores. Nevertheless the engine that drives most of this work is the staging, which is the real equivalent of a script or libretto; in most of these works it is the stage director, not the composer, who is the true *auteur*.

One important theater group that emphasized the composer's role was Lenox Arts, later renamed Music-Theater Group. This company commissioned and developed several music-theater collaborations between Foreman and composer Stanley Silverman including *Elephant Steps* (1968), *Dr. Selavy's Magic Theater* (1972), *Hotel for Criminals* (1975), *Africanis Instructus* (1986), and *Love and Science* (1987). Closely related are the same company's productions of music-theater works by choreographer

The Trojan Women originally premiered in 1974, inaugurating La MaMa's Annex theater. The photo depicts a scene from the 2004 revival by the Great Jones Repertory Company of La MaMa. Directed by André Serban, music by Elizabeth Swados. Photo: Richard Greene. Photo courtesy of The La MaMa Archive / Ellen Stewart Private Collection.

Martha Clarke with composer Richard Peaslee[1]—*The Garden of Earthly Delights* (1984; based on Breughel), *Vienna Lusthaus* (1986; inspired by Freud), and *The Hunger Artist* (1987; after Kafka)—and director/visual artist Julie Taymor with Elliott Goldenthal—*Juan Darien: A Carnival Mass* (1989; based on a South American tale). Taymor and Goldenthal also created *The Transposed Heads* (American Music Theater Festival, 1985; based on a Thomas Mann story) and *Grendel* (Lincoln Center Festival, 2006; based on John Gardner's retelling of *Beowolf* from the monster's point of view). Both of these teams also produced Pulcinella pieces.

New York: lofts, galleries and church basements; dance theater

The history of new music theater in New York is also linked to the development of performance art. This also comes out of an "off" performance scene

---

1. Peaslee has also worked extensively with Peter Brook and the Royal Shakespeare Company (*Marat/Sade* among others), Peter Hall and the National Theatre, and Joseph Papp and the New York Public Theater.

largely associated with downtown but quite independent of the off-Broadway theater. This is the loft and gallery scene of the New York art world—or, more accurately, art and dance world. As Greenwich Village became gentrified and rents began to rise, the artistic community began looking for a home still farther downtown. The discovery of large abandoned industrial establishments in parts of New York below Greenwich Village—notably the Soho area south of Houston Street and afterward the adjacent Tribeca area on the fringes of Wall Street—prompted a whole generation of artists to redeem and redevelop these unwanted spaces, turning them into studios, lofts, and galleries. With varying amounts of renovation, many of these were large enough and suitable enough (high ceilings, wooden floors) also to serve as performance spaces.[2] Associated with these downtown loft spaces were a number of old churches that had largely lost their congregations and were in the process of redefining their missions—often mixing social and political work (for example, draft counseling) with a ministry for the arts. Like the lofts, studios, and galleries, these churches had a very valuable commodity to offer artists: space. At the very least, there were basements and crypts, and often enough the main sanctuaries of the churches were available and suitable for performance as well.

Although a certain amount of theater performance took place in old churches, theater often involved extended runs, and most churches preferred other forms of performance activity, notably music and dance, that were more easily adapted to performance in an active church. At least one major wing of contemporary dance, the so-called Judson Dance movement, was born in a church (Judson Church on Washington Square in Greenwich Village). Dance movements like this were busy breaking the conventions of dance—even of modern dance—and moving into areas of theater, dance theater, improvisation, and what would shortly become known as performance art.[3]

There was a relatively large group of composers and performing musicians (many on the fringes of jazz as well as other forms of new music) active in the downtown community. Some of these artists had their own lofts or performed regularly in loft, gallery, and church spaces. Important jazz collectives, generally devoted to new, cutting edge, or unconventional forms of jazz, developed in these precincts. The loft performances

2. Many of these spaces were illegal as residences, studio space, or areas suitable for public performance, but after long battles with the bureaucrats of New York City, a certain amount of tolerance was permitted followed eventually by changes in the codes and regulations.
3. There were performances of musical theater as well. One of the pastors of Judson Church, Al Carmines, composed and produced a whole series of topical musical theater works at the church, which had a considerable following.

organized in the 1970s by saxophonist Sam Rivers at his Studio Rivbea were legendary. At another extreme, the Cage disciple Phil Corner regularly held events in his Soho loft, presenting performance and concept pieces of his own and of his colleagues that were attended by members of the downtown community including artists, writers, performers, and others. Activities and groups (Fluxus is a well-known example) that came out of this downtown scene were dedicated to a kind of performance art or theatrical actions that came close to theater and music theater.

The stylistic range of downtown was wide and included various varieties of performance and conceptual art. Among the major movements associated with New York loft culture, perhaps the best known is minimalism. The large industrial lofts were suitable for the production and display of large-scale works, and the constructions of art-world minimalists like Donald Judd, Richard Serra, Dan Flavin, John Chamberlain, Agnes Martin, Robert Smithson, Fred Sandback, and Sol LeWitt came out of the Soho lofts and galleries, which, unlike most conventional artist studios, were big enough to hold their oversize creations. When composers like Philip Glass and Steve Reich organized their own ensembles and began performing their phase and process music in these precincts, it was inevitable that the same name would also be applied to their work, and it was with the downtown New York community that this work first made its way (see Chapter 14).[4]

Another major development that came out of the loft, dance, and church scene was performance art. Although originally dominated by theater performers (monologists and other soloists; also the lively group known as "the new vaudevillians"), there was a strong music theater element in performance art from the start. Performance art was also closely associated with new dance, and when dance moved out of church basements and lofts into dedicated spaces like Dance Theater Workshop and the Joyce Theater, performance art and its associated music theater artists moved with them. The so-called Bessies (annual awards for modern dance) were quickly extended to include performance art. Two of the best known of these performers, working in a strongly musical or music-theater fashion, are Laurie Anderson, who is primarily a monologist mixing speaking, singing, and instrumental music with visuals (*United States*, 1983; *Stories from the Nerve Bible*, 1993), and Diamanda Galás, who makes extreme use of a classically trained voice along with electronic accompaniments and processing to create images of oppression and violence against women. She made her debut at Avignon in 1979 in a work of Vinko Globokar but has

4. Various sources credit Michael Nyman or Tom Johnson for having applied the name "minimalism" to what its American exponents prefer to call "process" or "phase music."

since created a series of her own works often collaging music from various sources. Other solo vocal performers who create their own work, many associated with the downtown performance scene, are treated in Chapter 17 on extended voice.

New performance spaces and complexes specialized for new music as well as for performance and media arts also sprang up and became important centers. The short-lived but influential Space for Innovative Development on the lower outskirts of midtown Manhattan was an old church complex that housed The Open Theater, the Alvin Nikolais Dance Company, Quog Music Theater, a jazz collective, the Multi-Gravitational Dance Company, and others. The list of active downtown performance spaces is a long one, and many of them—P.S. 122, The Kitchen, The Flea, Roulette, The Knitting Factory, Here and others—have continued over the years to offer extended programs of music, dance, performance art, and music theater.

Beyond Downtown: Brooklyn and out-of-town

Eventually, these movements expanded beyond the boundaries of downtown New York, in great part though the establishment of larger institutions. The best known of these is the Brooklyn Academy of Music (BAM), not far across the river. BAM, under the direction of Harvey Lichtenstein, was originally specialized in modern dance but early adapted itself to the creative work of theater and performance artists like Robert Wilson and Laurie Anderson. BAM's Next Wave Festival became a major showcase for innovative performance arts from all over the United States as well as from abroad. Miller Theater, under George Steele, and Symphony Space (and its downstairs Thalia Theater) are well-known performance spaces for new work on the upper west side of Manhattan (forming presumably the uptown branch of downtown). The American Music Theater Festival in Philadelphia (forty-five mainstage productions of varying size and character in more than a decade) was entirely devoted to music theater as an art form; however, it no longer exists in its original form. In recent years, the Lincoln Center Festival under Nigel Redden has hosted important new work often from abroad or from other parts of the United States and it has started to commission or co-commission new work. Other performing spaces scattered around the country (Minneapolis; Hartford, Connecticut; Ames, Iowa; Montclair, New Jersey; Los Angeles, etc.) have become important way stops for touring productions and also produce original work.

An important factor in the decentralization of artistic activity was the growth of the nonprofit regional theater around the country—in many ways an extension of off-Broadway. A number of these theaters—the American Repertory Theater in Cambridge, directed by Robert Brustein and more recently by avant-garde theater director Robert Woodruff, is an outstanding example—were and are hospitable to new music theater.

For a number of years, the Banff Center in Alberta, Canada, had a thriving music theater program (founded by Michael Bawtree), one of the most important and earliest defined programs of its kind in the Americas. Canada also has or has had several companies devoted to new opera and music theater, notably Montréal's *Chants Libres* and Toronto's *Tapestry*, *Autumn Leaf*, and *Music Gallery*.

The Left Coast

The Pacific coast of North America ("the Left Coast") has been an active center for new musical activity going at least as far back as the 1930s when many European emigré composers settled in the Los Angeles area. Among the maverick Americans who came from the West Coast, we can mention Henry Cowell, Harry Partch, John Cage, and Lou Harrison. Partch's last years were spent in La Jolla near San Diego where the local branch of the University of California at San Diego (UCSD) was a major center for contemporary music and new performance arts (Robert Erickson, Kenneth Gaburo, Roger Reynolds, and Pauline Oliveros). Reynolds, who was one of the founders of the ONCE Festival in Ann Arbor, Michigan (with Robert Ashley and Gordon Mumma), has written several music-theater pieces including *The Emperor of Ice Cream* (1962) and *I/O: A Ritual for 23 Performers* (1970). Oliveros, who was born in Texas and currently lives near Woodstock, New York, is known for her meditative and ceremonial pieces, which often include physical actions and audience participation.

Paul Dresher was born in Los Angeles; studied in San Diego with Erickson, Reynolds, and Oliveros (also in India, Africa, and Indonesia); and lives in San Francisco. He first came to prominence as the composer for the George Coates Ensemble, a group devoted to large-scale multi- or mixed-media performance pieces with strong visual elements: *The Way of How* (1981), *ave ave* (1983), *Seehear* (1984). Dresher, along with singer/composer Rinde Eckert, subsequently broke away from Coates, formed the Paul Dresher Ensemble, and created a series of music-theater pieces that included elements derived from rock music and contemporary themes, often with political implications: *Slow Fire* (1985–86), *Power Failure* (1989), and *Pioneers* (1989–90), all with Eckert as the leading performer. The single character of *Slow Fire*[5] is a Vietnam veteran trapped in the violence of his own imagination; it is scored for electric guitar, drums, and percussion.

---

5. There is a version for two characters but most productions of this work are Rinde Eckert monodramas.

Premiere of *Slow Fire*, Project Artaud, San Francisco, 1988; l. to r.: Paul Dresher, Rinde Eckert, and Gene Reffkin, drums. Photo: Marian Gray.

The Dresher Ensemble also produced work by other composers with rock/pop in their backgrounds, notably *Ravenshead* by Steven Mackay, a solo work for Eckert based on the true story of a sailor who appeared to have won a solo round-the-world sailing race by having radioed false positions; his boat was later found in the Atlantic with no sign of life aboard.

Eckert has increasingly appeared as a solo performance artist and his own work has included *And God Created Great Whales* (2000; commissioned by the Foundry Theatre and performed off-Broadway at the Bleecker Street Theater), in which he plays a composer racing to finish an opera based on Melville's *Moby Dick* before he loses his mental capacities. Other work has been created for the American Repertory Theater in Cambridge, Massachusetts (*Highway Ulysses* and *Orpheus X*) (see also Chapter 17).

Further Reading

Andran, Henri. *Total Art: Environments, Happenings, and Performance*. New York, 1974.

Gann, Kyle. *American Music in the Twentieth Century*. New York, 1997.

Kostelanetz, Richard. *The Theatre of Mixed Means: An Introduction to Happenings, Kinetic Environments and Other Mixed Means Performances*. New York, 1968.

Kostelanetz, Richard. *Esthetics Contemporary*. Buffalo, NY, 1978.

Kostelanetz, Richard. *Metamorphosis in the Arts: A Critical History of the 1960s*. Brooklyn, 1980.

Kostelanetz, Richard. *Writings on Glass: Essays, Interviews, Criticism*. New York, 1997.

Nyman, Michael. *Experimental Music: Cage and Beyond*, 2nd ed. New York, 1999.

Rockwell, John. *All American Music: Composition in the Late Twentieth Century* (New York, 1983).

chapter 14

Minimalism and Music Theater

What you see is what you see.

artist Frank Stella on minimalist art

Philip Glass

The arrival of minimalism on the new music scene in the 1960s marked a distinct break with the steady narrative of modernism as it developed out of twelve-tone music and the electronic music studios of the post–World War II period. Parallel in many ways to Stravinskyian neoclassicism after World War I, minimalism brought tonal centers back into contemporary music. The recognized classic of the genre was Terry Riley's *In C* dating from 1964, a piece based on the idea of musicians reconceptualizing—almost in a Cage-ian context—the notion of performing in C major. Sometimes the early work of Morton Feldman is associated with minimalism. Most of it uses a mixture of determined and nondetermined elements, but almost all of it is made out of soft, isolated and detached sounds from which any kind of process or structure has been removed, hence tonality is not a functional factor. Minimalism is here achieved by minimal amplitude, be it musical dynamic or of affirmative musical gesture, hence in some respect the opposite of the opera composer's "broad brush." More important in the nascent development of minimalism were the works of La Monte Young, whose early conceptual pieces inspired the Fluxus movement but who turned to stasis and long-held vocal drones from in the late 1950s onward.[1] An overt connection with neoclassicism came later and can be heard in many minimalist and minimalist-influenced works from John Adams to Michael Nyman. There are also connections with world music and with the more experimental precincts of pop music. Minimalism, based on phase and process, is not a style but a method or methods that can be applied to a variety of musical materials, styles, and esthetics.

Miminalism was born and long flourished outside the precincts of organized classical musical life, and its creation and diffusion rested largely on the composers themselves acting as performers or directing their own performance ensembles in the manner of pop groups or modern dance companies. The Philip Glass Ensemble built a substantial following for the music of its eponymous director by performing in downtown Manhattan lofts and galleries where the notion of minimalism first appeared in the art world. Glass was involved with the theater early in his career through his first wife, the director JoAnne Akalaitis, one of the founders of Mabou Mines, an experimental theater collective. Many of his stage works can be classified as music theater including *The Photographer* (1984; rev. 1996), a multimedia work with JoAnne Akalaitis; *1000 Airplanes on the Roof* (1988), with a text by playwright David Henry Wong based on the accounts of people claiming to have been kidnapped by aliens; and *Monsters of Grace* (1999), a multimedia collaboration with Robert Wilson. Glass has also written some twelve operas, mostly for traditional opera house performance as well as several works for live performance with film in the manner of a live sound track.

Standing halfway between the music-theater works and the operas is the piece that many consider Glass's masterpiece, the work that took minimalism out of downtown and onto a world stage. *Einstein on the Beach* was a close collaboration from its inception between Glass and Robert Wilson. Wilson was already known for his huge, static—one could also say minimalist—stage works often designated as operas although, in at least one case, there was no music at all. Much of Wilson's work had been based on historical figures like Queen Victoria and Joseph Stalin, and the new collaborators considered Chaplin, Hitler, and Gandhi before they agreed on Albert Einstein. Another essential part of Wilson's work

1. These works also included slowly changing visual elements by the artist Marian Zazeela and were a direct influence on Stockhausen's *Stimmung*, composed after hearing one of Young's drone pieces.

that was also congenial to Glass was the substantial length that would permit a leisurely unfolding of the scenic and musical elements of the pieces; *Einstein* lasts five hours, not particularly long for a Wilson piece of that time.[2] The scenes—Train 1, Trial 1, Night Train, Trial 2/Prison, Building, Spaceship—were connected by dances and also by the so-called *Knee Plays*, Wilson's term for the mostly spoken texts with music, performed downstage to permit the all-important scene changes. Aside from Einstein himself (who appears in costume and plays the violin at intervals throughout) and a few prototypical figures, there are no characters and there is no plot and no written text. Wilson provided a series of "story boards" or drawings, which serve as the "libretto." The idea was that the structure of the music was to be closely interwoven with the stage action and lighting.

The entire piece could be considered a poetic meditation on the march of technology from steam locomotive to spaceship, and the work ends with a clear reference to a nuclear holocaust. On the way, there is an ominous trial scene whose significance is never explained. Many of the spoken words are by Christopher Knowles, a neurologically impaired young man with whom Wilson had worked during his days as a teacher of mentally handicapped children (this was a formative experience for him). Glass also uses numbers or *solfège* syllables as texts in very effective and characteristic ways. The musical techniques are based on a relatively few elements worked up to a jewel-like perfection and at high levels of delay, buildup, and forward motion. Repetition of small modules is organized by additive processes (the slow addition or subtraction of notes to a basic pattern) or cyclical structures (simultaneous rhythmic patterns of different lengths that get out of phase and eventually back in synch).[3] A major character of the work is the pulsing, forward motion, which alternates with droning, static sections. This produces juxtapositions, intense detail, and an extended musico-dramatic movement that sets up the long corridors of time passing that characterize the work. Although productions have always been in a traditional proscenium theater (virtually a necessity for Wilson's concepts of design, lighting, and staging), the time span itself and the fact that the audience is allowed to come and go from their seats ad libitum during the multi-hour process go a long way toward defeating the norms and expectations of traditional theater.

2. The recorded versions were shortened by Glass himself to fit on vinyl discs. The later CD version is somewhat more complete but still not at the full length of the theatrical version.
3. Hence the terms Phase and Process Music.

Robert Wilson: Trial scene from *Einstein on the Beach*. Drawing courtesy Robert
Wilson & Byrd Hoffman Watermill Foundation, © 1976 Babette Mangolte &
Byrd Hoffman Watermill Foundation; © 1976 Philippe Gras & Byrd Hoffman
Watermill Foundation, 1976; © 1976 Byrd Hoffman Watermill Foundation 1976.

From music theater to grand opera

Although *Einstein on the Beach* is often referred to as an opera, it has few characteristics of traditional opera other than excessive length. In addition to there being no plot or through-written text/libretto, there is no heroic vocal writing for standardized operatic vocal types; instead the small group of nonoperatic vocalists is stationed in the pit with the instrumental ensemble. In addition to Einstein the violinist, the orchestra consists of the Philip Glass Ensemble—electronic keyboards, amplified flute, saxophones, clarinets, plus amplified voice. The premiere was at the Avignon Festival and in spite of its size, the work toured widely. The American premiere was at the Metropolitan Opera but it was produced by Wilson's own organization and was not (as is sometimes assumed) a production or presentation of the Metropolitan Opera; later revivals were at the Brooklyn Academy of Music (BAM), Wilson's home stage in New York.

Most of Glass's later stage work—notably *Satyagraha* and *Akhnaton*—are in the vein of traditional opera with defined roles written for trained operatic voices in the traditional categories and accompanied by standard orchestral and choral forces; unlike *Einstein*, they were intended to be produced in opera houses by opera companies. Nevertheless, there are music-theater elements even in these and other later work. *Satyagraha*, for example, has a specific subject (Gandhi's early career in Africa) and there are specified roles. But it is also nonlinear in many respects. The libretto is taken from the *Bhagavad Gita* and is sung in Sanskrit all the way through so that there is a detachment between what the singers are saying and what they are doing. Even where the texts may form a commentary on the action, no modern audience will understand them in performance.

John Adams, another major composer associated with the early group of minimalists, is well known for his theatrical works, but most of these belong to history of opera. The best known (*Nixon in China,* 1987; *The Death of Klinghoffer,* 1991) are collaborations with stage director Peter Sellars who took an *auteur* role in selecting the subject matter and putting together the creative team (writer Alice Goodman, composer John Adams, director Peter Sellars, choreographer Mark Morris). *Doctor Atomic* (San Francisco, 2005) and *A Flowering Tree* (Vienna, 2006) have librettos by Sellars himself and Lucinda Childs as the choreographer. All of these works have defined roles written for trained operatic voices in the standard categories and accompanied by a largely standard pit orchestra. They also use story librettos based roughly on relatively recent historical events of contemporary significance (these works and others of similar inspiration have been dubbed "CNN Operas"). Nevertheless, these are far from *verismo* operas or operatic music dramas in the post-Wagnerian mode. They are informed by a music-theater sensibility in the way they adapt news events of relatively recent vintage and in the striking sectional form that Sellars (and Alice Goodman) have developed. This permits Adams to use closed forms and a kind of abstract and gestural musical style that owes something to Stravinsky and Weill.[4]

Steve Reich

The early work of Steve Reich uses recorded vocal texts that are looped in a series of overlapped cycles on a time delay. In 1966, however, the composer founded his own ensemble, Steve Reich and Musicians, and most of his music after that date is instrumental or uses voices mainly as part of the instrumental ensemble. Unlike his colleagues, he came to theater rather late and then in a rather different form. Both of Reich's collaborations with his wife, video artist Beryl Korot, might be described as multimedia works, updated descendants of the multi- or mixed media form that was so popular in the 1960s (see Chapter 18). As in older works of the genre, *The Cave* and *Three Tales* use text, visuals, and sung and instrumental music without a narrative or plot to hold things together or drive them forward. In these so-called video operas, unity is achieved by the use of a focused, thematic subject matter and by techniques of integrating what is seen and heard through new methods of exploring the music of language, a theme that was important in Reich's early work and to which he now returned.

The Cave (1990–93), described as a "music and video theatre work," is based on video-taped interviews and commentaries with and by Israelis, Palestinians, and Americans concerning the reputed burial place of the patriarch Abraham at Hebron, Israel, and the biblical stories of Abraham, Sarah, Ishmael, and Isaac, common to the history and beliefs of both Muslims and Jews. In addition to the interviews, texts from the Bible and the Koran are also used. Adapting a technique he first used in his *Different Trains,* Reich has sampled the speaking voices of the subjects of these videos and by modulating the sound with electronic/digital controls, he has turned them into a musical score for four singing voices, woodwinds, percussion, keyboards, and solo strings. The musical score is performed simultaneously with a six-screen projection and multi-channel sound play-back of the videos.

The more recent *Three Tales* (2002), described as "a documentary digital video opera," is a similar work but with some differences. The underlying

4. Sellars and Adams did attempt a music-theater work in a popular mode, *I Was Looking at the Ceiling and Then I Saw the Sky* (1995), with a libretto by June Jordan and a cast of pop singers accompanied by synthesized sound and a rock band; it was not considered very successful.

Scene from *The Cave* by Steve Reich and Beryl Korot, showing video projections and live performers, London 2006. Photo: Ben Rubin.

subject matter is oddly close to that of *Einstein on the Beach*. The widespread, pervasive, and eventually dangerous growth of new technologies is shown through three events of the last century: the Hindenburg disaster of 1937 when the giant German Zeppelin, pride of the Nazis, exploded and burned in New Jersey; the atom bomb tests on the Bikini atoll in 1946–1954 (and the accompanying dislocation of the native residents of these islands); and the cloning of the sheep Dolly in 1997. Each of the tales forms an act and uses a video that mixes historical film, contemporary videos, interviews, photographs, texts, and other material created and recreated with the computer, transferred to video, and projected onto a single large screen. The live musicians—two sopranos and three tenors plus four percussionists, two keyboardists, and a string quartet abetted by recorded audio—perform a score that is also partly derived from the spoken material but is more music driven. Among other things, there are the following: a riff on Wagner; settings of the two creation stories from Genesis in the original Hebrew; and some new text/music techniques that include something Reich calls "slow motion sound" (in which the subjects being photographed are shown in slow motion without changing their pitch) and "freeze frame sound" (in which a single vowel or consonant is extended for long periods of time). In both works, all the live musicians—singers and instrumentalists—are amplified. Unlike Philip Glass who has moved to operatic voices in his theater, Reich describes the singing style required for these works as somewhere between Alfred Deller and Ella Fitzgerald—that is, between early music and jazz.

The spread of minimalism

A number of other composers in the minimalist orbit (or strongly influenced by minimalism) have ventured into the realm of new opera and music theater. The three founders of the New York ensemble *Bang on a Can*—Michael Gordon, David Lang, and Julia Wolfe—comprise a kind of second generation, hard-edged, more angular version of minimalism. All three collaborated musically with cartoonist Ben Katchor and experimental theater director Bob McGrath on a music theater work entitled *The Carbon Copy Building* based on Katchor's *Village Voice* strip entitled "Julius Knipl, Real Estate Photographer." The work, scored for four non-operatic singers (each taking several different roles) and four instruments (electric guitar, percussion, keyboard, and clarinet), makes use of low-tech projections to screen Katchor's cynical and amusing view of two identical structures in two very different neighborhoods of old New York. The result is a comic strip piece that is part opera, part show, and part funky social commentary. Lang has also recently collaborated with experimental playwright Mac Wellman on *The Difficulty of Crossing a Field,* based on an Ambrose Bierce story about the disappearance of a slave owner from his Alabama plantation in 1854.

Scene from *The Carbon Copy Building,* libretto and drawings by Ben Katchor, music by Michael Gordon, David Lang, and Julia Wolfe. With the kind permission of Bang-on-a-Can.

Minimalism has had an influence in northern and Eastern Europe where it has taken on particular local forms. Louis Andriessen came out of the serialist orbit but broke away for a complex of political and esthetic motives. He has been influenced by jazz and also developed his own European style of minimalism—dryer, grittier, more hard-edged than the usual American version. The energy and independence of his music have been very influential on younger composers in Northern Europe, many of whom have studied with him. Many of his earlier works are specifically designated as music theater although they almost never have conventional dramaturgy. His trilogy of pieces for voices and ensemble, *De Tijd* ("Time"; 1979–81), *De Snelheid* ("Speed" or "Velocity"; 1982–83) and *De Materie* ("Matter"; 1984–88), have a kind of monumental oratorio-like theatricality, and his collaborations with the British filmmaker Peter Greenaway—*Rosa: A Horse Drama* (1994) and *Writing to Vermeer* (1998)—are, at the very least, nontraditional operas in an aggressively theatrical mode. Andriessen's use of percussion and a varied instrumentation as well as his insistence on amplified, nonvibrato voices, also can be considered music-theater choices (see also Chapter 12).

The British composer Michael Nyman, best known for his film scores, has also written extensively for dance and theater in minimalist style that is more strongly based on European tradition than that of his American colleagues. His best-known theatrical work—perhaps more of a miniature opera than a music-theater work—is *The Man Who Mistook His Wife for a Hat* (1986) with a text of Christopher Rawlence based on a famous case study by neurologist and author Dr. Oliver Sacks (see also Chapter 12). Other British composers influenced by minimalism include Gavin Bryars, who has written three operas, and John Tavener, whose dramatic cantata *The Whale* (based on the biblical story of Jonah) was performed by the London Sinfonietta in 1968. Tavener, who joined the Russian Orthodox Church in 1977, was strongly influenced by its musical traditions, and his music is related to Eastern European minimalism. Like Tavener, Polish composer Henryk Górecki, Georgian Giya Kancheli, and Estonian Arvo Pärt are known for their religious, not theatrical, works; however, Kanchali has written an opera entitled *Music for the Living* (1982–1984) and music for dozens of films. Pärt's evocative music also has been popular with film directors, although little or none of it was actually written to be used in films.

German minimalism also has a national twist. Stockhausen's *Stimmung* absorbed the conceptual minimalism of Cage, Young, and Fluxus, which reappears also in the spiritual shift that informs his later work. Another flavor of minimalism was the so-called *Neue Einfachheit* or "New Simplicity" and which includes the work of such composers as Wilhelm

Killmayer, Wolfgang Rihm, Wolfgang von Schweinitz, Detlev Müller-Siemens, Manfred Trojahn, Peter Michael Hamel, Hans Christian von Dadelsen, and Hans-Jürgen von Bose. The compositional style vaguely connects back to the works of Hindemith and Karl Amadeus Hartmann, who had been discarded as "modern composers" by the Darmstadteers in the early 1950s. The *New Simplicists* adopted traditionalist notation along with quotations of romantic music—a German intellectual's interpretion of simplicity. This musical style, avoiding the ivory tower trap of conceptualization, suits the musico-theatrical situation more obviously than the avant-garde. Composers like Rihm, Bose, and Trojahn have actually done important pieces for the (German) *Musiktheater* scene.

Probably the biggest single influence of minimalism on music theater has been the reintroduction of modal/tonal elements, particularly into vocal performance. Closely connected to this is the dominance of nonclassical vocal techniques, many of which are related to early music, jazz, or pop vocalism and often employing microphone amplification. The composer-based ensemble using electronic and amplified instruments, extensive percussion, and amplified voices is a major element in much minimalist music and dovetails easily with the non-orchestral character of music theater and its characteristic use of theater and pop voices.

Further Reading

Mertens, Wim. *American Minimal Music*. London, 1983.
Potter, Keith. *Four Musical Minimalists: La Monte Young, Terry Riley, Steve Reich, Philip Glass*. New York, 2000.
Schwarz, K. Robert. *Minimalists*. London, 1996.

chapter 15

The Show Must Go On

Yeah yeah, whoa wo oh oh Ooh, I'll top the bill, I'll overkill
I have to find the will to carry on On with the show

from "The Show Must Go On" by Queen,
sung by Freddie Mercury

Songspiel and vaudeville; Kurt Weill

The disappearance of popular song from the stage and the separation of musical theater from the music hall, vaudeville, and cabaret entertainments with which it was formerly allied are subjects that are mostly beyond the scope of this volume. What can be said is that the separation has been accelerated by the independent development of mass media (film and television) but that it had been in progress long before the twentieth century. Popular song disappeared early from the Italian operatic stage and French court opera but held on in the *singspiel*, in the English ballad opera, and in eighteenth-century popular theater. It returned briefly to the opera in the early Romantic period but was overwhelmed by the operetta (more a middle-class than a truly popular entertainment) and was finally submerged by the esthetic of Wagnerian and post-Wagnerian music drama. It had so totally disappeared by the 1920s that its revival—in Europe at least—took on political as well as esthetic significance. Adorno, Schoenberg, and Boulez all took the point of view that folk, popular, pop, and/or non-Western musics were played out artistically and compromised by having been commercialized so that they could no longer be relevant to contemporary music.[1] Brecht, Weill, their followers in the theater, and the folk and rock musicians of another era had a different opinion.

The origins of the *Songspiel* or "Song Play" can be found in six poems of Bertolt Brecht concerning the founding of the imaginary Florida city of *Mahagonny*. Originally, Brecht sang these songs to his own tunes, accompanying himself on the guitar.[2] The 1927 Donaueschingen Festival was devoted to music theater (the subject was in the air) and Brecht and Weill were commissioned to write a one-act music-theater work. Weill composed new settings for the *Mahagonny* poems, connecting them with instrumental interludes. Brecht turned this into a miniature theater piece by staging it in a boxing ring, evoking a sporting event that was popular with the masses. Brecht had a theory about *Spass* (usually translated as "fun" although "enjoyment" might be a better, if less proletarian, English version); since music, theater, and boxing all provided a measure of *Spass*, it made sense to combine them all in a single work. This was, of course, entertainment with an edge as well as a "think-about-it" component, ideas that led on to notions of irony (the famous *Verfremdungseffekt* or "alienation effect") and the *Lehrstück* or "teaching piece."

Mahagonny was shortly followed by the *Dreigroschenoper*, the *Threepenny Opera*, adapted from John Gay's *Beggar's Opera* and apparently co-authored with Elizabeth Hauptmann but credited exclusively to Brecht. The eighteenth-century original used popular melodies of the day, and following this logic, the latter-day version employed a sequence of bitter, ironic, jazz-tinged musical numbers scattered throughout. Except for one quotation from the old piece, all the music was newly composed, but like the popular and folk melodies used by Gay, these were kept simple enough to be sung by actors rather than trained singers. Oddly enough, this work was not originally part of the planned collaboration between writer and composer but was thrown together in great haste for a Berlin theater that had a production fall by the wayside. The idea of an "opera for actors" was not so much a politico-esthetic inspiration of the authors as a given under

1. There is a lack of distinction between the terms for folk and popular music in many European languages and this was compounded by a confusion about the differences between jazz, pop song, show music, rock, and commercial music—not so much in the popular ear but in the critical community (with Adorno as perhaps the worst offender).

2. The songs and the tunes can be found in the Brecht *Hauptpostille*, a collection of his early poetry in the form of a chapbook or pseudo-hymnal. Brecht's melody for the Alabama-Song is the basis of Kurt Weill's setting, a fact that has been used to demonstrate both Brecht's influence on Weill and also Weill's vast musical superiority in transforming the material.

the circumstances. Another given was the small orchestra of eight musicians, not a theater orchestra but a clone of one of the popular German dance bands of the day trying to pump out their best versions of what they thought was American jazz. In short, Weill turned these possible negatives into major assets, and some of the numbers of this *Songspiel* quickly turned into real hits. Among the many well-known songs, perhaps the best known is the so-called *Moritat vom Mackie Messer* (Mack the Knife) sung by a street singer to open the performance. The *Moritat* was the traditional German popular ballad, which, like the Anglo-Irish topical ballad, was based on a sensational subject—murder, rape, blighted love, disaster. In the German tradition, the street singer often also used crudely painted canvases to depict, explain, or highlight his stories, which were often accompanied by a hurdy-gurdy and invariably ended with a moral. All these "primitive" or popular elements were invoked in Brecht's text, Weill's music, and Caspar Neher's staging design. The score also used neo-baroque elements in a dissonant modernist counterpoint that complemented or extended the songs.

Ironically (the word is a propos), this hastily thrown together work proved to be one of the greatest popular successes of the twentieth century. Literally thousands of performances were racked up within a year. Not even the biggest Broadway hit can boast those kinds of numbers, but Broadway shows are generally restricted to one theater while the *Dreigroschenoper* was played all over German-speaking Europe and eventually all over the world. Its tunes were immediately picked up by the popular German jazz and dance bands, a film version and various recordings appeared in short order, and it has been in virtually continuous production ever since.

Happy End was an attempted sequel using an American gangster story cribbed from Damon Runyon's *Guys and Dolls* by Elizabeth Hauptmann writing under the nom de plume of Dorothy Lane. Even though it has some of Weill's best songs, it was a major failure. This is usually attributed to the fact that the opening night performance concluded with Helene Weigl, Brecht's wife, declaiming a Communist tract from the stage, a largely irrelevant provocation that turned the public and the critics against the piece. It is, unfortunately, the songs that are irrelevant, an overenthusiastic example perhaps of the *Verfremdungseffekt*. In *Mahagonny*, the show was built around the songs. In *Happy End*, great songs seem to have been tossed willy-nilly into a so-so script.

Weill then turned his attention to producing an operatic version (or, as it turned out, several versions) of *Mahagonny*. Although Brecht wrote a substantial libretto (again aided by Elizabeth Hauptmann), he did not like Weill's operatic ambitions. Opera for Brecht was "culinary" (the bourgeois hedonist's multi-course dinner cooked up by formula) and he was particularly disdainful of the composer's use of a large orchestra; he much

Wedding scene from the original Berlin production of the Kurt Weill/Bertolt Brecht *Dreigroschenoper (Threepenny Opera)*. Note the use of painted drops with images and texts in the tradition of the *moritaten*. Theater am Schiffbau-erdamm, Berlin (1928), Erich Engel, director; Caspar Neher, set design. Photo courtesy of the Kurt Weill Foundation.

preferred the broken-down sound of the eight-player dance band. He also, no doubt, did not appreciate the composer's much greater importance and power in the opera house. Weill later set a few more of Brecht's lyrics, but with the single exception of the unclassifiable *Die Sieben Todsünden*, written in exile, *Mahagonny* was their last music-theater collaboration.

Die sieben Todsünden der Kleinbürger (to give the work its full title which translates as "The Seven Deadly Sins of the Petty Bourgeoisie") came about because of a commission from an English impresario who was trying to impress his dancer girlfriend. Both composer and writer had fled the new Nazi regime in Germany and the work was performed in Paris in 1933. Ironically, this final collaboration proved to be their most original, harking back in many ways to the first version of *Mahagonny*. There is no conventional narrative and the casting is unusual. The lead role of Anna is divided between a dancer and a singer (Anna I and Anna II), and the members of the family—father, mother, and siblings—are played by a male quartet. The series of vocal numbers are connected by powerful orchestral interludes, which also serve to accompany the dance.

Shortly thereafter, Weill emigrated to New York where he became a major figure in the Broadway musical theater before his early death in 1950. Brecht also ended up in America, but after a period in California trying to get work in Hollywood (and an attempt to get Weill to write a Broadway score for a newly revised musical version of his *Der gute Mensch von Sezuan*), he was called up before the infamous House Un-American Activities Committee of the United States Congress and after giving ambiguous testimony almost immediately went back to Europe, returning to the newly founded Deutsche Demokratische Republik where he founded and directed the famous Berliner Ensemble. The standard European view of the work of these two men long favored Brecht, whose effect on theater grew all through the latter half of the century. Weill's influence continued to be strong in America, both in popular music and in the musical theater world. But even as his music, his ideas, and his influence were taken seriously in New York, the Adorno view,[3] that his American productions are inferior and more commercial than his European work, was widespread in Europe and has only recently begun to be questioned. As Brecht has become a classic and a historic phenomenon, his theoretical influence has receded. Weill has also reached the status of a classic and even his lesser-known work is often revived but his active influence remains strong in the English-speaking world, less so in Europe.

Theater opera on Broadway

The Broadway scene that Kurt Weill entered in the mid-1930s was by no means the purely commercial arena that has sometimes been depicted. Social consciousness, left activism, and high-art modernism rubbed elbows with popular dramas, comedies, musical revues, serious imports from Britain and Europe, and even a certain measure of classic drama. The arrival of refugees in increasing numbers provided a certain amount of new blood and an increasing level of sophistication. Finally, the musical theater experienced a boom with a number of serious attempts to raise the level to high-art standards. This meant musicals that flirted with modernism, *engagé* subjects, and operatic dimensions.

One of the first attempts to introduce modernist music-theater ideas to Broadway was perhaps the most unlikely: Virgil Thomson's setting of Gertrude Stein's *Four Saints in Three Acts* for an all-black cast. This diatonic score with its references to American hymnody and folk song was by no means retrograde and it anticipates latter-day minimalism in many respects. The abstract and surrealist nature of the piece, the sets made out

3. Originally stated in Adorno's 1950 obituary of Weill in the *Frankfurter Rundschau*.

of cellophane, and the partly colloquial singing styles added up to a work that was out of sync with the notions of what constituted opera, romantic or modern, but it hardly constituted commercial musical comedy. It had its premiere in 1934 as part of a series of performances entitled *Friends and Enemies of Modern Music* at the Wadsworth Atheneum in Hartford, Connecticut, and then, surprisingly, transferred shortly thereafter to a Broadway theater. This unprecedented move created a good deal of stir, and in its curious way, it paved the way for other things to follow. *Porgy and Bess*, another work with an all-black cast, this one by the Gershwin brothers with playwright Dubose Heyward and poet Langston Hughes, was produced on Broadway in 1935, its original operatic form having been cut down to musical theater dimensions.[4] Weill's *Johnny Johnson* and Blitzstein's *The Cradle Will Rock,* both with political agendas, appeared a year later. A series of operatic or semi-operatic productions in New York theaters followed, including Douglas Moore's *The Devil and Daniel Webster* (1938; after Stephen Vincent Benét), Benjamin Britten's *Paul Bunyan* (1941; text by W. H. Auden) and *The Rape of Lucretia* (1946), Jerome Moross's *The Golden Apple* (1954; text by John La Touche), and most of the major works of Gian Carlo Menotti, including *The Medium* (1946), *The Consul* (1950), and *The Saint of Bleecker Street* (1954), all to his own librettos. To this list should be added Duke Ellington's large-scale but unsuccessful version of *The Beggar's Opera* (*Beggar's Holiday*; 1946, text by John Latouche) and the generally successful attempts of Richard Rodgers to create popular works on serious themes with both Lorenz Hart (*Pal Joey,* 1940) and Oscar Hammerstein (*Oklahoma!,* 1943; *Carousel,* 1945; *South Pacific,* 1949; *The King and I,* 1951; and an ambitious high-toned failure by the musical name of *Allegro,* 1947). Although these works differ in many ways, they all employ some kind of popular vocabulary in an extended form with music as a driving force—often *the* driving force—of the dramaturgy. Many of them are through-composed or at the very least employ extended musical development well beyond the simpler requirements of good theater songwriting. Taken together, they constitute a kind of movement to produce music theater of substance in the context of a highly commercial theater environment. It is of note that this activity all dates from the same decade and a half that marks Kurt Weill's American years.

The American Kurt Weill

Kurt Weill came to New York in 1935 to write the music for *The Eternal Road,* a hugely ambitious (overly ambitious some would say) theatrical

---

4. The Metropolitan Opera had expressed interest, but no opera company in the 1935 world was capable of putting an all-black cast on the stage.

pageant on the theme of the Jewish diaspora with a libretto by novelist Franz Werfel and produced and staged by another *emigré*, the flamboyant German director/producer Max Reinhardt. Weill was also involved early on with the activist Group Theater and wrote the music for a surrealist anti-war piece entitled *Johnny Johnson* (1935). Several major Broadway hits followed: *Knickerbocker Holiday* (1938; with the well-known playwright Maxwell Anderson), *Lady in the Dark* (1941; book by Moss Hart, lyrics by Ira Gershwin), and *One Touch of Venus* (1948; with a famous *New Yorker* poet of light verse, Ogden Nash). These were all popular pieces on topical themes: freedom, feminism, and bourgeois conformity.

Much of Weill's later work falls into the theater opera category and includes a highly influential slice of urban life called *Street Scene* (1947; with Elmer Rice and Langston Hughes, the not-so-distant ancestor of *West Side Story*); a folk opera based on the well-known American folk tune *Down in the Valley* (1948; text by Arnold Sundgaard); and *Lost in the Stars* (1949), an anti-apartheid South African story adapted by Maxwell Anderson from the novel by Alan Paton.

Weill took his place in New York theater quickly and easily and he took his task very seriously. He was in touch with major writers and theater artists almost immediately and recruited some of the best of them to be his American collaborators. He was a prominent and public advocate for the idea that the popular musical theater vernacular could evolve into the New World equivalent of what opera had been in the Old and, it should be added, many of these works are still performed.

There are two major landmarks in Weill's American history that lie somewhat outside the theater opera scenario. One, already mentioned, is Marc Blitzstein's translation of the *Dreigroschenoper*, which ran in a down-town (i.e., off-Broadway) New York theater for 2,611 performances over a period of eight years starting in 1954. Blitzstein, who was Weill's first and most important American disciple, created a small body of *engagé* popular work that is occasionally produced, but he is mostly remembered for his *Threepenny Opera*. The adaptation made changes that were heavily criti-cized by the Weill/Brecht purists (although, in fact, there have been many versions of this work over the years). But they made the work accessible to the New York audience for the first time. Weill's wife, Lotte Lenya, played the whorehouse madam and was given the *Pirate Jenny* song, which she sang nightly to powerful effect.[5] As pointed out earlier, this production is often considered one of the cornerstones of off-Broadway as a modern theater phenomenon in New York. To some degree The Living Theater,

5. Her success in this role enabled her to resume her career in the theater, in film, and in the recording studio.

the Open Theater, La MaMa, Theater for the New City, Mabou Mines, the Ontological-Hysterical Theater, the Performance Group (later renamed the Wooster Group), and all their contemporaries and successors are its offspring.

Love Life, which appeared on Broadway in 1948, is perhaps the oddest and the most original of Weill's American works. It is also simultaneously one of the least well-known and most influential of his works, a paradox that can be explained by the fact that it had a big effect inside the profession but was not well remembered by the public. It appeared during a recording strike and, as a result, there was no cast album. It is the least operatic of Weill's later works but it requires very large performing forces, so its potential outside the precincts of Broadway is limited and it has never had a Broadway revival.[6] The subject of Alan Jay Lerner's libretto is the battle of the sexes set against a huge panorama of American economic and political history. The whole show— and it is truly a "show"—is cast in the form or forms of a traditional

"Punch and Judy Get a Divorce," ballet from the 1948 Broadway premiere of *Love Life*, book and lyrics by Alan Jay Lerner, music by Kurt Weill; Elia Kazan, director; Boris Aronson, set design; Michael Kidd, choreographer. Photo courtesy of the Kurt Weill Foundation.

6. There was a major revival at the American Music Theater Festival in Philadelphia in 1990.

vaudeville *olio* or music-hall variety show,[7] complete with master of ceremonies, jazz band, black and white vocal ensembles, magic act, solo and ensemble dance numbers, lots of songs, hymns and gospels, specialty solos, a high wire act, a minstrel show, and so-called blackout scenes of drama and comedy, with or without musical numbers. Some of the flavor of this piece can be gathered from the black vocal quartet that comments on the preceding scene by singing a number entitled "Economics"; the punch line is "... good for economics but awful bad for love."

Weill (and Lerner) had invented what came to be known as the *concept musical*. This idea influenced a generation or two of the more innovative theater artists of Broadway including Bob Fosse, Harold Prince, Tom O'Horgan, Stephen Schwartz, Stephen Sondheim, and their successors.

The Weill heritage

The downtown theater movements of the 1960s involved the creation and production of small-scale music theater in a popular mode. This was a continuation or resumption of the small-scale and political music-theater movements of the 1930s but also in the direct line of Kurt Weill and the Weill/Brecht collaborations. Weill's major American disciple, Marc Blitzstein, wrote and composed *The Cradle Will Rock* in 1936–37. This was a kind of political cartoon in music-theater form about a steel-worker strike; it was produced by Orson Welles's Mercury Theater with funding from the federal Works Progress Administration. The day it was scheduled to open in New York, the federal funding was blocked by a group of right-wing congressmen, the theater contract was abrogated, and both musicians and cast were forbidden to go on stage. Literally at the last minute, with the cast and public already gathered at the now-closed theater, Welles found an available theater and marched everyone to the new locale. Blitzstein, seated at an old upright piano on an empty stage, was prepared to play and sing the entire work by himself but the cast, scattered throughout the house, stood and sang on cue from their seats. The effect was sensational; the story made the front page of the New York papers and ensured the success of the work, which was, ever after, performed with upright piano accompanying a cast on rough benches with no sets or elaborate costumes.[8] Blitzstein's

7. The word "olio" means a jumble, a mixture, a mélange of things. It was used in vaudeville to refer to a variety show made up of various skits, musical numbers, and specialty acts.
8. The story is told, with some embellishment and chronological shifts, in the Tim Robbins film *Cradle Will Rock* (1999).

later work—*No for an Answer* (1941; in a mode similar to *Cradle*); *Regina* (1949), an operatic version of *The Little Foxes* by Lillian Hellman; *Ruben, Ruben* (1955); *Juno* (1959; based on Sean O'Casey); and *Sacco and Vanzetti* (1959–64; commissioned by the Metropolitan Opera but left incomplete at his death)—continued to have resonance in the New York musical theater, although none of it ever quite equaled the impact of his *Threepenny Opera* translation. Blitzstein was a close friend and colleague of Leonard Bernstein,[9] and there is a direct line to works of Bernstein like *On the Town* (1944), *Wonderful Town* (1953), and especially, *West Side Story* (1957). Stephen Sondheim, who wrote the lyrics for *West Side Story*, picked up the torch as a composer in music-driven works like *Company* (1970), *Follies* (1971), *Pacific Overtures* (1976), *Sweeney Todd* (1979), *Sunday in the Park with George* (1984), *Assassins* (1990), *Passion* (1994), and others. The post-Sondheim generation of Bill Finn, Michael John LaChiusa, Adam Guettel, and Jonathan Larson continues to dominate the serious side of New York musical theater.[10]

Weill's influence on popular music and musical theater has never entirely disappeared. It continues to resonate in the New York theater in populist pieces with social themes like *Cabaret* and *Chicago* (1966 and 1975; both by John Kander and Fred Ebb), the Sahl/Salzman collaborations (*The Conjurer, 1975; Stauf, 1976; Civilization and Its Discontents, 1977; Noah, 1978; and The Passion of Simple Simon, 1979*), the musicals of Bill Finn (*In Trousers, 1979; March of the Falsettos, 1981; America Kicks Up Its Heels, 1983; Falsettoland, 1990; The Twenty-fifth Annual Putnam County Spelling Bee, 2005*), Mikel Rouse's *Dennis Cleveland* (1996; a "talk-show opera" inspired by the Jerry Springer TV show),[11] Jonathan Larson's *Rent* (1996), Adam Guettel's *Floyd Collins* (with Tina Landau; 1994), Michael John LaChiusa's *The Wild Party* (with George C. Wolfe based on the verse novel of Joseph Moncure March; 2000), and even recent off-Broadway pieces like *Urinetown* (1999; Mark Hollmann and Greg Kotis) and *Avenue Q* (2003; Robert Lopez, Jeff Marx, and Jeff Whitty). This kind of performance piece—small scale with social commentary, unsentimental music, and some measure of non-linear, satirical bite—has retained its cachet as the leading edge of musical theater in New York.

9. One of Bernstein's earliest successes as a conductor was directing a production of *The Cradle Will Rock* at Harvard University.
10. It is notable that although Sondheim began in the Broadway theater as a protégé of Oscar Hammerstein II, his recent work and that of the post-Sondheim group has found a more congenial home in the precincts of off-Broadway and its London equivalent.
11. Not to be confused with *Jerry Springer: The Opera* by Richard Thomas from England (2002).

Although the major impact of Weill was on the musical theater, there has also been more than a trace of influence on the course of new opera in the United States. William Bolcom's first collaboration with Arnold Weinstein was a surrealist anti-war music-theater piece in a *Dr. Strangelove* mode entitled *Dynamite Tonight* (1963). This very Kurtweillian work, which had a long and checkered history off-Broadway and in regional theater, was followed by *Greatshot* (1967–69), commissioned by the Yale Repertory Theater, and a series of cabaret songs, which have been very widely performed. Subsequently, the Bolcom/Weinstein collaboration moved toward the classical musical with *Casino Paradise* (1990; commissioned by the American Music Theater Festival) and opera with *McTeague* (1990–92; with Robert Altman), *A View from the Bridge* (1997–98; adapted from the Arthur Miller play with Miller's participation), and *A Wedding* (2004; again, a collaboration with Altman after one of his films).

There is a trace of Weill influence on Anthony Davis, whose opera on the life of Malcolm X—entitled simply *X*—was premiered at the American Music Theater Festival in 1985 and later performed at the New York City Opera. Other operatic works of Davis include *Under the Double Moon* (1989; a science fiction opera with a libretto by Deborah Atherton), *Tania* (American Music Theater Festival, 1992; a theater opera about Patty Hearst with a libretto by Michael-John La Chiusa), and *Amistad* (Chicago Lyric Opera in 1997; libretto by Thulani Davis about a slaveship uprising). He also wrote the music for Tony Kushner's play *Angels in America: Millenium Approaches* and *Perestroika* (1993).[12] Davis, who had his own improvisational ensemble, *Episteme*, has made it a practice to include improvisational elements in his operas although the overt references to jazz in his work are restricted and generally have dramatic significance (i.e., the scenes of Malcolm X as a street hustler).

Weill also has continued to influence more than one generation of pop and jazz performers, mostly from the serious side of folk and rock. *Lost in the Stars*, an album of Weill interpretations by a variety of contemporary, jazz, and pop artists, including Sting, Marianne Faithfull, Van Dyke Parks, Henry Threadgill, John Zorn, Lou Reed, Carla Bley, Tom Waits, Elliott Sharp, Todd Rundgren, and Charlie Haden, was put together by producer Hal Willner in 1985.

Kurt Weill in Europe; *The Black Rider*

One of the curious facts about the Kurt Weill connection is that while his influence can still be found in New York, it hardly exists in Europe except

12. *Angels in America* was turned into an opera by Peter Eötvös; premiere at the Théâtre du Chatelet in Paris in 2004.

perhaps in a very diluted form.[13] Elements of Brecht/Weill survived in East Germany and may be found in works like the Udo Zimmermann *Weisse Rose,* but in Western Europe, there are only a few theater artists and composers whose work is connected in any way with that tradition: Hans Werner Henze, several British composers beginning with Cornelius Cardew, the Dutch composer Louis Andriessen, and the Viennese group around Kurt Schwertsik and HK Gruber, all of whom have already been discussed. Heiner Goebbels (who will be discussed further in Chapter 18) has written a work called *Eislermaterial,* referring to (and quoting extensively from) Brecht's other major musical collaborator. There is also the strange case of the Swiss director Christoph Marthaler, whose work is close to music theater.

Marthaler, who started his career as a musician playing the oboe in theater orchestras, began to develop his own theatrical language from the *mise-en-scène* of the *Liederabend* or song recital, a basic concept out of which many of his later works grew. The visual characteristics of his work are closely connected to the stage and costume designs of Anna Viebrock. Marthaler goes back and forth between theater and opera, and as he is an habitué of the in-between, his works for the theater have a musico-theatrical character. He is one of the few director/artist/*auteurs* in today's music theater who has the power to divide the audience, making political what is most human. He is an original in his background, career, and work. One of his early pieces, *Murx den Europäer! Murx ihn! Murx ihn! Murx ihn! Murx ihn ab!*[14] was performed at the prestigious Berliner Theater Meeting in 1993. He used his own experience in a Berlin bar where the barkeeper had refused to serve him saying, "No beer for Jews!" Marthaler, who is actually from a Protestant family and often uses Catholic imagery, deals with the poverty of the soul in modern society. Music makes this even more human. A major creation was the staging of Schubert's *Die schöne Müllerin* with Marthaler's troupe of actors from the *Zürich Schauspielhaus*, an ensemble well versed in an uncompromising style that includes, among other things, grotesque slowed-down movements of falling. In Marthaler's hands, singing Schubert songs becomes an existential event; he performs surgery on the Schubert *lied*, operating on the music itself and extracting its contemporary qualities of disillusionment and unhappy love. Although he does not act

13. In German-speaking Europe (less so elsewhere), the old chanson/cabaret, *engagé* theater piece, and associated musical styles have retained their association with the sound of the politics of other eras and regimes, and, as a result, they have fallen out of favor.
14. Something like "Kill the European! Kill him! Kill him! Kill him! Kill him completely." The slang word "murx" also suggests the name of "Marx."

like a composer, he introduces musical ideas (a song takes on a jazzy flavor, another is spoken in mannered slowness, another is cut short right after it starts, etc.). He also relies on his own troupe of excellent artists so that the intertwined dramaturgy of the musical and the theatrical is indissoluble. In 2005 he directed *Tristan und Isolde* at Bayreuth where his dramatic tinkering with the musical score was, of course, not allowed and he had to work with a cast put together by the Festival. This unsuccessful experience showed that he is much more creative in his own environment when he has control and can cook from his own music theater recipes!

Not surprisingly perhaps, one of the most successful incursions of the Kurt Weill tradition in modern Europe came from two Americans working in the theater. The three Robert Wilson/Tom Waits commissions came not from the opera or any other musical institution but from theater companies: *The Black Rider* and *Alice* (after Lewis Carroll) from the Thalia Theater in Hamburg, Germany, and *Woyzeck* from the Betty Nansen Theatre in Denmark. Waits, it should be said, had previously worked with considerable success at the Steppenwolf Theater in Chicago, one of the most innovative nonprofit regional theaters in the United States. Wilson, of course, has crossed all the lines between theater, opera, and performance art.

The Black Rider, based on a piece of German folklore that is also the basis of the opera *Der Freischütz* by Carl Maria von Weber, is the best known of these collaborations. The immediate sources of the story were a novel by August Apel and Friedrich Laun from 1810 and an English version by Thomas de Quincey published in 1823. The musical was commissioned by Jürgen Flimm, then director of the Thalia, and was first performed there on March 31, 1990. The success of the work is partly to be explained by the fact that this is an American retelling of a German redemption story about someone who made a pact with the devil and has to go into exile. Wilhelm sings, "...don't cry for me, for I'm going away, and I'll be back some lucky day." This was less than a year after the fall of the Berlin Wall.

Another remarkable thing about *The Black Rider* concerns the choice of an author. This is the story of a man who has made a pact with the dark side and who subsequently kills his beloved with a bullet gone astray. *The Black Rider* was actually written by a man who had made a pact with the dark side and killed his wife with a bullet gone astray. This would be William Burroughs, and it was the writer's last major work. The concept of the piece belongs to Robert Wilson, who conceived it as a black comedy and staged it in a presentational style in which the actors explain, to each other and to the audience, the moral of the story as well as their characters and what they are doing.

The Black Rider is not realistic, it is not psychological, and its use of expressionism is almost quotational, postmodern. It is tightly choreographed

The Black Rider: the casting of the magic bullets. Direction by Robert Wilson, original music by Tom Waits, script by William S. Burroughs, costumes by Frida Parmeggiani. Photos courtesy Byrd Hoffman Watermill Foundation and Clarchen Baus-Mattar, 1990.

with a typical Robert Wilson use of time. People and things appear and disappear. Objects are misshapen and transform from one thing into another. It is child-like, cartoonish, and two-dimensional at the same time that it is complex and (in spite of the story) nonlinear. Everything is odd, colorful, funny, and threatening at the same time.

Tom Waits has been quoted as saying that he had been "trying to find a music that could dream its way into the forest of Wilson's images and be absurd, terrifying and fragile." Many of the Tom Waits songs, in his rough, American gospel mode, grow out of the text, but others seem quite peripheral to the action. Much of the music is actually arranged and extended by Waits's collaborators, Greg Cohen, Gerd Bessler, and the band itself (*The Devil's Rubato Band*), which played an important role in developing the score. Although the music plays a major part in the success of the work (most people probably think of the work as Tom Waits's *Black Rider*), Waits himself did not actually perform in the original production. However, he worked very closely and successfully with the musicians and the cast in putting it together and he left his unmistakable imprint on their performance style.[15] The score is, so to say, Kurtweillian, not only in the sense that it often sounds like Weill, but also in the way that it provides a solid anchor for a musical play organized in numbers. Although, many of the numbers and most of the scene music, much of it by Waits's associates, grow out of the dramatic situations and can be considered music-theater numbers rather than show songs, they do not always or necessarily advance the action and sometimes they actually stop or even negate the dramatic movement. Often they express something that the character—or the actor playing the character—needs to convey to the audience. The use of American pop styles is sometimes at odds with the Germanic folklore and Wilson's surrealist/expressionist stage style. Also, the use of both German and English and the presentational manner of the performance—with the actors talking and singing directly at the audience as much as at each other—produces an oddly "off" effect that tends to give the entire structure something of the character of camp cabaret in a *grand guignol* manner. *New York Times* critic John Rockwell called it a cross between *Cabaret, The Threepenny Opera,* and *The Rocky Horror Picture Show.*

Can the Kurt Weill (or Weill/Brecht) model continue to represent a new form of music(al) theater any longer? Does it provide a still-useful template for a presentational theater in which closed forms, pop music, irony and alienation, music-hall or vaudeville tradition, politics, and the *Verfremdungseffekt* continue to play a role? A related issue here is whether

15. The recording made by Waits himself in California a few years after the premiere differs from the theater score in significant respects.

the new music theater, as a successor to opera, will continue its avant-garde role as a class marker or whether it can recapture its function as a populist art form through its traditional association with pop music. At the moment, this issue seems to divide music theater in Western Europe (with its avoidance of pop music) from the American equivalent (pop music permitted in both the Weill/Brecht and experimental theater traditions and also around the edges of minimalism).

However, it can be said that *The Black Rider* represents a rare moment when the style of the contemporary off-Broadway musical, descended from Weill and his successors, reentered European music theater in an important and successful way. Whether this is a unique event—due to the offbeat talents of Wilson and, especially, Waits—or the start of something else remains to be seen. (See Chapter 21 for a further discussion of high and popular art.)

Further Reading

Banfield, Stephen. *Sondheim's Broadway Musicals*. Ann Arbor, MI, 1993.

Bentley, Eric. *Bentley on Brecht*. New York, 1999.

Farneth, David, Dave Stein, and Elmar Juchem. *Kurt Weill: A Life in Pictures and Documents*. Woodstock, NY, 2000.

Goodheart, Sandor. *Reading Stephen Sondheim: A Collection of Critical Essays*. New York, 2000.

Gordon, Eric. *Mark the Music (Marc Blitzstein)*. New York, 1989.

Jarman, Douglas. *Kurt Weill, An Illustrated Biography*. Bloomington, IN, 1982.

Kowalke, Kim. *Kurt Weill in Europe*. Ann Arbor, MI, 1979.

Kowalke, Kim. *A New Orpheus: Essays on Kurt Weill*. New Haven, CT, and London, 1986.

Sanders, Ronald. *The Days Grow Short: The Life and Music of Kurt Weill*. New York, 1980.

Schebera, Jürgen. *Kurt Weill: An Illustrated Life*. New Haven, 1997.

Schebera, Jürgen. *Speak Low (When You Speak Love): The Letters of Kurt Weill and Lotte Lenya*. Berkeley, CA, 1996.

Taylor, Ronald. *Kurt Weill: Composer in a Divided World*. Boston, 1991.

Thomson, Virgil. *Music with Words: A Composer's View*. New Haven, 1989.

Tommasini, Anthony. *Virgil Thomson: Composer on the Aisle*. New York, 1997.

Willet, John, ed. and transl. *Brecht on Theatre*. New York, 1964.

chapter 16

The Art of the In-Between

"...it's a no man's land, it's a no man's land..."

from the Serge Gainsbourg song "No Man's Land"

A stage director's art form?

In the art of the in-between, extra-musical elements could replace both traditional theater narrative and the inner, motivic structuring of musical form, putting both the traditional librettist and composer out of work. This rather large opening has served to let in those theatrical spirits whom neither composers nor writers/librettists have learned to control: the *metteur-en-scène* or stage director as *auteur*.

Guy Erismann, at one time a co-producer of the Avignon festival, illuminates how a particular art form came to life in those early years.[1] Music theater did not yet have entrée into the theater and was considered either a "bizarre outgrowth" of freaky musical activity by musicians who had no idea about theater or an affair of theater people who had no idea about music. A stagnating contemporary music scene was paralleled by a crisis in the theater at the same moment that opera was undergoing a renewal

---

1. Michel Rostain and Marie-Noel Rio, eds., "Aujourd'hui l'opera," *Recherches* 42 (January 1980): 63.

and experimental theater was becoming less verbal and more musical. Not surprisingly, the stage director quickly became the *auteur*, the central figure of certain forms of new music theater, notably in France. In the early 1970s, there were no composers who had a routine of writing such pieces or who had experience working in such an art form, and there was no musical or theatrical institution in place to give it form. Under those circumstances, many composers—Kagel, Aperghis, Cage, Stockhausen, Goebbels, and others—themselves decided to become the stage directors of their own music-theater works. Only later, with the renewed interest in grand opera, did composers rediscover that traditional and prestigious platform, causing many of them to throw away their revolutionary anti-bourgeois ideologies to go back to writing operas.

As the new experimental theater became less and less verbal and incorporated live music into its essential tool kit, the work of stage directors like Lavelli, Brook, Serban, Breuer, Wilson, Sellars, and Mnouchkine became closely identified with the sound of live vocal and instrumental music as an essential—often THE essential—element of their creations. At the same time, ensembles like the Living Theater, Open Theater, La MaMa, ATEM, Quog Music Theater, Théâtre du Soleil, Mabou Mines, the Performance or Wooster Group, and La Fura dels Baus expanded their conception of theater to emphasize physical movement as well as nonverbal sounds and more traditional music making as essential elements in performance.

The French director and writer Jean-Michel Ribes has pointed out that music theater is more about the fusion of the arts than their juxta-position or addition. This fusion demands the co-creation of the artistic elements through the close collaboration of composer, writer, designer, singer/actors, and musicians. But someone has to be in charge. It cannot be the writer and his script, which no longer provides a controlling direction. And the composer is no longer the traditional provider of the all-controlling musical and orchestral score. So it is almost always the director who now has to be in charge. Ribes and many stage directors talk about the musical basis of staging, but this is a notion that is often based on a lack of musical knowledge. Timing is a major issue for most directors today, and most of the time (certainly in traditional scoring), that function is completely usurped by the musical score. On the other hand, the modern staging theories of Craig, Meyerhold, Stanislavsky, Brecht, and others were almost all developed out of opera or musical theater and mostly based on existing scores that were already composed with the timing built in. Either we do away with the director's obsession with timing and let the music take over or we create a different kind of music theater in which the musical timing is plastic and can be molded by the director and the performers. These are not merely theoretical questions but everyday concerns in the creation of new musical theater works of every kind.

Pierre Barrat, former director of the *Atelier du Rhin*, proposed a differentiation of new music-theater creations into three types:[2]

- Either the theatrical action comes from the action of the music without any concerns about a justification through drama (e.g., Ligeti or Kagel), or
- The music, text, and language are at the center and the preexisting libretto and score directs the action and the scene (this is the traditional type), or
- The voice is central with the text as the semantic and/or acoustic carrier of the message or the story; the medium may even be purely vocal/musical (this third type necessarily places the actor/singer/performer at center stage).

With regard to Barrat's third type, it has to be said that in one important respect music theater is very much in sync with popular music. The voices in both pop music and music theater do not follow an idealized singing model (just as the dancers in modern dance do not follow the idealized model of ballet). What is valued instead is character and individual recognizability. The presence of a certain performer is often a condition for the performance in many works that have been developed for, with, or by specific performers. This model is not only limited to the singing voice; any group of specific performers, musicians, singers, or actors might be the starting point for a piece and a project. This will also have an important impact on the economics of a project as well-known artists might be expensive but they might also be able to sell the work of an unknown composer or an unpopular theme to producers or to the public.

The musicologist's history of music and dramaturgy is based on the idea that change comes about through the work of particular composers and that this is the benchmark for measuring the evolution of music (opera included). But a director's theater, even one in which music plays a major role, may be organized on very different criteria that include storytelling, conceptualization, and even entertainment. The last, one of the predominant reasons for the very existence of music and theater, has not been considered to be scientifically valuable as an area of study; as a result, it has been almost completely neglected, with its history fallen into oblivion. The so-called street is a subject sometimes taken into consideration by governments, foundations, and patrons of the arts who wish to demonstrate social consciousness, but the truly popular arts are traditionally left to make their

2. Ibid., 77–89.

way without support or comprehension from the musicologist, critic, or arts bureaucrat.

Experimental theater

The Avignon Festival (see Chapter 11) and the downtown New York theater have served as major centers for experimental work of this kind, much of which is director driven and dependent on collaborations between directors, choreographers, musicians, actors, singers, dancers, and media artists. The French term *théâtre musical* often refers to this kind of music theater.

Although contemporary theater, like modern dance, had taken on ritualistic and musical forms as far back as the early years of the century, the development of nonsensical, nonverbal, or surrealist dramaturgy became a dominant feature of new theater after World War II and particularly in the 1960s and after. The history of experimental theater is mostly beyond the scope of this volume, but the growing importance (both artistically and socially) of these kinds of theatrical experiments, the emergence of a new type of creative *auteur*/director, and the intersection of new currents in music theater and dance with the work of new companies such as the Living Theater, the Open Theater, and La MaMa are all phenomena that need to be noted here. The La MaMa *Greek Trilogy* of André Serban and composer Liz Swados; the Ontological-Hysteric theater of Richard Foreman (with or without the Kurt Weillian, music hall, and deconstructed show-music scores of Stanley Silverman); the *Oedipus at Colonnus* and *The Warrior Ant* of Lee Breuer (music by Bob Telson) and other Mabou Mines directors; work of the English director Peter Brook (active in France) going back at least to *Marat/Sade* (1967; music by Richard Peaslee); the collaborations of choreographer/director Martha Clarke and Richard Peaslee (*The Garden of Earthly Delights*, *Vienna Lusthaus*, and others); productions by the British group *Le Théâtre de la Complicité*; the Tiger Lillies' *Shockheaded Peter*; and many other productions of this sort could all be easily enrolled in the history of music theater.

On the edge of music and theater

Even in music theater, it makes sense to try to construct a historic continuum, but the path from Wagner, Debussy, and Puccini does not present a straight line to the stage door of a Broadway or West End musical house any more than it does to any hotbed of new performance art. The history of the evolution of new music theater has to account for what we are calling "the in-between" by taking us through the overheated early modernist years, which spawned a bewildering variety of new forms: new cabaret and the revue; emerging film-art; expressionist music theater and experimental dance; Oskar Schlemmer and the Bauhaus with their cubist ballets and futurist theater productions; theatrical experiments and innovations like those of the Russian Vsevolod Meyerhold, who used music as a time-structuring grid and emotional force even though that music was not actually heard in performance; Bertolt Brecht, whose anti-psychological "epic theater" broke with traditional theories of catharsis and mimesis but used jazz, cabaret, and popular song to create both distance and closeness; Antonin Artaud, who wanted to overcome the false and illusionary nature of our perceptions with the ritualistic directness and purity of his famous "theater of cruelty" (but not necessarily the theater of sadomasochism or sexual aggression that is often invoked in his name).

Artaud, although the least obviously musical of all these, has been a favorite of composers looking to rethink the pairing of music and theater. Artaud wrote the text for Varèse's *Astronome* which, unfortunately, was never completed. *Tutuguri* of Wolfgang Rihm is a ballet on a text of Artaud for speaker, large orchestra, and tape (1981–82). The same composer's *Die Eroberung von Mexico* ("The Conquest of Mexico"; 1987–91) is a music-theater work with a text by the composer after Artaud; and his *Séraphin* (1994) is described as an "essay without text" also after Artaud. Hans-Joachim Hespos invented an Artaud-influenced genre based on a scenic concept using titles such as "Scenic Event," "Scenic Adventure," "Milieu/Scene," "Thermodynamic Ritual," and "Video Scene or Fragment of a Departure." (Ironically, *Opernwelt,* an influential German opera magazine, selected Hespos's *iOPAL* as the leading *opera* creation of 2005.) As with Georges Aperghis, there is an intense collaboration with and between musicians and actors. Steven Holt, writing about the work of Hespos, observed that given the presence of "political and economic structures [that] encourage if they do not enforce the abdication of individual responsibility for one's actions, it is a brave composer indeed who would subject these social constrictions to an immanent critique by rendering his works vulnerable to them."

Vinko Globokar, born in France of Slovenian origin but also active in Germany, is a brilliant trombone player and composer who emerged from the Berio circle. His *Discours* pieces and works like *Voie, Kolo, Les Emigrés,* and *L'Armonia Drammatica* deal with issues of community and society. Many of his pieces have to be realized collectively by and with the performers. *Individuum/Collectivum* is a collection of music-theater ideas, comparable to Kagel's *Staatstheater.* He takes his models from nature and society and turns them into music theater. In 1979, he wrote *Un jour comme un autre* for the Avignon Festival; this work is based on a letter of a woman who has been imprisoned and tortured. The roles that carry the narration are distributed to both singers and instrumentalists (the woman is a soprano, the lead interrogator is a contrabass clarinet, the person who carries out orders is a percussionist, public opinion is an electric bass guitar, and another victim is represented by a violoncello). Although there are musical values in the work, the dramatic structure is impossible to understand without the staging.

Melodrama

The original meaning of the term *melodrama* referred to texts spoken or declaimed by actors and accompanied by music. This kind of in-between has a long lineage going back at least to 1770 and *Pygmalion*, a *melodrama* or *scène lyrique* by Jean-Jacques Rousseau and one Horace Coignet. This idea was picked up in Germany by Georg Benda, who set a German translation of *Pygmalion*. His *Ariadne auf Naxos* and *Medea* were also much admired and the technique was used by Mozart, Beethoven, Weber, and Schubert. Berlioz made extensive use of *mélodrame* in his *Lélio* as did Richard Strauss in *Enoch Arden*. This line takes us to the notion of speech-song as interpreted by Debussy (with traditional notation) in *Pelléas et Mélisande* and in early works of Schoenberg: *Erwartung* (which is designated as a "Monodrama" with a solo part in conventional musical notation) and *Pierrot Lunaire* (with translations of French symbolist poetry set to the so-called *Sprechgesang* for which the composer invented or adapted a variant notation). Related ways of using the voice are also encountered in works by Berg, Honegger, Busoni, Henze, and Britten; see also the music theater of Harry Partch (Chapter 8). For a recent example, see Michaël Lévinas's *Euphonia* (Paris, 1998; after Berlioz).

The use of spoken or speech-song declamation always has something very special about it and it is used for very intimate confessions. It plays an important role in popular cabaret, variety, and nightclub performances and, by extension, the so-called backstage movie, a staple of the Hollywood musical starting in the earliest days of sound movies with films like *Forty-second Street,* dating from the early 1930s, to the *Moulin Rouge* movies of John Huston (1952) and Baz Luhrmann (2000).

Melodrama and the spoken word reemerged in performance art, starting with Cage's radio drama *The City Wears a Slouch Hat* (1942; with Kenneth Patchen) and the storytelling in Cage's *Indeterminacy: New Aspect of Form in Instrumental and Electronic Music* of 1958 (in spite of its title, the piece consists of ninety spoken anecdotes that must be told in the time span of a minute each). More recent examples can be found in the work of Philip Glass with Robert Wilson (*Einstein on the Beach*) and JoAnne Akalaitis (*The Photographer*) as well as the solo performances of Laurie Anderson and the American "monologists" (see Chapter 17). That the reemergence of spoken word with music occurred at the same moment as the emergence of rap is probably not a coincidence.

Jazz, drums and noise

The sound of jazz and the music hall penetrated new dance before it became a major element in new opera and music theater. The Erik Satie *Parade* (designated *ballet réaliste*) includes new instruments like lottery wheel, typewriter, tubes, high sirens, and *bouteillophone* (literally "bottle-o-phone") as noise sources and manages a jazz sound in the theater as early as 1917. In the theater and dance music of *Les Six* (Milhaud's *Le Boeuf sur le toit* is a famous example), nightclub sound is never very far away; *l'adorable musique mauvaise* was Francis Poulenc's famous characterization. Scott Joplin's opera *Treemonisha* (1911) uses ragtime and John Alden Carpenter's *Krazy Kat* (1921; based on a well-known and rather surrealist comic strip) and *Skyscrapers* (1926; commissioned by Diaghilev) use jazz idioms and jazz instruments (sax, banjo, percussion). Interpretations of jazz played a major role in the *Zeitoper* of the 1920s and 1930s, notably in Ernst Krenek's *Jonny spielt auf* (1925–26), George Antheil's *Transatlantic* (1930), and the works of Kurt Weill.

Nevertheless, in spite of a long history of efforts to create some form of jazz opera or jazz music theater, the results have been, at best, sporadic. Later attempts to use rock and more recently rap have also had limited results—at least, to date. Most forms of popular music are too personal to their creators and too dependent on their performers being "in the vein" night after night to respond successfully to the conditions of theater. But letting in jazz and other forms of pop music was not only a matter of opening the door to the street but also had social and political meaning. Kurt Weill's postulation was that music theater had to deal with the *Zeit*, the present time, not merely to be up-to-date but also, if possible, with the insolent intention of scaring or amazing the well-brought-up and the well-to-do. *Épater les bourgeois* also meant letting loose a whole vocabulary of sound (dissonance, percussion) and new types of sound makers as well. The extension of the sound vocabulary "to make music out of everything" was proposed in dead seriousness by Busoni, Varèse, and Pierre Schaeffer and with humor by Satie and Cage; the theatrical aspect often justifies the presence of noise by allowing "un-musical" sounds to be made acceptable. With Satie and Cage, with Picabia and Picasso, with the noise instruments (*intonarumori*) of Luigi Russolo and the futurists, the actions needed to produce the noises themselves took on theatrical qualities. And, of course, the presence of a pop music sound, often with a percussive jazz or rock beat, has always provided theater directors with the kind of dramatic urgency and sexual innuendo that they require in their theatrical visions.

Institutions in No-man's-land?

In looking at the years from the mid-1960s to the early 1990s, it becomes clear that music theater has not been purely a story of composers and musical composition. The very notation of music is secondary to the production process and, in particular, the process of creation through rehearsal. Music theater happened in an ill-defined no-man's-land. Boulez called it "opera for the poor," a place where not-so-well-trained musicians, composers, actors, or singers could hide their insufficiencies, a playground for the avant-garde amateur. The Avignon Festival was, without a doubt, the first major institution to define music theater as an art form and to experiment with various mixtures of music and theater (plus dance and media) in a long series of productions starting in the 1960s. The difference between most of these works of *théâtre musical* and what was being defined as *Musiktheater* or music theater elsewhere is that these works were not necessarily music driven. By and large, these were pieces in which the stage director or choreographer was the true *auteur* and in which the music was often taken from a variety of sources and composers. Nevertheless Avignon was a place where new music-theater ideas could reach the stage and a number of major works had their premieres at the Festival (for example, the Robert Wilson/Philip Glass *Einstein on the Beach*; see Chapter 11 for more on Avignon).

In additional to those festivals that were receptive to such activity (Avignon, the American Music Theater Festival founded in 1983, and the Munich Biennale founded in 1988) and a small number of performance ensembles, a common solution (mostly in Europe) was to create an opera studio inside the big opera house to produce new pieces or workshops of new pieces. In many cases, this was actually an excuse not to produce new work in the big house and it often proved to be a temporary activity, the first thing to be suspended when there were financial constraints on the company. In North America, music theater tended to take place in the context of the nonprofit performing world: downtown spaces for new dance; performance art centers that mix far-out jazz with new music and music theater; the off-Broadway or "off-off" fringe theater; at universities (usually through their theater or dance departments); and through a small number of festivals and performance ensembles.

All such institutions, even those with demonstrable publics, are financially dependent on subsidy, and subsidy is, in turn, dependent on defining the necessity for it. Is there a need for new music theater or, indeed, for the new in-between? Can any of this tell us something—presumably something about our contemporary lives and society—that the old music theaters, well-defined and institutionalized as "opera" and "musical," cannot? Can this work be defined by existing institutions or do we need dedicated new institutions? How can such projects—works, performing groups, companies, theaters—be financed and their work distributed? How do we deal with such matters as time, not merely a parameter of the work itself but needed (and in large amounts) to create and produce convincing new work? What are we subsidizing? A theater? A festival? A music-theater theater? The work of a collective? A performance ensemble? A composer? A writer? An *auteur*/stage director? An experimental workshop/atelier? All these questions have been asked many times before and the answers were, of course, never found. Decades after the invention of new music theater, most of the original hype about this pluralistic or interdisciplinary form is either repeated ad nauseum or has vanished. It might be time to find new ways to reopen the subject.

Further Reading

Erismann, Guy. In "Aujourd'hui l'opera." Edited by Michel Rostain and Marie-Noel Rio. *Recherches* 42 (January 1980): 63.

chapter 17

Extended Voice

Ski Ba Bop Ba Dop Bop

Scatman John, 1995

Roy Hart

Roy Hart was born in South Africa and came to England in 1945 or 1946 (sources differ) with a scholarship to the Royal Academy of Dramatic Art. In London, he studied voice with Alfred Wolfsohn, a singing teacher from Berlin who had escaped from Nazi Germany in 1939. Wolfsohn was not a conventional voice teacher but a man with an extraordinary mission. He had been a stretcher carrier in Germany during World War I and the cries of wounded and dying soldiers suggested to him that such sounds, although extreme, might be part of the natural human repertoire of vocal expression and could be summoned up through a teaching method that put a healthy performer in touch with deeper physical and psychological forces inside his or her body. This led to the conclusion that the human voice was capable of a far greater range, both in pitch and in expressive sound making, than had previously been thought possible (or desirable) and that the way to develop that range was through the individual's physical and emotional makeup.

Hart, who became Wolfsohn's best-known pupil, used Wolfsohn's methods and philosophy to establish and develop the teaching and performance principles that led to the formation of the Roy Hart Theatre, first in Great Britain and afterward in the south of France. The starting point of this so-called extended vocal technique[1] was "the cry," a nonverbal, nonmusical form (or forms) of expression deriving from and conveying strong emotional states. The principle of "the cry" and of the biological and psychological basis for singing was extended to the entire range of possible sounds that humans can make including those traditionally regarded as rude, animal-istic, or aggressive (see frontispiece). Above all, it was extended to the process of widening the performer's vocal range to the point that women are able to perform in low male registers while men reach down to the lowest fundamental tones and climb all the way up to the highest falsetto registers. In the Hart technique, five octaves are considered normal; Hart himself is said to have had an eight-octave range. Other features of the technique are the ability to produce vocal double-stops as well as to sound fundamentals and overtones simultaneously producing multiple or chorded sounds, also known as multiphonics. Belches, farts, growls, the so-called vocal fry (a kind of low rasp), squeals, squeaks, and screams of all sorts become equally part of the usable voice repertoire.

To observe and study the accomplishments of these actors and singers, many well-known artists of the period—mostly, but not entirely, from the music and theater worlds—visited the Roy Hart Theatre.[2] In 1968–69, Peter Maxwell Davies wrote his *Eight Songs for a Mad King* for Hart. This piece, based on the madness of the English king George III, intentionally drew on the full range of Hart's technique and has become a standard reference for extended vocal technique. George is said to have conversed with his pet birds, and the stage is set with bird cages, each with a musician inside. Hart premiered the work in 1969 with Davies' performance ensemble, *The Fires of London*, in the Queen Elizabeth Hall in London. Although he stopped performing it a few years later, others have taken it up successfully and it has been one of the most widely performed extended-voice compositions, suggesting that many of his vocal techniques can (as Hart himself maintained) be learned. Composers who wrote for or were directly inspired by Hart included Hans Werner Henze and Karlheinz Stockhausen as well as Birtwhistle, Xenakis, and others. However, after the move to southern France in 1975, until his

1. Hart did not like the term *extended voice,* as he insisted that what seemed to be an extraordinary extension of the vocal powers was in fact part of the natural, if neglected, human vocal repertoire.
2. Among the visitors were John Cage, Harrison Birtwhistle, Peter Brook, Jerzy Grotowski, Aldous Huxley, Colin Wilson, George Steiner, Harold Pinter, Jerome Robbins, Jean-Louis Barrault, Edith O'Brien, Irene Worth, and Yannis Xenakis.

death a few years later, Hart devoted himself largely to working with his own ensemble. Members of the Roy Hart Theatre continue to teach his techniques. A notable example is Richard Armstrong who has lived and worked in Canada for many years, teaching at (among other places) the Banff Center, which was, for several years, a leading center in North America for the study, creation, and performance of experimental music theater.

The American monologists

The interest in extended vocal techniques was widespread at the time. György Ligeti's *Aventures* and *Nouvelles aventures*—both written in the early 1960s as concert pieces but later adapted for the theater—use an invented vocabulary of sounds. The American singer Cathy Berberian, active in Europe in the late 1950s and 1960s, performed Cage's *Aria with Fontana Mix*[3] in a wide range of vocal styles; Luciano Berio's *Thema (Omaggio a Joyce)* (1958) with its electronic transformations of her voice and her own *Stripsody* (1966) based on comic-book sounds also enlarged the notion of what vocal performance could be. Meredith Monk's The House, Kirk Nurock's Natural Sound Workshop, and Eric Salzman's Quog Music Theater, all founded in the late 1960s or early 1970s in New York, were ensembles devoted to the exploration of nontraditional uses of the voice, often in a physical and theatrical context; many of the techniques developed were quite similar to those used by Hart.

A whole generation of solo performers took up nontraditional vocal production, often extending their vocal explorations still further with microphones and electronic processing. The tradition of the monologist and solo act in cabaret and vaudeville was carried forward in the new performance art (in Europe, the single English word "performance" is often used with a similar meaning). Although the so-called new vaudevillians and new monologists were not always musical in their outlook, a number of well-known vocal performers were working in a vein that was very close to music theater. This repertoire was sometimes composed by composers (or composers working with writers and directors) but many, perhaps most of these performers have specialized in the creation of their own works. These performances usually have a predetermined structure but they are not necessarily based on musical form or musical notation; they are often put together in rehearsal in the manner of a dance ensemble or contemporary theater group. Improvisation may be a major element, and many of these works belong in the category of solo performance work, which is created or varied in the moment of actual performance.

3. Actually two Cage pieces performed simultaneously.

These vocalists are by no means similar in background. The vocal basis or starting points range from so-called natural voice singing (Meredith Monk) to traditional classical vocal techniques (Rinde Eckert, Diamanda Galás, Kristin Norderval, Pauline Vaillancourt) to jazz and cabaret (Theo Bleckmann) to a range of vocal techniques related to the Roy Hart technique with or without electronic extensions (Laurie Anderson, Lynn Book, Pamela Z).

There is no one way to go about all this. The expansion of the repertoire of what can be done with the voice, aided or unaided by microphone amplification and electronic/digital means, is as personal and generic to the individual performer as the sound of the basic voice. Not surprisingly, most of these performers work as soloists by themselves or with a limited number of other singers or accompanying instrumentalists. Microphones, amplification, and processing—to alter and vary the voice and to create accompaniments in the very act of live performance—are common techniques with most of these performers.

Meredith Monk

Meredith Monk's work stands out in a number of ways in this group of extended voice practitioners. It is based on the natural voice; amplification is used mainly to project rather than to alter the vocal sound, and although she often performs solo, much of her work is ensemble based. She organized one performance ensemble (The House, founded in 1969) for theater pieces and another (Meredith Monk & Vocal Ensemble, founded in 1978; Theo Bleckmann and Monk herself are members) for musical performances. She was originally known as a choreographer, and her work methods are often closer to those of a choreographer or jazz musician—creating works on her own body or voice or on the voices and bodies of the members of her ensembles rather than through conventional notation. Her vocal music is almost entirely wordless, and yet she uses the forms, the music, and even the communicative structures of nonverbal speech, mixing it up with equal parts of emotive sound, invented vocal "noise" as well as her characteristic simple, repeated, and extended melodic and rhythmic forms, all framed by an overt and structured physicality. Finally, along with all the extended techniques, it should be emphasized that her musical ethos and her vocal inventions are fundamentally melodic in a direct and appealing mode.

Although her more recent work has tended to focus on purely musical and vocal performance, she has created a series of highly original number of music-theater works in a dance/mime/theater mode—*Vessel* (1971), using vivid imagery, theatrical settings, lights and costumes, physical movement, her highly-developed vocal style, and, to a lesser degree, a limited number of instrumentalists who participate in the action. These works include *Education of the Girlchild* (1973) in which she turns into her own grandmother en route to Ellis Island and the New World[4] and *Quarry* (1976), in which she plays a sick child whose fragile space is surrounded by the rise of fascism, represented by the Chaplin-like garbled song-and-dance of a tinpot dictator and the mass movements of his followers. Other works from this period include *Specimen Days* (1981), *The Games* (1983; with Ping Chong)[5] as well as a nontraditional "opera," *ATLAS* (1991), based on the travels of a nineteenth-century English woman in the Himalayas. ATLAS is operatic mostly in its size and ambition, but she herself performs the lead in a decidedly nonoperatic fashion otherwise, the work is largely cast with opera singers whom she has trained in her musical and vocal techniques. The visual and aural imagination at work in the earlier pieces are amplified here by the picaresque form, by the large cast, by fantasy scenes of an almost sci-fi dimension and by the use of a pit orchestra.

Meredith Monk performing the lead role in her 1976 music theater work *Quarry* in the premiere production. Libretto, music, direction, and staging all by Meredith Monk. Photo: Nat Tileston.

4. Monk herself regards this character as prototypical rather modeled on anyone specific. In her own words, she "plays one woman's life from old age to youth."
5. Some of these works carry the designation "opera" but all rest more comfortably in the music-theater category.

Quog Music Theater and the American Music Theater Festival

Foxes and Hedgehogs (1964–67) is a large-scale concert work by Eric Salzman in dramatic form for four singers, two instrumental ensembles, tape, and electronic extensions on a text of John Ashbery. The title comes from a fragment of poetry by the Greek poet Archilochus, which states that "the fox knows many things but the hedgehog knows only one big thing" and the conflict between "one big thing" and "many things" provides the dialectic of the piece. The piece is in two parts, separated by a kind of pop song for soprano accompanied by a piano played in tone clusters. Part I, largely based on a running narrative that Ashbery modeled on an old-fashioned boy's adventure story, is highly directional and fast-moving. Part II, after the song, is made up of small fragments of text and music that are selected and ordered by the conductor, using simple hand signals. At the end, the live musicians and a tape collage of rock sounds clash head-on.

The Nude Paper Sermon (1969), a commission from Nonesuch Records, was created as a multilayer work (multimedia in sound) for eight-track recording—state of the art at the time. It is scored for actor, chorus, and Renaissance consort (countertenor, soprano, and baritone with lute, viola da gamba, and an array of Renaissance wind instruments performed by a single player). Sung texts are again by John Ashbery but there is a major spoken text, written for the work by Wade Stephenson (Steven Wade) as a kind of amalgam of the words of people who use language to manipulate others (politician, radio DJ, teacher, preacher, etc.). Electronic sounds are used to define the surface of the loudspeakers through which the piece is to be heard while "artificial" echo on the live performers creates the illusion of physical depth and perspective—the musical equivalent of Renaissance perspective or of the sound of Renaissance music performed in a resonant church. Although the original was created to be recorded, there is also a concert/theater version in which the chorus is seated in the audience making nonverbal emotive sounds as the actor reads the headlines from the morning newspaper. The singers move in procession through the hall and organize the singing of an onstage "Om" in which the audience is asked to participate before it is broken up by a loud, doomsday explosion. These pieces require a wide repertoire of vocal styles and sounds including the above-mentioned nonverbal emoting, which also functions as a separate ensemble piece under the title of *The Ten Qualities.*

In 1970, Salzman and a number of performers (mostly vocalists but including an accordionist, a trombonist, and a percussionist) began meeting regularly to work on issues dealing with physical movement, sound making, and theatrical action. Quog Music Theater was organized partly on the model of the improvisational theater and dance companies of the time. A major part of the work was the development of a whole series of techniques for extending the range of vocal sound production, not only in register but also in vocabulary. Some of the results of this work were performance pieces including *Larynx Music* (1966–67), *Helix* (1972), *Saying Something* (1972–73), *Biograffiti* (1972–73), *Voices* (1972, originally for radio and based on ancient texts), *Lazarus* (1973–74), and *Signals* (various versions from 1970 to 1988). *Ecolog* (1971) was commissioned for the Artists' Television Workshop of public television in New York and was broadcast as a simulcast with a noncommercial New York radio station where Salzman was music director. The piece is in five sections and uses ensemble improvisation, open form (spotlights serve as both dramatic and musical cues in one scene), and extended vocal techniques in conjunction with the visual realization of video artist Jackie Cassen. A live performance version of this piece was presented by Pierre Boulez at his New York Philharmonic Perspective Encounters. Quog also gave public workshops and demonstrations based on the techniques and improvisation exercises that had been developed by the group.

Starting in the 1970s and continuing into the next decade, Salzman worked on a series of words-and-music collaborations with Michael Sahl employing some of these elements but in a Kurtweillian music-theater mode. In 1983, after Quog Music Theater ceased to be active, Salzman cofounded the American Music Theater Festival in Philadelphia—possibly the first major institution exclusively devoted to music theater as an art form—and served as artistic director of the organization for twelve years, presenting forty-five mainstage productions of operas, musicals, and music theater, most of them premieres.[6]

6. Works produced at the Festival include *Strike Up the Band* (by George Kaufman; music and lyrics by George and Ira Gershwin), *Trio* (by Hilary Blecher; music by Noa Ain), *X* (by Thulani Davis; music by Anthony Davis), *Seehear* (by George Coates; music by Paul Dresher), *Gospel at Colonus* (by Lee Breuer; music by Bob Telson), *The Juniper Tree* (by Arthur Yorinks; music by Philip Glass and Robert Moran), *Queenie Pie* (by Duke Ellington and George Wolfe; music by Duke Ellington), *Slow Fire* and *Power Failure* (by Rinde Eckert and Paul Dresher; music by Paul Dresher), *The Transposed Heads* (by Sidney Goldfarb after Thomas Mann; music by Elliott Goldenthal), *The Man Who Mistook His Wife for a Hat* (by Christopher Rawlence and Michael Morris after Oliver Sacks; music by Michael Nyman), *Revelation in the Courthouse Park* (by Harry Partch), *1000 Airplanes on the Roof* (by David Henry Hwang; music by Philip Glass), *Dangerous Games* (by Graciela Daniele and William Finn; music by Astor Piazzolla), *Casino Paradise* (by Arnold Weinstein; music by William Bolcom), *Hydrogen Jukebox* (by Allen Ginsberg; music by Philip Glass), *Love Life* (by Alan Jay Lerner; music by Kurt Weill), *Frida* (by Hilary Blecher and Migdalia Cruz; music by

Salzman's later works, notably *The True Last Words of Dutch Schultz* (text by Valeria Vasilevski; 1997), *Cassandra* (text by Eva Salzman; 2001), and *The Jukebox in the Tavern of Love* (madrigal comedy for the Western Wind vocal ensemble on a text of Valeria Vasilevski, 2005), make extensive use of extended vocal techniques. *Cassandra* was written for Kristin Norderval, who not only sings the role but also accompanies herself, largely on a computer, which processes her own vocal sounds to create these accompaniments. *The True Last Words of Dutch Schultz,* created with the collaboration of Theo Bleckmann (who played the title role), uses a "found" text: the real last words of the notorious New York gangster as they were transcribed by a police stenographer during a hospital interrogation after Schultz, the reigning boss of the New York crime world and the F.B.I.'s most wanted man, was shot by a rival mobster. His delirious responses, described as a "surrealist, stream-of-consciousness gangster poem," were put into the form of a nonlinear libretto by Valeria Vasilevski. The title role, which includes improvisation on several levels, covers a wide range of styles and techniques using a kind of deconstructed jazz and pop singing as well as vocalizing on the overtones, the so-called vocal fry, and a variety of other nonconventional sounds. Dutch's mob is a male quartet, modeled on the traditional American barbershop quartet. The members of the quartet also have individual roles: a priest, a corrupt policeman, a rival gangster, and an old-fashioned iceman, a traditional symbol of death.[7] Dutch's mother and his girlfriend are the only female members of the cast (the mother has also been performed in falsetto by one of the mobsters). The voices of the interrogator and of a radio newscaster are part of the soundscape of the piece—heard but never seen. Another voice heard in several places is that of the writer William Burroughs. Burroughs, himself a kind of literary gangster, was fascinated by the text and wrote an (unproduced) film script based on it. Here he reads the original document, and the sound of his

---

Robert Xavier Rodriguez), *Steel* (by Derek Wolcott; music by Galt McDermott), *Atlas* (by Meredith Monk), *Amphigorey* (by Edward Gorey; music by Peter Golub), *Tania* (by Michael John La Chiusa; music by Anthony Davis), *Bobos* (a hip-hop opera by Ed Shockley; music by James McBride), *Stories from the Nerve Bible* (by Laurie Anderson), *Floyd Collins* (by Tina Landau and Adam Guettel; music by Adam Guettel), *The Mystery of Love* (by Sekou Sundiata), *Schlemiel the First* (by Robert Brustein and Arnold Weinstein after Isaac Singer; music by Henkus Netzky and Salman Mlotek).

7. Ice appears as a motif throughout. The Iceman spends a good part of the piece scraping ice and the scraping itself and the drip of the ice as it melts is amplified. Dutch skates in "The Racket" to the accompaniment of a kind of deconstructed "Skater's Waltz."

Theo Bleckmann as Dutch Schultz and Simon Admiraal as The Iceman, from the Michiel van Westering/Opera Centrum Nederlands production of *The True Last Words of Dutch Schultz* by Valeria Vasilevski and Eric Salzman, Amsterdam 1999. Photo: Ben van Oosterbosch.

voice, woven in at certain moments, suggests the reincarnation of Dutch himself, creating yet another vocal and dramatic layer. A film collage, used in some productions, made up of images of Dutch, his contemporaries, and his times, is accompanied by some deconstructed swing and ends with a song by Dutch's girlfriend. The instrumentation consists of keyboards (sampler, synthesizer, and acoustic piano), *scordatura* (drastically mistuned) violin, tuba, drums, and a percussion score that includes a so-called Foley table of acoustic sound effects of the type used in old radio drama and film noir (machine gun, body falling, brakes squealing, car crash, glass breaking, toilet flush, water dripping, etc.). The use of live sound effects in a percussion ensemble was actually pioneered by Cage in his 1942 radiophonic collaboration with Kenneth Patchen, *The City Wears a Slouch Hat,* and this rather coincidental fact has resulted in the two works being paired as a double bill.

Further Reading

Galás, Diamanda. *The Shite of God*. New York, 1996.

Jowitt, Deborah. *Meredith Monk*. Baltimore, 1997.

Kostelanetz, Richard. A *Dictionary of the Avant-Gardes*. New York, 1993.

Kranz, Stewart. *Science and Technology in the Arts, a Tour through the Realm of Science/Art*. New York, 1974.

Nagan, Doron. "Salzman wil muziektheater voor iedereen." *Algemene Dagblad*. Holland, 1997.

Quinn, Jim. "Divine Dissatisfaction: Reinventing Opera." *Seven Arts*. Philadelphia, 1993.

chapter 18

New Media and Music Theater

(McLuhan enters, to applause, moves to the podium.)
McLuhan: Good evening. I wonder if you have heard this
one about the teacher who asked his class: "What does
this century owe to Thomas Edison?" To which a student
replied: "If it weren't for Edison, we'd have to watch TV by
candlelight." (He waits for a laugh. There isn't one.)

From *Marshall McLuhan—The Musical* (1994), book by Frank
Maher, music and lyrics by Gerald Reid.

Stage technologies, old and new

In traditional opera, vocal music dominates, with instrumental music and
text not far behind; physical action, staging, stagecraft, dance, and design
are important but clearly secondary and meant to follow and underline the
text and score. One of the characteristics of the new "total theater" is the
far more equal use, even in relatively modest contexts, of other disciplines
and other media, which often operate on parallel tracks and may comple-
ment or even contradict the score and text. This is a major difference from
the Wagnerian *Gesamtkunstwerk* in which all art forms merge into one big
affirmative message stream. The modernist and postmodernist versions are
fragmented and even contradictory in their use of the various disciplines
and their artistic applications. The Cagean notion of a "useful dialogue"
between the various artistic elements is not a peace negotiation but something more like a debate in which the participants provide or create a sort
of a surplus value out of their differences.

In addition to the traditional media of stage and theater, performance
technologies now also include those audio and visual media that have come
into wide use through developments in electronic and digital technology.

We should not forget that virtually all these new technologies are part of what we can call the "electronic complex." They all depend on the availability of electricity and its controllers, the vacuum tube (formerly), and now the microchip. As simple and banal as this might seem, it shows not only an ecological aspect of modern arts but also the influence of the real world on our artistic and idealistic arts! On the other hand there are much deeper meanings behind the electronic complex. The word technology derives from the ancient Greek *techné*, which, according to some, suggests the platonic ideal of "technique," the forms and methods of which one must know and study to create anything in a proper manner. Against this elitist and intellectual notion, one can set the Aristotelian view that *techné* is only a part of *praxis* or action. It is not only the use of a video-beamer or some intricate computer software that constitutes "technology" in theater but a whole intellectual and philosophical approach based on either knowledge of what has been done before (i.e., "the rules") or on practical experience. The use of technology in music goes back at least as far as the first holes drilled in a hollow animal bone to make a flute. Violin making is the product of a complex and still not completely understand baroque *techné* and the piano is nothing if not a music-making machine whose rise to the top of the world of music is an artifact of the Industrial Revolution. None of these technological achievements exist without the breath or the fingers (or the brain) of the musician who employs these tools ("tool" is, after all, another word for "instrument").

If music is a technology-driven art form, music theater is perhaps the most technological of all the arts. The arrival of *new* technologies has typically provided it with a focus as well as themes for new work. The experimental use of new media as an end in itself provides a brief but notable chapter in the history of music theater (see Chapter 6 as well as below). More recently, however, as these technologies have become widespread, easily available, and much less expensive, they have become integrated into larger performance techniques or simply bundled into new theater conceptions. New media may serve new music theater in various ways, and there is a point at which the two simply merge. Is the medium of a musical film the music (or the music theater) or the film?

Trading on opera's reputation: cinema

The close relationship between opera/music theater and cinema has been often noted but, surprisingly, not very well studied. Sergio Miceli, an Italian specialist on the subject, tells us that this is partly because of the short-sighted interests of musicologists. Even the most recent opera reference books have little to say on the subject. But the view is equally shortsighted from the other side. Film musicals have been studied from a film point of view but often with little or no mention of the music or the composers. In most film musicals (e.g., the musicals of Vincente Minnelli), the director is the *auteur* and the composer is no more important than the screenwriter, the designer, or the choreographer. Nevertheless, even silent films were accompanied by music. All the early sound films featured music and many of the best known are full-blown film musicals. Some of these are original works, others are based on theater musicals, and a number of them are musicals about performing musicals. There were some ambitious efforts along the way. The famous Busby Berkeley musicals featured choreographic fantasies that were only possible on film. Georg Wilhelm Pabst's biting *Dreigroschenoper,* although obviously based on the stage work, is so different from the original as to be considered an independent work of Pabst. Stanley Donen's *Seven Brides for Seven Brothers* (1954; music by Gene de Paul; choreography by Michael Kidd, based on the story of the rape of the Sabine women set in the American West) is essentially a through-composed original dance musical. Jacques Demy's *Les Parapluies de Cherbourg* (1964; music by Michel Legrand), one of the few successful French-language musicals of recent decades, was created as a film. This genre was picked up again by Alain Resnais in his musical films *La Vie est un roman* (1983), *On connaît la chanson* (1997), and *Pas Sur la Bouche* (2003). The last, originally an operetta by André Barde and Maurice Yvain, has been reworked by Alain Resnais so that it is in effect a new piece. Gian Carlo Menotti himself refashioned his 1946 one-act opera *The Medium* for film (1951), giving it the feeling of an original work for the film medium rather than a reproduced live performance.

Nevertheless, in recent years the genre has had many difficulties in being accepted on any level beyond that of camp or at best children's fare. The convention that film and television screens are a kind of window through which theater viewers look at the reorganized external world works against the acceptance of the singing voice on the screen. It is true that the convention of background music has always been acceptable and it is rare for any film to be entirely without music. But as film and television have come to rely more and more on "realistic" narrative, it has become more and more difficult for characters to break into song without appearing ridiculous or without suggesting *kitsch* and camp. Dramatic pacing and movement is a related problem. Music timing, which dominates opera and most music theater, is much slower than that demanded by modern mass media film and television editing—and this not only for commercial reasons.

A number of interesting ways have been found to get around these problems. *Pennies from Heaven,* originally created for television by the English writer Dennis Potter, uses old popular recordings throughout; somehow the way actors seem to break out into familiar pop songs (even though we know they are only lip-synching to these old and familiar recordings) is less jarring than the effect of opera singers going from dialogue (usually stilted) to a full-blown, full-throated operatic sound. This may be partly because microphone singing in a pop mode is closer to speaking than opera singing, a fact that has led some music theater composers—in live as well as media situations—to prefer the pop singing voice to the operatic. Film biographies of well-known performers and composers provide multiple opportunities for musical performance without breaking the conventions of "realism" in cinema. A few films in the rock opera mode that was popular in the 1960s and 1970s have had a certain currency; *Evita* (1996) by Hal Prince from the Andrew Lloyd Webber/Tim Rice musical of twenty years earlier and *Hair* (1979) by Milos Forman from the Rado/Ragni/McDermott musical of the late 1960s are two examples. Perhaps the best and most effective of these rock opera/musicals was an original work; *Performance* (1968) was created for film by Nicolas Roeg and Donald Cammell with music by Jack Nitzsche and starring Mick Jagger of the Rolling Stones. It is a dark, noir-ish, surrealistic music-theater film about mobsters, sex, drugs, and rock 'n' roll in 1960s London and it manages to follow a cartoonish story thread without concern for a consistent picture-window realism, making it one of the most successful examples of its genre.

The history of opera on film has not been a really fruitful one. In the early days, pioneers like Thomas Edison, Georges Méliès, and others produced silent film versions of operas, lending credence to the theory that cinema is the legitimate heir to what opera was in the nineteenth century and perhaps also to boost cinema's standing by trading on opera's reputation as high art. This surprising history includes works like Robert Wiene's 1926 *Rosenkavalier* (for which Strauss himself wrote an instrumental reduction as accompaniment) and the already-mentioned Pabst *Dreigroschenoper*. As already suggested, many of the first sound films were musicals, and as early as 1932, Max Ophuls made a *Bartered Bride* and Abel Gance produced a film version of Charpentier's *Louise* in 1938. Jean-Marie Straub and Danièle Huillet's *Einleitung zu Arnold Schoenbergs Begleitmusik zu einer Lichtspielszene* (1972) is a real film that employs a score written for an imaginary film; their *Moses und Aron* (1974) is after Schoenberg's opera. Better known are Franco Zeffirelli's *La Traviata* (1982) and Giuseppe Patroni Griffi and Brian Large's *Tosca* (1992). These last-named films tend to distract from the drama, losing dramatic force amid their reconstruction of period locations or details. In the case of Zeffirelli, who has been active as stage director, there was little difference between his opera stagings and film versions, which were all focused on minutia. The *Salome* (1992) of Derek Bailey catches Peter Hall's stage production of the Strauss as a performance reality.

In a more creative vein, the films of the German director Hans-Jürgen Syberberg are of epic length and try to evoke the atmosphere of Wagnerian operas. Syberberg's *Parsifal* (1982) literally explores the creative potential of a nonrealistic approach to operatic filmmaking in a highly original way. In spite of a few such examples, the most common and widely used method of putting opera (and other forms of music theater) into a reproductive medium are the filmed stage productions of repertory operas, suitable for sale as DVDs.

Between film and video

As a medium very close to film, video has become the omnipresent visual format of today. Television formerly required very large and heavy equipment, but the invention of the digital camera has changed the situation. Two aspects of the use of video in new music theater can be found in Thomas Desi's *Hoffmanniana after Tarkovsky* (2004) and *Closed Concert Tele Vision* (2005). The *Hoffmanniana* is based on a script of the Russian filmmaker Andrei Tarkovsky[1] on the life and fantasies of the enormously influential German writer E. T. A. Hoffmann and is made with the idea of using video in the style of film. Tarkovsky's films are known for their slow camera work and a certain theatricality, which suggest the possibility of music theater. A prerecorded voice, representing the artist (a sort of blend of Hoffmann, Mozart, and Tarkovsky), speaks and sings about his inspirations and concepts in creating this piece. The film restages images from various Tarkovsky films as well as three Donna Annas, multiple versions of a character who appears in Mozart's *Don Giovanni* and also in one of Hoffmann's stories. Mozart might seem to serve very well as a point of reference for three typical opera singers in rococo costumes except that these are not opera singers at all but jazz and pop singers who reinterpret Donna Anna in terms of 1980s Italian pop sensibility (Tarkovsky lived in Italy during his last years although we don't know anything about his relationship with Italian pop music). Another layer of sound is the electronic score for the film, which is by turns abstract and illustrative. There is a strong postmodern aspect to this multiple and layered setting of Mozart (a distant compositional echo of an eighteenth-century opera composer), viewed by Hoffmann (a nineteenth-century fantasy writer), re-viewed by Tarkovsky (a twentieth-century filmmaker), and "re-reviewed" by Desi (a twenty-first

---

1. Tarkovsky staged a *Boris Godunov* under Claudio Abbado at Covent Garden, London, in 1983.

On the left, stills from films by Andrei Tarkovsky; on the right, the restaging of these in Thomas Desi's *Hoffmanniana*. Bregenzer Festpiele 2004. Photo: Thomas Desi.

century music-theater composer). On this level, *Hoffmanniana* functions simply as a rearrangement of fragments from different periods, selected, rewritten, and re-viewed through the filters of the present: a poetic merger of video technology, electronic pop, and postmodernism. The paradox of the camera's narrow angle versus the eye's space perception in the theater makes the projected onstage film appear as a window into the unreal, the imagined, or the remembered. The limitations of projection in matters of light and sound serve to bring out the points in which live performance really does offer more life!

This desire to connect the levels of media projection and live acting was also the main point of *Closed Concert Tele Vision* (2005). Here German extended-voice singer/actor Salome Kammer appears as a opera singer and gets lost in a vast off-stage building as we follow her on the CCTV screens. Whereas video in *Hoffmanniana* imitates the high art of high-resolution film, CCTV deals with the esthetics of the low-fi, low resolution CCTV cameras. Video is not a generic medium any more. It has become *the* global visual medium.

Music theater and surveillance cameras: *Closed Concert Tele Vision* by Thomas Desi; Salome Kammer, soprano, Vienna 2005. Photo: Thomas Desi.

A bridge between high and popular culture: television

The relationship between opera and television has been no better understood than that between opera and film. A 1995 study by Youssef Ishaghpour on opera and television has little to say on the subject except that cinema destroyed opera, just as television would destroy cinema. Jennifer Barnes (2002) tells us that in the United Kingdom and the United States between 1951 and 2002, more than fifty operas were commissioned for television. These include live broadcasts (generally of photographed stage productions) and video recordings in a studio (offering more creative possibilities). Operas made for television that have had some success include Gian Carlo Menotti's *Amahl and the Night Visitors* (NBC, 1971, and rebroadcast almost every year since at Christmas), Igor Stravinsky's *The Flood* (NBC, 1962; with George Balanchine), and Benjamin Britten's *Owen Wingrave* (BBC, 1971). Britten's earlier television experiences include *The Turn of the Screw* (Associated Rediffusion, 1959) and *Billy Budd* (NBC, 1952, and BBC, 1966). A more recent example is Gerald Barry's *The Triumph of Beauty and Deceit* (1995), part of a projected series of six hour-long television commissions from Channel 4 in Great Britain.

We note, however, that the subtitle of Jennifer Barnes's report is *The Fall of Opera Commissioned for Television*. The duration and slow pacing of opera on television is a problem that often cannot be overcome by fancy cutting. The limitations of the genre—at least with regard to the very different ideas of how opera and television are supposed to work—are constricting. As a bridge between high culture and the popular, the genre might be renewed with the creation of more innovative works expressly designed for television. These would probably relate not so much to traditional opera as to the music videos (or music clips as they are known in many places) made famous by MTV.

Most new technologies, particularly in their early stages, reproduce works from previous media if only to establish their bona fides and produce a marketable product. If theater is to be defined as a measurable space within which actors can move, speak, and sing, then, by definition, a series of projected moving images on a flat screen is something else. The traditional solution is to regard media production of any kind as a reproductive act. Almost all classical music recording (as opposed to pop music studio recording) tries to reproduce the ambiance of live performance, literally evoking the sense of physical space through the use of a recorded or even artificially produced acoustic. Opera and other theatrical performances on film or video traditionally reproduce live performance or create a simulacrum on a studio soundstage. A popular Hollywood conceit starts a scene or a musical number as if it were being played live on a stage and then opens it out from there into a limitless virtual space. The Ingmar Bergman *Zauberflöte,* which begins as if it were a performance in the eighteenth-century Drottningholm Theater, is a well-known example of this technique applied to opera.

The bigger and more interesting question is whether film and/or television can function as a creative medium for new opera and music theater. The newer technologies, high definition optical discs (DVD, Blu-Ray) in particular, with their potential to reach larger and more diverse audiences, offer a chance to rethink the media/opera equation if the means can be found to create or adapt new works directly and not simply reproduce stage performances.

Televised opera: Robert Ashley's *Perfect Lives*

In the development of video as an independent art form, it is notable that there has always been a close association with new music. The MTV format has been so successful in pop music that most bands in recent years have released music videos together with their CDs. Music videos have sometimes been considered a legitimate form of music theater and have created what is virtually a whole school of music-theater directors, some of whom have gone on to direct major television and film (occasionally stage) projects. The Kitchen, a major New York performance arts center, was originally founded as a center for video and music by the video artists Woody and Steina Vasulka. Harvestworks is a center for art and technology at which video plays a major role; Kristin Norderval (see Chapter 17) has been an artist-in-residence there. Beryl Korot's work with Steve Reich has already been mentioned; both of their big collaborations, *The Cave* and *Three Tales,* are performance works built on and around the use of video, and the music is even derived in part from the sound tracks of the videos (see Chapter 14). Two of the major artists in the still relatively new medium of video, Nam June Paik and Bill Viola, started out as composers—Paik in the Cage/Fluxus orbit, Viola as a recordist and creator of environmental sound and sound environments.

Composers who have produced original works for broadcast television include Mauricio Kagel (*Ludwig Van*), Robert Ashley (see below), and Eric Salzman (*Ecolog* with Quog Music Theater; *Feedback* with visual artist Stan Vanderbeek). These works tend to use the medium itself as their theater of action. For example, one scene of *Ecolog* is both musically and scenically directed with the improvisational use of spotlights and multiple cameras picking out performers who must choose from their predetermined repertoire of responses when the light hits them. The growing separation of film and television (video) production from large-scale theatrical or broadcast distribution, the increasing availability of equipment, a drastic drop in cost, and the growth of the Internet as a means of distribution have all made it easier to produce original film and video works for at least limited distribution.

Robert Ashley, who came out of the Ann Arbor, Michigan, *Once* group (with David Behrman, Alvin Lucier, Gordon Mumma, and Roger Reynolds), is linked to the work of the pioneers of mixed media and performance art to which he adds a special flavor of interactivity. In his piece *Public Opinion Descends upon Demonstrators* (1961), the electronic sounds are triggered by the audience's behavior and reactions. Related pieces, many of them described as operas or electronic music theater, are *Interludes for the Space Theater,* "sound-producing dance" (1964); *She Was a Visitor* from *That Morning Thing* (1967); *In Memoriam... Kit Carson* (1963); and *Purposeful Lady Slow Afternoon* from *Wolfman Motorcity Revue* (1968). The merger of electro-acoustic music, psycho-acoustic research, mixed media, video, television, and cinematographic language led Ashley to the idea of televised opera, an original format of musical dramaturgy in which television was the originating (and not a reproductive) medium. This approach broke with the familiar habits of television and cinema. *Music with Roots in the Aether* (1976) is made up of fourteen videos of about one hour each. Artists like Behrman, Lucier, Mumma, Philip Glass, Pauline Oliveros, Terry Riley, and Ashley himself are interviewed in continuous shots without cutting; the idea is to create a visual *mise-en-scène* of those artists representing the "consciousness of being American," a task that also becomes the subject matter of Ashley's later works.

Perfect Lives (Private Parts) (1978–1980) is a kind of a summation of this period of Ashley's work, uniting the previous experiences of live performance and television opera into a work that consists of seven 30-minute episodes. It has been called "the first American opera," a label that is, of course, not accurate either literally or figuratively; in fact, the work is not comparable to traditional operatic writing. Nevertheless the term *opera* as used to describe his work functions as a kind of upside-down metaphor, referring to the huge gestures of late romantic opera in all dimensions. The music-theater television cycles of Ashley were becoming Wagnerian in their recalibration of ordinary bourgeois lives into something mythic. *Perfect Lives* was first broadcast by Channel 4 in Great Britain in April 1984 and was the starting point for the works that followed, including a complex series of intertwined works including *Atalanta (Acts of God* 1982–89), *Improvement (Don Leaves Linda)* (1985), *eL/Aficionado* (1987), *Now Eleanor's Idea* (1986–89), *Yellow Man with Heart with Wings* (1989–90), *Foreign Experiences* (1994), *Balseros* (1997), *Your Money My Life Goodbye* (1998), *Dust* (1998), and *Celestial Excursions* (2003). These are all described as operas and although mostly conceived for broadcast, they have also been shown on the stage using video playback and live video as a pre-showing for a future television series. Many of them have been subsequently seen on television in Austria, Germany, Spain, and the United States, and at film and video festivals around the world. If this is opera, it is opera that has migrated from the opera house to the virtual world of television.

The structures of the pieces themselves are part of a paradox. Using a vernacular approach in language, Ashley's own words are based on surprisingly small and even trivial events. The unusual dimensions of the pieces remind us of antique myths re-elaborated as taking place in contemporary suburban society. Driving in cars, a robbery, a golf game, parties, and other such events constitute the episodes. The absence of "normal" narrative logic or pace is characteristic of Ashley's style. Based on the spoken word, the message of those pieces comes through language, which, in a reworked, reflected manner, transforms ubiquitous reality. Speech-sound is the center of the transmission but there are also "songs" that refer to antique myths such as the *Iliad*. The sound of the voices in different situations is accompanied by percussion and piano playing.[2] Very low-key and distinctively "cool" ways of speaking in different "tonalities" are used to stand for moods such as aggressive, friendly, and so on.

2.   Much of the latter is provided by Ashley's collaborator, the pianist and composer known as Blue Gene Tyranny (Robert Sheff) and generally using improvisational and prerecorded musical accompaniments built out of repeated melodic and harmonic patterns ranging from the simple to the complex.

Robert Ashley in *The Supermarket*, one of the seven episodes from his television opera *Perfect Lives*.

As television time is expensive, time is carefully measured. Ashley developed "metrical templates" that coordinate every line to 3 beats in a basic tempo of 72 beats a minute. In *Improvement*, durations of 2.5 seconds' duration in one act and 3.33 in another produce different rates of speech. Larger formal structures are measured out in strips of time that are arranged, rearranged, intertwined, and packed into various larger formats like soap operas or *telenovelas*. Concerning the visual, Ashley tends to transfer theatrical experience into television with formalized movements of the camera that underline the coherence of the ongoing opera. These "soap opera" operas are a new form of media music theater that use the medium of television in a truly original way to respond to the habits of a society that lives with the television medium daily.

A theater of mixed means

Even before the introduction of sound into film, film images were already being incorporated into live theater and opera performance. There is a well-known film sequence in Berg's *Lulu*, and Schoenberg wrote music for an imaginary film scene that was realized cinematically only long after his death. The notion of incorporating colors and visual projections into live musical performance goes at least as far back as Scriabin whose *Prométhée, le poème de feu*, Op. 60 (written between 1908 and 1910), was scored for large orchestra with solo piano, wordless chorus, and a colored-light projector that was operated with a keyboard. Further experiments in mixing visual and aural media took place in the following decades but the notion of mixed-media performance work did not really come into its own until the new technological developments of the post–World War II period. One was the arrival of electronic or electro-acoustic music. Another was the development of cheap and effective projection equipment. The popularity of the so-called light show commonly used in conjunction with amplified rock 'n' roll performances was another. And there was the growth of video and video projection formats that were convenient, easily available, and relatively inexpensive. All of this was further affected in a major way by the application of digital and computer technologies starting in the 1980s, which made audio and video even simpler, easier to handle, and less expensive as well as interchangeable and interactive.

Opera and the various forms of music theater are the original mixed genre. Theater, music, and dance have been the essentials but other arts participate as well. Although visual elements originally played only a supporting role, they increased in importance with the development of visual technologies that has permitted the use of image, light, and color in live performance and the evolution of esthetic positions that regard all the elements as having equal importance.

In a narrower sense, the mixed-media genre has been described as the mixture of live (often live/processed) and electro-acoustic sound (the Varèse *Déserts*; the Milton Babbitt *Philomel*; Berio's *Omaggio à Joyce*). With the addition of projected visual elements, such efforts turned into major performance pieces and the notion that mixed- or multimedia was the modern *Gesamtkunstwerk* was very prevalent in the 1960s following the San Francisco Tape Music Center and the Trips Festival of 1965 and the nine EAT (Experiments in Art and Technology) events that took place in New York a year later with both artists and scientists/technologists taking part. The collaborations of composer Morton Subotnick and visual artist Tony Martin are generally credited with having created the light show based on liquid projections, which shortly became a staple of rock concerts.[3] More recently the Montréal based group "4D art" (Michel Lemieux and Victor Pilon) developed "virtual video-projection" techniques, which produce

3. For the history of media performance in San Francisco including tape music, light shows, multi-media, and music theater see the recent publication *The San Francisco Tape Music Center*, edited by David W. Bernstein (Berkeley, CA, 2008).

projections with a three-dimensional feeling that seek to render invisible the borders of performance, scenography, cinema, video, dance, poetry, visual arts, lighting design, music, and sound exploration (see Chapter 6).

A series of events at New York's Electric Circus (the most notable of which was *Reunion*, a chess game between John Cage and Marcel Duchamp; the chess moves triggered a variety of sound-making activities) and the *New Image of Sound* concerts at Hunter College all featured live performance events at which visual projection, sound technologies, and music interacted in one way or another. Other examples include the Cage/Hiller *HPSCHD*; Cage's *Roaratorio, an Irish Circus on Finnegan's Wake,* the Salzman/Vanderbeek *Feedback;* the Subotnik/Martin *Play!* and many others. *Feedback*, a collaboration with filmmaker and visual artist Stan Vanderbeek, is a modular piece—in effect, a structure for an environmental, participatory work into which an infinitely expandable range of live performance and media elements can be plugged. In some of the versions of this piece, dozens (even hundreds) of performers were involved, with the public coming and going ad libitum over periods of many hours. One of the major realizations of this was organized in 1968 by the Friends and Enemies of Modern Music at Syracuse University, the director of which was Louis Krasner, the violinist who had given the premiere of the Berg Violin Concerto! Another major performance of *Feedback* was organized in 1969 in Buenos Aires by Alberto Ginastera[4] (with the collaboration of Argentine artist Marta Minujín) at the *Instituto Torquato di Tella* where Salzman was teaching a course in multimedia at Ginastera's Center for Advanced Music Studies. Another multimedia work of Salzman, *Can Man Survive?*, was commissioned for the centennial of the American Museum of Natural History and exhibited in 1969–71; it used the cyclical forms of minimalism with the techniques and scale of multimedia to create an ongoing walk-through environment reflecting the environmental crisis.

Such productions mixed live performance with processing: electroacoustic sounds (generally on tape) with light shows, slide and film projections, improvisation, mime, and dance; there was also typically a strong measure of audience participation. The distinctions between tape and electronic sound produced by studio synthesizers and those produced by pop music instruments (electronic guitars, electronic keyboards) tended to disappear, a merger that was very reflective of both the politics and esthetics

4. Ginastera's operas, including *Don Rodrigo* (1964), *Bomarzo* (1967), and *Beatrice Cenci* (1971), using twelve-tone and serial techniques, were well known in the United States.

of the time.[5] Although, the vogue for such big (and expensive) productions has passed, it is possible to say that in a wider sense, the mixed-media genre has become almost synonymous with the new music theater. The availability of digital video opens up new creative areas that have been the subject of major proposals although yet to be truly mastered. As a medium for artistic expression, video or video art is not identical with television as it does not necessarily suffer from the commercial restraints of the latter. And, of course, digital video provides the most complete and effective way to preserve the ephemeral performance arts, music theater included, for documentation, study, and re-creation.

Digital interactivity

Tod Machover and Zack Settel are both American composers who have worked at IRCAM in Paris and have used interactive computer technology in somewhat different ways. Settel, now active in Montréal, uses "live inter-active electro-acoustic processing systems"—essentially performer inter-activity—as a basic principle of his work. *L'Enfant des glaces* ("The Ice Child" or "The Ice Maiden") is called an "electr-opera." It was created on a commission from the Montréal company *Chants Libres* in 2000; the concept of the piece as well as the stage direction is by Pauline Vaillancourt who also played the title role. The subject matter was inspired by the discovery of the mummy of a young woman—apparently a victim of ritual sacrifice—which had been preserved in an Andean glacier in Peru. Besides the appearance of this young woman as she rises up from her tomb in the ice, there is a second character—mainly a speaking role—who is an amalgam of the scientist who discovered the tomb, a Spanish *conquistador*, and, without too big a stretch, a modern-day economic *conquistador* at play in the fields of the global economy. The piece is built on the contrast between these two figures: Old World and New, conqueror and conquered, male and female, even ancient and modern, traditional and new. Two short poems of Gérard de Nerval and Francisco de Quevedo, translated into various unfamiliar languages (Armenian, Japanese, Persian, Russian, Finnish, and Pular, an African language), serve as the fragmentary texts for the piece. There is also a video projected on a wall of water as well as a complex and hallucinatory stage set. The computer runs software developed by Settel that has the function of taking the vocal sounds generated by the performers and using them to control synthesizers, samplers, and processors. On another level,

5. Symbolized perhaps by the multiple uses of the Moog Synthesizer. All this has, of course, been transformed by the evolution of music hardware into computer software.

L'Enfant des glaces in the Chants Libres production by and with Pauline Vaillancourt and Jean Maheu, music by Zack Settel; Montreal, Musée d'art contemporain 2000. Photo: Yves Dubé.

the text, as articulated by the performers, is also modified by a program that both analyzes and processes the sounds. In effect, the text actually controls the electronic processing of its own sounds. The sounds of the text itself and how it is articulated (sung, spoken out loud, whispered) and the character of the vocalizing (legato, staccato, trills, accents, etc.) are analyzed by the computer and used to produce control signals which then shape the sounds being produced by the synthesizers and samplers as well as the signal processors that modify these sounds.

Todd Machover served as composer-in-residence and director of research at IRCAM from 1978 to 1984; since then he has been affiliated with the Massachusetts Institute of Technology in Cambridge, Massachusetts. His *Valis,* based on Philip Dick's book of the same name, was commissioned by the Pompidou Centre in Paris for its tenth anniversary in 1987. This adaptation of the Dick novel—by the composer with Catherine Ikam and Bill Raymond—has been described as an "environmental performance piece of operatic dimensions." It calls for seven singers, an actor, piano and percussion, extensive video displays, prerecorded tape, and live computer manipulations. His *Brain Opera,* versions of which have been presented in various forms almost literally around the world (New York, São Paulo, Lisbon, Palm Beach, Los Angeles, Toronto, Milan, Munich, Copenhagen,

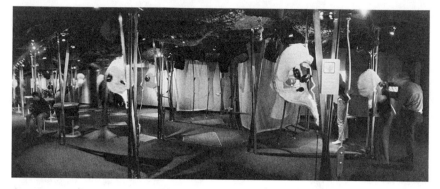

Brain Opera installation by Todd Machover at the Haus der Musik, Vienna. Photo courtesy Haus der Musik.

Tokyo, Paris, Linz; now permanently installed at the *Haus der Musik* in Vienna), is actually made up of two separate elements under a single title. One is an installation of the composer's so-called hyperinstruments, set up to allow the spectactor/visitor to interact with them through actions, movements, and speech which trigger or create sounds. This creates a sort of music or music-video arcade which Machover calls a "Mind Forest." In this interactive environment, the visitor can go "Harmonic Driving," performing on "Singing and Speaking Trees," "Rhythm Trees," "Melody Easels," and the like.

Brain Opera is also a composed performance piece in which the composer uses his hyperinstruments to make a typically complex and theatrical mix of styles, elements, forms, rhythms, and colors from everywhere and anywhere but all directed at definable performance results. Performer choice, even accidental movement, may alter these results somewhat but the work bears the composer's strong personality as he has defined it through a mix of traditional compositional elements, his computer work, and the notion of interactivity. The complex transformation of what is nowadays everyone's experience of almost everything makes Machover the guru of overload and a major anti-minimalist in contemporary music-theater creation.

Rethinking theater as a medium

Heiner Goebbels, German composer of music theater, born in the year of the famous Black Mountain College "happening," thinks dramaturgically. In effect, he uses theater and theater technologies as a medium within the larger precincts of his music-theater concepts. The separate elements from Cage's experimental world are here shrunk to the selection of texts that have no dramaturgical aim in themselves and the selection of pre-existing pieces of music to become part of the sound fabric of the works. Goebbels says that he dislikes the "doubling" of text and stage, so language and staging are laid out on parallel but nonreinforcing tracks. Music, pre-existing or newly created, adds still another layer. This creates another version of the "useful dialogue" of Cage. From the confrontation of heterogeneous, incoherent materials, a discourse or dialogue arises.

Goebbels developed the music-theater piece *Max Black* in 1998 in collaboration with the actor André Wilms (one of a series of three such collaborations). An important aspect of this particular piece is that there is no score that can be analyzed. There is the text, spoken by the performer, and there is the machinery of sound production and of light and fire with a list of cues. This might not be that surprising or new, but it introduces another border between music theater and the other theater arts, a border that has to do with the creative process. This piece was not theoretically conceived and composed in the ivory tower but created from scratch on a stage with its possibilities and necessities constructed around a particular performer.

This piece uses pyrotechnical devices in a musico-theatrical space. Fire, as we learn, serves as a metaphor of thought. Velocity as a theme can be found in thought and also in fire. The actions of the solo performer are often quick and forward moving. There is no constructed drama or story in the classical sense but rather a set of philosophical ideas, centered on the character of a real person. Max Black was an American scientist of Russian origin and inventor of the so-called fuzzy logic. His view was that fuzziness and vagueness have in common an openness that is opposed to rigid systems. Thinking and morality are often very much restricted by the boundaries of inherited systems, tradition, or habit. Max Black worked by crossing such borders through playful experiments.

But this is not a "bio pic" showing anything particular that might have actually happened in Max Black's life. He merely serves as the "human factor," a talking head spitting out texts of many other clever people including Paul Valéry, Georg Christoph Lichtenberg, Ludwig Wittgenstein, and even the historical Max Black himself.[6] These provide the philosophical

---

6. In *Eraritjaritjaka—museé des phrases*, another work in the series of collaborations with André Wilms, the quotations are all from Elias Canetti. In this piece, there is a string quartet on stage playing a variety of things, and a video camera, which follows Wilms out of the theater, into a taxi, and presumably to his apartment where he cooks an omelette. The apartment, with Wilms and the String Quartet in residence, turns out to be hidden on stage just in back of a screen on which the video images have been projected and which also contains a childish scrawl of a house with a window, which eventually opens up to reveal what lies behind it.

and thematic fields that, along with the visual elements and sounds created in the piece, are accompanied or even opposed by various fantastical actions. These actions, performed by Wilms, consist mainly in the demonstration of physical phenomena and take the form of experiments, demonstrations that have a charming and surprising visual quality on the stage. The end result is something like speaking about a theme while showing aspects of it and meandering around it in circles. Nondramatic theater and nondramatic subjects tend to be cyclical or circular rather than directional (as in dramatic pieces). Time loses its onrush and changes from pointedness to a leisurely passing flow. But if we do not expect anything, what keeps our expectation (i.e., our interest) going? Before we try to look for some answers to this question, we need to know more about the piece itself. The texts are from philosophical sources, as well as from the Paul Valéry *Cahiers*. The latter are the poet's daily journals on which he worked on every morning for three hours for over fifty-one years; they are mostly in French but also with English and German texts mixed in (Wilms, who is from the Alsace region of France, is an excellent actor in several languages). Quickly we understand that this is about self-reflection, self-consciousness, and the role of language in our thinking. With the freedom of the artist, the composer cuts up the results of scientific research to remount them in a monologue that resembles the stream-of-consciousness model. There is no expectation that anything special will happen that might set up a story. A series of phrases on language, on thinking, and on useful thoughts is laid out for us. The mathematical formulas help establish the familiar theatrical image of the genius in his laboratory creating a homunculus or looking for Faustian enlightenment. Even if Max/Wilms seems to be talking to himself, we get the feeling of being taught something when he shows his experiments or writes something down on a blackboard or on paper.

The piece lives because of the possibilities offered by the microphone. It simply could not exist or be performed without amplification and live-electronic processing, mechanisms that gives life to its soundscape.[7] Whatever the composer's intentions might have been, the work's coherence comes from speaking about machines through the intervention of machines. The smallest action comes alive through microphone amplification. When a small movement comes across at the same sound level as an obvious sound production (such as an explosion or a piano played by a wheel on

---

7. According to Goebbels, all sounds are live-electronically processed by a program called LISA (Live-Sampling), developed by the STEIM studios (Michael Waisvisz) and "throwing back whatever the performer creates himself."

the keyboard), there is a distortion of acoustic proportions. This makes one think about how we are going to make certain discoveries through the medium of performance, discoveries that, however small, play a major role in the life of our hero-scientist.

There are many kinds of soundscapes in this work. The idea of music is equal—but not more equal—to that of other elements in the performance. Among the major roles for music are the concepts of "feelings" and nostalgic atmosphere such as that suggested by the Ravel A-minor Piano Trio heard in the middle. The sound sources coincide in many places with the actions of the performer—but not always. Even the fact that we don't always recognize where the sound comes from contributes to the effect of complexity. What we are presented with on the stage is the model or representation of a single scientist who creates thoughts, images, and sounds in his playful research, a path that we can follow without really being able to follow its logic or necessity; it is a path full of impulse, intuition, and improvisation, and of surprises that we cannot anticipate. There is otherwise no dramatic action and nothing at all about human relationships. Models and clichés in human relationships in the traditional theater call for us to anticipate behavior, and it is our very expectation that is confirmed or overthrown. But here every action and every moment is a surprise. The price of this constant re-innovation of the piece (as the performer says "I invent myself") is the lack of "psychological depth." We are—and the piece is—driven by the surprising and often beautiful sounds seemingly produced by the performer. But we also know that the piece has a team of stage hands and technicians working behind the scene to control the technical facilities and help with the samplers and keyboards, all this to intensify our impression of a polyvalent actor going restlessly from one idea, one object, one place to another as if he could ever come near to a "solution" or to enlightenment. This comes close to a magic show and gives the piece its high concentration on the performer and its density as well as its entertaining qualities.

Why did Goebbels choose these particular texts, verbal and musical? They create an intellectual nest, a substrate as a biologist would say, for the development of an "instrumental theater" where the "instruments" have been extended to include anything that makes sound. There is nothing bizarre or alien in it. Although the figure of the scientist follows the cliché of the "crazy professor," we are much nearer here to the true craziness of the professor than will ever be found in film or television. This is partly because of the quality of the texts, which express truly existential problems, and partly because of the physical presence of a live performance that is intensified by the use of fire. The pyrotechnics never become independent or mere "effect" but are logical outcomes of the professor's own logic. The acting itself and the exclusion of any other person on stage (who would instantly destroy this intense situation by creating a relationship) acts like a microscope on the actions of a single human being who carries the burden of knowledge and lucidity.

In this context, the music does not exist as something external. Everything, music included, has reached the same sense of distance, the same degree of justification for its existence. Is this still music theater? Do we care? Because of the character and uniqueness of the protagonist, we find ourselves imitating him. We participate in those of his experiments that populate our aural space with various odd sounds. We start to expect such sounds and to be able to follow their creation. We listen to his voice and we know that because of the music of language, he is speaking to us also for musical reasons. Perhaps there are some people—the funders, the theater company, the public relations officer, or the critic—who need to put the piece in the right drawer, who care whether this really is music theater. But why should we care? Pieces like *Max Black* have been and remain a provocation to traditionalist institutions.

Further Reading

Barnes, Jennifer. *Television Opera, the Fall of Opera Commissioned for Television*. Woodbridge, UK, 2002.

Bolter, Jay David, and Richard Grusin. *Remediation: Understanding New Media*. Cambridge, MA, 1998.

Bianconi, Lorenzo, and Giorgio Pestelli. *Storia dell'opera italiana*. Vol. 4, *Il sistema produttivo e le sue competenze*; Vol. 5, *La spettacolarità*; Vol. 6, *Teorie e tecniche, immagini e fantasmi*. Torino, 1988.

Cohan, Steven, ed. *Hollywood Musicals: The Film Reader*. London and New York, 2002.

Dahlhaus, Carl. "Traditionelle Dramaturgie in der modernen Oper." In *Musiktheater heute*. Mainz, 1982, pp. 20ff.

Feneyrou, Laurent, ed. *Musique et dramaturgie, Esthétique de la représentation au XXe siècle*. Paris, 2003.

Ishaghpour, Youssef. *Opéra et théâtre dans le cinéma d'aujourd'hui*. Paris, 1995, p. 12.

McLuhan, Eric, and Frank Zingione, eds. *Essential McLuhan*. New York, 1996.

McLuhan, Marshall. *The Gutenberg Galaxy*. Toronto, 1962.

McLuhan, Marshall. *Understanding Media*. New York, 1964; repr. 1994.

Miceli, Sergio. *Musica e cinema nella cultura del Novecento*. Milan, 2000.

Morricone, Ennio, and Sergio Miceli. *Comporre per il cinema. Teorie e prassi della musica nel film*. Rome, 2001.

Sandner, Wolfgang. *Heiner Goebbels: Komposition als Inszenierung*. Berlin, 2002.

Simpson, Alexander Thomas, Jr. *Opera on Film: A Study of the History and the Aesthetic Principles and Conflicts of a Hybrid Genre*. Ph.D. dissertation, University of Kentucky/University of Louisville, 1990.

Steenstra, Sytze G. *We Are the Noise between Stations: A Philosophical Exploration of the Work of David Byrne, at the Crossroads of Popular Media, Conceptual Art, and Performance Theatre*. Maastricht, The Netherlands, June 2003.

"...and how did *you* like it?"

Around 1960, one of the authors (ES) was a fifth-string critic at the *New York Times*, covering the new music of the day (Cage and Varèse, dodecaphony at the ISCM, Fluxus events, and proto happenings) as well as neoclassical oboe sonatas and minor cast changes at the old Metropolitan Opera. New operas were not performed at the Met (or anywhere else for that matter), and music critics did not cover the off- and off-off-Broadway theater or the dance world where a lot of the really new music and new music theater was just beginning to be heard.

On this particular evening, the author found himself at intermission with his opposite number, an elderly gentleman who was covering for the other major morning paper (now long extinct). This distinguished critic had graduated from Boston Latin School and Harvard University at the turn of another century and, as he never failed to remind anyone who would listen, he had been in the house—it was the same house that we were still in—when Olive Fremsted sang the American premiere of Richard Strauss's *Salome* in 1907 (a *scandale* that was not repeated for many years thereafter). Presumably that long-ago evening had made a deep impression on him as he talked about it constantly. The irony was that although 1907 performances continued to be extremely vivid to him, contemporary performance circa 1960 generally eluded him completely. He often slept through concerts, being intermittently awakened only by audience applause.[1] This required him to go to the newspaper files and write a condensed summary of previous reviews of the same artists (how he reviewed debuts was never clear).

On this particular evening, however, this elderly gentleman showed some remarkable signs of life. We were in the press office and the company's press representative was conversing animatedly in Italian with an Italian visitor. Our distinguished critic, not to be outdone, began to give his impressions of the evening's performance in what passed for fluent Ciceronian Latin, an accomplishment that he had apparently acquired at the aforementioned Boston Latin School. This was so remarkable that it seemed worth the effort to try to persuade him to write his review in that elegant ancient language. If nothing else, it suited the theme of the opera of the evening which was, as I recall, Bellini's *Norma*, set in

---

1. If, as sometimes happened, the audience failed to applaud and the performers plunged ahead to the next piece on the program, he would be left with the impression that one of the works listed on the program had been omitted.

ancient Roman times. The newspaper in question was famous for its eccentricities and, in any case, late night reviews, if not actually obscene, went into the paper essentially unedited. Our distinguished critic was walked back to his office, rehearsing all the while the exact wording of this elegant classical review, which, without a doubt, would have made journalistic history.

Alas, the review the next morning was his usual compendium of previous clichés, all indubitably in warmed-over English.

Our elderly friend's choice—to rehash some received ideas or try to express something new in an incomprehensible manner—might represent the state of music criticism when faced with new ideas. Resistance to the experimental forms of modernism eventually gives way to their acceptance and that, in turn, provokes resistance to the novelties of the next generation. We saw this with the generation of Schoenberg, who told Virgil Thomson that the music of Kurt Weill was the only music he knew that had no value whatsoever. It recurred again with the critical establishment that came to support dodecaphony and had, therefore, to reject everything else that followed. Even Adorno, who supported Schoenberg and set up the famous dichotomy of Schoenberg versus Stravinsky, attacked Weill's work in America in his famous 1950 obituary in the *Frankfurter Rundschau,* a judgment that has been mindlessly repeated ad infinitum ever since. Adorno could not even support the new serialism, which his own writings had helped to nurture. And then the serialists, unmindful that they were simply repeating their own history from the other side, attacked the next generation of new ideas. IRCAM opened its doors to music theater and related kinds of performances only after Boulez ceased to be its director.

The essential conservatism of classical music in the twentieth century, especially as compared to the visual arts and the other performing arts (theater, dance), is striking even when the most advanced forms of modernism are theoretically being supported and espoused by critics and musical institutions. The institutional foundations of classical music—its Latin vocabulary so to speak—are the same today as they were 150 years ago: the conservatory, opera companies, symphonic orchestras, and concert halls with all their accompanying institutional structures and critical apparatus. Underneath all this lies the basic underlying assumption, largely derived from nineteenth-century German idealistic philosophy, that music is the highest form of the arts because it is the purest and the most abstract. Ironically, this is a critical position that places music at the apex of artistic expression precisely because it is the most difficult of all the arts to explain in words. This is the great paradox that has led to the triumph of instrumental music as the highest and least contaminated form of musical expression (not to say all artistic endeavor) and it is at the root of the split between modernist music and all forms of opera and music theater.

The standard critical formulae of the twentieth century can be summarized in a few words: the universal conviction that innovation is (theoretically) desirable combined with an active and deep-seated dislike of anything truly new. This induces critics to espouse the innovations of the generation past (as "real innovation") while trivializing what they have just heard ("nothing new"). The other major criteria are purity of form and an absolute horror of anything that smacks of commercialization and kitsch. All of this leaves only a very poor vocabulary for the critical evaluation of new work in general and opera and music theater in particular. The result is that critics are seemingly constrained to review new work by rehashing old formulas or by writing their reviews in Latin.

Further Reading

Cott, Jonathan. *Back to a Shadow in the Night: Music Journalism and Writings: 1968–2001*. New York, 2003.

Grant, Mark N. *Maestros of the Pen: A History of Classical Music Criticism in America*. Boston, 1998.

part iv **After the Show:**
         Taking It Apart

chapter 19

Toward a Theory of the New Music Theater

> ...the gathering was splendid and today's performance of *Don Juan* (Mozart's *Don Giovanni*) was the object of the conversation. Everyone was united in praising the Italians and the energy of their performance. Little remarks, thrown here and there, made it clear that everyone had a sense of the deeper significance of this opera of all operas. Don Ottavio was well liked. Donna Anna was too passionate for one fellow. In the theater, he explained, everything should be properly moderate and anything too aggressive avoided. Wasn't he shocked by this story about rape and murder? At this moment, he took a pinch of snuff and looked incredibly stupid to his neighbor, who insisted that the Italian lady was certainly a beautiful woman but paid too little attention to her appearance. It was exactly in this scene that she let her hair down and covered her profile! Then someone else began to hum softly (Don Giovanni's aria) "Fin ch'han dal vino" whereupon a lady remarked that the Italian Don Juan was her least favorite; he was too dark, too serious and didn't make this frivolous and merry character as light-hearted as he should have been. The big explosion at the end of the piece (where Don Giovanni is dragged down to hell) was praised by all. Fed up with this rubbish, I ran up to my room.
>
> from E.T.A. Hoffmann, *Don Juan*

Analysis and criticism

Ernst Theodor Amadeus Hoffmann, a multi-talented artist of the early romantic period, composed the first German romantic opera (*Undine*, 1814), but is today mostly remembered for his short stories. The story entitled *Don Juan* concerns an early nineteenth-century performance of the

Don Giovanni by that other Amadeus. His account of audience reactions some two hundred years ago is amusingly contemporary. In addition to the usual clichés, there is the deep division between those in the know and those on the outside. Music, being closed in on itself, presumably without any reference to anything outside itself, demands knowledge to be understood. On the other hand—and this is the paradox—the direct affective impact of music does not necessarily call for any specific knowledge at all.

What then constitutes musical "understanding"?

In his review of Sebastian Claren's book about Morton Feldman's *Neither*, Eberhard Blum, an important flutist of contemporary music who worked closely with Feldman, stated that attempts to describe or analyze Feldman's music, no matter how detailed, leave him cold as do all attempts to approach a musical artwork in such a way. Blum professes to be happy that Claren did not find Feldman's musical "secret." "As long as we listen and play the music," he argues, "the enigma is solved without needing to put the solution into words."

The reconstruction of signification and meaning in the historical spoken drama and its connections to philosophical interpretations of the past make up an exciting and enlightening enterprise that provides a clear-sighted view of history. Alas, there is this strange feeling that all the efforts to put together text, singing, music, action, lighting, and costuming in opera and music theater do not make it any easier to grasp the message, that is, the overall meaning. Setting a text of high quality and complexity to music risks garbling it with an almost complete loss of its quality as a text. But insofar as such a setting is the result of proven traditions and in-depth thinking, we know that this cannot really be the case. This paradox demonstrates the hard-to-describe "otherness" of music theater as compared to music or drama, considered separately.

The emotional, nonverbal route and the more conscious, scientific method have something in common. Whether we want to find out "how it works" out of sheer human curiosity or for strictly professional reasons, the notion of understanding is central to both positions. Merely speaking about an experience means sharing it with others, exchanging viewpoints, judging and evaluating what makes culture in one way or another.

Most of us would agree that culture is made up of actions—creating, producing, or "consuming" music theater pieces, for example. So, what role does theory play? At what point do criticism and analysis come into play? Condensed into a simple question, we might ask, "What is analysis good for?"

Do we need a dense net of cross-references to help us understand the performers in their attempts to carry us away in thoughts and dreams? If we were from some distant place and not conscious of the possible connotations of a piece, would we be able to have the same understanding as someone from the culture? Or does music, supposedly the most universal of all the arts, appeal directly to our senses above and beyond the cultural foreknowledge?

References for understanding

The first reference point for understanding—especially in the nonverbal art of music—is the purely esthetic. Without specific knowledge, we depend on intuition and fantasy to solve a problem or decipher an experience. The traditional touchstone of esthetic theory was beauty and the artist's job was to create beautiful objects, whether physical, verbal, or aural. Most twentieth-century theory tells us that this notion of the beautiful has been corrupted in modern times and is now useless as a reference for meaning.

One might well ask, with music-philosopher Peter Kivy, why the esthetic principles of Aristotle on beauty would not apply to music theater anymore: "something that is too small cannot be beautiful, something that is too large cannot be beautiful because we cannot take in the whole"[1] As a result of the steady commercial exploitation of beautifully designed objects and images of human beauty, we learn that being seduced by the beautiful leads to the conclusion that it is only a commercial object. This makes it difficult to accept beauty as the central idea of a noncommercial work of art. In this way, the arts re-form themselves as counter-criticism against the commercialism of the culture that wants to market beauty as a saleable item. For example, contemporary drama strips the stage of its beautiful embellishments and puts conflict on center stage as a sort of a "counter-beauty" or even outright ugliness.

As beauty has become a problematic and consumerist reference for judging modern art, we have to look out for other possible references to understand and capture meaning. Another counter-critical option would be *"art for art's sake,"* that is, art that has no purpose but is only an esthetic object that follows its own logic: "It doesn't mean anything so it must be art." However dynamic, transitory, and dependent on cultural context art may be, beauty may again take its place in society and become a more dominant theme in the arts if properly treated as abstraction: beautiful objects made for the sake of creating beautiful objects.

The problem is that music tends to appeal directly to our senses, often circumventing what we might think we know about it, with the result that we instinctively decide what is pleasing and what is not. This is the simplest

1. Peter Kivy, *Osmin's Rage, Philosophical Reflections on Opera, Drama, and Text* (Princeton, NJ, 1988), 51.

and most basic form of criticism, and biologists would tell us that—in sexual matters at least—there are good biological bases for deciding what (or, rather, who) is beautiful (for example, smooth skin and regular features as indicators of good health or good genes). In the same way, loud, complex gibbon or howler monkey "songs," although not necessarily conventionally "beautiful" to our ears, might indicate a healthy male owner of a territory and thus serve to scare away competitive males but attract females. Human culture is, no doubt, more complex than baboon culture, but in neither case is music expected to be always merely dull and pleasing. Perhaps it might be in order for us to place the powerful—the overwhelming, the sublime—next to the beautiful as a criterion for art.

The images of the beautiful and the sublime, questionable in their reductionist view as they may be, nevertheless lead us to the problems and trials of "drama-made music" from Monteverdi to Wagner at least. All of European music history is laid out before us in a coherent stream of traditions, but, as Kivy tells us, history tends to blur the discontinuities. Furthermore, the closed nature of those historic events cannot apply to the openness of today's creation. Kivy, a good Aristotelian, views the construction of opera as a nonmusical art form. All this shows us that most of the mystery about traditional opera and music theater comes from the way both try to connect two different syntaxes: text and music. Music—as a principle of organization as well as sound-as-an-art—requires patterns, forms, and manageable human proportions. In this view, even pieces that are nearly five hundred years old seem fresh and full of structural inspiration. Galilei tells us that "it is not enough merely to take pleasure in the various harmonies heard between the parts of a musical composition unless one also determines the proportions in which the voices are combined."[2]

Criticism: a system in itself

If we look more closely at our task, analysis reveals itself to be a subset of possible approaches toward a work. Although music criticism is sometimes thought of as more journalistic than theoretical, the word has been adapted as an umbrella term that includes journalistic reviewing as well as analysis. The Greek source of the word means "to divide." And this is exactly what analysis, criticism, and reviewing has to do: that is, divide the overwhelming and complex whole of a performance or a new work into manageable chunks. The aim is to pin down the manifold references and connotations, follow the traces, evaluate them, and construct a meaning and sense out of the material under consideration.

2. Kivy, *Osmin's Rage*, 49.

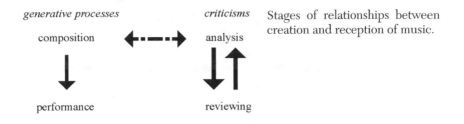

generative processes   *criticisms*   Stages of relationships between
                                                             creation and reception of music.

composition   ◀·—··▶   analysis

↓   ↓↑

performance   reviewing

Artistic creation is a process that is always aimed at a specific moment: the time when the work is being communicated to the public. At this precise time, the piece is "happening." The question of whether the performance is itself creation or only interpretation is relevant only afterward. But there is then a third step (after creation and performance) that consists in looking back at the concept, the composition, its interpretation and performance. In the broadest sense, this looking back is criticism. Analysis is understood as a textual criticism of the concept or score of a work, whereas journalistic reviewing is another subset of criticism dealing with the performance.

Patterns, models, and ideals

If we examine our instinctive reactions more closely, we find a conscious layer where we look out for patterns. We look for samples, patterns, models, and even ideals that we already know or think we know, and we use them for comparative purposes. These samples are not just theoretical words but practical experiences. Recognition is the precise word for what this is: the repetition of a cognitive act. The original cognitive act—which could go back to early childhood—might be difficult to recall in exact detail, so criticism and analysis work mostly by the comparative method. This is where the concept of the *Gestalt* comes in and this also explains why we have problems with vagueness, lack of definition, or variability. When the objects or samples that we have to deal with are in a state of change or metamorphosis, their perception can be a difficult task and we tend to drift away from the job of figuring out what they actually mean.

Analysis also has to be discursive. This means finding the problem and working it out into a solution in exactly the same way that a composer deals with the problems presented by his concepts and his ideas. For example, the subject of a fugue might impose the problem of whether the answer should be tonal or real or what the countersubject might be. In this sense, the composer is always analyzing—consciously or intuitively—by referring to the same models that his audience will use.

If we know the samples and models, the works of art will speak to us. In this way, the creation of art and its reception are closely linked through the use and recognition of samples, models, and ideals that we have in common.

This is a technical approach, and analysis, as the word itself implies, needs specific musical and theoretical knowledge and skill. Its academic study requires confrontation with a system on its own terms, often in hermetic theoretical language, full of technical jargon about comparing bar numbers or calculating "pitch-class-sets."[3] Inside the professional music theory business there have been ongoing discussions, if not wars, about how to describe, define, categorize—that is, analyze—music, all of it in order to construct a specialized academic system that follows its own "scientific" rules. According to Nicholas Cook, "The principal types of musical analysis current today do not have any real scientific validity, and we therefore need to rethink what it is that they can tell us about music."[4] The same author questions also if a supposedly scientific analysis can explain what "the listener" actually will be hearing. This concept of the imagined listener will be treated below. For the moment, we need only say that despite the claim in many analytical texts as to the existence of the ideal listener, we are unlikely to ever meet any in real life. Finally, if there are no scientific criteria for deciding what a certain artistic constellation really is, searching for it could be considered a waste of time. Somewhere, Albert Einstein said that mystery is important in both science and art.

Often the meaning of an art work lies in the models that the artist, consciously or not, makes reference to and not in what the actual composition shows. By skillfully simplifying, reducing, even de-coloring and de-ornamenting, it is possible to trace back from the actual composition to its models. These models—schemes, samples, clichés—have to exist somewhere earlier in history and this is information that can be acquired by anyone through study or through careful observation, comparison, and recognition. Take, for example, the abstraction known as "aria form." Then compare the purely theoretical models (there are more than one) with actual arias by George Frederick Handel, John Cage, or Georg Friedrich Haas. The essence of the art lies in the differences between the model and the final text while the "meaning" remains in the model.

The system of society

We like to "re-cognize"; hence the popularity of repetition in our socio-cultural system. Michael Brenner, director of Germany's biggest musical

3. A statistical method invented by music theorist Allan Forte—under the influence of the serial composer Milton Babbitt—in the late 1970s to define the use of certain pitches, relationships, and patterns in mostly atonal music.
4. Nicholas Cook, *A Guide to Musical Analysis* (London, 1987), 224 ff.

production company, says that the audiences "ask for music which is known already."[5] The constants in our lives are often shattered and fragmented; nostalgia and revivals are subforms of a constant in which experiences are repeated. These are "closed cases"—such as, for example, the experience of meeting old friends without the unease of the unknown. The familiar style of the musical numbers, the internal appearance of repetition and its uses as well as return and reprise throughout the larger form are all hallmarks of how the music works in these popular musical shows. If we study the dramaturgies, not only of musicals but also of popular theater and literature, we find that familiar schemes and formal models are much more commonly used than individual creative inventions. The cultural system of society organizes the samples.

When referring to general cultural conditions and traditions, we all follow the cultural system that has been established by a particular society. The organization of society includes values that are called in to help judge objects or actions. Pure perception is followed by a process of evaluation that might accept or reject the object or the action as pleasing, meaningful, useful, and so on. Part of this process might involve reading criticism or attending a lot of live performances. In the modernist period, this would likely involve some kind of system such as serialism. Or it might be that, as Feldman liked to say, "I am the system." Although Feldman was not quite an autodidact, he composed according to methods of his own devising, mostly inspired by the so-called abstract expressionist painters who were his principal colleagues and influences. Being self-taught does not necessarily mean that as an artist or as a "consumer" of art, you are any less adept, and it might even be proof of outstanding analytical capacities. In most cases, however, the self-educated spend a lifetime with the special status conferred by a sociocultural system that labels them uneducated.

All of this weakens the importance of musicological hermeticism, especially when it concerns something that actually is accessible to anyone with healthy ears. The job is, as always, to find the right path, making "claims not too ambitious or too modest."[6]

We are still a distance away from a theory in which analysis is understood as a subset of criticism. This is not so much about making claims as it is about asking the right questions, about addressing a creative potential that might have the power to change viewpoints, about challenging fantasy, about imagining new explanations or new answers to old questions. Finally, it is about questioning one's own perceptions.

5. Interview in *DB-NEWS* (newsletter of the German Railway Corporation), January 2006, p. 42.
6. Cook, *Guide to Musical Analysis*, 232.

When the question of situating a work in its proper sociocultural and artistic context is answered, the focus might go to the text. In opera and music theater, the "text"—in the metaphorical sense of that term—is summed up by the cast of characters, the dramatis personae which usually appears on the second page of the score or libretto and on the principal page of the program. This casting—not just the cast list but the actual physical presence of the performers—embraces the visual, textual, and audible elements of the work that is to be performed. Music theater that avoids the human element as its center of interest is only underlining this reality by avoiding it. Most music theater deals with the human body even when it makes the body disappear.[7]

But this is not the end of it. The sociocultural system is also exclusive. The demon of categorization hounds us: those things that are too difficult to be easily categorized will likely be dumped first. The presumed desirability of the "new" is actually ambiguous. An appearance of newness or of being pleasing will help make something fashionable and acceptable for a while and also help it to be easily forgotten afterward. Radically new things are rarely welcomed. They have to prove that they can become and remain a part of our large cultural model or sample collection.

We also have to consider other levels as well. We might ask, for example, whether a piece is situated in the right place. Some works might be at home in a nightclub, another only in the refectory of a monastery; a third might need a theater building. The question of what constitutes a theater has been opened up in experimental work (see Chapter 7); the limitations of playing only in old-fashioned theaters might cause music theater to become even more context-ridden. In the 1950s and 1960s, it was fashionable to go into factories to play for (or to confront) the workers. In the 1970s and 1980s, it was the fashion to go into abandoned factories. Have factories become unfashionable since the 1990s? Or are we dealing here with a real socioeconomic factor (i.e., the flight of blue-collar jobs to other parts of the world)?

The music-theater object

Basically there are only two questions that need to be posed: "What is it about?" and the ubiquitous intermission question, "How do you like it?"

---

7. An interesting example of a piece that brings in both the analytical process and the body as a stage element is Dick Raaijmakers *Dépons/Der Fall* (1992, 1993) in which he transfers Muybridge's photographic studies of movement into music theater. The same subject had been previously treated as music theater by JoAnne Akalaitis and Philip Glass in *The Photographer* (1983).

Answers differ but even the most abstruse doctoral dissertation finally has to do with expressing an opinion, creating a reference, deciding on value, and understanding the message—in short, all forms of analysis. In any case, we have to keep in mind that answers do not necessarily lead to "the" truth and that an exciting response or an elaborate explanation can refer to a deadly boring piece (or the other way round.)

Is it the job of the analysis to tell us if a piece is boring in performance? The gap between concept and reality sometimes becomes all too clear. What could create artistic significance and value as seen from an analytical, theoretical point, considering the newness of the work and its relationship to previous cultural achievements in the field? Does it or does it not match the audience's interests or demands? How much does that matter? And not least, what are we actually talking about, what is our "object"?

Music, being simultaneously precise (through notation, the score) and vague (because of its ephemeral character), has only a very thin connection to the real, physical world. This makes it quite tolerant to all sorts of misinterpretation, voluntary or otherwise. Fortunately, no one will break a leg or lose his life because of a bad analysis—say, a miscount in a twelve-tone row or the claim that the Bach-Fugue in B minor, BWV 869, contains the first example of twelve-tone music—wrong historically and wrong esthetically. Would this make anyone look at or listen to that particular piece of music in a different way?

The first example of twelve-tone music? Theme of the Bach Fugue in B minor from *Das Wohltemperierte Klavier, Book I.*

We might think of analysis as something that reconstructs what the composer has done. It may decipher codes or hidden messages such as the hidden names in Schumann's or Berg's works. It can discover the interrelationships of the characters in Wagner's *Tetralogy* through the *Leitmotif* or the truth of a political attitude, as in the symphonies of Shostakovich or Dallapiccola's protest music. Whoever persuaded Communist Party commissars to call composers like Shostakovich, Lutoslawski, or Eisler *bourgeois formalists* was actually performing some kind of analysis even if this was only based on an impression of confusion and "cacophony," an opinion about the presumed social and political function of music rather than on any real structural analysis (as would seem to be implied by the word "formalist"). Although the mere musical notes alone do not tell us anything specific, the connotations that come from the social and historical background of music do certainly bear meaning. Even without text, music can be full of references, emotions, and signification. As Peter Kivy expresses it, this is an examination that comes down between operatic practice and philosophical theory where the formal and the representational coalesce in an optimal way. Where this happens, the results are largely about human emotion. In other words, the purely musical form must be satisfying or, as Kivy writes, "What music can't do, opera can't do."

Without discussing the question of whether music itself is a "language," we can acknowledge that music theater of all sorts usually employs verbal texts as well as stage actions which, if understood by the audience, do carry meaning and might even get into conflict with the connoted meanings of the music.

Music that evokes other music is usually connected to special events or specific societies. It carries those images with it and needs the trained or educated listener to detect the messages. More common is the case when a specific song is stripped of its text and the citation consists of only the melody, or bits of it. The whole story of the song may be evoked by just a small piece of it and the amount of musical information needed for recognition can be astonishingly small. In the Nazi era, the BBC used four timpani notes, G-G-G-Eb, the opening of Beethoven's Fifth Symphony, to introduce their news broadcasts. If someone in Germany were detected listening to those four timpani notes, it could have meant a death sentence—even though the source was one of Germany's greatest composers!

A musical death sentence?

In brief, meaning in music may come from what the music brings along from the nonmusical, real world. Nevertheless there is a difference between "pure" music and music combined with words or action. Music for film or any form of theater is no longer pure music and, in this larger context, our perception of it is changed. And this is where our analytic problems begin.

The music theater object is a complex intertwined artwork and it has to be considered as a whole. This whole is often extended in length (some might remember their parents listening to opera for what seemed to be days at a time and asking "Why are operas always so long?") but in other ways as well. The relationships between the various ingredients are difficult to judge and the resulting effect in performance becomes more and more difficult to pin down as more elements are added in. It is the analyst's job to slice and dice the whole into handy, manageable portions. The list below shows the analyst's agenda on the subject of music theater—not so different from the inquiring listener/watcher's list:

Phenomenological

- What do the words say?
- What happens at the same time in the music (melodic/vocal lines; instrumental accompaniment)?
- What are the singers doing at that moment?
- How do they look (physiognomy, gestures, movements, costumes)?
- Where are they on the set and how do they interact with each other and their environment?
- What are the reactions and possible interactions with the audience? Is there a perceivable effect of the 'here and now' moment?

Historical (the "context")

- What are the historical references of the story, the social situation, the language, the musical style, the visual and architectural style?
- Is there a gap between expectations and realization?
- If there is a gap, it is a result of incompetence ("poor performance"), over-compensation ("huge success," "surprise"), or innovation ("unknown," lack of reference or knowledge on the part of the public)

Emotional

- Are we touched? Are we shocked?
- Do our reactions, feelings and observations change or tire or fade?
- Is it the personality of a particular performer or the particular persona that attracts our attention?

This can be brought into another, more straightforward scheme:

The music theater object is composed of static aspects: the concept, the composition (the score), the motivations of the composer, and the formal implications of the work. The dynamic aspect is represented by "subjects" (not to be confused with the "subject matter" or narrative of the work), which include the cast (the actor/performers and their interpretations) but also the earlier mentioned "ideal listener," invented by the music theorist or analyst but also often addressed by composers themselves as they imagine their "ideal audience."

abstract / concept

dynamic / subjects

music theater "object"

The music theater object as process or product.

From a phenomenological point of view, music theater could be equally well regarded as either a process or a product.

Another way of looking at music theater is to regard it as the result of the overlapping of several systems of expression that causes those systems to merge into a new supersystem. But that way of thinking does not make things any easier.

In the Kantian view, opera (or music theater) is a product. The more correct analogy may be that it is a process of addition, "the sum of its parts," as in a work with noncommunicating activities on separate tracks such as Stockhausen's *Originale* or the Cage *Europeras*. Or it actually may be the product of multiplication, where music, text, and action are synchronized and "surplus value" is formed as a result. If this were the case, opera would need different specialists to judge and analyze the different intertwined arts. For example, score, text, and *mis-en-scène* would require three different critics to work together in the analysis of a piece.[8]

Of course, these simple mathematical analogies with sums or products as end results do not really do justice to a truly organic symbiosis of

8. When the works of Menotti or Bernstein were performed on Broadway, the *New York Times* sent both theater and music critics to review. Most of the time, the music critic would praise the dramatic qualities of the piece while attacking the music while the theater critic would praise the music but criticize the theater.

elements in a music-theater performance where the interaction is dynamic and ongoing.

The end result of a process—the final cut, so to speak—is not necessarily the final curtain on opening night. Theatrical works develop their drama-turgical impact through a series of performances. Changes may be made by the creators (composer, librettist), by the director, or by the performers through their performance experience. The behavior of the audience, the reaction of the public, or the report of the critics may have an unplanned or even subliminal influence on the performers. Live performances vary from evening to evening, from audience to audience, and from place to place. All of this constitutes aspects of the dramaturgy of a work.

This generating process, of course, starts early in the development of the piece. Sometimes the development of a work—sketches, conversations, letters—can be as fascinating and enlightening as the completed work itself. The *critique génétique*, developed by French structuralists in the 1970s, allows us to look in a more scientific and academically acceptable way at the generating process. Although developed for research on literature, this is still a rather young field with many possibilities for both music and music theater. In some respects, it has to be regarded as the history of the making of a work, which collects all sorts of documentation to examine its origins. In this view, the process of the work-coming-into-being is a text that includes the history of its creation (including its preparation in rehearsal) leading to performance.

Beyond libretto: meta-text

Changes in performance space (stage, auditorium, seating, location, venue), performance time (duration, starting time, canned theatrical or pre-produced "time"), social conditions (abandoning the social dress code, opening up of the opera to various classes, even the change in the cost of tickets) are all profound differences that helped call into being new and different types of libretti. And the developing interest in the phonological phenomenon of speech and language brought into question the semantic qualities of text itself. All these higher deconstructive processes take us to another level, that of "meta-text."[9]

9. "Metatext is all, or almost all, interpretation. In its first freshness, it widens one's eyes, offering an unaccustomed vision of a text. But soon the vision is replaced by an image, and then (if the metatext is as effective as it is inter-esting) by a statue, indeed an icon, of the author.... Metatext accommodates the text to new circumstances, insuring its relevance now, guaranteeing its irrelevance in the future, until another metatext can be imagined" (Samuel Kinser, *Rabelais's Carnival: Text, Context, Metatext* [Berkeley, c. 1990]). http://ark.cdlib.org/ark:/13030/ft596nb3qo/.

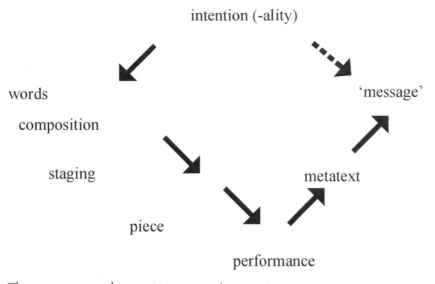

intention (-ality)

words   'message'

composition

staging   metatext

piece

performance

The message an author wants to pass on is many steps away.

The definition of meta-text as interpretation makes sense for new music theater. Many pieces are difficult to understand solely on the basis of a written story because the text is often inaudible, fragmented, or otherwise distorted. The concept of meta-text embraces the *whole* concept/composition of a music-theater piece. We can easily leave out the prefix "meta-" and just speak of "text" in music theater. Text in this sense includes the libretto plus a lot more.

The scheme above summarizes in a flowchart the process of theater. This is to be understood, not in a practical sense, but as an abstract formal skeleton. Psychological and philosophical areas are touched on.

What is intentionality? What is the difference between the piece and the performance in terms of temporality? What do we eventually "understand"? Which "text" (or meta-text or message) is finally created in our understanding? What differences come into view by considering the culture, the audience, the conditions of particular performances?

There is, at the very least, a flash of "intentionality"' in every performance, a moment when the performance is actually about something. Visual art in the twentieth century has taught us to be cautious about defining the rules of what art is or has to be. Music and music theater are somewhat more complex because of the on- and off-stage team involved in getting any production onto the stage. "Intentionality" guides the team to create, in a given space and time, a text that is something more than the piece because the piece is also a concept. The performance, as an action, creates this "text," which inevitably carries a message. Whether this message is the one intended by the artists depends on both the piece *and* the performance. Pieces without a written score, without a libretto, or even without a performance concept exist only in someone's imagination or, as an "open text," in the realm of the virtual. In any case, a message will be transmitted to the spectator. It is in the difference between the intended message and the actual transmission, or between the intended message and the spectator's understanding of it, that things can go wrong. "What did the artist want to tell us?" we ask. Is it irony or just our (or the audience's) stubbornness?

The intentionality of a performance defines the space for the performance in many possible ways. The recognizable signs that modify a specific space draw the borders between, on the one hand, an inside space consisting of the performer and the performance and, on the other, an outside space made up of the audience, the spectators, and the rest of the world. As spectators, we have no problem recognizing the chatting, laughing, and coughing in the audience or the emergency exit lights or accidental events like noise from the street as belonging to the outside space. We are used to making judgments about such objects or events in everyday life so we have no trouble separating them from others intended by the performers to be part of that inside space that we designate as the performance. The recognition of these two spaces is a phenomenon of live theater and live performance in general. With dynamics and overlaps, it remains a basic part of the essential significance of live performance. As opposed to this, projected and media art lack the warm bodies of the performers and thus do not address the complex questions that derive from the fact that, in live performance, "it is happening only here and now." In some electronic media art performances, the onlooker himself becomes a performer as he enters a space that looks like a stage but where borders between the spaces are intentionally blurred. Putting the audience into the performance space or, conversely, putting performance elements into the audience creates surprise by placing elements of the outside on the inside or inside events in the outside, thus creating a sort of theatrical hyperrealism. Performances in public spaces tend to play a great deal with this phenomenon. Participatory theater encourages boundary crossing from the other side by reversing the usual audience habits. Instead of being voyeurs, the public turns into exhibitionists.

Working these levels was a basic part of the new music theater starting with the early experiments in Russian theater.[10] They are found everywhere

10. Examples are Aleksej Krucenych's *Pobeda nad solncem* ("Victory over the Sun"), premiered in St. Petersburg in 1913, and Alexander Tairov's (1885–1950) "synthetic theater."

in Mauricio Kagel's instrumental theater. Luigi Nono, in his articles *"Appunti per un teatro musicale attuale"* ("Notes on a contemporary music theater," 1961) and *"Possibilità e necessità di un nuovo teatro musicale"* ("Possibility and necessity for a new music theater," 1963),[11] calls movement the most important difference between the static traditional opera and new music theater. Kagel, in his own manifesto (1960),[12] also refers to kinesis, in particular the onstage movement of musicians, as a basic characteristic of instrumental theater. For Kagel, a stage properly equipped with multimedia would reflect the relationship between the music and the space. Kagel wants the musicians to move and to act in such spaces and, whether or not these movements constitute "acting," they would be the typically controlled exaggerations and stereotypical gestures of musicians in performance action. Or perhaps they are just the insignificant gestures of normal human behavior. Kagel conjectured that noise and sound, musical or otherwise, are often only the by-products of scenic performance. He was interested in observing this minimalistic and ephemeral margin of theatrical and musical performance. The role that the musician plays is himself or herself and the self-reflective nature of Kagel's instrumental theater becomes instantly evident. In this "instrumental theater," sound-producing gestures are created and transmitted, replacing spoken text but forming a meta-text in the sense defined earlier.

In Kagel's *Pas de cinq* (1965), five actors in dark glasses with canes and umbrellas wander slowly through a labyrinth of ramps and turning stage elements, tapping out rhythms. This is the composer's way of dealing with the theater as a myth of itself from which different "stories" can be distilled. These stories are without spoken text but are composed of movement, light, and sound. Recent music theater sometimes prefers to deny, rather than tell, a story or narration in a dramaturgically comprehensive way (this tendency is also found in the visual arts since Joseph Beuys). The German word *Verweigerung* or "deniers" is the name for artists who founded their work on a specific kind of opaque retreat close to the kind of existential thinking known from the work of Marcel Duchamp and Samuel Beckett and their musical confreres John Cage and Morton Feldman; Helmut Lachenmann, Salvatore Sciarrino, and the more recent German *Wandelweiser* composers are examples. These are the esthetics, not of the sensational, the shocking and the larger-than-life but of the small and the inconspicuous with their compelling demands to be looked at and listened to from close up.

11. See Jürg Stenzl, "Stories/Luigi Nono's 'theatre of consciousness', Al gran sole carico d'amore," Teldec New Line 1999 (an essay in the booklet for the recording on Elektra/WEA 2001).
12. See Heile Björn, *The Music of Mauricio Kagel* (Aldershot, UK, 2006).

Earlier we said that singing belongs to another world. But that hardly suffices to describe what most modernist and contemporary composers are up to. The proverbial saying is that "when emotions become too strong for speech, you sing; and when they become too strong for song, you dance." This tells us that dreams, desires, decisions, and emotional outbreaks are traditionally sung and danced but it also tells us that the emotionally less important, the banal and insignificant, are excluded. The question "What is the piece about?" has obviously undergone a major reshaping. In the time of modernist abstraction, surrealism and dadaism, artists turned away from narrative story to personal experience, to the confession of intentions, obsessions, or methods. The art work abandoned the communal to become the result of individual vision, the Freudian "other" that we find in dream and hysteria, or simply the banal and accidental outcome of the everyday.

Subjects

Subjects are, in brief, the warm bodies of a cold-hearted concept: to act out what we would never expect or want to experience in "real life." They are the analyst's "music-theater object." To make an object out of a subject requires a rather sadistic curiosity as it is necessary to pose the question of "what would he or she do if I put him or her in this or that situation?"

The core of the actor's profession is the fascinating procedure that requires one person to "play" another. The underlying issue in this process is the question of distance or closeness. Brecht insisted on distance so that both actors *and* audiences always remain conscious that they are partici pating in a play with actors performing designated roles. This idea, which has had a lot of influence in the theater, was never really accepted in the mass media, and many performers in all media—including live theater and opera—are still working hard at "becoming" the character they are playing in order to be "convincing" (the dead end of this line is "reality TV"). But what is "convincing"? Does it mean "realistic" or "natural" and how are these defined? There is a whole complex here that has been studied in the literature of theater and performance research. Felsenstein speaks of the need for the actor to transmit a message—to his or her partner on stage as well as to the audience—in a spontaneous way. The notion of "realism" in theater covers a huge range from total abstraction as in Peter Brook's work all the way to Franco Zeffirelli's glittering golden necklaces. Between these extremes there are many in-betweens, none of them more or less convincing because of the degree of realism employed!

The triangular axis of interpretation, improvisation, and (co-)creation is demanding. And the precise borders required in new music theater are hard to define as nearly every project has its differing demands. The composer/*auteur* might expect a strict execution of precisely notated structures, creative input through improvisation in rehearsal/performance, or almost anything in-between.

The problems of co-authorship with collaborators (directors, performers) can be fuzzy from a legal or copyright point of view. Recently, choreographers and stage directors have staked out their claims in this area, going as far as claiming co-authorship and developing their own forms of notation comparable to the composer's score. Other collaborators can sometimes get in on the act as well. Michael Bennett's *Chorus Line* grew out of workshops in which dancers told their personal stories, elements of which were adapted into the final version of the piece, and several of the original workshop participants claimed co-authorship. Jonathan Larson, the composer of *Rent,* also wrote the original book and lyrics (distantly based on *La Bohème* but set on New York's Lower East Side). After failing to reach the stage for a number of years, the work was largely rewritten with the help of a professional dramaturge and became a popular success, transferring from off-Broadway to Broadway. The dramaturge then sued the Larson Estate for her portion of the royalties; originally she was paid only a small flat fee for her work.[13]

Such problems are still fuzzy and require the tolerance of the performers and/or a good contract between collaborators. This is why, in many cases, groups or companies have been formed on a cooperative or collective basis. In these situations, which may be motivated by social or even political ideals, the theater becomes a work of many and the dynamics of the traditional hierarchies may change. Some of these companies work with specific themes such as ritual (e.g., Hermann Nitsch's Orgien Mysterien Theater) or physical theater that may include the manipulation of the audience. The Spanish/Catalan La Fura dels Baus performed in venues without barriers between stage and audience space, enabling them to push audiences to drop their voyeuristic passivity and react (more recently they have returned to a traditional proscenium setting). At this point, we are close to the "musicking" concept discussed earlier.[14]

13. To our knowledge, no audience participant in an interactive work has yet claimed co-authorship.
14. Christopher Small in his observations of Afro-American musical practice had noticed the active roles taken by the members of a society in making music together. In this view, music is not a thing or a product but a spontaneous act of a society. This idea can work very well for opera and music theater as it implies a theatricality of making music in a social or ensemble setting that includes many elements of society, from the youngest to the oldest, and all united for a feast of dancing, singing, eating, and drinking. Small calls this entire complex "musicking." Like the actions of a deejay in a

A Fura dels Baus production: *Accions* (1983, Sitges). Photo: Fura dels Baus.

club, this is a sort of music making on the go with its own built-in system of feedback and autoregulation as the musicians react spontaneously to each other and to the audience.

All this helps to show how the understanding of a piece does not derive purely from the piece itself or the references it carries along with it but also includes expectations about how the piece should go—how it *should* sound, look, or feel; what it can transmit or communicate in the way of narratives, experiences, or illuminating explanations about the world. These concepts form (and perhaps de-form) new work in a theater culture that includes press releases, media interviews, advance articles, and the like. Analysis and criticism are therefore not only retrospective but creative as well and part of a back-and-forth Ping-Pong game of social/intellectual action and reaction.

The mood of the temporary or geographically stereotyped audience may also come into play. In some places, artists fear audiences either for their aggressiveness or their passive attitude. This might have something to do with local cultural traditions of good behavior or free expression. Of course, artists love best those evenings when the audience reacts, "vibrates," "is present"; when the artists applaud the audience and the audience itself experiences a kind of temporal identity, reacting as a single unit and without consciously trying encourages the performers to do their absolute best.

The imaginary audience

There are roughly two groups of artists: the more communicative types, who create close to the real world, and the introverted ones, who prefer to create for themselves in the ivory tower. Whether one creates for others or for oneself, there is usually the image of a listener, a viewer, an audience. The use of formal schemes in the compositional process, based on traditions of skillfulness and craftsmanship, are all about how to structure those expressions. The early expressionists had problems with the intended disorderliness of their automated expressions. This becomes insurmountable in the dimensions of the theater. There has to be that punctuation that we call dramaturgy—*timing, narration, surprise, suspense*—in the classical meaning of those terms (or tools). They have no function except to make communication possible.

There is, of course, a line between theater created on models and samples, formal rules and traditions, in which an author's individuality is largely absent, and the spontaneous and individual expressions of a creator who shows or explains an original view of the world. When this latter individuality leads to problems of communication (reducing redundancy, hiding behind an esoteric or too abstract and personal language), then a whole apparatus of accompanying by-texts emerges, addressing the ideal listener who is listening, of course, to the ideal piece. But this ideal listener is, alas, only the artist's puppet, created to understand everything automatically and behave exactly as the artist requires. Analysis often falls into this trap by imagining this same idealized protagonist and then trying to convince the reader that he or she is that ideal listener and therefore able to understand the most difficult constructions of logical methodology, process, or hidden symbology.

Analysis often tends to tell the listener what he should be hearing (as in Heinrich Schenker's method, for example). The listener becomes a prisoner in a war of competing systems. If, by chance, we don't hear or understand what we are supposed to hear and understand, then we are obviously mishearing or misunderstanding. What is never clear is why we cannot just be entertained without having to be right or wrong about what we think we have heard!

One way to interpret nineteenth-century opera is that it provided a catharsis for the bourgeois nightmares that were its actual subject matter.[15] Contemporary Bollywood movie productions—music theater in filmic form—deal with subject matter that is a complex of family dramas and community life. As is well known, European romantic opera exaggerates its collective tensions and projects them onto theatrical crime, murder, illicit passion, violence, and death. Societal taboos are "worked out" through the music drama. In these cases, there is no need for the ideal listener since the real audience is already part of that society that is out there looking at itself.

Workstyles of the *auteur*

Opera is traditionally regarded as a collaboration between artists, and the collective act of creation and performance by a team can be lively. However, new music theater, like film, usually has an *auteur*. This might be the composer but it can also be the stage director, sometimes a producer, or even a performer who has assembled the team with the aim of creating something around his or her own personal artistic skills or specialties.

There is a place where music theater and its *auteur* become the meeting point of all sorts of ideas from the static (concepts, texts, compositions) to the dynamic (performance, projection, process) and this is the point at which we can locate the concept of a "universal music theater."[16] It is possible, even likely, that this *auteur*-theater is the most characteristic innovation of twentieth-century music theater.

In fact, there has almost always been an *auteur* in the popular musical theater (John Gay, Emmanuel Schikaneder, and Noel Coward are some

15. The German philosopher Alexander Kluge in a panel in Vienna in 2002.
16. Manos Tsangaris, "Conversations," in *Musik Texte 91*, November 2001, Berlin.

names that come to mind) but the concept has not been always extended to works of the past about whose origins we know little. In any case, the presence of a controlling figure (whom we have designated as the *auteur*) does not mean that there are no other influences shaping the work. Medieval and Renaissance art were produced by workshops under the direction of master craftsmen. Baroque and classical composers were able to sustain their high levels of productivity by employing assistants and copyists. Bach and Haydn employed whole workshops of copyists, and even composers like Schumann and Liszt leaned heavily on assistants; Joachim Raff and others are known to have helped Liszt with his orchestration. Wagner asked Mathilde Wesendonck to recopy his own pencil draft in ink, and he had other disciples who helped prepare the piano scores and even orchestration. Ferde Grofé orchestrated the original version of the Gershwin *Rhapsody in Blue,* and most popular musicals employ orchestrators and arrangers so that the composer can be on hand inside the theater to participate in the rehearsal process. In film music, it is common for the designated composer to use specific assistant-composers and not just in Hollywood; Hanns Eisler asked Paul Dessau to write certain film sequences for him. Stockhausen long maintained a medieval workshop's worth of assistants for the realization of many of his large early works (whole sections of pieces like *Momente* were written by his "apprentices"). Meredith Monk used an assistant for the orchestral scoring in her opera *Atlas* and Giacinto Scelsi is said to have had others transcribe his music into score from his piano improvisations.

The score as extended text

Hegel, in his *Ästhetik*, defined opera as a text, extended by all possible means. (See also Chapter 5 on Text.) Music would, of course, be (just) one of those means. He would presumably ask the drama critic to review new operas. On the other hand, Ernst Krenek (in 1927) argued that it is the performers in performance who actually create the work. What then is the score? Is it just a necessary tool to facilitate the performance of the piece or does it also anchor the work in various ways by responding to the rules of the system of artistic production? This creates the paradoxical situation of operas that have never been performed but exist only in score. If Krenek's view is correct, these might be said to exist only as virtual operas and even then perhaps only when someone who is musically literate sits down to read the score and imagine the scenic action!

The written score permits a quasi-scientific "analyzability." It overcomes the ephemeral character of theatrical and musical performance by providing a fixed object that seems to embody the essence of the work. The entire mechanism of traditional classical/romantic musical culture in Western culture has rested on that written score; one even speaks of the score as if it were synonymous with the music. The score is the basis of a whole structure of education, journalism, theory, criticism, and pedagogy as well as the industrial organization of music (mass production with replaceable parts). The dominance of the score may even control the lyrics, stage directions, settings and costumes in opera and it also sustains the machinery that creates and assures the dominance of Western music throughout the world.[17]

The score has less importance and authority where recording media and the influence of jazz, pop, and electronic music are predominant. This is actually a problem for the literacy of the academic world, which largely defined intellectual values for centuries but is now feeling the crushing power of mass culture, which has entered the universities and musicological institutes. The lack of scores in pop, world, and electronic music is noticeable in the coverage of these kinds of musics where the traditional tools and terms of musical analysis cannot be applied.[18] The same holds for mixed media and many musical/theatrical works.

Can the authority of the score be questioned?

The score-as-document as been identified with the work itself for so long that it has become the sole basis for the study of the work itself, the so-called *Urtext*. It should be pointed out that analysis of the classics of the repertoire from the point of view of the score (as it has been handed down to us) has little to do with criticism in the strict sense of the word. For one thing, there seems to be nothing left to be criticized. These works have become untouchable as they cannot be questioned for their value, their messages, or the way they have been put into final form. This is particularly true in the case of operatic classics whose librettos and scores have often achieved an artificially fixed form that does not correspond to anything that was actually written by the creators.

17. This was not always the case. In the eighteenth century, the librettist's name—and sometimes that of the machinist!—usually appeared ahead of the composer's. As the composer—whose position was something like that of the screenwriter in the modern film—came to the fore in the late classical and romantic periods and through-composed scores became the norm, the work became more and more identified with the score and its creator. Curiously enough, the evolution of the popular musical followed an almost identical pattern at the distance of about a century.
18. Although, to a great extent, recorded music replaces the score in these cases, great efforts have been made to transcribe nonnotated music from the recordings for pedagogical, analytical, or musicological purposes (or simply to produce music that can be printed and sold). How to reduce nonstandard music making to standard notation is, of course, a subject of endless debate.

Even in the heyday of European tradition, the existence of the score was of very little interest to the public. Full scores of operas, operettas, and other music theater works were rarely even published and were (and often remain) difficult to find, being often available only in limited quantities.[19] In addition, the notion of the definitive score of an opera or music theater work is often a chimera, even with the classics of the genre, as stage works were constantly the subject of revisions and often exist in multiple and equally "authentic" alternate versions.

Many composers have tried or try to insert themselves into the traditional music business and into the social system (or some other system of "civilized culture") by continuing to turn out—now generally with computer or other assistance—highly elaborated scores. Nevertheless, major works are performed and even recorded that do not have a written score, a fact that flies in the face of the European tradition that works of art are documents. The truth is that there are other methods of creating musical work that are at least as spontaneous, at least as well adapted to performers' needs, and as honest as the highly elaborated written score.

The score as the ideal

In spite of all these caveats, we start with the score, which is traditionally the most important of the music-theater objects. It contains the music with the lyrics attached, plus instructions for performers and musicians and ideas about staging including, at times, drawings. What the score generally does not contain is a set of ideal images for the visualization of the work, even when there are clear indications or sketches by the creators themselves.

In the cinema, the images on film are the piece itself. Only rarely is the design part of the original conception of an opera or music-theater piece and then only when the *auteur* of a new work is also the designer of the work (e.g., the Robert Wilson/Philip Glass *Einstein on the Beach*, the "story board" designs for which function as the libretto; see the illustrations in Chapter 14).

Although not quite "set in stone" (as is sometimes said), the score—at least since Wagner—provides the unchangeable framework. This makes opera and certain kinds of music theater different from the other performing arts that have no such immovable center. The phenomenological

19. Oddly enough, the original reason that scores were not published and were difficult to find was to prevent piracy of popular works in a day when copyright protection was not available or was very weak. Full scores of operettas and musicals were almost never published; as a result, they have sometimes been drastically altered or have even disappeared over time. Today, the opposite reason often prevails—that is, lack of commercial appeal!

point—and it never fails to fascinate—is the existence of a virtual or ideal-ized piece that lies behind (if not above and beyond) the score. It will never be seen or heard by the public but it breathes life into the performance that they will actually see. Because of its nature as a virtual work, it is perpetu-ally ready to come into real existence and it offers all sorts of possibilities in some domains even as it shuts off possibilities in others.

All this creates an ideal of the intended final piece, the perfect and ideal parent to the previously mentioned ideal listener—both unknown to ordinary mortals. In opera as in classical concert music, nearly everything is crafted after an ideal, an overwhelmingly perfect and larger-than-life model that we never actually get to see or hear in real life. Music theater shares some of these ideals, particularly with regard to the singing voice. Even when the desired singing voice is more closely related to pop or to jazz than it is to the full operatic instrument, there is almost always an ideal of beautiful singing lurking somewhere in the background. Sometimes, in order to create a more natural "reality," composers try to replace singers with actors, narrators, or unsung recitation of one sort or another. Sometimes an *auteur* is commis-sioned who asks Tom Waits to do the music and to train actors to sing in the same gravelly way that he does. But beyond this, questioning the singing voice would mean questioning the whole enterprise and the art form itself.

The score as transformed libretto

The different meanings of the term "text" as discussed in Chapter 5 can be recapped here. The libretto or lyrics should not be confused with the meaning of "text" in the philosophical sense where we might speak about "avant-text" (in generative criticism) or "meta-text" (in analytic philosophy) or just about text as a process in itself (in structuralist thinking). The word can also be understood as the concept or concepts from which the piece is derived, the intention or intentions that shape the "abouts" and the "hows" of the future piece. It is from this point that the libretto is built and the music added. But this is not purely a procedural issue but also a dramaturgical matter. The title of Salieri's opera (and a favorite catch-phrase ever since) is *Prima la musica, poi le parole*—"First the music, afterwards the words." But the historical reality has been mostly—if not quite always[20]—the reverse. The music has to deal with the text and its

20. Popular song provides the biggest exceptions, with lyricists often asked to provide words for existing music—sometimes replacing or translating older lyrics, sometimes adding a text to a popular instrumental or dance tune, but sometimes just accommodating a composer's inspiration. On occasion, this has had influence in the theater (for example, all the songs in Gay's *Beggar's Opera* have new lyrics fitted to older popular tunes).

dramaturgy, eventually imprinting its own musical timing onto both words and action. Other texts—criticism, analysis—follow after.

In spite of the musical claims made by Salieri, Mozart, and others, this "reverse" situation held for a very long time but, as with many other issues, the advent of modernism changed the rules.

Timing and musical dramaturgy

The timing issue has always been the most significant aspect of music theater. The musical setting, far more than a side effect, exercises an almost complete control over all actions. The notion of the score as an absolute value and the power of musical time to control all the other elements of performance is related to the control that society exerts on its members through the conservation and protection of its values. Opera's strongly hierarchical inner organization may be one reason why it seems to be such a conservative art form.

Since timing is the driving force in music theater, the temporality of the music will be the leading issue in this method. Measurements might be in real time (seconds) or relative, musical time (bars of music with attached meter and tempo). But all this remains bogged down in a world of statistical transposition that might have little to say about our main interest in a piece. The overall duration of most pieces is not a major problem as most works conform to a standard duration—generally now between fifty and ninety minutes without an intermission.[21] (See, however, the method of Robert Ashley discussed in Chapter 17.) The most pressing immediate issues are whether there is a narrative and, if so, what is the subject of the narrative: a story, a parable, a factual history of note from ancient or recent times. Whatever the story or information to be conveyed, it has to be compressed, not only into a short and fictive stage time but also in a way that follows the music.[22] This is a double time bind in the transposition of large real-time spans of life into narrative text and then again into musical performance time.

As the narrative will probably have no inherent timing, the dramaturgy might make use of some striking incident or incidents. Important changes may be brought into play by constructing an assumed linearity and punctuating this with actions that create surprising shifts in that linearity, thus provoking consequences.

21. The usual reason given is that an intermission, especially in a short, concentrated piece, would break the audience's attention.
22. The compression of historical time on the stage (or in a film) is often a problem. The turning points in real life are quite different from the classic narrative requirement for build-up, climax, and denouement.

A paradoxical use of narrative might show a situation that takes place or evolves in real time or pseudo-real time. For example, if a meal were to be cooked on stage, the performance time would then have to follow this activity. This is not purely a theoretical idea. In Heiner Goebbels's *Eraritjaritjaka— museé des phrases*, André Wilms is seen to cook an omelette and eat it, an event that appears to take place in real time in a real kitchen but is actually seen as a video projection (we never really know if it is happening live or indeed, if it is happening in someone's apartment or somewhere backstage in the theater). The whole piece plays with the idea of the passage of "real" time in "real" locations partly onstage and partly appearing, perhaps deceptively, as a seemingly live video. Andy Warhol's *Sleep* (which shows a man sleeping for six hours) and his *Empire* (which shows eight hours in the "life" of New York's Empire State Building) deal with the passage of time by not dealing with it. The closer you get to real time on the stage or in the media, the more you have to deal with nonactivity or uneventfulness as compared to paradigmatic dramatic time, which is collapsed and fictional.

A written score or a timed-out audio playback inevitably conditions the performance of a dramatic, dance, or performance piece in very specific ways. In new music theater, the timing issue is crucial and the only way to test it out is in "real time" with an actual run-through. This control over content was also the basic concept of Meyerhold's theater in the early twentieth century: his performers would rehearse to a musical score that was not used in the actual performance. A similar case is common in dance where, whether working with music or not, performers use counts that create a metrical score known only to the performers.

Of course, spoken theater also creates its own performance rhythms but this is more about feeling than a truly composed time structure. Theatrical action has its own aleatoric timing, mostly a natural speed of speech and/or physical movement. It will float somewhat freely unless it is weighted down by other factors. When there is a score with extended musical sections, this provides the essential background for any musical performance in or out of the theater. Stage directors who move from spoken theater to opera are straitjacketed by not being able to change the given musical timing of a scene. Walter Felsenstein and the East Berlin *Komische Oper* famously overcame this problem with an enormous amount of rehearsal time; Felsenstein's formula was 100 to 120 times the actual playing time of the piece. This luxury was available in East Berlin and in the Bavaria of Ludwig II but even well-subsidized contemporary state theaters cannot afford these amounts of rehearsal time or this kind of idealism any more.

Looking for possible correspondences between physical, verbal, and musical timing is always of interest. Music has been used to illustrate physical timing in live performance and in media, sometimes in minute detail.

In fact, the practice of using music to track movement is widely known (and not only in the cartoon business) as "mickey-mousing." Synchronization in both animation and film photography was achieved in several ways. Traditionally the music was added after the final cut, with the score being recorded by the musicians as they followed the projected image. A more modern method employed by many recent directors is to cut the score to the music (sometimes to a dummy score that then has to be imitated by the composer!).[23] "Mickey-mousing" and the more generalized tendency to align music and film editing can be thought of as a form of doubling, much like the way actors and singers will "indicate" by physicalizing what they are saying or singing (directors will often spend a considerable amount of time trying to check this tendency).

Musical *topoi*

Although they are out of favor at present, there is a long history to the creation of parallel or duplicating vocabularies, going back at least to the ancient art of rhetoric: "see what you hear, hear what you see." The so-called figures—also known as *topoi* or tropes—played a major role in university studies and scholarly education up to the late eighteenth century and appear in music from at least the sixteenth century on.

As already suggested in Chapter 5, the relationship of text and musical patterns is so ancient and widespread that we can assume there is a lot of forgotten knowledge and practice in this field. One area of rediscovery of buried tradition lies in what was known as rhetoric or the art of discourse. Revived in the Renaissance, after Greek models, it appeared in music in the sixteenth century. Generally speaking, it is a method of composing large structures out of small samples, using parallels in meaning between music and text.

Here, out of an endless list of possible examples, is the moment in Mozart's *Le Nozze di Figaro* when the Countess tries to get out of Cherubino's grip.

"Ripping motif" from *Le Nozze di Figaro* by W. A. Mozart.

23. A famous example was Stanley Kubrick, who kept his dummy score for 2001 in preference to Alex North's commissioned score.

The musical idea of ripping can also be applied to a curtain (Bach: *St. Matthew Passion*) or to the soul (Mozart: last act of *Don Giovanni*). The notion of "paralleling" is meant to imply that the words and the music describe the same idea. It is difficult to use music to describe an object literally but music and text coming together with a stage action become a music-theater "object." These *topoi* are staples of medieval and baroque artistic craftmanship but they do not fit well with avant-garde esthetics. The technique of paralleling creates a doubling of the expression, as if somebody were telling us what we already know or can see for ourselves. This element of redundancy is not congenial to modernist modes of expression.

The essentially new or the "unveiling"

After the timing issue, there is a second element of a dramaturgy to be uncovered: what the German philosopher Martin Heidegger called the *Entbergung* or the unveiling. We can go out into the street and observe a real place that might or might not show us "something" happening. Is theater a medium that could allow such nonevents to take place? A film or sound recording is an object and can be said to exist even if the original performers are gone and no one is watching or listening but a theatrical or musical performance requires actual live performers and the passage of time. In English, the word "theater" is used to designate the characteristics of a certain kind of architectural space but it also may refer to something created by performers or by a stage designer, or even something that looks "staged" and "theatrical."[24] The Warholian reflux of theater into common life shows us something about the importance of theater in society, but what interests us more is the possibility and necessity of "staging." Staging sets up performance by putting performers into focus, catching the attention of onlookers by throwing light on something or someone, that is, physicalizing, pointing to, putting in relief, unveiling.

There is a whole complex of what an ongoing performance constructs in the mind of the audience but that remains otherwise invisible. This notion goes back to the ancient Greek or Aristotelian dramaturgy. It is more dominant in spoken theater where the performance shapes the relationships between the protagonists on an emotional level. This kind of theater, descended from realistic, missing-fourth-wall concepts, is closed off and voyeuristic. It is based on the fiction that the audience is peeping into a

24. The word "theater" is also used in different contexts (for example, a "theater of war") when it refers to a place where something is going to happen. The word "scenario" is also used to describe any hypothetical narrative about to be played out.

room and overhearing the private relationships between the protagonists of the drama. Music theater is more open, more directed out toward the audience, and because of the effect of sung language, it is more focused on a clash of affects, pushed by the sound/music and also by the visual realization. The French philosopher Gilles Deleuze speaks of the "affection-image"; we tend to read the emotion (the "affect") rather than to look at the performer's face esthetically. This is why masks, puppets, and the techniques of expressionism work so well in theater even though they are anti-naturalistic. It also helps explain why opera is sometimes visually so voluptuous as compared to spoken theater. Opera and music theater are not only presentational; they are exhibitionistic.

Composition as *mise en scène*

An increasing number of writers have taken to speaking about "music and dramaturgy" or "composition as *mise en scène*" rather than about music theater, but this only sounds like a more technical version of the same thing. Other terms now in vogue are "dramaturgy" and the "dramaturge" who practices dramaturgy. The German terms *Dramaturgie* and *Dramaturg* are somewhat different animals from their equivalents in the English-language theater. In America, the notion of dramaturgy and, specifically, the rather new concept of a professional dramaturge are often connected with traditional ideas about the "well-made" play. In any case, before good work can be done there has to be knowledge of the issues.

Many performance pieces that might aspire to the condition of music theater—because of the presence of both music and theater—do not really fit the criteria because one element merely decorates the other (scene music used in a spoken drama; a letter that is read or intoned in an otherwise sung opera). We might end up asking where the sources and artistic home base of the creators are to be found. Perhaps such terminological issues are tedious but it is worthwhile to distinguish between theater that sings and theater that is driven by music and musical timing.

Taking up the challenge of "putting music to words" means entering the world of dramaturgy. The combination of words and music imprints musical time onto the text and, equally, onto the actions that go with it. In this context, we might cite Verdi, who asked his librettist to produce a *parola scenica*, scenic language.

Here is Morton Feldman's account of how he approached Samuel Beckett to collaborate on his piece *Neither*:

"[Beckett] said to me, after a while, 'Mr. Feldman, I don't like opera.' I said to him, 'I don't blame you!' Then he said to me, 'I don't like my words being set to music,' and I said, 'I'm in complete agreement. In fact it's very seldom that I've used words. I've written a lot of pieces with voice, and they're wordless.' Then he looked at me again and said, 'But what do you want?' And I said, 'I have no idea!' He also asked me why I didn't use existing material. We had a mutual friend who told him I wanted to work with a Beckett text. He wrote back to this friend suggesting various things. I said that I had read them all, that they were pregnable; they didn't need music. I said that I was looking for the quintessence, something that just hovered."

This is a case in which text has to be written in a very specific manner so that something essentially new (i.e., Feldman's "quintessence") results from the symbiosis of text, music, and action. A sort of hidden layer of meaning and communication, affects, emotions, atmospheres, and relationships is created behind the visible and the audible part of the performance.

This communication is connected to another observation. Although pieces from the classical period have very strong models and formal traditions are very strong, the dramaturgy (text/music) follows the logic of the stage actions and their consequences. The piece unfolds in this logic and "on its own," seemingly without the presence of the author. All this changes from the moment in history when that logic and those model forms are weakened or abandoned. Our performance arts are no longer driven by the ideal of beautiful form any more but rather by individual expression. The author becomes more and more present as we go from interpretative commentary into psychological interpretation. Music takes on more and more of the role of a "sounding unconscious" but, of course, consciously set forth by the composer who may also offer explanations in the form of didactic and introductory speeches, interviews, or written studies and demonstrations.

The reaction against the so-called mimetic theater, the loss of a communications system based on well-known rhetorical devices, the need for new concepts, the creation of individual composing methods as well as the taste for dadaism (i.e., the nonsensical, the contradictory, and the vague) all have combined to produce a new necessity to explain everything. These by-texts—written before, during, and after the works they purport to explain—often come from the composers themselves who, particularly in Europe from the 1950s on, developed a huge corpus of explanatory writing.[25] The new texts, only rarely set to music themselves, are nevertheless a vital part of the art works they purport to explain although, somewhat curiously, they are rarely presented together with the work to which they refer. These

25. Many American artists—John Cage is a good example—refuse to explain their work but have, nevertheless, produced a parallel body of nonexplanatory text that complements their nonverbal work.

tracts partly replaced the functionality of the score, now much weakened, and helped to lift some bizarre new work into a high-brow and intellectually ambitious place.

One side effect of this was that the explanations about intended methods, goals, and references replaced a traditional dramaturgy that was more concerned with real-world results in performance. Some of the hidden layers of these works were thus unveiled and exposed to our direct perception.

Music theater can well be understood as the product of such layering. It is not merely multidisciplinary but also in itself multipartite and, as a composite form, it shows the interaction of its layers.

These examinations of the whole can also create their own references (i.e., meaning and sense) in different fields: historical (the history of opera, for example), the technical/theoretical ideas of the stage director (e.g., the writings of Felsenstein or Brook), the merely philosophical (Alexander Kluge, Peter Kivy, Carolyn Abbate, etc.), popular and journalistic (the "Opera Goers Guide," "Who's Who in Opera," etc.), psychological/interpretative (e.g., Slavoj Žižek's writings on opera), and so forth.

Autonomy in a sea of facts

There are few clear frontiers anywhere in art or, for that matter, in life. The fuzziness of our world calls for models that do not squeeze the facts into theory but rather make theory and analysis accept the fact that categorization is just one, perhaps outdated, way to rationalize the sea of facts and the details of life.

The most important requirement of analytical, critical thinking is to understand that we are not talking about fixed laws but ways of thinking and, as a result, ways of being able to enjoy art. Most artistic issues cannot be approached through ideas about good and bad rules and relationships. The more intricate and clever these relationships are, the more we need to find methods, perhaps equally intricate and clever, to catch their meaning.

An essential factor is the listeners' autonomy, which enables them to find, in their own way, the references and the meaning or sense while, at the same time, re-cognizing the manipulative powers of all sorts of expression. This might be one answer to the question "What is analysis good for?"

Further Reading

Abbate, Carolyn. *In Search of Opera*. Princeton, NJ, 2001.

Blum, Eberhard. Review of Morton Feldman/Samuel Beckett *NEITHER*. *Positionen*, November 2000.

Brenner, Michael. Interview in *Deutsche Bahn-NEWS*, January 2006, p. 42.

Brook, Peter. *The Empty Space, A Book about the Theatre: Deadly, Holy, Rough, Immediate*. New York, 1968.

Claren, Sebastian. *NEITHER. Die Musik Morton Feldmans*. Hofheim, 2000.

Cook, Nicholas. *A Guide to Musical Analysis*. London, 1987.

Deleuze, Gilles. *Cinema 1: The Movement Image*. Translated by Hugh Tomlinson and B. Habberjam. London and New York, 1986.

Fuchs, Peter Paul, ed. *The Music Theater of Walter Felsenstein: Collected Articles, Speeches and Interviews by Walter Felsenstein and Others*. Toronto, 1975; repr. London, 1991.

Hegel, Georg Friedrich Wilhelm. *Ästhetik*, hg. F. Bassenge. Berlin, Weimar, 1965, p. 536.

Heile, Bjorn. *Recent Approaches to Experimental Music Theatre and Contemporary Opera Music and Letters* 87, no. 1 (2006): 72–81.

Kant, Immanuel. *Kritik der Urteilskraft*, complete works. Vol. 10, §52. Frankfurt am Main, 2004.

Kinser, Samuel. *Rabelais's Carnival: Text, Context, Metatext*. Berkeley, CA, 1990.

Kivy, Peter. *Osmin's Rage, Philosophical Reflections on Opera, Drama, and Text*. Princeton, NJ, 1988.

Kluge, Alexander. *Herzblut trifft Kunstblut—Erster imaginärer*. Berlin, 2001.

Krenek, Ernst. *Zur Sprache gebracht, Essays*. Munich, 1958, pp. 25, 29.

Ruf, Wolfgang. "Musiktheater—Oberbegriff oder Spezies." In *Colloquium:The Musical Theater*, pp. 132ff. Brno, 1980, pp. 132ff.

Schultz, Klaus, ed. *Aribert Reimann's Lear*. Munich, 1984.

Tsangaris, Manos. "Conversations." In *Musik Texte* 91. Berlin, November 2001.

Zizek, Slavoj. *Opera's Second Death*. New York, 2002.

chapter 20

Notation versus Improvisation?

It don't mean a thing (if it ain't got that swing)

Duke Ellington/Irving Mills, 1932

Notation, improvisation, and the theater

The invention of musical notation and its increasing sophistication over the centuries has created a box within which classical musical performance in the European tradition has had to be stuffed. None of the other performing arts are created or transmitted in this manner and even musical culture is not, in most times and places, subject to the overarching domination of notation. The usual alternative to notation is said to be improvisation, a notion that ranges from mild *rubato* to ornamentation to free jazz, but in many ways this is a false dichotomy. The real alternatives to notated music are text-based musical declamation and aural tradition, which may or may not be jogged by written reminders. Both (they are not mutually exclusive) have been especially important in the history of the various operatic, musical, and music theaters.

Dance and mime are created and transmitted by physical example as conveyed in rehearsal (modern attempts at notation are, at most, purely supplementary). Post-Renaissance theater is text driven but a lot of contemporary theater is also created physically in rehearsal. Most non-Western and popular musical traditions depend on aural transmission. In these cases, notation is not necessary or is, at most, a mnemonic device to remind performers of "how it goes." When texts are declaimed musically—as in various forms of chant and recitative—the words will determine a lot about the musical shape. A little-discussed fact of music history is that until recently, few singers could read music, and even today, many singers learn their roles by ear.[1]

The underlying issues that have driven the increasing complexity and precision of music notation are ensemble coordination and timing. The development of modern notation in Western music was an attempt to structure rhythmic regularity in a manner that would permit numbers of musicians performing together to coordinate the simultaneous articulation of different melodies and different pitches so as to produce an intelligible series of harmonic effects. The sacrifice of individual rhythmic freedom and ensemble flexibility in timing to produce ensemble harmony is, in essence, the history of Western music from the middle ages until the twentieth century.

This great achievement has always presented special problems in the theater. With precisely notated rhythmic music in control, the physical movement and interaction on a stage can no longer be the direct result of text declamation or dramatic timing. Performers are, to put it simply, completely constrained by musical notation and its predetermined rhythmic boxes. No matter what the stage director or the actor thinks, four beats must pass between the beginning of one measure of 4/4 and the next.

There were two traditional solutions to any potential conflicts that might arise because of this. One was to limit the number of instruments that could accompany voices intoning a text to a keyboard or a plucked string that could produce a full harmony but could still be flexible enough to follow the vocalists. This was the "dry recitative" (*recitativo secco*) solution. The other was to alternate fully accompanied rhythmic songs with unaccompanied dialogue (the "number opera" solution). The invention of the *stile rappresentativo* in the late sixteenth century simply meant that text could be freely declaimed in a continuous fashion (i.e., uninterrupted by speech) against chordal punctuations. Even after rhythmic music was reintroduced into opera, first as dance music and then afterward in the form of arias and vocal ensembles, singers continued to learn their music by rote and were expected to embellish their melodies more or less ad lib and were

---

1. Human voices mature late, and by the time most singers develop their singing abilities, they are well past their school days.

regularly offered open—that is, non-boxed-in—spaces to add interpolations and cadenzas.[2]

Although opera was generally music directed from the keyboard or by
the first violinist ("the concertmaster") of the orchestra well into the nineteenth century, a limited amount of dramatic recitative was composed out
and accompanied by the full orchestra, mostly with held chords and chordal
punctuations. But it was only with the advent of the Wagnerian music drama
and the Wagnerian-era conductor that the control of theatrical timing passed
definitively from the stage to the pit—to the conductor working with the
composer's score. This was not only a matter of esthetics; the very length of
the piece, the technique of through-composition ("endless melody"), and
the size of the performing forces made temporal and notational control a
necessity. At the same time, the last vestiges of improvisation disappeared
from instrumental performance and from those corners of the opera where
they had survived largely in the form of *rubato*, held notes, and cadenzas.

Improvisation returned to classical music in the twentieth century in a
limited way through the influence of jazz (at first, jazz was almost exclusively
an aural art form) and the revival of early music practice that insisted on
ornamentation and other forms of performance practice as essential parts
of pre-romantic music.[3] The idea that new music and music theater could
be created from something else other than a base in strict notation was slow
to take hold; even Cage's early work was still based on traditional notation.
The creation of new work with strong performer input came about largely
in three ways: (1) the development of alternate forms of notation (mostly
the so-called graphic notations of the 1960s and 1970s), (2) the introduction
of open form (still tightly controlled by the creators), and (3) the influence
and methods of choreographers and creative stage directors, working with

2. Ironically enough, these cadenzas were purely musical events and had
   nothing to do with text declamation.
3. Jazz, non-Western music, and European baroque and classical music share
   an essential feature: regularity of the beat. *Rubato* meant literally stealing
   time from one part of a measure to another or even from one measure to
   another (i.e., across bar lines). Steadiness of meter is supported by a continuo
   instrumentation—keyboard, cello, and bass; piano, drums, and bass; or some
   variation on the idea of a rhythm section. Traditional improvisation usually
   means working across or against a known steadiness of pulse. Starting in
   the romantic period, however, continuo instrumentation disappeared and
   rubato came to refer to changing measure lengths for expressive purposes
   and, ultimately, changes of tempo, now controlled by the soloist, by the
   conductor, or both. As romantic *rubato* increases, improvisation decreases.
   Eventually, rubato is actually notated by the composer so nothing further
   can be added. This is the dead end of interpretative freedom.

performers in extended rehearsal periods and without text (or with only text fragments) and without a controlling score.

Note that these developments do not necessarily have much to do with improvisation in the traditional musical sense. In most cases, the composer still keeps control. Only in the third scenario is music created—for purely musical or for musico-dramatic purposes—without the notational box and possibly subject to the physical movements of dancers or actors on a stage. In such cases, composers may work directly with the performers or through the intervention of a choreographer or creative stage director. In the end, even without written notes, the music may be quite fixed or subject only to the small variations that occur during physical performance. The timing is under the control of the performers, however, and not under the tight rein of a conductor.

The obvious analogy is with the way dancers learn a new work from a choreographer (and the way that a choreographer may "compose" a new piece "on" his or her dancers). Of course, if a dance is being made to a preexisting musical score, performed live, or prerecorded, then the music creates the timing even if—as in the case of many Cage/Cunningham collaborations—that refers only to the elapsed time between the start and the finish of the work. If the score is created in collaboration with a choreographer or with dancers, the situation can be reversed, with musicians following the dancers or through some kind of interaction.

In the parallel case of a contemporary theater piece (especially one that is not purely text based), the process of creation may take an even longer rehearsal or workshop period but neither text nor scene music (if either are used) determines the stage timing. The timing itself then becomes a major focus or even the subject itself of the creative work. Again, music theater works have been created using such techniques, but this is also not really improvisation even though the permissible variables may include different rhythms or even different melodies from one performance to the next!

Performer choice begins to enter the game when the possibility is built into the music. Certain musical parameters may be fixed while others are left undetermined in advance. If the pitches are known, the rhythms may be chosen by the performer—or vice versa. Musical fragments can be learned in advance but ordered and reordered by the performers in performance. Is this improvisation? Is it any different from a jazz performer playing a made-up melody against the chords of a well-known song?

Although the notion of free improvisation does certainly exist, most improvisation takes place within a known structure where certain elements or parameters are fixed while others are left open to variability and performer choice. In ensemble works, the improvisational element is likely to be reactive: a performer responds to what another performer is doing or reacts to an unpredictable stage or electronic event. Finally, it needs to be said that, even in the case of traditional improvisation, certain formulas tend to become fixed with repetition. An improvised piece, if played often enough, starts to take on a fixed form. This is, no doubt, how certain works of the great improvisers of the past—we can go back at least as far as Bach and Beethoven for good examples—turned into written-out fantasias or sonatas.[4]

How well do these techniques work in a theatrical context? True improvisation is very little used in ensemble choreography if only because of the major physical limitations of the medium (unless the level of activity remains very low, there can be actual physical danger involved in unpredictability). In ensemble theater, where the physical level is not too high or where a lid is kept on it, a higher level of choice may be available although a "free jazz" level of improvisation is rare.

Here is a rather arbitrary twelve-step scheme for the range of variability in musical performance starting with precise notation and leading to free improvisation:

1. Traditional, precise notation (e.g., Mahler, Webern, Babbitt, Ferneyhough)
2. Traditional notation modified by performance traditions such as *rubato, ritardandi* and *accelerandi*, ornamentation or embellishments, fermatas, cuts, repeats and other elements not written in the original score (so-called baroque and classical performance practice)
3. Alternation of notated music with free sections (cadenzas, riffs, held notes, etc., as in the classical concerto, and in aria singing well into the twentieth century)
4. Notated music followed by variations on the notated music; variations on a melody; variations on the harmony or on a bass (as in both classical and jazz practice)
5. Performance from a "lead sheet" or performance based on rhythmic riffs only within a determined number of bars: melody alone, melody and bass, drum or bass riffs only within a determined number of bars (traditional jazz, baroque music, some non-Western music, and more recently, in live/electronic interactions)
6. Pitch notation with open rhythmic choice (used in chant and other forms of pitched speaking that require speech rhythms with a fixed melodic outline; also used by certain open-form composers such as early Morton Feldman)

4. This explains the existence of multiple notated realizations of certain pieces.

7. Graphic notation (meaning determined by the composer; some parameters may be precise, others not—usually free pitch within roughly indicated time, registral and rhythmic frameworks). This has been used to create a vagueness of meaning that might open up different solutions (e.g., Sylvano Bussotti whose detailed graphic scores are intended to inspire the performers to put them into audible—and visible—form)

8. Open form (i.e., more-or-less precisely notated music in fragments that can be reordered by the performers). This idea challenges the performer to take some of the structural responsibility for putting a piece of music together (John Cage, Earle Brown; adopted by Boulez, Stockhausen, and other Darmstadteers)

9. Concept art (in which performers work from ideas in the form of verbal instructions but make their own choices about the details); this may also apply to ways of using given text elements. (Examples: "action notation" like Kagel's *Sonant* which uses texts as a manual for how to perform the music; La Monte Young's *Compositions* from the late 1950s and early 1960s which consist of one-line instructions; Terry Riley's *In C* consisting of assorted fragments of C major music with a set of flexible verbal instructions for putting them together)

10. Musical development in rehearsal (composer working with performers in the manner of a choreographer with dancers; certain pieces that use graphic notation need to be rehearsed in this fashion; many jazz composers work with minimal notation and put the music together in rehearsal; the same process has been used by theater composers working closely with stage directors who need flexibility in timing for theater work that is in evolution)

11. Ensemble development in rehearsal; working with a director as well as or instead of a composer or musical leader (this was the classical group work in such ensembles as Aperghis's ATEM in Paris or Quog Music Theater in New York, both in the 1970s)

12. Free solo or ensemble improvisation (as in so-called "free jazz" or in recent forms of electronic/computer improvisation)[5]

The lower numbers in this sequence are typical of traditional musical practice in the baroque and classical periods; (4) and (5) reflect common practice in traditional jazz; with (6) to (8) we are approaching techniques widely employed in new music after World War II; (8) and (9) reflect the

5. There are, of course, always habits, traditions, styles, and ideas that determine the final sound result. Even concert electronic improvisation is often based on specific concepts of sound, computer programming, or social/artistic ideas.

influence of Cage. The later numbers describe music-theater practices, many of them borrowed from modern dance and experimental theater in which performers work with a director or choreographer over an extended period to put pieces together in workshop/rehearsal form without a score. Composers, perhaps dissatisfied with the musical direction offered by stage directors and choreographers, have also adopted these techniques as way of producing an ensemble-created music theater with a strong musical orientation. Free improvisation without the intervention of a composer or director reflects a performer's art and is little used in music theater.

Economic implications

Opera and music theater, the most expensive of the performing arts, always have had to deal with financial issues. This is a shadow on operatic history that is little discussed. Although most music theater and so-called small-scale or chamber opera can hardly be classified as *arte povera*, these formats cost less, are more flexible, and are easier to organize.

Given all this, it might seem as if programming based on improvisational methods would be a practical way to go, but the opposite is true. Rehearsal time is often now cut to extremely short periods, and with a score, contemporary performers, specialized in sight reading and quick learning, can prepare their parts in short order. The drawback in this highly industrialized process is a much less coherent ensemble. Developing a piece of music theater from scratch as a series of collective improvisations demands an ensemble of performers who need to get to know each other. The lack of a common language or commonly known compositional rules and the inexperience and unease of many performers are obstacles that must be overcome.

In short, improvisation demands a much higher active and creative participation from the performer than notated music. Another problem is that improvisation involves creation rather than interpretation and this does not fit so easily into a classical music business that is based on repertoire and interpretation.

There is a significant difference here between improvisational practice in traditional jazz (where there is common agreement about styles and limits) and the more experimental forms of contemporary music (with no common language, no common rules, and literally everything or anything is possible). If, in an open-form piece by Cage, a musician starts to play a bit of Mozart, it might seem that there would be nothing wrong with this. In fact, it could be shown that the musician who interpolated Mozart, probably to make fun, simply didn't understand the concept, the meta-text, of the piece. In an improvisation, open-form, or aleatoric piece, performers

are particularly obligated to understand the meta-text if they are to integrate their contribution into the whole.[6] As art becomes more and more
individualized, there is more and more that needs to be known about the
"abouts" and it often becomes necessary for the musician (and sometimes
the audience as well) to understand the meta-text and the concept of the
work being played. The question then arises as to whether the score is of
help in these matters.

Music as play

If using a score short-circuits all these problems, why bother with improvisation at all? Or why not just ask performers to come together without any
preparation at all, if all they are going to do is improvise anyway?

There is something unforeseeable, unpredictable, and even competitive about improvisation. The idea of musical competition appears in jazz,
in Indian music, and in other cultures as well. It is a recurring theme in
those meta-operas—operas about opera—that virtually constitute an eighteenth-century subgenre. Mozart's *Schauspieldirektor* is a famous example
but there are many others, and it reappears in more recent times in Tom
Johnson's *Four-Note Opera* (see Chapter 8). Improvisation underlines the
"play" in playing music or in putting on "a play." The expression is common
in many languages but in most cases there is very little play involved. Children's play is amusement and perhaps some kind of practice for life (but
nobody wins or loses). Play can be a way of exploring as well as a kind of
improvising with physical objects (materials) or with other people. A "play"
in the theater suggests some kind of ancient meaning, which might imply an
element of unpredictability or at least surprise. If we know a story or a piece
too well, the element of curiosity and surprise is gone. With more improvisation and less predictability, theater (not to mention music theater) might
become more interesting. There could even be winners and losers, just as
there are in games and sports. The human dimensions would be at least as
large and perhaps deeper in the setting, the conflicts, and the goals. As in
composition, the core activity of improvisational performance is making
decisions. From nearly infinite possibilities, decisions are made not by the
composer in advance but by the performer in the moment. There would

6. When Feldman's graphic score for the Merce Cunningham *Summerscape*
   was being rehearsed by the New York City Ballet Orchestra, the oboist
   kept playing satirical, intrusive riffs as his "interpretation" of the indications in his part. At a certain point, Feldman simply announced that he had
   made a mistake in orchestration and eliminated the oboe entirely from the
   score.

have to be goals and a rule or set of rules. Music is phenomenologically focused on itself and exceeds the complexity of individual decisions. These phenomenological constraints require that improvising musicians cannot act totally autonomously and individually. They must pay attention to what they are producing not only as individuals but as an entity. There cannot be two or three "musics" at the same time, as the multiple sound sources must mix into an overall sound. Improvising in an ensemble requires social-artistic competence from all participants to allow them to integrate their individual contributions into the context of the whole.

With notation, social considerations for the participants need not be observed. The score organizes not only the musical timing but also the social interplay of the group members, who may not have to work any of this out for themselves. Improvisation, especially in the theater, needs a special type of performer or musician, able to individually express himself or herself and simultaneously able to integrate into the whole context. The performers themselves then become the actual subject of the work that they are performing.

The responsibility to act as a co-composer may be a burden that not all performers will appreciate. But it might be a way for them to express them-selves not only as individual artists but also as a group, and it will affect how the whole work will be shaped. The formal problem is centered on how to catch the audience's interest through suspense and surprise. Complex structural events are literally impossible to predict and difficult to control in the course of improvising. Because of this, improvisational groups tend to abandon such ideas, and audiences learn not to expect them. When improvising from scratch, for example, it is very difficult to achieve pieces that need to build up a dynamic over the course of many hours where surprise and climax become possible. In such cases, notation not only has artistic and economic roles to play but also a psychological one for the performers!

Finally, it is often difficult for the audience to recognize improvisa-tion. In many ways, it is really of little or no importance to the listener or onlooker whether the artists are improvising and whether the public is aware of it. Sometimes a very carefully staged interpretation makes the actors or singers sound like they are inventing and not reciting; even so, a certain amount of unpredictability generally creeps in. What probably counts most for the audience is simply being entertained, and however one explains the idea of entertainment, timing is certainly a big issue. Opera scores of the past show many signs of the problems that composers had with timing. The marking *vi-...-de*, indicating a cut, is found in many scores and suggests that someone changed his mind about timing by short-cutting extended material.

Because of harmonic issues, cuts have to be hidden, even if it means that certain passages have to be rewritten. Composers themselves—Mozart, Verdi, even Wagner—have provided different versions of their operas for different performances, and operatic scores have always been less sacred than pure concert pieces. *Carmen* was written as an *opéra comique* with spoken dialogue alternating with musical numbers; after the composer's death, someone changed it into a full-blown grand opera by turning the dialogue into accompanied recitative. Italian operas have often been cleaned up dramaturgically by taking out the *cabalettas* (the fast final sections of certain arias) or even by removing entire acts (as in Verdi's *Don Carlo*). When a certain tenor in the Viennese production of *Don Giovanni* could not manage "*Il mio tesoro*," Mozart wrote the simpler "*Dalla sua pace*" as a substitute (now most tenors want to sing both, which presents dramaturgical problems that most audiences are willing to overlook). Many, perhaps most, operas have been rewritten or chopped for a whole host of reasons (to suit different casts, opinionated impresarios, or impatient audiences). The most bizarre versions of this process are the *potpourris* ("hotpots" into which all sorts of leftovers are tossed and recooked) in which one famous melody chases another. Resizing, rewriting, rescoring, changing texts or translations, cutting out boring bits, changing order of scenes—literally everything has been done to opera and music theater to make the theater and the music feel as if they were being improvised and created right on the spot. This is the ideal, the model: the sense that "it is happening now!" It is in the true nature of theater and music theater that it is created, lives out its life span, and expires in each performance. In that sense, all theatrical performance needs to have the aura of an improvisation that lives in its moment.

Further Reading

Engle, Ron, and Tice L. Miller. *The American Stage: Social and Economic Issues*. Cambridge, 2006.

Sperber, Martin. *Improvisation in the Performing Arts: Music, Dance and Theatre*. Ed.D. dissertation, Columbia University, 1974.

chapter 21

Popular or high art?

His is the only music in the world in which I find no quality at all.

Arnold Schoenberg to Virgil Thomson in 1935
on the music of Kurt Weill

Do we need an art class structure?

What the composers and literati of the aristocratic Florentine literary club known as the *camerata* invented in the waning years of the sixteenth century did not, strictly speaking, start out as opera nor did these distinguished gentlemen pretend that it was anything but declaimed Greek tragedy. Their own name for it was *stile rappresentativo*, a fancy way of describing a method of "representing" or reciting the words in performance—in Italian, it is true, not in Greek—with a simple musical accompaniment. Although the term literally suggests "theatrical style," it refers to a musical method better known to us as recitative that was used for songs and even madrigals as well as those larger theatrical works generally based on classical subjects of the serious or tragic variety (although the tragic endings were generally altered with a deus ex machina).[1]

---

1. The *deus ex machina*, literally god appearing out of a (theatrical) machine, is generally thought of as a device to provide a happy ending to a tragedy, but the larger significance of a higher power that can override mundane concerns and lesser beings was hardly to be overlooked in an autocratic age.

What the *camerata* had accomplished was the creation of an aristocratic performance mode that appealed to a small, highly educated public and was clearly distinguishable from the popular entertainments that have passed for musical theater ever since Roman times. They did this by ignoring the most essential feature of those popular entertainments: the folk-tinged ballad or song. Those early operas are pure recitative, and even the work of Monteverdi tended toward a through-composed form based on heightened recitative that occasionally thickened into arioso or was interrupted by choral, scenic, or dance music performed by the larger ensemble of voices and instruments. Greek tragedy has both choruses and dance so both were acceptable to the high standards of our avid company of humanists and Renaissance courtiers. Because of the need for ensemble togetherness, these larger passages tended to be rhythmically simpler than the recitatives and ariosos and therefore more immediately melodic.

Inevitably, the melodic elements took over. Long before the end of the seventeenth century, melodic airs and arias had moved in, nonclassical subjects were introduced (epic poetry, saints' lives, pseudo-historical subjects), comic elements began to appear, and opera had become popular enough in its land of birth—where it was, after all, being sung in the local vernacular—to allow the establishment of public opera houses. Ironically, the choral and dance element largely disappeared from the public houses (for economic reasons) and recitative became the storytelling link between solo numbers that were melodic, highly rhythmic, and, often enough, full of bravura and display. For two centuries the *opera lirica* dominated both the high-brow and popular theater in Italy while the serious spoken theater, which had been revived in Renaissance Italy on Roman and Greek models, faded badly. Only in the popular theater—the improvised *commedia dell'arte*, the puppet shows, and the written-out comedies, often in dialect, of later writers like Goldoni—did the tradition of spoken theater stay alive, and even then with a mixture of dialogue and songs.

Opera traveled quickly to France where the young Florentine Giovanni Battista Lulli—better known as Jean-Baptiste Lully—introduced the Monteverdian model. It also appeared early in the German-speaking world and somewhat later in Russia, England, and elsewhere. Outside of Italy, opera per se was and is an imported, aristocratic enterprise in a foreign language. In the major centers (or wherever it was economically feasible), Italian singers and musicians were imported as prestige items. Ironically, whereas Italian public opera houses basically presented solo operas with small casts and minimal orchestras (the stars brought in the public so everything else was dispensable), opera in the major centers north of the Alps was well funded and supported larger casts, larger orchestras, bigger choruses, longer rehearsal periods (hence the possibility of more complex numbers), and more resplendent productions. In most of the world, opera was and remains a high-art form imbued with strong class markers.

The dialectic between popular and high art in music theater has been with us ever since. There is no reason to think that opera, even in its international heyday, actually displaced popular forms of music theater. Quite to the contrary, popular theater, which was largely some kind of music theater, existed all over Europe but it was never very well documented; only in its later incarnations (when, for example, important composers took up the form) did it produce texts and scores that have survived.

In general, popular music theater requires performances in the local language, juicy melodic songs (airs, arias) with a folk or pop influence, charismatic performers to sing them, spoken dialogue or easy-to-follow recitative, and comic or soap opera subjects. These subjects can be surprisingly complex but they almost always deal with the interaction between the classes and/or with various kinds of forbidden or thwarted love alliances. A good dose of kinetic energy is also required, preferably in the form of song and dance. High art, on the other hand, requires tragic or "serious" subjects with simple, traditional stories, preferably in a foreign language. It is also characterized by high-end vocalism (in range and virtuosity), elaborate costumes, and *décor* with spectacular scenic effects. Dramatic and even through-composed scenes alternate with big multipart solo numbers.

This simple class division was complicated when, starting in the late eighteenth century, the middle class began to make its weight felt in both size and wealth. Up to a certain point, the new merchant class chose to emulate the taste of the upper classes but it very quickly developed its own preferences. A major influence was the growth and popularity of the novel, which was a preferred form of entertainment for the now literate middle class and the fast-growing publishing industry that grew up in its midst. Two of the biggest musical-comedy hits of all time (not only in Italy but all over Europe) were Niccolò Piccinni's *La Cecchina ossia La buona figliuola* of 1756, based on Richardson's *Pamela*, and Pergolesi's *La Serva Padrona*, a story about a servant who seduces her master and gets him to marry her. Comedies and serious operas based on popular English and French novels continued to appear throughout the rest of the eighteenth and much of the nineteenth centuries.

New forms of music theater, under a variety of names, gained popularity in all the Western countries where the new bourgeoisie thrived. The *opera buffa* (*opéra bouffe* in French), the "little opera" or *operetta*, and their more recent successor, musical comedy, might seem to make fewer artistic or musical demands on its performers than grand opera but they require attractive and charismatic performers. The stereotypical stories involve matters of class, sex, mistaken identities, wealth, and other issues of concern to the bourgeoisie. The singing style was a somewhat lighter and more theatrical version of the operatic projected sound that was needed to fill large acoustic environments. A lighter sound was possible because operetta theaters as well as operetta orchestras were smaller and lighter than their grand opera opposite numbers. Elegant décor, lightness of touch, and comic themes involving the upper and lower classes were essential.

As opera lost its aristocratic patronage in the late eighteenth and nineteenth centuries, it came to be patronized more and more by the upwardly mobile middle class. Opera struggled to maintain its high-art status, largely through a series of reforms. Class divisions and theories about art were an essential part of the various disputes over what opera and music theater ought to be: *la Querelle* (or *Guerre*) *des buffons* (French baroque opera challenged by the new, simpler, more popular Italian *opera buffa*); the dispute between the supporters of the classic French opera of Lully and the new theories and music of Rameau; the ballad opera of John Gay satirizing the Italian (or Italo-German) opera of Handel and his contemporaries; Gluck's high-minded classicism as a reform of old-fashioned Italian and French opera; the struggles of Berlioz to get his romantic ideal of opera on the stage; the battles and triumphs of Wagner's "music of the future" over Meyerbeerian grand opera.

By the end of the nineteenth century, the center of truly popular musical life had moved to the revue, vaudeville, and music-hall houses found in cities around the world, and after the advent of mass media, this culture (and most of its artists) passed almost completely to the film and television studios. By the time theater and musical artists like Les Six, Stravinsky, Brecht, and Kurt Weill took up the form of the popular musical in the 1920s and 1930s, they were as much reviving a moribund art as trading on the vitality of a thriving popular form. The distinction is important because of the confusion between the truly popular entertainments of earlier times and the essentially middle-class and even upwardly mobile ambitions of the musical theater. At the same moment composers were trying to revive and revitalize the popular *songspiel*, the authors and composers of Broadway musicals—from *Show Boat* to *Carousel* to *Phantom of the Opera*—were trying to make the musical more "artistic" by making it more operetta- or opera-like!

During this period, seriously operatic music-drama—whether traditional or in the modernist orbit—remained largely in the Wagnerian mode. The real successors to high-art opera and music drama were a handful of atonal and twelve-tone operas, almost all with big tragic/expressionist subjects, and a series of modernist performance works ranging from *Le sacre du printemps* to the Antheil/Leger *Ballet mechanique* to the *opéras minutes* of Milhaud to the Russian futurist performances to the never-completed *Astronome* of Varèse based on a libretto by Artaud. It was this line, largely cut off in Europe by World War II, that was continued in America by Cage, Harry Partch, Robert Ashley, and others. New music and, more slowly, experimental music theater were reestablished in Europe by the large-scale experimental work of Stockhausen, Kagel, Ligeti, Berio, Nono, and others. In a curious way, this post–World War II modernism carries many of the high-art ambitions formerly associated with grand opera. Just as the opera patron brings a certain level of education and connoisseurship into the theater, so must the public for new music and new music theater come into the performance arena with a sense of structure and form. Atonality requires a tonal sense to validate its extensions or violations. Similarly, experimental music theater starts from the premise that audiences will expect certain rules and relationships to apply (although, ironically, a piece that is labeled "experimental" creates the expectation of violation). These strictures apply not only within each work and performance but also between the performers and the performed-to, even as the rules and relationships are upset, teased apart, rearranged, or drastically violated.

Traditional opera—its subject matter and its formal relationships as defined from baroque opera up until Wagner at least—is often described as an art that defines its class by celebrating the *status quo*. Modernist art, which originally attacked the *status quo*, long ago lost its ability to provoke the existing social order, but by challenging middle-class assumptions about art (sentimentality, happy endings, *kitsch* in the form of upper-class emulation, etc.), it allies itself to a degree with popular art. As stated elsewhere, modernist art tends to create its own inner utopias rather than attempting to build external utopias by reforming society. To sit through Cage's four minutes and thirty-three seconds of silence or the four hours and thirty-three minutes of the relentless sound waves of *Einstein on the Beach* becomes a class marker and an affirmation of one's position in life—internal acceptance perhaps rather than a recipe for external change.

Does middle-class music theater still exist? In the Euromusicals of Andrew Lloyd Webber and Claude-Michel Schoenberg, the operetta has morphed into something resembling a phantom of the old opera. In contrast, the contemporary American musical seems to consist largely of "juke box musicals" (song-and-dance collections of pop songs) and raucous retro works modeled on the old Broadway musical comedies (*Hairspray, The Producers*).

It can be argued that in the last decades of the twentieth century, the central dynamic of middle-class entertainment has passed from the passive realm of theatrical performance to the active (and interactive) domain of club culture. Dance clubs, with their quasi-theatrical *mise-en-scène* and their tendency toward extravagant exhibitionism, have something of the character of a Westernized form of "musicking" (see Chapter 19).

Is there such a thing anymore as a serious popular music theater?

The American musical broke away from the Viennese operetta when it introduced Afro-American elements including jazz dance and the blues-derived popular song into its fabric, and it has always renewed itself by drawing on the deep well of jazz and pop music. If this is the case, then what is obviously needed are not more Kurt Weills but serious popular artists working in the musical theater. By and large this hasn't happened, but it is not for want of trying.

Most successful popular theater composers have been, like Weill, not actual creators of popular music but theater craftsmen or classically trained composers who have adapted or emulated some of the qualities of jazz and pop and translated them into a theater context. The list of these "translators" is fairly long. It includes Jerome Kern, Eubie Blake, Kurt Weill, Marc Blitzstein, Leonard Bernstein, Bob Telson and others.[2] Only in a relatively very recent period have active popular musicians had the kind of recognition (and to some degree the skills) that would permit them to be taken seriously as artists. In the past, the few who have tried to work in the theater have had very limited success. Scott Joplin had to pay out of his own pocket for the performance and publication of his opera *Treemonisha,* and it took decades before there was any recognition of this work. Gershwin had better luck, but *Porgy and Bess* was severely edited to be turned into a Broadway musical and film; no opera house would produce it until long after his death (although it is now universally recognized as a major opera). Duke Ellington tried several times without success—notably with his own version of *The Beggar's Opera* (*Beggar's Holiday* of 1946 with John La Touche and John Houseman) and with his *Queenie Pie,* produced only after his death. The Tom Waits/Robert Wilson collaborations came about because of commissions from a German theater resulting in a German expressionist interpretation of the Broadway musical (see Chapter 15)!

There are difficulties with the "serious" pop artist in the theater that have not yet been overcome. A common view is that the commercial structure and high costs of the Broadway or West End musical theater do not permit serious creativity from any quarter, pop or otherwise. The need for an expensive Broadway production to hold its own and sustain the long runs needed to pay back the substantial investments required sets up too high a barrier.

2. Astor Piazzolla might be included in this list for *Dangerous Games* and *Maria de Buenos Aires,* but the former was arranged by others from his work and the latter remains relatively little known.

The pop performer and composer Paul Simon made a major unsuccessful attempt to circumvent this problem by independently producing his own musical on Broadway with his own money, which enabled him to keep complete control; the subject (a sensational and well-remembered New York murder story) and a cast of outstanding Hispanic pop stars brought a popular audience into the theater for *Cape Man* but not in large enough numbers for the work to hold its own on the Broadway stage.

Another instructive example is the Lee Breuer/Bob Telson *Gospel at Colonnus,* an unconventional retelling of Greek tragedy in the form of a black gospel service with the Five Blind Boys from Alabama collectively playing the blinded Oedipus. This is a genuinely popular music-theater work with a truly original theatrical form. It was developed in the nonprofit theater (BAM, American Music Theater Festival). It toured widely and was recorded for public television and on CD with success. But it failed on Broadway because after it exhausted the elite part of the New York audience in its initial run, it could not continue to fill the theater with middle-class suburban audiences and out-of-town tourists, which provide the bulk of the Broadway audience for long runs. The mass public, which could provide a large potential audience for such projects, has long ago lost the habit of going to the theater for entertainment or enlightenment. The high cost of a ticket was an obstacle. Another major factor was that it proved extremely difficult to get convincing gospel-style performances eight times a week out of a union chorus, which had to "play" the gospel choir on Broadway. Previous productions of this work had always used real (i.e., authentic) local gospel choirs, a fact that in itself produced a public for the piece and helped turn tour performances into local community events.

There are other, more generic problems that should be noted. One is that most popular composers are essentially songwriters and need musical help to produce anything more elaborate than the bare bones of songwriting (words set to a melody accompanied by a few chords). It is, of course, common Broadway practice to use arrangers and orchestrators;[3] this allows the composer to participate in the rehearsal process (when big changes may be made) while permitting the orchestrations to be done at the last minute, an important consideration if revisions are in progress. Nevertheless, the contemporary view is that orchestration is an essential part of composition and that something important is lost in this process (significantly, the one Broadway composer who insisted on doing his own orchestrations was Kurt Weill).

---

3. They were used in the Robert Wilson/Tom Waits *Black Rider.*

Another issue is that the soul of much pop music lies in performance rather than in composition. It is difficult for performers to reach that charismatic level of intensity and communication—those epiphanies that constitute a big part of the genius of pop music—in a theatrical context, especially when they must sustain the level night after night in the "cold" atmosphere of a theater (as opposed to the "warm" atmosphere of a club or arena). As the *Gospel at Colonnus* example suggests, it can be even more difficult to convey these things secondhand through theatrical performers who have to be trained in a limited rehearsal period. The subject of most pop music is almost always the "I"—the performer/composer's own experiences, thoughts, moods, and so on. Most theater, on the other hand, requires something else: a sense of the other, a certain objectivity with the ability to project ideas, actions, and characters outside of oneself, up onto a stage, and into the body and voice of a stage performer or performers who may have very different talents, roles, and motifs from one's own. Finally, it is very rare that a pop composer can move in or close to the position of the *auteur* in these projects which are almost always director-driven.

Although these difficulties have been occasionally overcome (see the discussion of *The Black Rider* in Chapter 16), they are obstacles to the creation of a genuinely popular music theater through the collaboration of librettists and theater artists with creative pop musicians. In a few cases, it has been possible to take larger pop ideas—mostly "concept albums" created for the vinyl or compact disc—and put them on the stage; The Who's *Tommy* and Pink Floyd's *The Wall* are examples. For the moment however, most new popular music theater—insofar as it still exists—still depends on the "translators."[4]

Further Reading

Grant, Mark N. *The Rise and Fall of the Broadway Musical*. Boston, 2005.
Jablonski, Edward. *Gershwin*. New York, rev. 1998.
Peyser, Joan. *The Memory of All That (Gershwin)*. New York, rev. 1998.

4. It can be argued that pop and rock concerts constitute a sort of popular theater with dancers, laser lights, staging, and various qualities of "showmanship." The model for these live performances is, of course, not traditional theater but the music video, and the narrative (insofar as there is one) is the marketing of a musical product. Nevertheless, it would be a mistake to overlook these events as contemporary forms of popular musical theater.

chapter 22

Is Anyone Listening?

If it goes on like that I will get tinnitus!

an elderly lady overheard during the intermission
of a contemporary music concert

Audience at a production of Muziektheater Transparant, Antwerp, Belgium,
2000.

Who is the audience?

Looking at photographs taken at performances we can sometimes catch
a glimpse of the audience. Happenings, performances in galleries or on
streets, on canals, and in natural settings often show performers mixing
with the audience, creating a special form of street theater. Galleries that
host performances are typically rather small so the public ends up standing
or sitting on the floor with the performer or performers in the middle.
Sometimes it is not easy to differentiate performers from audience purely
by dress, but in other cases the distinction is clear. The audience photographed during an "action" by Yves Klein in 1960 Paris shows elegantly

Audience at an Yves Klein performance, Paris 1960

dressed members of society watching two nudes covered with blue color dragging themselves around on paper.

A picture that shows the grand staircase during intermission at the New York Metropolitan Opera in the 1980s gives us a good idea of the dress code of the day. In contrast, more recent audiences, dressed informally, have been willing, even anxious, to get involved as participants or at the very least as documentarians of public performances.

In the traditional theater, the audience completely disappears into the black of the auditorium as the theater lights go down and stage lights come up and seal the distinction between the performers and the performed-to. The proscenium arch, the "missing fourth wall" of realistic theater, the bright lights of the stage, and the unreal costumes all create a picture—a picture in motion to be sure—that stands out in opposition to the invisibility of the audience, huddled and immobilized in the auditorium.

At another extreme, we might have a work in which the performers disappear into the audience. In Dick Raijmaakers' *The Fall of Mussolini*, the audience is put on a scaffold or catwalk above and around the performance space. Many new theaters today have multipurpose or modular stages in which the floor or parts of it can be moved so that the audience/performance relationship can be changed as needed (see Chapter 7 for more on standard and nonstandard theater types). Ironically, these once-utopian possibilities are more widely available but much less used

Metropolitan Opera grand staircase during intermission; 1980s audience in dark suits and evening gowns. Photo: Henschel Verlag.

or appreciated than they once were. The Italian architect and librettist Valerio Ferrari[1] presented a concept for an opera house in which audiences would be placed alongside a stage in the form of a huge descending spiral. Stockhausen had a truly utopian vision for a hall with the public

1. Ferrari's opera *Oirat* about Albanian refugees drowned as they tried to reach Italy has music by the Albanian composer Aleksander Peçi.

suspended in midair and the music diffused in 360 degrees and three dimensions. Audiences today seem to divide into those who prefer very conventional situations in the traditional proscenium theater and those who patronize the type of event that reinvents everything anew with each piece.

Dealing with the audience in a new piece or production is not only a philosophical or ideological issue but also has its practical limitations. Fire laws or other security regulations apply in almost every theater in Western countries and this often becomes a subject of dispute between artist and producer. Switch off the emergency lights? Place objects in the emergency or fire lanes? Block the exits? Are there specific materials, actions, or sounds that could harm, injure, or discombobulate the audience? Break the law and the police or fire department may come and close down the theater!

Some companies, like the Catalonian La Fura dels Baus, are specialized in performance actions for which the audience is actually warned to wear waterproof clothing. This is certainly one form of the breakdown between performance space and audience space. Blue Man Group sells certain seats with a warning attached and also issues protective gear against flying paint.[2] More recently the audience has started to become part of the performance, both participating in and documenting the event on digital and mobile phone cameras. In general, however, the rules and regulations of public gatherings, intended to be protective of public security and well-being, are limiting. As everywhere, it is hard to say where security ends and overprotection starts. The problem is complicated by the enormous differences in audiences with respect to what they will tolerate. In some cases, a quiet whisper will evoke protests whereas thousands of people at pop concerts pass the time socializing, eating, drinking, screaming, and so forth. A case of serious injury at, say, an interactive performance could lead to major problems for the responsible producer or artist. It has happened at pop concerts with very negative aftereffects. There are no special art exemptions in civil law.

All this has been said to demonstrate that a work of performance art of any kind does not exist in a vacuum. It is takes place in a specific time and place. Although the piece itself might remain the same, a given performance in a certain place with a certain audience may totally change its reality.

2. Blue Man Group, which started out as a kind of "new vaudeville" anti-theater, has evolved into a popular, slightly mysterious, and childish play-time pursuit with a public made up largely of students while La Fura dels Baus and Nitsch are always very serious, grown-up and perhaps even frightening in their demand that audiences accept their transgressions.

What brings audiences into the theater?

Opera in its heyday was the top of the market, but nowadays opera houses, although still working with big budgets, have a lot of competition from cinema, pop concerts, dance clubs, and home media. The once-popular theater in the round and thrust stages were intended to give a more vivid immediacy to the performances—the updated version of the old bourgeois theater whose aim was to overwhelm rather than to partner with the public. Ironically, some once-progressive theater companies are now stuck with these thrust stages and no-longer fashionable theater-in-the-round theaters.

In many—perhaps most—of those cases, the audience is treated as if it were something fluid and easy to manipulate, easily timed and programmed, docile and willing to be led by the nose. But like the reality of the performance itself, the reality of audiences is actually complex, paradoxical, and constantly changing. In a series of performances of the same piece, it is a commonplace that different audiences react very differently.

The group psychology of audiences is not very well understood. The public sometimes behaves as a "stupid mass" and sometimes as a distinct intelligent individual. Performers commonly talk about this after a show, noting whether the audience was noisy or quiet, in a good mood, responsive, inspiring or slow, heavy, and unresponsive. Sometimes they will even note specific individuals who behave in unexpected ways. "You have been a wonderful audience" is a common remark from pop performers that causes the audience to cheer and increases the public's regard for the performer. Opera divas go even further than this, blowing kisses to their fans, bowing and kneeling, retrieving bouquets, and so forth. This is all part of the highly differentiated and complex art form of classical opera that also has a highly structured public and a set of rituals that controls the relationship between performer and audience. This begins when people buy their tickets (sometimes sleeping overnight in sleeping bags outside the opera house) and continues on the inside through the very structure of the opera house interior. Parquet, parterre, loges, ranks, and standing places all create a stratified temporary society inside the theater, inversely reflecting the society outside (the lower seats are the most expensive).

Other elements of operatic ritual are the socializing at intermission; the applause, which is counted in curtain calls (or, in modern theaters without a curtain, by the number of times that the stage lights are brought down and up); and the post-performance stage door lineup for autographs and glimpses of the stars. The collecting of recordings, photos, souvenirs, and memorabilia also provides a way the public can participate in this performing arts culture.

Family Circle
Balcony
Dress Circle
Grand Tier
Parterre
Orchestra

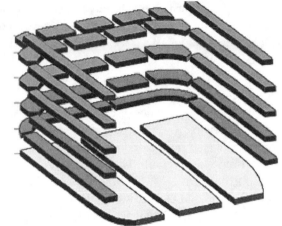

The Metropolitan Opera's stratified society.

This traditional culture of theater and opera does not depend on specific works and seems naive and easily penetrable. Not surprisingly, there have been many attempts to change it, but the system has proved to be more resilient and audiences more adaptable than expected. In some cases, audiences have come to acknowledge and accept the challenge in a very passive way. As a result, a situation has developed in which an opera house will play an extremely difficult avant-garde piece in front of an accepting opera audience, which simply goes through its normal pre-programmed reactions. There is not only no scandal but all the components of audience behavior are now identical to those at any opera performance!

As the costs of live performance go up and the public turns more and more to mass media, the situation for all the performance arts becomes more and more difficult. Unless there are big names involved, producers are willing to take fewer and fewer risks. The only questions that are asked are those that concern self-preservation, and in fact, the operatic system itself has become—with built-in redundancies and safeguards—a method for self-preservation.

In music criticism and musicology, it has become a habit to speak about music as if it were some kind of product. But music, of all the arts, is the least like a product and the most like a social action based on a process of transmitting and giving something. It is only in the smaller and more flexible music theater that these questions can be asked openly: What is given and to whom? What does the creative artist have to offer?

The historical past of music making shows a mixture of functionality (masses, cantatas) and entertainment (concertos, court opera, shows, pop music). One definition of a classical period in music would be a time when Mozart could write *La Clemenza di Tito* and *Die Zauberflöte* almost simultaneously; in short, when usefulness, entertainment value, and artistic quality were in some kind of balance. In all cases, there is always an addressee, someone to whom the work or the performance is dedicated. It might be a god or a royal patron. It might be all of humanity or just the customers drinking at the bar before or after the performance.

Who is watching whom? The audience is watching the performers but the performers are also watching the audience. Performers are always dealing with the public in ways that the creators or producers of the work they are performing do not necessarily appreciate or understand. What contact do performers have with their audience? In the archaic spectacles, described by Christopher Small in his book *Musicking,* the answer is, quite a lot. Small shows how strongly the audience in African culture is (or was) connected to the performers and musicians. Performances in most of the great ancient or traditional theaters may continue for many hours—even days—and take the form of a huge party in which everyone, even children, participate. In Indonesian and Balinese theater—at least before performances became tourist attractions—the line between public and participants was not always so well defined, and the inhabitants of entire villages may take part in certain events. John Cage used to note that in Bali there was no word for "art." Another characteristic of this kind of "musicking" is that the repertoire can, has, and does change over time, a fact not always taken into account by musicological purists.

Individualization and specialization in European theater has produced specific art forms for specific publics; at the same time, it has annihilated forms of expression without an audience and, on the flip side, it has not permitted or it has inhibited specific audiences to generate their own forms of expression. There are exceptions to this. One is children's theater, which is mostly music theater, mostly educational, and likely to be funny and playful, reflecting the way adults imagine children's minds. Unfortunately, children nowadays, even at the earliest ages, discover television as well as computer and video games and tend to regard them as being much more fun than theater or music. There is not yet, in a society where the image of the young, beautiful, and dynamic is everywhere, much of a concept of theater for the old.[3]

3. One of the authors (ES) has had the experience of a work (*Noah*) written for performance by a mixed cast of professionals and students being successfully adapted for professionals and seniors at a center for older people.

In the Americas, other exceptions are made for the urban poor and for immigrant audiences. What was once called "race music" turned out to be jazz, blues, gospel, and its progeny (up to and including hip-hop). Black and Hispanic theater is important in New York and California and has always been open to musical theater forms. There is even a movement to create hip-hop opera and music theater. *Bobos* (American Music Theater Festival in 1993) by Ed Shockley and James McBride is an early example, and there is now a Hip-Hop Theater Festival.

There are many paradoxes here. The stressed young urban professional dresses up for a couple of hours to go to a performance of a classical opera. But why? It is much easier for her not to dress up (or to dress down) and go to a nearby auditorium where there are plenty of seats and where, often at a lower price, she can meet her peers and see or hear something new in pop music. But perhaps this does not match the social aspirations of her peers or the unconscious desire to affirm traditional culture and the *status quo*.

Local or/and global

Many questions about audiences need to be asked. To whom is contemporary opera/music theater addressed? What might a potential audience for new music theater be interested in? Nineteenth-century society, originally addicted to amusements and escapes, turned to various forms of realism with the work of Zola, Ibsen, Strindberg, Verga, Dreiser, and others, work that reflected "real" problems and "real" tragedies. *Verismo* in opera was not far behind. Nowadays, however, theater presents itself in laboratory costume—in vitro so to speak—as a series of proposal for discussion. This attitude is connected to our vaunted knowledge explosion. Some spectacular remote events are now transmitted immediately into our homes and form pieces of a large puzzle. The result is that our knowledge of the world is as much global as it is local even though most of this is useless ballast in our minds, a mixture of curiosity and voyeurism. The commercial possibility of live, local performance, as contrasted to global media transmissions, is limited and tends to be ignored by the media. What claims can be made for live theater (let alone live music theater)? Does it really help promote a better understanding of the world or is this merely the kind of educational approach that audiences dislike?

It is very characteristic of music theater to be local but widespread. When NewOp was founded in 1992 (see Chapter 12), it brought together composers, writers, and producers of new music theater from different parts of the world who did not necessarily even know each other or each other's work. The globalization of music theater was, perhaps, an inevitability in a movement that had popped up in many places but had deep roots only in few. Increasingly, electronic (or, more correctly, digital) media have begun to dominate a mass music scene that absorbs and fuses everything available for sale on the global market. National trends and characteristics are losing their profile as European Community policy promotes quick exchange, artistic discussions, and cross-national projects. The trend is towards the application of free-market policies, which ensure that even the arts have to follow the economic rules, a very problematic path at best. The issue then becomes—for free-marketeers and arts bureaucrats alike—what art organizations and art works can be sold across the widest markets, a principle that tends to put at a disadvantage, or ignore entirely, small local institutions and local cultural conditions. These rules have put control into the hands of a few managers who tour one production or a selection of artists within the carousel of festivals that are often the only way to get in touch with non-mainstream performance art. The globalization represented by NewOp or by the Munich Biennale (see Chapter 9) resulted in a music theater that is necessarily a form of *Zeitoper* and has an audience that is widespread in the Western world and in Westernized cultures although not necessarily numerous anywhere in particular.

Audiences, media, and performance space

When we talk about media, a distinction has to be made between media that is part of the work under discussion and media that functions as the performance space by acting as the conveyor of the performance itself. Performance space in this latter sense includes theater as well as radio, television, and film. Performance media within a performance might include video, cassette tape, computers and mini-computers, even CD-ROMs, DVDs, Blu-ray discs, computer games, mobile phones, headphones, and mini-computers. Some of these are already well-known components of music theater and other performance arts; others might seem more peripheral. Nevertheless, it is perfectly feasible to introduce music theater to such media or vice versa. Joshua Fried, a New York composer, has a series of "headphone-driven" pieces involving performers who respond not to written-out music but to what they hear on their headphones. In his *Headphone Follies,* not so much a performance as an installation, it is hard to tell who are the performers and who is the audience. In *International Cloud Atlas,* Mikel Rouse's score for Merce Cunningham's *eyeSpace* (2006), each member of the audience has an individual Ipod and listens to a different random shuffling of the tracks (there are 3,628,800 possible permutations).

The computer game *Lara Croft,* in a series called *Tomb Raider 2,* is placed in and around the Venetian opera house *La Fenice* and the dramaturgy of

the game, which lies between cinema and theater and depends on the ambience of this traditional opera building (where many contemporary pieces
have been premiered), pushes us to think about future possibilities. In
this last example, the social aspect of live theater is essentially nonexistent
although the interactive functionality of the game transmits the feeling of a
live performance. King Ludwig II of Bavaria or on occasion the Pope might
have constituted the entire audience for an operatic performance, but the
proverbial command performance is available only to such exalted personages. Now, however, the transmission techniques of electronic media have
made performance-on-demand for an audience of one perfectly feasible
and there can also be performances without performers or in which the
spectator is the only actual performer. Interactivity and interactive media
put a question mark on a lot of traditional assumptions. Is interactive game
playing creative in any meaningful sense or is it merely "interpretation" (the
creative role presumably belonging to the developer of the game)?[4] This
leads to the question of whether an audience can be (or can be made to
be) creative at all. This question was posed in the 1960s and early 1970s in
the so-called *Wandelkonzerte* ("wandering audience concerts") of Ladislav
Kupkovic in which groups of performers and audiences were organized to
move inside compounds or even throughout a city. This differs from those
public art performances, happenings, and installations in which the art
activity merges into the flux of everyday urban bustle and becomes nearly
indiscernible from real life. The audiences at such events do not deliber-
ately gather at a certain time in the expectation of a performance but are
simply passers-by who happen on some action or performance and have
either a fragmented idea of what is going on or no idea at all.[5]

The public space, where the performance is free of charge, can draw in
people who otherwise never would enter a theater. The street or subway
(underground or metro) musician, the clown, the break dancer, and the
living statue are performing theater literally without the theater building.
Most outdoor performance venues are places where people gather and
such places are often chosen for their qualities of landscape or architecture.
What is missing is the frame and the dedicated audience; after all, anybody
can be on the street and nobody is excluded. Perhaps these can be viewed
as positive aspects of street performance. On the negative side, there is the

4. It should be added that writing music for computer games is now a recognized profession.
5. A classic example of this is the 1977 Times Square installation of Max
   Neuhaus in which the sound comes up through a grating in the sidewalk
   and becomes so integrated into the noisescape of its environment that the
   installation was almost completely forgotten and ignored for years before it
   was reinstalled in 2002.

likelihood that such performances will be simply overlooked by the very people who might be most interested. And, although street musicians are common enough, elaborate ensemble musical theater performances on the street or in the subway are, for many reasons, rare and difficult to carry off effectively.

Performances in the ancient open-air theaters of Greece and Rome took place in daylight.[6] Renaissance theaters were brought indoors but they used permanent sets that represented the street—as if the outside were being brought inside and plays were still being played in daylight.[7] Curiously, many modern open-air performances in Italy, often played in antique ruins, reverse this situation and bring the proscenium and set design of the closed theater back out into the open, generally competing with, disregarding, or even blocking out the surrounding landscape (and most often, with the aid of modern outdoor stadium lighting, performing at night). The ancient theaters were built to integrate nature and land-scape into the theater performance. These performances had to conquer and hold their audience's attention by being surprising or suspenseful. Otherwise the audience would prefer to eat, drink, and chat (as it still does—or did until recently—in provincial performances of ultra-familiar operas in Italy).

The baroque and rococo court theaters of the seventeenth and eigh-teenth centuries developed the art of the changeable set within the picture opening provided by the proscenium stage. The public was separated from the stage by the orchestra placed at ground level. However the rela-tively small size of the theaters and the horseshoe design of the *théâtre à l'italienne* meant that no one was very far from the stage, and sightlines and acoustics were generally good for everyone. The bourgeois opera houses that followed, although on a much larger scale, carefully imitated the court theaters in such matters. The rigidity and hierarchy of the seating arrange-ments and the ritual of theatrical procedures was preserved along with the increasingly traditional repertoire. Curiously enough, although most concert music and classical opera is quite profane in its nature, a religious aura is preserved in these performance rituals, perhaps a relic of the time when such events actually had a religious significance. Performances in lofts, galleries, and abandoned industrial buildings can be said to lie in-between the rigid traditions and rituals of formal theaters and the unspecific

6. The bullfights of Spain and southern France, which take place in outdoor arenas, might be cited as surviving examples of daylight theater. They might be considered as partly sport but they are certainly mostly theater with a strong flavor of ritual.

7. Two or three such theaters still survive in Italy. The Palladian *Teatro Olim-pico* in Vicenza is an outstanding example.

float and rush of street theater.[8] In all these situations, there are different expectations and different limitations.

To a certain degree, audience response is based on expectation, which is, in turn, based on prior knowledge. How does an audience get to know something about what they are going to see and hear? In this secondary and preliminary layer of communication lies the biggest problem of all art forms that do not have the consecration of institutionalization. Before the performance and its actual unfolding in time, there is a kind of pre-performance, a background event that prepares, publicizes, helps, and even promotes the understanding of the art work or the performance that has yet to appear. This may take the form of press releases, journalism, public relations, advertising, promotion, media coverage, or any number of other methods of binding a new work or performance to its potential public. Without the older coherence of a society where certain agreed-on languages, codes, and rituals are a well-established habit, the traditions for understanding may be blurred or missing and the activity of public relations[9] has to take their place. It represents a deep difference between those who claim that a new piece should be understandable at first sight without pre-information and those who say the opposite.

Berio said that his pieces for the opera needed the opera house and the opera public and he even went so far as to seat provocateurs in their midst. At the time—the 1960s—opera audiences were still coherent entities with predictable behavior, which made scandals easy to program. When the social and intellectual background of the theater- or operagoer is calculable, the assumption can be made that certain notions, themes, and texts will be recognized and understood. When those assumptions are no longer valid or when theater happens outside its protected areas (protected in the sense that there is a certain understanding and behavior to be taken for granted), problems of intelligibility arise.[10]

8. In the *Ruhtriennale* in Germany, vast factory buildings and coal-mine structures are used for theatrical events. There is some historical cynicism in changing sweatshops into high-brow art venues, as these vast spaces become fantastic stage sets that are fitted out as genuine theaters while their original uses are hidden or ignored.

9. Or, on a more serious level, the notion of "audience building" has been proposed to help develop a more profound preparation of the public for difficult or experimental work that lacks (or defies) common standards and codes.

10. An amusing example of this was provided by Daniel Nagrin's *Peloponnesian War* (music by Archie Shepp and Eric Salzman), which began with a disturbing collage of recorded performances of the American national anthem, a sort of musical flag-burning. Initially, audiences always stood up at the first notes but afterward, many felt betrayed or otherwise deceived; some members of the audience simply walked out. Over the long performance history of the piece—approximately the length of the Vietnam

There was a major discussion in the avant-garde as to whether there could be any kind of musical underpinning to new work without some connection to history. For Scriabin there was a metaphysical message in the concept of synesthesia; the audience became humankind itself, which had to be saved by listening to and watching his compositions. Twentieth-century artists and authors, particularly in Europe, have often employed a language that feeds directly into that "second layer," the explanatory by-text, the row of footnotes. Does this actually win over the audience or, on the contrary, does it create resistance? Such ideas can be stimulating, surprising, and inspiring, but it is not always the case that a great idea makes for a great musical or theater evening.

Why can't a work be self-explanatory? Why should a piece of music or a play need to be explained in simple words when the work itself is so highly complex or disturbing? Has the common denominator of theater consumers been lowered so much that the public cannot understand anything but the simplest discourse any more? Is the discourse of contemporary art too specific? Are new art, music, theater, and opera destined only for a specially trained audience?

When art and music represented the wealth of governments, they aimed at universality. Haydn said, "The whole world understands my language," and by and large that was true (of course, "the whole world" was a much smaller place back then). In most of the arts, universality was closely connected to *mimesis* but in music it depended on something else. Perhaps there is something innate or "hard-wired" in human beings when it comes to music. Or perhaps it was the connection to folk art and to a popular culture that has always favored music. We all react to the sound of the human voice, and in most cultures, vocal music is dominant. Where instrumental music comes to the fore, there is rhythm, perhaps equally hard-wired. Rhythm is connected to dance, and like the structure of the instruments themselves, rhythm has both a physical component and mathematically definable characteristics that make for hard-fact realities.[11] Even with all the variety that twentieth- and twenty-first-century music has shown, the psycho-physiological meanings of distinct intervals and kinetic rhythms continue to exist and have not yet been by any means replaced by other compositional concepts.

War—audience members (for whatever reasons) mostly stopped standing up at the first notes of the national anthem. In effect, the scandal became more and more difficult to program!

11. In terms of basic rhythm, many theorists associate duple meters with breathing and triple meters with the human heartbeat. However, combinations and more complex rhythms are well known in many musical cultures.

By the late nineteenth century, the leading masters of musical composition, many of them opera composers, developed different strategies to avoid or postpone the tonal cadence. We might well ask if this had anything to do with the social-political evolutions or revolutions of the same period. A cry for freedom was coming from colonialized peoples, subjugated minorities, Afro-American slaves, workers in heavy industry, prisoners, Jews in the European ghettos, and so forth. But who was crying to be liberated from the tonal cadence?

The cadence might be considered as the mimetic element in music. This harmonic-melodic and rhythmic pattern has a double importance to musical composition. It defines formal sections as well as whole pieces by setting the basic tonality and creating movement away from the center and back again. The play of tonalities and associated rhythmic movements create movement through expectation and, increasingly, by defeating expectation. Whole forms, notably the famous sonata form, are based on this. So are theatrical structures although we are less likely to be concerned about the tonalities of operatic scenes. *Die Zauberflöte* is, in a larger sense, indubitably in E-flat major, but unless the overture is performed as a separate concert piece, that fact is not generally noted. In any case, the cadence is part of the power of traditional opera and a point of connection between the arcane arts of composition and the musical comprehension of the public.[12] In effect, it was the link between purely musical form and the power of music to drive a theatrical narrative. As this power slowly ebbed away, a hole was created in the fabric of music, which has not yet been repaired.

No one would deny the importance of the core structure of tonality in Western art music. But is it just a relic from another, more hierarchical period, when politics and social organization were similarly organized? Can it be called a reign of musical terror or musical oppression with meaningful political parallels? It was certainly the product of a dynastic era of absolute monarchs and baroque social hierarchies, and as they disappeared, the reign of tonality seemed to become progressively weaker and weaker. Do the Declaration of the Rights of Man and the advent of meritocracy have esthetic applications? The parallels, however simplistic, are irresistible, especially since we know that the breakdown of the old order and the beginning of the breakdown of tonality and the cadence are almost simultaneous historic events. In an age of pluralistic democracy, wouldn't any sound have the right to be played and heard in the widest context? In fact,

12. It is also worth noting that "cadence" and "cadenza" are essentially two versions of the same word; improvised interpolation, in opera arias as well as concerto movements, usually takes place at the structural seams of the music as defined by these cadence/cadenza points.

this has actually proven to be the case. It is ironic that when innovation is everything and any new sound imaginable is a possibility, the term *music* itself becomes fuzzy (any sound or complex of sounds can be "music" if we so name it) and the notion of new music itself becomes a paradox.

There is another factor here, a twentieth-century addition to the political and social change of the previous century. This is the intrusion of technology into the process. The near-universality of amplified and loudspeaker sound long ago replaced acoustic sound transmission as the norm of musical culture. Although classical opera might seem to be the least affected of all the arts, it hardly escapes the omnipresent and democratic reign of audio—and now also video—technology. New halls and opera houses are built to sound like high-quality audio recordings. Performers learn music and musical interpretation as much by listening to recordings as through written music. Formerly rare and obscure repertoire becomes familiar to both performers and audiences. Difficult or unfamiliar contemporary music becomes much easier for performers due to the presence of examples that can be imitated or learned by ear. Through recordings, the history of music is pushed back and forth through the centuries and extended horizontally around the globe.

Only new, unperformed music seems to escape this and presumably must be learned in other ways. But even this is no longer completely true. New music is now often recorded before it is performed for an audience. Composers, even when writing for the voice, can routinely mock up electronic versions of their music for learning and rehearsal purposes, a scheme that is enormously aided by the portability and relatively low cost of modern sound systems and digital audio computing.[13] In addition to creating sound and music, sound systems make available any sound that can be or has been recorded; such sounds are not only available for direct musical use but they can also be sampled for further use and processing. With the intervention of microphones, amplifiers, and sound modification devices—nowadays mostly computer programs—any sound can be recorded, synthesized, processed in multiple dimensions, reworked, distributed, and redistributed.

All of this has had a huge influence not only on new music but on musical culture in general. This influence extends from pop music through all the layers of classical and contemporary music and is a major factor in new music theater as well. The new universality of a musical culture where everything can potentially enter the world-scene through media and mass media has produced a new complexity and new levels of overload. It has also produced a reaction, a strong countercurrent that favors "acoustic"

---

13. Although it should be noted that among all the instruments, the human voice is the one that is most poorly imitated by digital synthesis.

music, the nonamplification of voices, the paring-down of vocabulary, and the kinds of neo-tonalities represented by minimalism and its offshoots. This even has social and political ramifications as it did in Marxist days. The double-bind of total democratization may bring and even require a simplification of language. Looking at the avant-garde of the twentieth century from the vantage point of the early twenty-first, we can see how and why much of modernism was transitory. The utopian plan for a new society with potentially total freedom inside an anarchic but peaceful social order simply collapsed. Is there a new cultural order that will come to replace the old? What is certain is that change continues and that it is reflected in new audiences and new relationships between audiences and the performing arts, with music theater most certainly in the front lines of change.

Further Reading

Goldberg, Rose Lee. *Performance Art from Futurism to the Present*. London, 1988 and 2001.
Seeger, Horst, and Wolfgang Lange. *Oper heute*. Berlin, 1990.
Small, Christopher. *Musicking: The Meanings of Performing and Listening*. Lebanon, NH, 1998.

A Quick Summary of the Modern History of Music Theater

1900	1910	1920	1930	1940	1950	1960	1970	1980	1990	2000

1st phase, c. 1900–1930: experimental, abstract, and revolutionary character of modernism

Besides the revolutions in art (abstraction, atonalism, informal, psychological), the political element in the origins of new music theater is apparent

2nd phase, 1930–1970: serialism and political engagement

A few innovators experiment with theatrical structures in musical performance (*azione musicale*, *Instrumentales Theater*). After 1968, in a search for alternative forms outside the established operatic and musical institutions, there is an increase in the establishment of companies, theaters, festivals, and other institutional forms specializing in or devoted to "alternate opera" and/or music theater and in the number of established operatic and theatrical institutions which take on, sponsor, or commission new works of music theater and related forms of opera. Some create individual conceptions intended to overthrow the whole institution of opera and its musical traditions.

3rd phase, 1970–: technological (r)evolutions

Theatricalization of concert performance along with the extensive use of media. Music theater increasingly employs elements of the electronic or digital media as an integral part of performance or, in some cases, as its primary medium. Experimentation with installations and with nontheatrical venues (street theater, site specific performance). By the end of the twentieth century and particularly after the fall of communism, the political and socially radical impulses fade and the ideologically drawn lines between opera and music theater blur. Many composers turn to traditional nineteenth-century style, forms, and institutions, bringing some music theater elements into the opera house (and, vice-versa, some operatic elements into music theater). Minimalism and neotonality, often allied with avant-garde pop and non-Western musical elements, reappear in various guises and reinvigorate new music theater.

APPENDIX II
Selected Reading

General

Anhalt, Istvan. *Alternative Voices: Essays on Contemporary Vocal and Choral Composition*. Toronto, 1984.

Auslander, Philip. *Liveness: Performance in a Mediatized Culture*. New York, 1998.

Bawtree, Michael. *The New Singing Theatre: A Charter for the New Music Theater*. New York, 1991.

Kolleritsch, Otto, ed. *Das Musiktheater—Exempel der Kunst*. Wien Universal-Edition, 2001. Includes summaries in English.

Martin, George: *The Opera Companion to Twentieth-Century Opera*. New York, 1979.

Reininghaus, Frieder, and Katja Schneider, eds. *Experimentelles Musik- und Tanztheater*. Laaber, 2006.

Rockwell, John. *All-American Music*. New York, 1983.

Ross, Alex. *The Rest Is Noise*. New York, 2007.

Salzman, Eric. *Twentieth-Century Music: An Introduction*, 4th ed. Upper Saddle River, NJ, 2002. Chapters on "Opera & Musical Theater" and "Media & Theater."

Small, Christopher. *Music of the Common Tongue: Survival and Celebration in African American Music*. Hanover, NH, 1998.

Early Twentieth-Century History

Nielsen, Nanette. *Weimar Opera and Music Theatre: An Investigation of the Intersection of Ethics and Aesthetics*. Ph.D. diss., Musicology, Royal Holloway College, University of London, n.d.

Zurbrigg, Lloyd Alvin. *Greek Tragedy in the Theatre Pieces of Stravinsky and Milhaud*. Ph.D. diss., Music Education, New York University, 1968.

Music Theater and Libretto

Cohn, Richard G., Jr. *The Music of the Text: Challenges in Operatic Translation*. D.M.A., Performance, University of Illinois, n.d.

Heilgendorff, Simone. *Experimentelle Inszenierung von Sprache und Musik: Vergleichende Analysen zur Dieter Schnebel und John Cage*. Freiburg, 2002.

Müller, Ralph. *Das Opernlibretto*. Winterthur, 1966.

Robison, Clayne. *The Departure: A Theatre-Oriented Theory of Opera Translation Including an English Version of Die Abreise by Eugen d'Albert*. D.M.A., Performance, University of Washington, 1974.

Music Theater and Media

Berland, Jody. "Sound, Image and Social Space: Music Television and Media Reconstruction." In *Sound and Vision: The Music Video Reader*, ed. Simon Frith, Andrew Goodwin, and Lawrence Grossberg. London, 1993, p. 28.

Bernstein, David W., ed. *The San Francisco Tape Music Center: 1960s Counterculture and the Avant-garde*. Berkeley, CA, 2008.

Bornoff, Jack, ed. *Music Theatre in a Changing Society: The Influence of the Technical Media*. Paris, 1968.

Causey, Matthew. "Mapping the Dematerialized: Writing Postmodern Performance Theory," in *Postmodern Culture* 5, no. 2 (January 1995).

Fischer-Lichte, Erika. *The Aesthetics of Disruption: German Theatre in the Age of the Media*. Studies in Theatre History and Culture. Iowa City, 1997.

Katz, Mark. *Capturing Sound*. Berkeley, CA, 2008.

Rose, Brian G. *Television and the Performing Arts*. New York, 1986.

Wurtzler, Steve. "She Sang Live, but the Microphone Was Turned Off: The Live, the Recorded, and the Subject of Representation." In *Sound Theory Sound Practice*, ed. Rick Altman. New York, 1992.

Music Theater and Film

Cohan, Steven, ed. *Hollywood Musicals: The Film Reader*. London and New York, 2002.

Huckvale, D.P.H. *The Semiotics of Film Music in Relation to Nineteenth-Century Melodrama, Musical Declamation and Theatre Music*. Ph.D. diss., Musicology, Open University, n.d.

Simpson, Alexander Thomas, Jr. *Opera on Film: A Study of the History and the Aesthetic Principles and Conflicts of a Hybrid Genre*. Ph.D. diss., Musicology, University of Kentucky / University of Louisville, 1990.

Youngblood, Gene. *Expanded Cinema*. New York, 1970.

Music Theater and the Other Arts

Friedman, Ken, ed. *The Fluxus Reader*. New York, 1998.

Goldberg, RoseLee. *Performance: Live Art Since 1960*. New York, 1998.

Long, Robert L. *Arts Integration and Twentieth-Century Theatre*. Ph.D. diss., Musicology, University of London, n.d.

McNeill, William. *Keeping Together in Time: Dance and Drill in Human History*. Cambridge, MA, 1995.

Ruhe, Harry. *Fluxus, the Most Radical and Experimental Art Movement of the Sixties*. Amsterdam, 1979.

Young, La Monte, and Jackson MacLow, eds. *An Anthology*. New York, 1963.

Archeology and Ethnology

Killick, Andrew P. *The Invention of Traditional Korean Opera and the Problem of the Traditionesque: Ch'angguk and Its Relation to P'ansori Narratives.* Ph.D. diss., Ethnomusicology, University of Washington, 1998.
Mithen, Steven J. *The Singing Neanderthals: The Origins of Music, Language, Mind, and Body.* Cambridge, MA, 2005.

Music Theater and Pop

Beadle, Jeremy J. *Will Pop Eat Itself? Pop Music in the Soundbite Era.* London, 1993.
Steenstra, Sytze G. *We Are The Noise Between Stations: A Philosophical Exploration of the Work of David Byrne, at the Crossroads of Popular Media, Conceptual Art, and Performance Theatre.* Maastricht University, The Netherlands, 2003.

Music Theater and Production

Baumol, William J., and William G. Bowen. *Performing Arts: The Economic Dilemma.* New York, 1966.
Blau, Herbert. *The Audience.* Baltimore, 1990.
Freemal, Beth. "Theatre, Stage Directions and Copyright Law." *Chicago Kent Law Review* 71, no. 3: 1017.
Jacobshagen, Arnold, ed. *Praxis Musiktheater: Ein Handbuch.* Laaber, 2002.
Rackard, Benny Gene. *A Directorial Analysis and Production Guide to Three Musical Theatre Forms for High School Production: La vida breve, The Sound of Music, and The Chocolate Soldier.* Ph.D. diss., Music, University of Southern Mississippi, 1980.
Zentgraf, Christiane, ed. *Musiktheater-Management.* Europaeische Musiktheater-Akademie and Forschungsinstitut fur Musiktheater d. Universitat Bayreuth and Institut fur Theaterwissenschaft Universitat Wien, Thurnau. Vol. 1, 1992; vol. 2, 1993; vol. 3, 1994; vol. 4, 1995.

The Ingredients (What Is Music Theater About?)

Gier, Albert. *Das Libretto: Theorie und Geschichte einer musikoliterarischen Gattung.* Darmstadt, 1998.
Honolka, Kurt. *Der Musik gehorsame Tochter.* Stuttgart, 1959.
Kagel, Mauricio. "Über Wort und Stimme in Anagrama," *Nutida Musik* 5, no. 5 (1961–62).
———. "Über das Instrumentale Theater," *Neue Musik.* Kunst- und gesellschaftskritische Beiträge, no. 3 (1961), abridged. Reprints: *Nutida Musik* 5, no. 3 (1960–61); *Dansk Musiktidschrif* 37, 7 (1962); *Hefte des Ulmer Theaters* 63, no. 7 (1963); *Hefte der Kölner Bühnen* 4 (1963/64); "La

Musique et Ses Problèmes Contemporaines," *Cahiers Renauld-Barrault* 41 (1963).

———. *Mobile SpielräumeTheater der Zukunft*. Frankfurt am Main, 1970.

———. *Worte über Musik: Gespräche, Aufsätze, Reden, Hörspiele*. Munich, 1991. Includes conversations: "Über Die Erschöpfung der Welt" (with Werner Klüppelholz), "Über Aus Deutschland" (with Werner Klüppelholz), "Über die Sankt-Bach-Passion" (with Werner Klüppelholz), "Was ist an diesem Handwerk noch Wert, in Frage gestellt zu werden?" (with Wulf Herzogenrath und Gabriele Lueg), "Wer von uns allen wird darüber berichten können?" (with Dieter Rexroth), "Komponieren in der Postmoderne" (with Werner Klüppelholz); lectures: "Zur Eröffnung der Kölner Philharmonie," "Der Name der Freiheit," "Briefe nach Berlin"; essays: "Vom Selbstverständnis und von den Aufgaben des Künstlers," "Kritik der unreinen Vernunft," "Die mißbrauchte Empfindsamkeit. Johannes Brahms zum 150. Geburtstag," "An Gott zweifeln—An Bach glauben. J. S. Bach zum 300. Geburtstag," "Spezifisches über meine Hörspielarbeit," "Fortsetzung folgt"; radio plays: Rrrrrr...Hörspiel über eine Radiophantasie; Cäcila, ausgeplündert. Ein Besuch bei der Heiligen.

Kinser, Samuel. *Rabelais's Carnival: Text, Context, Metatext*. Berkeley, CA, 1990.

Maehder, J., and J. Stenzl, eds. *Zwischen Opera buffa und Melodrama*. Frankfurt am Main, 1994.

Nono, Luigi: "Appunti per un teatro musicale attuale" (Notes on a contemporary music theater), 1961, and "Possibilità e necessità di un nuovo teatro musicale" (Possibility and necessity for a new music theater), 1963. In *Texte. Schriften zu seiner Musik*. Zürich/Freiburg, 1975.

More on Single Authors

Carnelia, Craig. "Stage Craft: A Conversation with Stephen Sondheim," *Playback Magazine*, ASCAP (summer 2007).

Citron, Stephen. *Sondheim and Lloyd Webber: The New Musical*. New York, 2001.

Claren, Sebastian. *Neither, Die Musik von Morton Feldman*. Hofheim/Ts., 2000.

Fearn, Raymond. *The Theatrical Works of Bruno Maderna with Specific Reference to Venetian Journal and Satyricon*. Ph.D. diss., Musicology, Keele University, 1987.

Goodhart, Sandor, ed. *Reading Stephen Sondheim: A Collection of Critical Essays*. New York and London, 2000.

Herbert, David, ed. *The Operas of Benjamin Britten*. New York, 1979.

Krause, Anja. *John Cages Europeras*. Ph.D. diss., Musicology, University of Frankfurt am Main.

Lederman, Minna, ed. *Stravinsky and the Theatre*. New York 1949; repr. 1975.

MacKenzie, Kirk Loren. *A Twentieth-Century Musical/Theatrical Cycle: R. Murray Schafer's Patria* (1966–). Ph.D. diss., Musicology, University of Cincinnati, 1991.

McGiffert, Genevieve. *The Musico-Dramatic Techniques of Benjamin Britten: A Detailed Study of Peter Grimes*. Ph.D. diss., Theatre, University of Denver, 1970.

Perle, George. *Wozzeck*. Berkeley, 1980.

———. *Lulu*. Berkeley, 1985.

Sandner, Wolfgang. *Komposition als Inszenierung*. Berlin, 2002.

Schneider, Wayne. *George Gershwin's Political Operettas: Of Thee I Sing (1931) and Let 'Em Eat Cake (1933), and Their Role in Gershwin's Musical and Emotional Maturing*. Ph.D. diss., Musicology, Cornell University, 1985.

Steiner, Ena. "The Happy Hand: Genesis and Interpretation of Schoenberg's Monumentalkunstwerk," *Music Review* 41, no. 3 (1980).

Stenzl, Jürgen. *Luigi Nono*. Reinbek, 1998.

Swayne, Steven R. *Hearing Sondheim's Voices*. Ph.D. diss., Music, University of California at Berkeley, 1999.

Symonette, Lys, and Kim H. Kowalke (eds. and transl.). *Speak Low (When You Speak Love): The Letters of Kurt Weill and Lotte Lenya*. Berkeley, CA, 1996.

Weber, Eckhard Hans. *Das Musiktheater von Manuel de Falla vor dem Hintergrund der Nationalmusikbewegungen im ausgehenden 19. Jahrhundert*. Ph.D. diss., Musicology, Freie Universität, Berlin, 1994.

Weill, Kurt. "Musik und musikalisches Theater," in *Gesammelte Schriften*. Schott Mainz, 2000.

White, Eric Walter. *Benjamin Britten: His Life and His Operas*. Berkeley, CA, 1970.

White, Pamela C. *Schoenberg and the God-idea: The Opera "Moses und Aron."* Ann Arbor, MI, 1985.

Some Festivals and Performance Institutions

USA

Brooklyn Academy of Music (BAM)
A major center for contemporary performance works, including music theater, contemporary opera, and performance art, which are often a feature of its "Next Wave" festivals.
Peter Jay Sharp Building
30 Lafayette Avenue
Brooklyn, NY 11217
Tel: 718-636-4100
www.bam.org; info@bam.org

Center for Contemporary Opera
The Center for Contemporary Opera has been dedicated to the creation and performance of contemporary American opera and music theater for the past quarter-century.
P.O. Box 258
New York, NY 10044-0205
Tel: 212-758-2757
www.conopera.org; mail@cononpera.org

Music-Theatre Group
Music-Theatre Group identifies and shepherds collaborative, interdisciplinary works of music and theater from commission, through development, and into full-scale productions.
30 West 26th Street, Suite 1001
New York, NY 10010
Tel: 212-366-5260, ext. 22
www.musictheatregroup.org; mtg@musictheatregroup.org

American Opera Projects
American Opera Projects' mission is to champion innovative works of music theater, to expand the art form, and to identify, develop, and present new works by emerging and established talent.
138 South Oxford Street
Brooklyn, NY 11217
Tel: 718-398-4024; Fax: 718-398-3489
www.operaprojects.org; info@OperaProjects.org

CANADA

Chants Libres
Since 1990, Chants Libres' work in bringing together music, theater, visual arts, electronics, video, and other art forms around the human voice has led to many creations of contemporary new music theater.
1908, rue Panet, bureau 303
Montréal, Québec, Canada H2L 3A2
Tel: 514-841-2642
www.chantslibres.org; creation@chantslibres.org

Tapestry
Tapestry is dedicated to the creation, development and performance of new opera works through its unique and highly collaborative work process.
Tapestry New Opera Works
55 Mill Street
Building 58, The Cannery, Studio 316
Toronto, Ontario, Canada M5A 3C4
Tel: 416-537-6066; Fax: 416-537-7841
www.tapestrynewopera.com; information@tapestrynewopera.com

AUSTRALIA

Chamber Made Opera
Chamber Made Opera is Australia's leading development and production house for new Australian music-theater and music-based cross-art form works.
Arts House, Meat Market
1 Blackwood Street / PO Box 302
North Melbourne, VIC, Australia 3051
Tel: 613-93-29-74-22
www.chambermade.org.au

EUROPE

Munich Biennale
The Munich *Biennale—International festival für neues Musiktheater* is entirely devoted to new creations of music theater.
V.i.S.d.P.
Münchener Biennale
Ludwigstraße 8
D80539 München
Germany
Tel: +49 89 280 56 07
www.muenchenerbiennale.de; biennale@spielmotor.de

Sechs-Tage-Oper, Düsseldorf, Germany
The "Six-Day-Opera" is a festival that creates new music-theater pieces. Outdoor projects as well as projects involving whole villages and even an entire island have enlarged the boundaries of conventional music theater.
Europäische Vereinigung für Kammeroper und Musiktheater e.V. (EVKM)
Heyestrasse 116
D-40625 Düsseldorf
Germany
Tel: +49 211 929 35 82
www.6-tage-oper.de; info@6-tage-oper.de

Muziektheater Transparant, Antwerp, Belgium
"Muziektheater Transparant is a production company that shifts the boundaries between opera and musical theatre. The voice is placed firmly at the centre of our projects, and we continually blend the old and the new…"
Muziektheater Transparant vzw
Leopoldplaats 10 bus 1
B-2000 Antwerpen
Belgium
Tel: +32 (0)3 225 17 02
Fax: +32 (0)3 226 16 52
www.transparant.be; info@transparant.be

Avignon Festival, Avignon, France
"The mission of the Festival is to show-case French and foreign contemporary drama and dance creations and stage performances in general—about forty productions each year—to an ever-growing audience (around 100,000). There are about twenty, rather unusual, performance venues in Avignon and nearby the city including cloisters, churches, the famous Pope's Palace, an old stone quarry and school halls."
Avignon Festival et Compagnies
6, place des Carmes
F-84000 Avignon
France
Tel: +33 (0)4 90 82 20 47
www.avignonfestivaletcompagnies.com; info-doc@festival-avignon.com

National Theater of Quimper (Théâtre de Cornouaille), Quimper, France
The Théâtre de Cornouaille, directed by Michel Rostain and incorporating the Scène nationale de Quimper, Un Théâtre pour la musique, and Le Centre de la création musicale, is one of the national theaters of France specialized in various forms of music theater including the creation of new work.

Théâtre de Cornouaille
1 esplanade François Mitterrand
29337 Quimper Cedex
France
Tel: +33 (0)2 98 55 98 98
www.theatrequimper.asso.fr; contact@theatrequimper.asso.fr

Grame, Lyon, France
The *Centre nationale de création musicale,* directed by James Giroudon and Pierre
Alain Jaffrennou, sponsors the *Biennale Musiques en Scène,* which includes works
and premieres of contemporary opera, music theater, jazz, and electronic music.
9 Rue du Garet BP 1185
69202 Lyon Cedex 01
France
www.grame.fr; grame@grame.fr

Almeida Theatre, London, United Kingdom
"Since 1992, the Almeida Theatre has presented Almeida Opera, a season of
new opera commissions each summer. Building on the opera and music
festivals that the Almeida's founder Pierre Audi established in the 1980s,
Almeida Opera has established an exceptional reputation in London for the
production and commissioning of chamber operas and music theatre."
Almeida Street
Islington
N1 1TA London
UK
www.almeida.co.uk; info@almeida.co.uk

PLEX (Den Anden Opera), Copenhagen, Denmark
PLEX (which was until 2006 known as Den Anden Opera, København) calls
itself a "vibrant hub in the centre of Copenhagen where music theatre, installations, concerts and sound art converge. Artistic crossover is what PLEX is all
about, with interactivity and exploration playing a central role. Our aim is to
create a forum where artists, their work, and the audience can meet."
Copenhagen's Music Theatre Kronprinsensgade 7
DK - 1114 Copenhagen K
Denmark
Tel: + 45 3332 3830
www.plex-musikteater.dk

index

Note: Page numbers in *italics* indicate figures.